The Other Alliance

AMERICA IN THE WORLD

SVEN BECKERT AND JEREMI SURI, *series editors*

Also in the Series

David Ekbladh, *The Great American Mission: Modernization and the Construction of an American World Order*

Andrew Zimmerman, *Alabama in Africa: Booker T. Washington, the German Empire, and the Globalization of the New South*

Ian Tyrell, *Reforming the World: The Creation of America's Moral Empire*

Rachel St. John, *Line in the Sand: A History of the Western U.S.–Mexico Border*

The Other Alliance

STUDENT PROTEST IN
WEST GERMANY AND THE UNITED STATES
IN THE GLOBAL SIXTIES

Martin Klimke

PRINCETON UNIVERSITY PRESS

PRINCETON AND OXFORD

Second printing, and first paperback printing, 2011
Paperback ISBN 978-0-691-15246-2

The Library of Congress has cataloged the cloth edition of this book as follows

Klimke, Martin.
    The other alliance : student protest in West Germany and the United
States in the global sixties / Martin Klimke.
    p.   cm. — (America in the world)
    Includes bibliographical references and index.
    ISBN 978-0-691-13127-6 (hardcover : alk. paper) 1. Student
movements—United States—History—20th century. 2. Students—
United States—Political activity—History—20th century. 3. Protest
movements—United States—History—20th century. 4. Student
movements—International cooperation—History—20th century.
5. Student movements—Germany (West)—History. 6. Students—
Germany (West)—Political activity—History. 7. Protest movements—
Germany (West)—History. 8. Vietnam War, 1961–1975—Protest
movements—United States. 9. Vietnam War, 1961–1975—Protest
movements—Germany (West) I. Title.
    LA229.K54 2009
    373.1'81097309046—dc22   2009021743

British Library Cataloging-in-Publication Data is available

Publication of this book has been aided by the
Heidelberg Center for American Studies (HCA), University of Heidelberg.

This book has been composed in Sabon

Printed on acid-free paper. ∞

Printed in the United States of America

3   5   7   9   10   8   6   4   2

CONTENTS

ILLUSTRATIONS

IMAGES

Figures

ABBREVIATIONS

AH	America House / Amerika-Haus
AID	Agency for International Development
APO	Außerparlamentarische Opposition (also EPO)
APOB	Archive "APO und soziale Bewegungen," Free University of Berlin
ASTA	Allgemeiner Studierenden Ausschuß (Student Government)
BKA	Bundeskriminalamt (Federal Criminal Police Office)
BPP	Black Panther Party
BV	Bundesvorstand (National Office)
CF	Chronological File
CIA	Central Intelligence Agency
CND	Campaign for Nuclear Disarmament
CREST	CIA Records Search Tool, U.S. National Archives II, College Park, Maryland
CU	Bureau of Educational and Cultural Affairs, Department of State
CU/ OPP	CU–Office of Policy and Plans
DK	Delegiertenkonferenz (National Convention)
DOS	Department of State
EPO	Extra-Parliamentary Opposition (also APO)
ESU	Étudiants Socialistes Unifiés, France
EUR	Bureau of European Affairs, Department of State
FBI	Federal Bureau of Intelligence
FNL	Front National pour la Libération du Sud Viêt Nam (also NLF)
FRG	Federal Republic of Germany (Bundesrepublik Deutschland)
FRUS	Foreign Relations of the United States
FSM	Free Speech Movement
FSO	Foreign Service Officer
FU	Freie Universität Berlin (Free University of Berlin)
FY	Fiscal Year
GAI	German-American Institute
GDR	German Democratic Republic (Deutsche Demokratische Republik)
GUL	Georgetown University Library, Special Collections, Washington, D.C.
G/Y	Undersecretary of Political Affairs, Department of State

HEW	Department of Health, Education, and Welfare
HIS	Hamburg Institute for Social Research, Hamburg
IAYC	Inter-Agency Youth Committee (formerly known as Inter-Agency Committee on Youth Affairs)
ICDP	International Confederation for Disarmament and Peace
INFI	Internationales Nachrichten- und Forschungsinstitut (International News and Research Institute)
INR	Office of Intelligence and Research, Department of State
ISS	Intercollegiate Socialist Society
IUS	International Union of Students
IUSY	International Union of Socialist Youth
JFKL	John F. Kennedy Library, Boston, Massachusetts
JGS	Jeunes Gardes Socialistes, Belgium
LBJL	Lyndon B. Johnson Library, Austin, Texas
LID	League for Industrial Democracy
LNS	Liberation News Service
MAAG	Military Assistance Advisory Group
MACV	Military Assistance Command, Vietnam
NA	U.S. National Archives II, College Park, Maryland
NADC	U.S. National Archives, Washington, D.C.
NALSO	National Association of Labour Student Organisations, UK
NATO	North Atlantic Treaty Organization
NEA	North East Asia
NLF	National Liberation Front (also FNL)
NLN	New Left Notes
NPD	Nationaldemokratische Partei Deutschlands (National Democratic Party of Germany)
NPT	Non-Proliferation Treaty
NSA	National Student Association
NSA	National Security Agency
NSF	National Security File
OLC	Oxford Labour Club, Oxford, UK
PL	Progressive Labor
RAF	Rote Armee Fraktion (Red Army Faction)
RC	Republikanischer Club (Republican Club)
RYM	Revolutionary Youth Movement
SANE	National Committee for a Sane Nuclear Policy
SI	Situationist International
SDS	Sozialistischer Deutscher Studentenbund (West Germany); or Students for a Democratic Society (USA)
SED	Sozialistische Einheitspartei Deutschlands (Socialist Union Party of East Germany)
SHB	Sozialdemokratischer Hochschulbund (Social Democratic

Student Association)
SHSW   State Historical Society of Wisconsin, Madison, Wisconsin
SLID   Student League for Industrial Democracy
SNCC   Student Nonviolent Coordinating Committee
SPD   Sozialdemokratische Partei Deutschlands (German Social
       Democratic Party)
TU   Technische Universität (Technical University)
UASC   University of Arkansas Libraries, Special Collections,
       Fayetteville, Arkansas
USG   United States Government
USIA   United States Information Agency
USIS   United States Information Service
VDS   Verband Deutscher Studentenschaften (Association of
       German Student Bodies)
WFDY   World Federation of Democratic Youth
WHCF   White House Confidential File
WYA   World Youth Assembly
YPSL   Young People's Socialist League

ACKNOWLEDGMENTS

THERE ARE PERFECT BOOKS and those that actually get published. This work has been written in the latter spirit, viewing itself as the beginning rather than the final word on the many discussions that are being opened up in the following pages.

It took me about ten years to gather the sources for this book and finish the manuscript. During this time, I have enjoyed the unwavering support of my family, friends, and colleagues, who have been an integral part of this journey from the very beginning. A special expression of gratitude goes to my colleagues at the University of Heidelberg, both in the Department of History and in the Heidelberg Center for American Studies (HCA). The HCA invited me as a research fellow in 2005 and has been my academic home for several years. I am especially indebted to Detlef Junker, who cordially welcomed me to Heidelberg in 2001 and let me pursue this project, supporting and guiding my work both intellectually and on a personal level over the years in ways too numerous to mention. Also in Heidelberg, Wilfried Mausbach and Philipp Gassert's comments on matters of substance and style, as well as my intense academic discussions with them over the years, have helped me navigate the turbulent waters of the sixties on both sides of the Atlantic and have profoundly shaped this work.

I owe further gratitude to Akira Iriye of Harvard University. His insights into the global dimensions of American history, our many exchanges over the years, and his constant personal support have been an important part of my intellectual development and were of enormous benefit to this book. Also in Cambridge, my affiliation with the New Global History initiative and Bruce Mazlish's encouragement inspired me to see the value in a broadened historical perspective. It also led me to reframe my conclusions about the transnational dimension of 1960s protest in the spirit of a global history. Likewise, the scholarship and comments of Daniel Rodgers of Princeton University have guided and greatly enriched this work over the years.

This book is also a product of a transatlantic cooperation between the University of Heidelberg and Rutgers University, N.J., where I had the privilege of spending two academic years as a visiting scholar and adjunct lecturer. The generous support of the Volkswagen Foundation allowed me to conduct my work in the company of fellow academics, whose cooperation I deeply appreciate. I am particularly indebted to Belinda Davis and Carla MacDougall for the productive collaboration and their constructive suggestions during this time.

Responsibility for the content of this work rests with me alone, but many people have helped in its production. I was given the chance to present portions of this work at various conferences, workshops, and seminars at Columbia University, Harvard University, the University of California at Berkeley, the University of Wisconsin at Madison, the University of Mississippi at Oxford, Washington and Lee University, Vassar College, the University of Leeds, the University of Bielefeld, the University of Münster, the University of Zurich, the University of Vienna, the University of Helsinki, the German Historical Institute in Washington, D.C., the German Studies Association, the German Association for American Studies, the American Historical Association, as well as the Society for the History of American Foreign Relations. There and elsewhere, I benefited substantially from the comments and suggestions of Manfred Berg, David Farber, Ingrid Gilcher-Holtey, George Katsiaficas, Laura Kolbe, Charles Maier, Detlef Siegfried, and Franz-Werner Kersting. Wolfgang Kraushaar has shown his continuous support ever since the project was in its early stages and has been a guiding force over the years. Jeremi Suri has read and commented on various drafts of my work with a keen eye on the precision of my key arguments, which tremendously enriched my understanding of *The Other Alliance* along the lines of an international study. Maria Höhn's academic advice and her optimism and collegiality in the past years have become a reminder of the great benefits that abound in an open and honest scholarly cooperation and in intellectual friendships. Similarly, the insights of my colleagues Joachim Scharloth and Kathrin Fahlenbrach, as well as the many projects and papers from the affiliates of our international research network "European Protest Movements Since 1945," have illuminated for me the ways in which other disciplines look at this tumultuous decade. Finally, Jeremy Varon's passion and enthusiasm, combined with our discussions on lessons and legacies of the sixties, have helped me make better sense of my discoveries and further nourished this book.

I also owe an enormous debt of gratitude to the many archivists and archival institutions that patiently helped me in the past few years. Of these, I would like to single out the dedicated staff of the Lyndon B. Johnson Library (Charlaine McCauley and Jennifer Cuddeback) and the National Archives in College Park, Md. (Michael Hussey and Jennifer Evans) in the United States. In Germany, the untiring help of Reinhard Schwarz at the Hamburg Institute for Social Research and Siegward Lönnendonker from the APO-Archive at the Free University of Berlin was equally extraordinary. I would like to thank all of my interview partners and those who offered their advice for generously giving their time and trust, in particular Bernardine Dohrn, Helen Garvey, Tom Hayden, Rainer Langhans, Carl Oglesby, Robert Pardun, Patty Lee Parmalee, Michael Vester, and KD Wolff. Their insights gave me a personal window into the past and challenged me to rethink my own perspectives on the 1960/70s.

I was also lucky enough to enjoy the support and gracious assistance of many friends during the writing of this book. For their friendship and patience I thank all of them, especially Andre Tölpe, Matthias Voigt, Miguel Gonzalez, Jens Paulus, Peter Kupfer, Oliver Wehr, Boris Czerwon, Aki Kalliomaki, and Dieter Albe. I owe particular gratitude to all my friends who volunteered ungrudgingly to correct my work or facilitate it in various other ways, such as Lindsey Stokes, Helena Chadderton, Anette Neff, Tobias Dussa, Gerold Marks, Mischa Honeck, Alexander Holmig, Michael Frey, Thea Van Halsema, Frank Beyersdorf, Christian Müller, Philip Bracher, and Holger Klitzing, one of my earliest and most enduring readers. Danijela Abrecht's generous hospitality during my sojourns in Heidelberg and Mannheim, her patience in the transcription of interviews, and her professional coordination of our Volkswagen Foundation research project deserve a particular mention. So do Rebekka Weinel's excellent administration and management of our research project "European Protest Movements Since 1945," as well as her organizational support over the years, which has enabled me to continue to pursue this work.

My thanks also go to all of my colleagues at the German Historical Institute, Washington, D.C., who warmly welcomed me with a generous Fellowship in North American History in 2007. This allowed me to revise and complete this book. At the GHI, I am greatly indebted to its former acting directors Gisela Mettele and Anke Ortlepp, and its current director, Hartmut Berghoff. In addition, I am most grateful for the academic and linguistic knowledge generously shared by Betsy Hauck, David Lazar, Casey Sutcliffe, and Mary Tonkinson. Above all, I also want to thank Laura Stapane for her tireless efforts in helping me structure my work and procuring the copyrights for the images in this book.

At Princeton University Press, Brigitta van Rheinberg, Clara Platter, and Terri O'Prey were supportive and patient every step of the way, and I am indebted to them for their guidance and trust during the various revisions of the manuscript. Thanks are also due to Linda Truilo not only for her careful and thoughtful copyediting but also for her optimism and sense of humor with which she tackled my occasional lapses into Teutonic wording and sentence structures.

For financial support I would like to thank the Alpha Delta Phi Committee of the English Department of Amherst College, the John F. Kennedy Institute for North American Studies at the Free University of Berlin, the Heidelberg Center for American Studies, and the Society for the Promotion of the Schurman Library for American History at the University of Heidelberg, as well as the Volkswagen Foundation.

This book is dedicated to my parents Eva-Maria and Manfred Klimke, without whom this and so many other things in my life would not have been possible.

The Other Alliance

INTRODUCTION

The men who create power make an indispensable
contribution to the nation's greatness, but the men
who question power make a contribution just as
indispensable, especially when that questioning is
disinterested, for they determine whether we use
power or power uses us.
—*John F. Kennedy at Amherst College,*
October 26, 1963

We are not hopeless idiots of history who are unable
to take their destiny into their own hands. . . . We can
create a world that the world has never seen before; a
world that distinguishes itself by not knowing wars
anymore, by not being hungry anymore, all across the
globe. This is our historical opportunity.
—*Rudi Dutschke, TV Interview, December 3, 1967*

You could strike sparks anywhere. There was a
fantastic universal sense that whatever we were doing
was *right*, that we were winning. And that, I think,
was the handle—that sense of inevitable victory
over the forces of Old and Evil. . . . We had all
the momentum; we were riding the crest of a
high and beautiful wave.
—*Hunter S. Thompson,* Fear and Loathing
in Las Vegas, *1971*

THE ERUPTION OF STUDENT PROTEST in the 1960s was a global phenomenon, the magnitude of which was acknowledged by contemporary observers, enthusiastic supporters, and fierce critics alike. A CIA report on
"Restless Youth" from September 1968 stated, "Youthful dissidence, involving students and nonstudents alike, is a world-wide phenomenon. . . .
Because of the revolution in communications, the ease of travel, and the
evolution of society everywhere, student behavior never again will resemble what it was when education was reserved for the elite. . . . Thanks to
the riots in West Berlin, Paris, and New York and sit-ins in more than
twenty other countries in recent months, student activism has caught the
attention of the world."[1]

The extraordinary nature of the 1960s and the *annus mirabilis* 1968 are hardly disputable today. The long "sixties" are commonly remembered as an era of global change, producing a historical caesura, culturally as well as politically. In numerous countries, images of protest, generational revolt, countercultural indulgence, sexual liberation, and government repression circulate in the public memory of those years. Young people rebelled against what they saw as outdated traditional values and politics, expressing a widening gap between the generations. The outstanding historical characteristic of the sixties is that they transgressed the ideological fronts of the cold war. Not only the "First World" of Western capitalism but also the "Second World" of the Communist bloc and the "Third World" in Latin America, Africa, and Asia were shattered by largely unexpected internal ruptures.[2] As historian Eric Hobsbawm argues, the miraculous year "1968" was already an indication that the "golden age" was coming to an end. It was the climax of various developments that had been set in motion due to the immense speed of the social and economic transformations after the Second World War: a dramatic increase in university enrollment, a globalized media landscape that allowed an almost instantaneous spread of news and images, as well as an economic prosperity that fed the rising purchasing power of youth.[3]

Whether we describe sixties' protest as a revolution in the world-system, a global revolutionary movement, or a conglomerate of national movements with local variants but common characteristics, its transnational dimension was one of its crucial motors. As the French student leader Daniel Cohn-Bendit conceded, "Paris, Berlin, Frankfurt, New York, Berkeley, Rome, Prague, Rio, Mexico City, Warsaw—those were the places of a revolt that stretched all around the globe und captured the hearts and dreams of a whole generation. The year 1968 was, in the true sense of the word, international."[4] His British counterpart, Tariq Ali, even likened the impact of this year to a storm, which swept across the world and hit numerous countries in Asia, Europe, and the Americas.[5]

In recent years, many historians have begun to transform the sixties from an era mostly characterized by individual recollection and popular memory to one of professional, academic inquiry. In their judgment, the protest movements of the 1960s/70s were also a global phenomenon, representing social and cultural responses to emerging patterns of economic, technological, and political globalization.[6] Yet the exact processes through which activists from numerous countries established contact, shared ideas, and adopted each other's social and cultural practices are still largely unexplored.[7] Most works fail to analyze how activists from different geographical, economic, political, and cultural frameworks imagined themselves as part of a global revolutionary movement. This book traces the perceptions, shared traditions, and exchanges between student protesters during the 1960s, using the protest movements in two countries of the "First World," the United States and West Germany, as a case study. It illustrates how activists from different political and cultural frameworks tried to construct a collective identity that could lead to solidarity and cooperation, as well as a more global consciousness. In addition, it details for the very first time how the U.S. government monitored and reacted to the global student protest during the 1960s.

Perhaps the most significant condition for the emergence of the protest movements of the 1960s was the powerful economic upswing of the 1950s. In the United States, Great Britain, West Germany, and other countries, the 1950s heralded an economic boom that opened the door to a broad-based consumer society from which the middle class benefited the most. This sudden prosperity resulted in new social freedoms that expressed themselves in a growing recreational culture. It also went hand-in-hand with the discovery and increasing influence of young people as an economic factor. This young postwar generation, the so-called baby boomers, not only flooded the universities in the early 1960s and severely strained their capacities, but also possessed a formidable purchasing power that made them a lucrative target group for the fashion and music industries. Commercialization and the exploitation of youth culture by the culture industry were therefore already discernable at the beginning of the decade and continued all through the 1960s.

All of these processes and discourses were disseminated internationally thanks to the rapid advances in communication technology—in particular television and satellite communication. In July 1962, a year after the German broadcasting company ZDF was established, NASA's Telstar 1 broadcasted the first television pictures from the United States to Europe via satellite. In addition, international airlines expanded their services during the decade with a growing number of destinations and cheaper ticket prices. The cold war and the increasing cultural-diplomacy efforts of both superpowers to influence global opinion also helped promote transnational exchange well into in the first half of the 1960s. In short, technological innovation and an internationalized media landscape created a qualitatively new level of sociocultural networking across national borders well before 1968.

This system of international exchange provided a favorable climate for the emergence of transnational subcultures and protest movements that were to shape the ideas and actions of sixties' activists. Raging against consumerism and the spiritual decay of society in the 1950s, the Beat movement or the "Halbstarken" phenomenon provided an important source of inspiration for the young generation. Similarly, artistic avant-gardes like the Situationist International (SI), which drew on the existentialism of Sartre and Camus, Dadaism, Surrealism, and the Lettrists, offered an action repertoire which the Dutch Provos, the German Kommune 1, and American countercultural icons such as Abbie Hoffman, Jerry Rubin, and the Diggers readily copied from.

An equally rich source of inspiration was the African American civil rights movement. Its iconography, protest methods, and ethics made an impact far beyond the United States' borders. Figures such as Rosa Parks and Martin Luther King, Jr., strategies such as Freedom Rides, direct action, and civil disobedience, as well as the denunciation of a system of apartheid in the heart of the Western "free world," played a crucial role in the politicization process of Western activists. The Black Power movement then motivated student protesters to take a firmer and even militant stance against an establishment that appeared unwilling to compromise. Furthermore, it directed the students' attention to the Third World liberation movements and the legacies of European colonialist policies. This was especially apparent in the case of Vietnam. The U.S.-led war in Southeast Asia therefore soon became a symbol of the imperialist oppression of the Third World by the "free West."

Starting in 1965, the growing antiwar movement in the United States not only influenced the style of protests on an international level through the institution of teach-ins. In the footsteps of an international pacifist network that had protested nuclear armament since the 1950s, the antiwar movement was also able to gather a worldwide following of protesters by the late 1960s, all of whom had one thing in common—their opposition to the Vietnam War. As the conflict escalated, the Viet Cong, Che Guevara, and even Mao Zedong became international icons that represented the uncompromising struggle against the all-powerful, globally operating forces of imperialism.

Even the movement that provided much of the intellectual undercurrent for the protest of the 1960s, the New Left, was of transnational origins. Initially a European product that emerged in Great Britain under the influence of E. P. Thompson, Stuart Hall, and Ralph Miliband, it was carried over to the United States by, among others, the sociologist C. Wright Mills. The American SDS (Students for a Democratic Society) and its programmatic "Port Huron Statement" of 1962 helped shape the New Left's agenda even further and ultimately established it in a transatlantic context. Activists on both sides of the Atlantic had much in common—the rejection of traditional Marxism and its focus on the working class, a fundamental dissatisfaction with the cold war (its policy of nuclear deterrence and anticommunist ideology) and the condemnation of society's social and political apathy, materialism, and capitalistic competitive mindset. In addition, activists were inspired by each other's protest, visited each other's conferences, and imported new protest techniques and strategies to their local contexts.

The shared opposition against the war in Vietnam remained, however, the issue that most deeply connected activists to each other. For members of the West German SDS (Sozialistischer Deutscher Studentenbund, or German Socialist Student League), for example, Vietnam epitomized the global reach of imperialism and the necessity for a "global revolutionary alliance" between activists in the First World and the liberation movements of the Third World. Along this dictum, many student protesters sought to overcome the bloc confrontation of the cold war between East and West in favor of a greater focus on the North-South divide, and reached out to their peers in other countries for this endeavor.

This is not to suggest that national and regional idiosyncrasies were not still pervasive. Even though anti-imperialism, anti-capitalism, and international solidarity were diffuse-but-shared elements of the cognitive orientation of these movements, specific national issues generally determined the characteristics of protesters. In Belgium, the dominance of the French language at the Flemish university in Leuven triggered major protests among Flemish students, which had a strong nationalist current. In Italy, and even more in Germany, activists turned their anger on their parents' fascist past. In Greece and Spain, the dictatorships of the colonels and of General Franco were the main targets of criticism. International encounters therefore did not always lead to tight and permanent networks across national borders but sometimes also showcased the differences among activists. Such differences became visible, for example, during the World Youth Festival in Sofia in 1968, when the Bulgarian hosts clashed with the West German guests over an antiwar demonstration at the U.S. embassy.

Perhaps the most apt expression of this ambivalence was a panel discussion hosted by the BBC shortly after "the French May." The discussion featured such prominent student leaders as Daniel Cohn-Bendit and Alan Geismar from France, Tariq Ali from Great Britain, Karl-Dietrich Wolff from West Germany, Jan Kavan from Czechoslovakia, as well as Dragana Stavijel from Yugoslavia, among others. The interesting aspect is that all these participants agreed that youthful unrest, in its attempt to transform society, had transcended national borders. In a remarkable display of mutual solidarity, all of them rose up and sang the "Communist Internationale" together at the end of the program, each of them in their native tongue.[8]

Fraternizations like these were made possible by the rise of alternative lifestyles and countercultures, often of Anglo-American origin, as additional forms of dissent. New aesthetics emerging in art, music, film, and fashion joined with hippie ideologies and lifestyles and merged into a new set of symbolic forms, attractive to the young generation in both the East and West. Long hair, beards, colorful and exotic clothes, casual behavior, and a hedonistic search for pleasure and ostentatious informality became distinctive marks of a rebelling youth across the world. This is illustrated by the international success of artists such as Joan Baez, Bob Dylan, the Beatles, and Jimi Hendrix.[9] In addition, a global media landscape allowed iconic images to travel around the globe almost instantaneously, whether it was the killing of a Viet Cong by the police chief of Saigon, the frightened Vietnamese girl Kim Phúc running down the streets away from her village, or when National Guard units open fired on students at Kent State University.[10]

The transnational interaction among activists in the 1960s thus drew its strength from a collective protest identity that consisted of shared cultural and political reference points and was strengthened by a global medial discourse. The significance of these networks increased as their participants addressed problems encompassing an international dimension that people could also relate to on a local level (imperialism, bloc divisions of the cold war, and so forth). With universities as the breeding grounds of protest—a protest that drew support from prominent intellectuals such as Herbert Marcuse—the late 1960s saw the emergence of an international language of dissent.

In the case of the protest movements in West Germany and the United States, the exceptionally close political, economic, and cultural associations between the two countries during the cold war were particularly important for this transnational exchange.[11] Due to the specific conditions of occupation and reeducation and the Federal Republic's role in U.S. foreign policy after 1945, the transatlantic partnership between the two countries was extremely strong. In the first decade after the Second World War, American "cultural diplomacy" was aimed at a democratization of German political culture, in other words an "Americanization from above."[12] The years that followed, from 1955 to 1965, in contrast, can be viewed as a starting point for a "grassroots Americanization," whereby official political goals were complemented and even replaced by an immense cultural influence on West German society and the political landscape.[13]

With the increasing actions of the civil rights and free speech movement in the first half of the 1960s, the U.S. government's prestige began to change among the perceptions of the young generation both in the United States and Europe. What added to this dissatisfaction among the younger generation in West Germany was the legacy of the German past and the after-effects it still had on the young republic, which, in their view, had not successfully mastered its legacy under U.S. political influence.[14] Furthermore, the notion that the United States, once seen as a democratic model, guiding spirit, and leader of the supposed "free world," was waging an ever-escalating and questionable war in Southeast Asia led many to revolt against what they believed to be a cynical version of democracy.[15]

Similar feelings of disillusionment had already developed within the United States and found their way to Europe, where they fundamentally challenged the prevailing impression of the United States among segments of the young generation. Hence, the split perception of the United States was one of the dominating concepts for the New Left in West Germany, because it vehemently clashed with previous images.[16] As Richard Pells wrote with respect to the European perception of America in the 1960s,

> America might be racist and repressive, but it also supplied the leaders and the troubadours of the revolution: Malcolm X and Bob Dylan, Angela Davis and Joan Baez, the Students for a Democratic Society and Jefferson Airplane. A young person living in Austria, Holland, or Italy could denounce the imperialist in the White House and the Pentagon while at the same time learning from the media how to emulate the adversarial style of the American counterculture and the tactics of the civil rights and antiwar movements in the United States.[17]

These countercultural items and their import can hardly be labeled as anti-American, given their origins and strong roots in the United States.[18] They instead formed a critique of the official U.S. government, thus defining this dissent as predominantly anti-imperialist and, as such, a further expression of intense mutual relations between American activists and their European counterparts. Moreover, these shared sentiments reflected an additional degree of American (counter-)cultural influence. In other words, the dissent was (if at all) an anti-Americanism of "With America against America."[19] These ambiguous images were part of the intercultural, transatlantic network and discourse between the two movements. West German and European students selectively adopted, modified, and used American countercultural imports, thereby turning them into their own.[20] That this intercultural exchange created a common, though constructed, reality explains why the protesting students of the 1960s felt connected to each other, as if they were on an "international crusade." It turned the sixties into a shared experience across national boundaries.[21]

The aim of this study is to illustrate the ways in which this "other" cold-war alliance composed of students enabled them to connect to each other and form a counterpoint to their countries' official transatlantic partnership. By examining the interconnectedness of the American and German student movements and the government reactions their relationship provoked, the study seeks to contribute to an explanation of the internationality of the sixties and this decade's role in the postwar political order.

Chapter 1 retraces the origins of the New Left in both the United States and West Germany, starting with the cooperation between the American and German SDSs as initiated by German SDS member Michael Vester. The influence that Vester exercised on the formulation of the Port Huron Statement of the American SDS in 1962 forms the chronological beginning of my analysis, which illustrates the transnational nature of the New Left as early as the beginning of the 1960s, as well as the degree to which American protest ideas continued to be imported to the German SDS until the mid-sixties.

Chapter 2 examines the development of the transatlantic networks of protest between the two student organizations with respect to their common opposition to the war in Vietnam. After reviewing the attempts by the American SDS to internationalize the antiwar movement, the chapter explores the significance of American protest techniques of "direct action" for the ideological development of the German SDS from 1964 through 1966/67. American protest examples helped the anti-authoritarian faction in the German SDS led by Rudi Dutschke in its effort to win over the organization to its own political program. By integrating strategies of "direct action," such as sit-ins or teach-ins, from the American New Left into their own protest repertoire, German activists created a unique amalgam of revolutionary theories that merged with previous ideological influences from sources as diverse as Che Guevara, Herbert Marcuse, and George Lukács.

Chapter 3 describes the global revolutionary theory that emerged out of this synthesis and the various attempts of German and American student activists to realize it in the form of an anti-imperialist, second front in the urban centers of the First World. The challenges posed by the implementation of this projected global protest network are illustrated through a detailed examination of the international conferences and meetings of the New Left, as well as of alternating visits between German and American activists and other modes of transatlantic cooperation. Rudi Dutschke's plans to study with Herbert Marcuse in California, Bernardine Dohrn's visit to the German SDS 1968 national convention in Frankfurt, and German SDS president Karl-Dietrich Wolff's lecture tour through the United States in the spring of 1969 are just some of the many transatlantic connections exemplifying this global revolutionary program.

Chapter 4 then explores a previously unknown dimension of transatlantic intertwinement in the 1960s/70s, namely the reception of the civil rights movement and Black Power ideology in a West German context. By investigating the contacts between German SDS members and representatives of the Black Panther Party, I can show for the first time how solidarity and identification with Black Power fostered an increasing radicalization and greater militancy in the West German student movement.

For West German activists, Black Power epitomized the liberation from imperialism and capitalism from within the First World by fulfilling both Che Guevara's foco theory (sparking a revolution through both revolutionary action and the creation of conditions that make it possible) and Herbert Marcuse's minority theory (revolutionary change does not come from the working class but from society's outsiders and minorities). When combined with Frantz Fanon's theories of liberation from colonial oppression through the use of violence and the unresolved National Socialist past, Black Power formed an ideological symbiosis that not only reinforced the determination of West German activists but also played a significant part in the emergence of the Rote Armee Fraktion (Red Army Faction; RAF) and the terrorism of the 1970s.

The last two chapters of this study point out the various ways in which the "other" alliance contested the transatlantic partnership and official relations between West Germany and the United States. Using previously classified government sources, chapter 5 discusses how American officials evaluated the challenge posed by the transnational cooperation of protesting students in the Federal Republic and the United States and how the government initiated a comprehensive monitoring and cultural diplomacy effort to counter it. Focusing particularly on the interplay between the State Department and local mission officials, the chapter explores how American foreign policymakers viewed the rebelling West German youth, especially in light of the country's geopolitical significance in cold-war Europe and its long-standing relationship with the United States.

Taking West Germany as a case in point, chapter 6 demonstrates the overall institutional and strategic impact that the global dimension of student protest had on U.S. foreign policy in the 1960s/70s by introducing the work of the State Department's Inter-Agency Youth Committee founded under the Kennedy administration in 1962, which continued to advise American foreign policymakers until 1972 on how to confront youthful unrest.[22] The study concludes with a discussion of the significance of the "other" alliance and the transnational dimension of 1960s/70s' protest for the history of the cold war and the twentieth century.

Chapter 1

SDS MEETS SDS

The Origins of the Student Movements in
West Germany and the United States

When the 21-year-old German student Michael Vester started his 1961–62 exchange year at Bowdoin College in Brunswick, Maine, with the support of the Fulbright program, he had no idea that he was to become the earliest mediator of an emerging transnational New Left and, at the same time, take an active role in the creation of one of the most influential manifestos of the American student movement of the 1960s. Vester had been born in 1939 Berlin into a middle-class family and spent the first years of his life there before his family moved to Silesia. Committed to a leftist Christian communitarianism and pacifism, part of his mother's family had become politically active in the Weimar Republic after their belief in German nationalism had been shattered by the human catastrophe of the First World War. As a result of their commitment, some family members were forced to emigrate after the National Socialists came to power in 1933. The Second World War and the Soviet advance eventually forced the family to relocate to Holzminden in rural-industrial Northern Germany in March 1945, where Vester's father had been deployed as a soldier.

As refugees, they built up their life anew in this provincial setting during the postwar years while keeping in touch with the other branches of their internationally dispersed family that had spread to Great Britain, the United States, and Latin America. These contacts enforced Vester's orientation toward the Anglo-American branches of the family, who had left England around 1630 as politico-religious dissenters and had been known for their activity in the antislavery movement of the nineteenth century. Most prominent among these relatives was his grandfather's cousin, Thurman Arnold, who, as assistant attorney general in the Roosevelt administration, was in charge of the Antitrust Division in the Department of Justice and was an intrepid liberal and partisan of civil rights.

The German Protestant environment in which Vester grew up after the Second World War encouraged his decidedly antiwar position, which included opposition to the politics of West German Chancellor Konrad Adenauer and the Federal Republic's rearmament in the 1950s. Members of

Vester's family were inspired by the theologian Martin Niemoeller and, as part of a critical middle class, gradually turned to the Social Democratic Party and its representatives such as Willy Brandt. Vester's own political coming of age, however, occurred with the unsuccessful 1953 workers' uprising in East Germany and the 1956 revolt in Hungary, which symbolized the persistent harsh realities of Stalinism. His skepticism toward communism drove him to look for a third way between Western capitalist democracy and Eastern-style communism, a political philosophy based on humanist values. This search was fostered by the actions of the Western alliance during the Suez crisis in 1956, which for Vester signified the continuous interest of the old imperial powers in the Third World. At the age of 16, he was therefore deeply suspicious about any close alliance with either one of the two power blocs in the cold war. He channeled his protest into activism in high school student governments and advanced to the respective student representation on the state level. There he took on the task of political education, running information events on the crimes and legacy of National Socialism in Germany and Stalinism in the Soviet Union. Another politically formative outlet was his participation in Deutsche Freischar, one of the organizations of the Bündische Jugend, a youth movement going back to the 1920s and dedicated to outdoor group experiences. These groups began to rebel against the narrow conservative mood of cold-war society and moved to a neutralist stance against U.S. and Soviet cold-war politics. All of these activities finally brought him closer to the Sozialdemokratische Partei Deutschlands (German Social Democratic Party; SPD), which he perceived as a gathering pool for intellectuals disenchanted with the status quo in the young Federal Republic.

In 1959, Vester finished high school and started studying social sciences at the University of Hamburg. There he was immediately drawn to the SDS (Sozialistischer Deutscher Studentenbund, or German Socialist Student League), which was an ally of the SPD, and he was elected into its regional office. After moving to Frankfurt in 1960, Vester also organizationally drifted to the trade union movement where he met people who had been engaged in resistance efforts during National Socialism, such as trade union chairman Otto Brenner. After his academic year in the United States, he completed the practical parts of his sociological curriculum in the trade union's public relations department and in the educational department under Hans Matthoefer. Through the left-wing Social Democrat Matthoefer (who, in the 1970s, became minister of research under Chancellor Helmut Schmidt), Vester would also become acquainted with European and American labor organizations. His main activism, however, concentrated on the German SDS. Soon after his arrival in the Frankfurt chapter, he became the national vice president of the German SDS, and was also responsible for its international contacts.

At the beginning of the 1960s, the organization that Vester represented already had a long history to look back upon.[1] It was rooted in the Association of Socialist Student Groups of Germany and Austria (1922 to 1929) and its successor, the Socialist Student Association (1929 to 1933).[2] Despite these continuities to prewar times, the group was newly founded on September 3, 1946, out of an initiative of informal socialist student groups at German universities, and it adopted the name that it was to carry throughout the 1960s. Erich Ollenhauer, vice chairman of the Social Democratic Party (SPD), and Kurt Schumacher, the charismatic SPD chairman, in particular supported the meeting of these regional groups and the creation of this socialist student organization. From its inception, SDS was thus associated with the SPD in West Germany, which in the following years urged SDS to adhere to official party lines. The great diversity of the founding generation of SDS after 1945 is illustrated by its first two presidents: Alfred Hooge, who was involved in the socialist resistance during National Socialism, and Heinz Joachim Heydorn, who became a deserter. What initially united them and their membership was the conscious experience of the Weimar Republic, the immediate impetus to re-create a socialist youth movement, and the aim to prevent any future war by actively engaging in peace politics. With the first generational shift in the organization and the replacement of the founding members by people who had still been in school in 1933 and had later been soldiers or involved in other youth party organizations during National Socialism, the organization gradually began to change. This new stream of younger people was characterized by the experience of comradeship, a deep skepticism against any kind of nationalism, openness toward the political culture of the West, a lack of interest in complex theories of society, and an emotional distance to the values of the old labor movement. One member of this new generation was Helmut Schmidt, who was elected president of the SDS in 1947 and would later become West German Chancellor (1972–82). During his time at the head of the German SDS, Schmidt displayed characteristics that would mark his later career: an extraordinary organizational talent, disapproval of "utopian" visions, great sympathy for decisions based on Realpolitik, an international perspective, and diplomatic skills in dealing with competitors or internal rivals.[3]

In ideological terms the German SDS followed a policy that was outlined in the "Eschweger Guidelines" following a conference in February 1948 near Kassel. It envisioned a society that would enable people to develop their own personalities in harmony with each other, a democratically controlled government, and an economic order that would guarantee even the needs of the poor, otherwise exploited by capitalism, through a planned economy. The university, according to the SDS, was to offer free education and a material basis sufficient for living, because one's studies were, in the long run, work for the benefit of society itself. Responsibility for society as a whole and a strong interaction with the SPD were further dominant features of the student organization in its early years.

A further shift in the German SDS took place on October 23, 1958, when for the first time its leftist faction gained ground during the National Convention in Mannheim. The new leaders of the organization, especially Jürgen Seifert, Monika Mitscherlich, and Horst Steckel, were closer in their thinking to the critical theory of the Frankfurt School as represented by Theodor W. Adorno and Max Horkheimer as well as to the democratic-humanist Marxism represented by political scientists like Wolfgang Abendroth and Peter von Oertzen at the universities of Marburg and Göttingen. Political issues like the threat of nuclear power, the demand for negotiations between the two German states, and a possible German confederacy became prominent items on the new agenda. The Frankfurt branch of the SDS continued to exercise an enormous influence on the organization throughout the 1960s. As an informal discussion circle, the organization was close not only to the Frankfurt School, humanist Marxism, and the trade unions, but also to the cultural scene of the city, to which a substantial number of emigrants had returned after the Second World War. The leftward turn of the new leaders of the SDS, however, caused outrage in the party council of the SPD, whose most outstanding members were Herbert Wehner, Helmut Schmidt, and Willy Brandt. With the "Godesberger Program" of 1959, the SPD aimed to become a mass party through integration into the existing political system of the Federal Republic. As part of this process, leading reformers in the party council such as Brandt, Wehner, and Fritz Erler, hoped to distance the organization from its Marxist heritage or, at least, from its dogmatic incarnation in Soviet communism. The German SDS itself, although internally torn between various factions, frequently tried to reconfirm its loyalty to the Social Democrats but could not conceal the growing ideological divide. In this process of increasing separation, the concept of a "New Left" was to play a particularly significant role.

Encouraged by Michael Vester, Frankfurt SDS member Gerhard Brandt (who later taught industrial sociology in Frankfurt) was among the first to introduce the term "New Left" to the theoretical discussions in the organization. In 1961, he described the rise of the New Left in England in the SDS journal *neue kritik* summing up its most important characteristics: a departure from orthodox Marxism, a breakaway from the established party system, a criticism of authoritarian tendencies and apathy in society, a demand for social change, a general dissatisfaction with the cold-war situation, and an affinity to the Campaign for Nuclear Disarmament (CND).[4] He also presented a review of the New Left's most influential book, *Out of Apathy*, edited by social historian Edward P. Thompson, and analyzed the individual contributions by Stuart Hall, Alasdair MacIntyre, and Kenneth Alexander, among others. For Brandt, the goal of these authors was to liberate British society from the dominance of big business and the spiritual void of consumer society. Their means was a "reformist tactic within a revolution strategy," which included a strengthening of organized labor and a belief in the humanism of the working class. Although Brandt was critical of what he viewed as old-fashioned hope for the potential of labor, he nonetheless concluded that the British New Left as a whole combined the innovative dynamics of a socialist youth movement and the strengths of an already-respected political force. By declaring this new movement an example for the German SDS and demanding a more action-oriented strategy, Brandt's article was symptomatic of a push for new discussion within the organization.[5]

As a consequence, the theme of a New Left became dominant at the SDS national convention in 1961, where the organization's president, Michael Schumann, proudly declared, "[W]e feel that we belong to the movement which originates in England under the name 'New Left' and in France is called 'Nouvelle Gauche.' "[6] The president-elect of SDS caused even greater alarm for the Social Democrats when he referred to the SDS as a promising "point of crystallization of a New Left" with possible "organizational tasks."[7] The Social Democratic Party eventually moved to action when, in addition to this, a socialist support society (Sozialistische Fördergesellschaft, SFG) was constituted to help the student organization financially. This society even considered itself to be "the intellectual conscience of the social democratic movement." Deeming the German SDS an institutionalized version of inner-party opposition under the label "New Left," the Social Democratic Party's leading circle decided to break completely with its former ally. In its press statements, the SPD among other things explained the decision as a determined move against the New Left as such, which, according to the party heavy weight Herbert Wehner, was also trying to destroy Social Democratic forces in other European countries.[8] As a result, the SPD executive committee decided to set up its own student organization within its regional chapters in February 1960, thereby officially disassociating itself from the SDS, on November 6, 1961. Membership in the two organizations was from then on declared mutually exclusive.[9]

Facing institutional independence, the SDS allowed the concept of a "New Left" to become even more the focus of internal debate. It was during this period that ideas transported from the American scene started to play a more significant role. Until that point, the alienation between the SPD and SDS had also taken on different dimensions as far as ideological orientation and political concepts were concerned, yet the nature of the definite break left SDS with valuable qualities: the experience of exclusion, a newly gained self-confidence, and a strong intellectual curiosity that also transcended national borders. Indeed, these characteristics would become increasingly valuable in the future. In the years ahead, SDS tried to come to terms with its independence, both financially and theoretically. Ideological diversity and autonomy were celebrated, seen as a distinctive feature of the new generation in SDS. This generation increasingly sought and found a new theoretical definition and identity in a compromise between theoretical and practical socialism associated with the New Left. In other words, SDS as an organization of the "young socialist intelligentsia" from then on positioned itself as a representative of a New Left movement; this movement would not necessarily focus on the workers alone as agents for social change, but would additionally look toward the growing technical and scientific elite at the universities for alternatives to the existing order.[10] SDS understood itself less as a recruiting resource to lead a labor movement, but more and more as an avant-garde organization, which was to attract the educated middle classes and win them over to emancipatory goals for changing society. The concrete relationship between socialist theory and practice, however, still remained to be determined.

At the beginning of the 1960s, there were very few indications of an emerging student movement in the United States. The Student League for Industrial Democracy (SLID), the renamed heir of the early-twentieth-century Intercollegiate Socialist Society (ISS), had only three chapters (at the universities of Columbia, Yale, and Michigan), which operated largely as discussion clubs with a small membership of a few hundred students.[11] The organization had its part-time headquarters in a lower Manhattan office building, and yearly support of not more than $3,500 from its parent organization, the League for Industrial Democracy (LID). It defined itself as "a non-partisan educational organization which seeks to promote greater active participation on the part of the American students in the resolution of present-day problems."[12] In 1960, however, SLID adopted the name Students for a Democratic Society (SDS), which was to become known as the most vocal and popular American youth organization in the upcoming decade.[13]

The name change occurred only shortly after a conference at the University of Michigan, Ann Arbor, which secured the American SDS a prominent place in the public perception of student activism in 1960. Inspired by the lunch-counter sit-in in Greensboro, N.C., student interest and involvement in the civil rights movement spread all over the South; it also reached the North when 150 students gathered at the "Human Rights in the North" conference in Ann Arbor during April 28–May 1, 1960, eager to combat racial discrimination. The fact that students from Greensboro and members of the newly founded Student Non-Violent Coordinating Committee (SNCC) also participated in the conference generated extraordinary interest and brought publicity and recognition for the American SDS. The organization helped to put segregation and racial inequality in the United States on the political agenda of students in the North, who also found inspiration in the protest techniques and strategies of their Southern peers. The conference therefore provided a first meeting ground for two strains of student activism in the 1960s and formed a loose alliance between them; an alliance, however, which was marked by SDS's attempt to absorb the issue of civil rights into the larger political program of a burgeoning New Left movement.

The mastermind behind this strategy was 24-year-old student Al Haber, who had joined SLID in 1958 and afterward turned its University of Michigan chapter into the most active and fastest-growing chapter of the organization. Haber was an extremely talented and persuasive organizer, who very successfully recruited students for this multifarious organization around specific issues such as civil rights, disarmament, and poverty in America. Between 1960 and 1962 he became the first president and national secretary of SDS. With the help of equally ambitious student-organizers such as Richard Flacks and Tom Hayden, he was able to move SDS further away from the Old Left, whose doctrines they perceived as timid and ineffectual. Haber's strategy was to bring together existing campus chapters and groups of various organizations, to coordinate them, and to cater to their individual needs on a national level, thereby abandoning any ideological exclusionism and old battles from within the organization.

Tom Hayden, on the other hand, became the public voice of SDS in its early stages. He had grown up in a Detroit suburb, had a Catholic background, and was influenced by Jack Kerouac's *On the Road* and by the writings of Albert Camus, C. Wright Mills, and University of Michigan philosophy teacher Arnold Kaufman. A concept that Hayden derived from Kaufman's teaching of Aristotle and the Greek city-state ideal of polis, the concept of "participatory democracy," would later become a central SDS theme.[14] This particular notion that active political participation was essential for any civic education was energetically lived out by Hayden, who very soon immersed himself in civil rights work and various activities of the Student Nonviolent Coordinating Committee (SNCC) in the South, and who was on many occasions severely beaten up for his political commitment. His "Letters from the South" to the SDS chapter in Michigan had a lasting impact on the direction of the early SDS from 1960 to 1962. At that point, when little credible information was available on these activities, the SDS perceived itself as SNCC's ally in the

North. The few recruits that the SDS had at that time were sympathetic toward the civil rights movement, toward disarmament, and toward a vague feeling of democracy as a "radical idea."[15]

Organizationally, SDS was still tied to LID, but by 1961, under Haber's presidency, it had begun to establish some theoretical distance from its parent organization. The definitive ideological split, however, was to come in the summer of 1962, when fifty-nine SDS members attended a conference in Port Huron, Mich., at an education camp owned by the United Auto Workers. The aim of this conference was to create, discuss, and ratify an "agenda for a generation"; a vision that was able to attract a young generation dissatisfied with political conformity, social apathy, and the rationalization of modern society. The Port Huron Statement, which emerged from the conference, more than fulfilled this mission and became one of the most influential manifestos of the American Left in the twentieth century.[16] It turned out to be the key document for the formation of the SDS, and served as a break away from the Old Left ideology. It moved away from traditional cold-war loyalty and primarily focused on the problem of ethical existence, as its preamble illustrated: "We are people of this generation, bred in at least modest comfort, housed now in universities, looking uncomfortably to the world we inherit."[17]

The discomfort articulated by SDS stretched from the nation's apathy and complacency, to its supposed poverty of vision, and to the disruptive effects of the military-industrial complex on democracy in America. The organization dismissed any interpretation of the cold war as a struggle between good and evil. It rejected the assumption that there were no alternatives to a foreign policy based on the threat of mutual nuclear extinction. As a result, SDS demanded that the United States live up to its democratic ideals of liberty and social and political equality both internationally and domestically. It attacked the prevailing culture of anticommunism, as well as the existence of poverty on a national and global scale despite technological advances. Values and ideals were supposed to replace the moral bankruptcy and disillusionment of a capitalist society marked by ruthless competition. In this historical context, the Port Huron Statement was dedicated to achieving a radical democracy through the involvement of ordinary people in the decision-making process that affected their lives:

> We regard *men* as infinitely precious and possessed of unfulfilled capacities for reason, freedom and love. In affirming these principles we are aware of countering perhaps the dominant conceptions of man in the twentieth century: that he is a thing to be manipulated, and that he is inherently incapable of directing his own affairs. . . . We see little reason why men cannot meet with increasing skill

the complexities and responsibilities of their situation, if society is organized not for minority, but for majority, participation in decision-making.[18]

SDS argued that only a moral realignment of society could help alleviate its ills.[19] To realize that mission, the organization looked to various other social movements that addressed similar issues: the civil rights movement, the peace movement, organized labor, and the new campus activities. It found that these single movements and their programs were intertwined, but that they lacked a coherent channel of political expression, largely due to their rejection by the Democratic Party.

According to SDS, the university could fill this precise gap. The geographical distribution of institutions of higher education and their central position in society would be ideal for coordinating these various movements and taking on the role of engine and agent of social change. The result would be a *New* Left composed of young visionary people who would not shy away from controversy, who would aim at a synthesis of liberalism and socialism. This New Left would attempt to obtain political power through cooperation with an "awakening community of allies" outside the university, which in itself would serve as "a base for their assault upon the loci of power."[20] The American SDS, and with it the New Left in the United States, therefore started out as an open, nondogmatic, and democratic organization, which desired to emancipate itself and break away from the Old Left partly because of the latter's outdated, doctrinaire views shaped by anticommunism and the cold war, but even more so because of its loss of passion.[21]

These feelings among young college students were, however, not restricted to the United States. As Tom Hayden argued in his assessment of student social action in March 1962, "All over the world the young intellectuals are breaking out of the old, stultified order. Before you call them 'communist' or 'extremist' or 'immature', stop a moment; let yourselves be a little bit more insecure, so that you can listen to what they say and perhaps feel the pulse of their challenge."[22] What might have reconfirmed the internationalism of this sentiment for Hayden was the fact that a representative of a West German student organization bearing the same acronym had by then introduced himself to the leading circle of the American SDS.

Transatlantic Alliances

In 1961 when Michael Vester started his exchange year at Bowdoin College, the German SDS was undergoing transformations similar to what he was about to witness in the American SDS. Through his work in

1960–61 as vice chairman of the German SDS, who was at the same time responsible for its international relations, Vester had already met various American student activists and obtained contact addresses of several political youth and student organizations situated on the political left in the United States.[23] Once in the United States, he decided to get in touch with these groups. Vester quickly established a close relationship with American SDS. This became the earliest link between the German and American SDSs.[24]

Vester visited the National Office of SDS in New York City in early 1962 and spoke at length with Al Haber and Tom Hayden about the German SDS and its activities, such as an exhibition on Nazi perpetrators in the legal branch, its stance on the status of Berlin, and the New Left in Europe. Having become acquainted with Vester's ideas, Haber and Hayden, as well as other members of the American SDS such as Rebecca Adams, were convinced of the common ground between the two organizations and proposed a deeper exchange between them. This collaboration included being on each other's mailing lists as well as serving as hosts for mutual visits. The American SDS was even planning a charter flight to Europe for the summer to attend the summer camp of the International Union of Socialist Youth (IUSY) and the World Youth Festival in Helsinki, Finland, and inquired about like-minded people in Germany and elsewhere to whom they could turn. In addition, Haber asked Vester to become active in the American SDS by setting up new chapters on the northern East coast and contributing to the organization's informational material on international issues such as the division of Berlin:

> As we briefly mentioned when you visited the office, we'd like you to play some role in our organization, at least for the period you remain in the States. Bob [Ross] will probably be coming out from exams soon and will write again about the international bulletin he is doing. An analysis of the Berlin situation and context would also be valuable for inclusion in the program packet put out by Turn Toward Peace. . . . We are beginning a drafting of a political manifesto for the young Left in America, to serve as the basis for our con[v]ention in June. You could give us some valuable assistance on that. And of course, we'd like to make contact with people in the Maine, New Ham[p]shire, Vermont area. Perhaps you could do some traveling for us and aid in the setting up of some groups.[25]

Michael Vester gladly complied with this request and was not only integrated into the leading circle of the American SDS but was also asked for assistance and given the opportunity to participate actively in the formation of an intellectual position within the American SDS that would eventually result in the Port Huron Statement, the fundamental manifesto of the New Left in the United States. From the very beginning, he helped craft the international views of the American SDS and served as a major first-hand contact to the European New Left scene.

In the months after their initial contact, Vester's cooperation with the American SDS intensified. Continuously supplied with SDS literature and that of related organizations, he enjoyed regular correspondence with Al Haber on international issues such as the situation in Africa, particularly the case of Algeria.[26] He also produced short reviews and critical commentaries for the American SDS on the legacies of National Socialism in Germany, and an article summing up the German SDS's position on the political status of Berlin, entitled "Berlin: Why Not Recognize the Status Quo?" which was subsequently put on the American SDS publication list.[27] Furthermore, Vester asked for the specifics of Haber's travel plans to Europe so that he could connect the American SDS president with "people adhering to New Left thoughts," and he requested that several addresses of German SDS members be included on the American SDS mailing list. During these exchanges, Vester also took up Haber's request for organizational assistance to increase the SDS presence in Maine. Haber provided Vester with names of interested people in his area; Vester in turn informed Haber about potential local recruits for the American SDS at Bowdoin, where he had cofounded and was actively engaged in a campus group called the Bowdoin Political Issues Committee, which, among other things, sponsored the screening of the controversial film *Operation Abolition* on campus.[28] In light of the upcoming Port Huron conference, the American SDS president particularly encouraged Vester's recruiting efforts and suggested extending them to other colleges in Maine, such as Bates College in Lewiston: "If you know any of these people or could contact them in a fraternal capacity, that would be much appreciated. I would like to get a good delegation from [this] group and from Bowdoin to our convention."[29] Early on in the decade a member of the German SDS was therefore actively involved in organizing what he perceived to be a transatlantic counterpart of the emerging New Left scene in Europe. Vester not only helped expand American SDS's domestic network by preparing the groundwork for the organization's presence in Maine, but also shaped its international outreach by providing contact addresses in West Germany, as well as writing reviews and articles on international issues for the American SDS.

In the same way, Vester became actively involved in drafting the Port Huron manifesto. He became an important intellectual contributor to the manifesto's evolution, which was already in the planning phase.[30] Early on, Haber had requested Vester's participation in distributing first drafts of the convention programs and of the manifesto to the mailing list.[31]

Initially, Vester was uncertain if financial and time constraints would permit his attendance at the conference.[32] He was aware of the gradual evolution of the manifesto, and since he anticipated his absence at the convention, he sent lengthy comments and remarks to its main author, Tom Hayden, in advance. As will become evident, these suggestions were influenced both by his German background and by his perspective on the emerging New Left movement that he had witnessed and helped to instigate in Europe.

In general, Vester was very enthusiastic about the project, which explains his detailed response to Hayden's first draft.[33] He praised the "dramatic impetus which characterizes classic manifestos" but also drew attention to some stylistic shortcomings. More important, however, were his remarks about the manifesto's actual content. Vester urged Hayden to be more explicit about the "societal contradictions pointed out by socialist analysis," as seen, for example, in the gaps between political democracy and economic concentration of power, and between a rising arms budget and a decrease in public spending for education and general welfare. Furthermore, he pointed to the affluence in the United States and the poverty in the countries of its trade partners as well as the nation's claims for equality on the one hand, and the manipulation by the consumer society on the other.[34] Vester particularly criticized Hayden for his sections about the economy and the military-industrial complex, which he considered "a too detailed summary" of C. Wright Mills and lacking "a more explicit refutation of the theory of the countervailing powers (Galbraith & Co.) which exists only in the middle levels of the society, below the power elite."[35] In doing so, Vester emphasized the need for the manifesto to renounce popular economic theories according to which the influence of business in society was kept in check by trade unions and other lobby groups. He saw that this idea, originally put forth by John Kenneth Galbraith in 1952, was not only discredited by the rise of the military-industrial complex in the previous decade but was also in disunity with his socialist analysis of society.[36]

Apart from his criticism, Vester nonetheless considered the sections on the apathy and autonomy of the current student generation especially well developed and urged Hayden to put more emphasis on the final goals of the envisioned social change:

> The postulate to channel the unstructured protest into a meaningful struggle for a better society, *to transform the struggle against armament into a struggle for a genuine democracy*, deserves a clearer formulation. It was this task we failed to complete in Germany because we formulated it too late to give the protesters a time perspective, patience, and a morale. This implies that action is meaningful and

legitimated only through correlated theoretical digestion of the facts. . . . This is t[h]e theme of your whole manifesto; it has to be explicit from the beginning.[37]

In a similar vein, Vester complemented Hayden's views on anticommunism in American society with a particular German SDS perspective of it. He offered a comparative foil for the role of this specific form of cold-war ideology from a precise German context, explaining that "when faced with the issue we [the German SDS] introduced the term BLIND ANTICOMMUNISM; sometimes it is our own fault when our opposition against anticommunism is misinterpreted because we do not make that distinction. Also the emphasis that blind anticommunism has an integrative function for this society (in Germany it replaced anti-Semitism this way) could be stronger."[38] Vester's stress on this point has to be seen in context of the manifold influence by the Critical Theory of the Frankfurt School on the German SDS. The concept of the "authoritarian personality," developed by Theodor Adorno, among others, in Berkeley in the 1940s, and its attempt to describe certain character features that make people prone to antidemocratic behavior and action had exercised a substantial influence on young intellectuals in post-fascist Germany. Accordingly, they perceived anticommunism as a dangerous ideological tool that played on the very same personality traits of authoritarian submission and aggression that were used under National Socialism. It is striking, however, that in conjunction with Hayden's draft, Vester applies this theoretical model not in a one-dimensional way with respect to existing anticommunist ideologies but considers it an equal danger for an emerging New Left:

> In this context you could imply that persons, frustrated by capitalism, turned to blind anti-capitalism, the correlate to blind anticommunism; I mean that weak personalities think they have to feel a part of [an] *established power*; due to this authoritarian tendency, they sought in communism what capitalism denied them, surrendering the chance of autonomy, which today can find no backing of a great established power. You should emphasize the critical psychological situation of the autonomous personality who has no backing but his hopes.[39]

Vester also warned Hayden of not simply reiterating the "uncommitting generality of the American creed" in the section on values, but to underline that good values can unfold their power only in a good society, where they can gain broader currency.[40]

Interestingly enough, Vester also differed with Hayden on the role of the intellectual as defined by American sociologist C. Wright Mills, who in his "Letter to the New Left" (1960) had advanced the idea of students and intellectuals as a driving force for social transformation. In Vester's view, however, "the intellectuals by themselves, can be a motor of social change, but *not the agency*, the moving power itself!" For him, this was a profound difference, since there was a danger of overestimating the social impact of intellectuals while at the same time, like Mills, who was disillusioned, overlooking the potentials of the labor movement. In the eyes of Vester, "Only a labor movement can be the strong force to actually bring about the changes desired."[41] Nonetheless, Vester stressed that the focus of the manifesto should be concentrated on the situation of youth and its political environment at home and abroad, rather than abstract class struggle. The need to transform the social structures that motivated the general apathy of youth and society at large was crucial for him. He therefore appreciated Hayden's analysis of the "intellectual flexibility" and independence that were landmarks of the New Left both in West Germany and the United States.

All in all, Vester offered constructive criticism of Hayden's first draft, which represents more than merely a reflection of the different perspectives of the two groups. Both considered themselves part of the New Left; however, as was the case with Vester, a greater stress on socialist analysis and its theoretical application, a clearer direction of protest, and a closer relationship to the labor movement and its representative organizations were indicative of a distinctively German or European perspective. For Vester, the sole emphasis on the intellectuals and a neglect of the potential force of the labor movement in transforming society seemed an unrealistic vision. He therefore pleaded for precise wording in the manifesto with regard to the analysis of power relations in society, the underlying socioeconomic reasons for the state society was in, the goals of protest, and possible ideological pitfalls. Nonetheless, these existing differences should not overshadow the common ground and fraternal relations that are ingrained in Vester's comments on Hayden's precirculated draft. As Vester wrote, "My point is not to bring new things but to express what I think to be the *emphasis*—among those things we agree upon."[42] They were united in their transcendence of bipolar cold-war ideologies, their dissatisfaction with a foreign policy of deterrence and with the prospect of mutual nuclear destruction, as well as in their increasing interest in Third World liberation movements. Domestically, both sought to overcome a climate of political apathy and fear and to push back the increasing influence of the economic sector on people's lives and decisions. Their vision overlapped in the creation of a society that would confront social and economic injustice and allow active participation of its citizens in the decision-making process. Despite their differences, the New Left in both the United States and West Germany was dedicated to replacing the cold-war culture in which it grew up with a particular model of a society based on ideals and values and on a more just and peaceful world order. These rather abstract sentiments provided a feeling of similarity and community that enabled mutual personal exchange and cross-fertilization between the two organizations. Most important, even if Vester had not participated in the Port Huron conference, his influence on the development of the manifesto would have remained significant. His remarks circulated among the SDS membership and found entry into various papers of other SDS activists, who paid close attention to his suggestions and integrated them into their own notes.[43] As a matter of fact, Tom Hayden even complained during the National Executive Committee meeting on May 6–7 at Chapel Hill that only one response to his draft had come in, which made Vester's elaborated response all the more prominent.[44]

Michael Vester eventually participated in the Port Huron conference, and his ideas were discussed and incorporated even more strongly as a result of his presence. Participants of the conference, such as leading SDS member Richard Flacks, attest to Vester's influential role in developing an international perspective that connected the outlook of the American SDS, which was primarily shaped by domestic events, to the emerging New Left in other countries. According to Flacks, "[T]hat we were independently coming to parallel notions about a New Left seemed to me to be a real reinforcement and validation of what we were doing. . . . One of the things Vester brought was a kind of European understanding of foreign policy issues which none of us probably had that much of, and the whole German question was a very big question in the early 1960s."[45] Similarly, Tom Hayden argued that Vester brought in an encouraging international perspective: "We were very much a movement based on conditions in the US, especially racism and the powerlessness of young people. But we saw the cold war as the reason why dissent was chilled and our spending priorities were on weapons rather than investments at home. So we were very interested in what Michael Vester, then a student visiting from Germany, had to say about the cold war and its effects on Europe. He helped internationalize our understanding of what we faced."[46]

The reactions of Robert Ross, an influential early member of the American SDS, point to another consequence of Vester's influence. Since Ross hailed from a Jewish background, his interaction with Vester and with the ideas of the German SDS profoundly changed his image of Germany. He and many others felt that this evolving student organization in Germany, with its policies of opposing authority, questioning Germany's past, and challenging current cold-war politics, provided a safeguard against the reappearance of German nationalism. The desire of the German SDS to come to terms with the past, together with a shared socialist view of the world as presented by the New Left, created sympathy on the American side and formed the early basis of what can be considered a collective identity between the two student organizations. As Ross commented,

> These characteristics were very, very encouraging to me. One: they were militant, they were activists. Two: they were anti-fascist. I am of Jewish background. Very important to me that there were young people in Germany that I could identify with. . . . So, here are these guys that had the same initials. It was accidental, but whatever. They called themselves socialist. They emphasized, for everything I knew, democracy. They were kind of rebels. You associated. It was very important, and at least encouraging.[47]

Another crucial unifying factor was Vester's stance on the cold war in Europe as it correlated with and extended the analysis of the American SDS. When the topics of the cold war in Europe, NATO, and the role of the divided city of Berlin came up as part of a marathon plenary discussion to determine the direction of the final version of the manifesto, Vester's comments and proposed revisions to the draft were ratified in total by a "comatose assent" of the conference participants.[48] As Richard Flacks recalls, Vester had prepared a written statement to revise the original draft, which, after his presentation, was simply integrated into the final version of the Port Huron statement as it was put together by Tom Hayden.[49] The positive reception of Vester's ideas could be attributed to the fact that he had already submitted an analysis of the Berlin situation at Haber's request in February 1962, in which he demanded recognition of the status quo and further concessions of both superpowers—demands that were in line with the position of the German SDS.[50] As Vester had elaborated in this article,

> The Berlin wall is a consequence of the cold war and the division of Germany. . . . It had to be expected that a regime which makes people flee would prevent them to flee. . . . Why cannot the problem be solved by a mutual recognition of the status quo: West Berlin's freedom on the one side—East Germany's border lines on the other? . . . In the long run it will be impossible to keep Berlin out of the cold war which dictates affairs in Central Europe. The diametrical confrontation of military blocs constitutes only a labile equilibrium and does not remove the threat of war. Only a military disengagement and a neutralization of all the trouble zones in the world can constitute a genuine TURN TOWARD PEACE.[51]

When comparing this article to the respective section in the Port Huron statement, the linguistic and content resemblances between the two are evident:

A crucial feature of this political understanding must be the acceptance of status quo possessions. . . . [I]t had to be expected that a regime which was bad enough to make people flee is also bad enough to prevent them from fleeing. . . . As a fair and bilateral disengagement in Central Europe seems to be impossible for the time being, a mutual recognition of the Berlin status quo, that is, of West Berlin's and East Germany's security, is needed. . . . The strategy of securing the status quo of the two power blocs until it is possible to depolarize the world by creating neutralist regions in all trouble zones seems to be the only way to guarantee peace at this time.[52]

The same is true with regard to the characterization of West Germany as "authoritarian" and the harmful consequences of a possible German reunification.[53] The influence of Vester and the pieces he wrote for the American SDS on the political situation in Germany and its implications for world peace are thus clearly discernible.[54] Specifically, his stance on the question of Berlin, which the drafters of the Port Huron Statement placed in the section on disengagement and disarmament in the cold war, figured prominently in the final version.

It is thus conclusive to argue that the "agenda for a generation" was at least partially created under the influence of a representative of the German SDS, who successfully integrated his organization's views into the final draft of the document. In fact, Vester's article on Berlin remained on the literature list of the American SDS long after the Port Huron conference ended, and it was, among other things, disseminated as a European view on the cold war through the Liberal Study Group at the annual convention of the National Student Association (NSA) in 1962.[55] This transnational cross-fertilization mediated by Michael Vester is thus another very pronounced example of the international nature of the New Left at the beginning of the decade. Similarly affected by the stalemate of the cold war and the dogmatic perspectives of their parent organizations, activists on both sides of the Atlantic sought alternative models of society and reached out across national borders for stimulation and exchange. In doing so, they turned the emergence of the New Left into a transatlantic experience.

The Formation of an International New Left

The personal discussions that Michael Vester enjoyed with Al Haber, Richard Flacks, Robert Ross, and Tom Hayden during his stay in the United States not only formed the basis of personal relationships, but also influenced institutional cooperation. Soon after Vester's arrival in the United States, the German SPD-SDS split became a topic in his correspondence with Haber. Accordingly, when SPD documentation on the separation with its former youth organization reached the American SDS, Haber immediately relayed it to Vester. In turn, Vester gave him further details on the conflict and on pending court orders prohibiting the SPD from portraying the German SDS and the European New Left as infiltrated by communists.[56] As a result, the American SDS voiced its protest against the expulsion of students and other intellectuals from the ranks of the German SPD and demanded a correction of the party's statements:

> We stress that in this statement of protest we do not approve of everything the Socialist Students of Germany ever did. With deep regret we have to believe that the SPD had to resort to dishonesty in order to justify the expulsion of students, professors, and other intellectuals. The SPD still owes us an explanation.[57]

In another letter to the SPD drafted by Vester, Haber on June 6, 1962, continued to insist that the German SDS was not infiltrated by communists: "The SPD thus failed to invalidate the statement in our letter that any known opponents of communist regimes support the SDS." He elaborately questioned the party's claims and particularly defended the status of the New Left in Europe.[58] At the same time, he brought up the conflict within the International Union of Socialist Youth (IUSY) concerning the continuation of the German SDS's membership, which had erupted after the separation process when the German SDS had been downgraded to the status of a cooperating organization.[59] Haber argued that the American SDS "would also be interested in the SPD's opinion toward the IUSY report on the German SDS, which emphasizes that the SDS is not communist-infiltrated but fulfills a valuable function at the German universities." Despite his sharp protest, however, Haber also struck a softer chord with regard to a potential meeting with the SPD that summer. He concluded by saying that "although our correspondence has not yet produced much agreement, keeping in touch leaves the way open."[60]

The American SDS's defense of its West German counterpart illustrates that both organizations had been aware of each other through their common membership in and conferences with the IUSY.[61] The fact that these protest letters sent off by the American SDS were drafted by Michael Vester in consultation with the executive council of the German SDS in Frankfurt was indicative of the fraternal relationship that Vester had already established with his U.S. counterparts. Based on this tradition and with Michael Vester as a crucial mediator, both openly supported one another in the face of massive institutional pressure from their parent organizations as well as attacks by international socialist associations on a New Left ideology that both groups could identify with. The American and German SDSs are thus the most strongly developed example of a transnational New Left operating on both sides of the Atlantic at the beginning of the 1960s, thereby preparing the groundwork for future international cooperation later in the decade.

Members of the American SDS also worked for a further integration of efforts with the German SDS. Robert Ross seriously considered publishing an international bulletin through the American SDS. In a draft prospectus from December 1962, Ross complained about the lack of understanding within the organization about the intricate mechanisms and problems of foreign policy. Stressing the need for the peace movement to present a positive alternative to existing models of cold-war rhetoric, he argued,

> Often we have been guilty of startlingly naive myopia—the belief that if this and that problem is solved the world will be well on its way to peace, freedom and security. In the peace movement, and more broadly, in the entire field of international relations and foreign policy, our actions have been negative, reactive and sporadic. . . . But nowhere, it seems, has a coherent understanding of the basic power configurations of world politics emerged.[62]

He emphasized that the focus of peace activists should thus not only center on questions of nuclear testing, but also include the broader perspective of power politics in a time of bloc confrontations. According to Ross, an international bulletin from the New York office of the SDS could identify and analyze specific areas of foreign-policy concern and contribute to a more informed SDS membership. The bulletin was designed to appear more-or-less on a monthly schedule, with individual issues focusing on one specific area and its connections to the international political system. Students from Ann Arbor and other campuses were supposed to be the main suppliers of articles, with the editorial line being "consistent with that of the Bulletin; an attempt to put together coherently, and radically, the political values and relevant information."[63] Although the bulletin never materialized, because the issue of reforming the organization's bureaucracy and structures seemed more pressing, plans for such a publication give testimony to the growing interest among SDS members in issues affecting the world outside the United States and the American role in international politics.

Even before entertaining the idea of an international bulletin, Ross had been dealing with the international side of the student movement. In 1961, a year before the Port Huron conference, he proposed that student revolts in various countries be viewed as an interconnected phenomenon:

> These students are part of a world-wide revolution. There is no use dividing that revolution into anti-West or pro-Soviet slogans. . . . The social ferment that is sweeping the undeveloped nations of the world,

and which is having its effect in the Western nations as well, frequently finds the student population in the vanguard of action. The examples of Japan, Algeria, West Africa, and Latin America are not inconclusive. . . . In protests, demonstrations, riots, and revolutions students have been exerting their demands for a better world. This is often due to unique factors of the culture in which they live, but there are several common denominators amongst them.[64]

Ross distinguished between student actions in the West, which were mostly a reaction to the cold war, and those in the underdeveloped countries, which were motivated by a new nationalist drive.[65] The unifying factor in his view, however, was that the world itself and its political order had come into question for students in both places. Even more, they felt they could alter the global political situation through their own actions for the good of humankind.[66] To further connect the American campus scene to these rapid developments, Ross considered his proposed bulletin and the informational basis it would provide as yet another way to reach out internationally to other student movements through foreign policy issues.[67] He was already arguing at the end of 1962 for an institutionalized channel for international exchange of information and cooperation. This demand, however, remained unrealized until 1965, when early opposition to the war in Vietnam made the idea of a greater international network of America's critics more attractive and promising in its capacity to affect worldwide public opinion.

On the other side of the Atlantic, the German SDS attempted to institute a project similar to that of the bulletin, this time in the form of an international newsletter (Auslandsbrief). Published quarterly by the international office of the organization, it was supposed to inform its membership about international events and the foreign activities of SDS. The incentive for the endeavor also stemmed from the lack of publicity for foreign socialist debates.[68] Accordingly, the first issue featured thematically structured literature lists, short reports on SDS's international appearances and contacts, and translated articles from a variety of countries.[69] The English-language bulletin *German News* was a further attempt to inform foreign students and organizations about the work of the German SDS and the situation in Germany. This was superseded in 1962, however, by the international edition of the *SDS-Informationen*, the *German Correspondence*.[70] The efforts of the German SDS in this area and its interest in international cooperation and outside presentation were twofold. On the one hand, the emergence of a New Left with its distinct ideological shaping in neighboring European countries did not go unnoticed by the leaders and membership of the organization, and so the initiative for broader transnational perspective was also inspired by a direct need for more information. On the other hand, the growing domestic difficulties in the aftermath of the split with the Social Democratic Party left the organization with a crucial need to defend its standing abroad and clarify its ideological position, especially after the SPD had accused it of being communist-infiltrated. The international sphere afforded the German SDS the chance to find validation and further development of its theoretical program dedicated to a New Left. International outreach thus took on a completely different dimension for German activists than it did for their American peers. For the Germans, it was both a reaction to developments already in progress in their immediate vicinity and a response to a desperate domestic situation that threatened the organization's political and financial survival.

This also explains the active role that the German SDS played early on in pushing for the setup of a transnational infrastructure for the burgeoning New Left movement. During the IUSY congress in Vienna in October 1960, the German SDS delegation, chaired by Vester, took a leading role in bringing together for a separate meeting the representatives of various youth organizations who considered themselves part of a New Left. The delegations included the Étudiants Socialistes Unifiés (France), the National Association of Labour Student Organisations (England), Politeia (The Netherlands), SSF (Norway), the ESB and Jeunes Gardes Socialistes (Belgium), the Nigerian youth organization of the National Congress of Nigeria and the Cameroons (NCNC), and individual delegates of other organizations.[71] Officially constituted as a working group under the title "Vers le Socialisme" (Toward Socialism), their association was designed to have an operational base in Britain, a "center of information" run by the Oxford Labour Club (OLC), and in Belgium, a so-called "center of action" run by the national office of Jeunes Gardes Socialistes (JGS) in Brussels.[72] Monthly circulars were supposed to inform affiliated organizations of further developments. As a result of this assembly, its participants proudly declared, "[T]he work of the international new left will begin."[73]

Although the eventual outcome and significance of these meetings were marginal, these efforts can be considered the first endeavors to institutionalize a transnational affiliation based on a loose ideological understanding of a New Left in the 1960s. This emerging common sentiment would soon find its expression in the foundation of the *International Socialist Journal*, whose first issue at the beginning of 1964 would feature international contributions from Ernest Mandel, Raymond Williams, Jürgen Seifert, Theo van Tijn, and Tom Hayden, among others.[74] For the German SDS, the cultivation of these foreign contacts was of crucial significance for maintaining its domestic and international standing after its separation from the SPD.[75] Accordingly, the German students tried to keep this international New Left network alive; before the 1963 IUSY convention they once again tried to initiate a separate meeting of various organizations that belonged to this group in order to discuss a common strategy. Their plan was to establish an independent and bloc-free socialist wing in the IUSY based upon the slowly blossoming New Left movements in various countries.[76]

The office for international affairs (Auslandsreferat) in the German SDS was institutionally responsible for these connections.[77] Its role was to further international membership exchanges through close contact with foreign organizations and international publications such as the *German Correspondence*, a quarterly English-language newsletter that reported on the main fields of the German SDS's work and the political development in the Federal Republic. The aim was to foster an international form of solidarity that could lead to "new forms of joint struggle."[78] With the gradual evolution of the network of the international New Left, the need for a considerable amount of staff dedicated to this task became increasingly apparent. In April 1962, the executive council of the German SDS therefore asked for the cooperation of the local chapters.[79] Due to the essential importance of international cooperation in order for the German SDS to enrich and further develop new theoretical approaches, each local group was to determine a contact person responsible for entertaining connections with foreign organizations. This person would represent the German SDS at international seminars and provide information on foreign events and the situation in other countries through international journals.

The crucial emphasis that the German SDS placed on these networks is also reflected in the correspondence with American organizations. Mutual requests for fraternal greetings, the sending of delegates to national conventions, and the exchange of contact information on student organizations in Africa and Latin America were a frequent occurrence.[80] Furthermore, the German and American SDSs also signed joint international statements as a symbol of mutual cooperation. Especially in the case of nuclear disarmament, cooperation between the two groups was facilitated by a firmly established international peace movement and its national affiliates, whose roots extended back into the 1950s. The American and German SDSs were closely linked to this peace network due to personal continuities in activist networks and a shared ideological opposition to an ever-escalating arms race and fear of the "bomb."[81] In the United States, for example, the Student Peace Union (SPU) occupied a prominent place among leftist student organizations as the leading group for nuclear disarmament activism, as is reflected by its marked rise in membership at the beginning of the decade.[82] The later SDS President Todd Gitlin was a case in point. Gitlin was initially drawn to activism through the Harvard peace group Tocsin, which, in conjunction with SPU, Student SANE, and SDS, mobilized about 5,000 students for the largest White House demonstration since the Rosenberg trial in 1951. On February 16–17, 1962, they picketed in front of the White House against President Kennedy's nuclear test plans.[83] Through his work with Tocsin, Gitlin was very much aware of the efforts of the peace movement in Europe, such as the British Campaign for Nuclear Disarmament (CND).[84] As part of his activities, he even got in touch with the short-lived German socialist periodical *Opposition und Ziel*, which printed several of his articles.[85] Although Gitlin later became chairman of Tocsin, he eventually resigned from this position and, after graduating from Harvard University, went on to become elected president of the American SDS at the 1963 national convention.

It was therefore no surprise that when the Young People's Socialist League (YPSL) and other U.S. student organizations joined together to present a statement on disarmament to the United Nations for Easter 1963, the German SDS promptly responded to their call to turn it into an international student statement. After participating in the Easter marches for peace and the disarmament campaign in West Germany, the German SDS, according to Vester, especially welcomed "the positions of active neutralism and supporting the United Nations."[86] The demand by Peter Myers, International Secretary of YPSL, for "better international lines of communication" in order "to promote a greater understanding and cooperation among youth of all countries" was illustrative of putting international solidarity into practice. Incidentally, the call for international disarmament was forwarded to the German SDS by the British National Youth Campaign for Nuclear Disarmament and Peace; this indicates that student activists could already rely on a very strong and efficient transatlantic network, often centered in the United Kingdom.[87]

Sympathetic American academics working in Europe were of equally crucial importance in facilitating the continued development of the international network between the United States, Great Britain, and continental Europe, particularly West Germany. For example, from the 1950s until the mid-1960s, American sociologist Norman Birnbaum taught at the London School of Economics (1953–59), Oxford University (1959–64), and the University of Strasbourg (1964–66), after having spent time at the universities of Marburg, Mainz and Heidelberg in 1952/53. In Europe, he joined the circle around the *New Left Review* and was therefore able to witness the creation of the British and the European New Left first hand. As the "academic American of the British New Left," Birnbaum served as a contact to the American New Left scene, for example, to people such as C. Wright Mills and to the editors of *Studies on the Left* and *Dissent*. During his time in London, he introduced American visitors such as Michael Harrington to the British New Left. In addition, he supplied American activists such as Tom Hayden with information on what was happening in Europe, as he did while on a lecture tour to Ann Arbor, Chicago, and Berkeley in the summer of 1962. At the same time, he remained in close touch with a whole range of European activists, particularly with the German SDS members, whom he visited while in Berlin various times in 1963/64 to lecture on the situation in America. Birnbaum's role as a "messenger between two worlds" did not cease after his return to the United States in 1966. He continued to give lectures on the European student movement while remaining in close touch with its activists, just as he had done in Europe on the American scene.[88]

Similar forms of transatlantic exchange also took place when the American and German SDSs worked on related topics or wanted to announce their work abroad. In 1959, the German SDS had sponsored the exhibition "Unredeemed Nazi Justice" (Ungesühnte Nazijustiz), which documented the past of many acting judges and prosecutors in the Federal Republic with regard to their role under National Socialism. The exhibition aggravated SDS's relationship to the Social Democratic Party and caused a stormy public debate about the origins of the judicial system in West Germany. By 1961, the main organizer of the exhibition, Reinhard Strecker, was able to show it to audiences in Oxford, London, Amsterdam, and Utrecht, among other cities. Due to its success, the German SDS also attempted to export the exhibition across the Atlantic. During his time in the United States, Michael Vester had already discussed the issue of former Nazis in the Federal Republic on a radio show. In early 1961, he proposed to Michael Harrington, the well-known American socialist and leader of the League for Industrial Democracy (LID), the production of a sequel, as well as publications to generate public attention in the United States on Nazi war criminals.[89] Vester also tried to enlist the help of the American SDS in forming a committee to facilitate the efforts of the German SDS in prosecuting former Nazi criminals in the legal branch.[90] Eventually, the Student Peace Union (SPU) picked up the issue and used it to initiate general cooperation with the German SDS.[91] Since the exhibition had provoked very little media interest in the United States, Reinhard Strecker and the German SDS were eager to seize the opportunity of having SPU produce a pamphlet based on German SDS material.[92] Although it remains unclear whether the actual brochure was eventually printed, the communication related to this issue is only one example of the thematic variety of these early transatlantic networks. Both the German and the American SDSs attempted to benefit from each other by sharing the results of their political work—for example, in the case of university reform—and they sought to magnify their public presence through the help of their transatlantic peers. The depth and diversity of their exchanges, regardless of whether they were on a personal or organizational level, thus forms one of the most striking characteristics of the early New Left.

The SDS-SPD split, and the institutional isolation resulting from it, was one of the most significant forces driving German SDS into the arena of international cooperation. After gaining independence from the party, the disillusionment of SDS members with respect to the old socialist forces only increased, and this in turn influenced their attraction to the New Left in other European countries. As Michael Vester wrote to Joel Geyer of the socialist journal *New Politics*, "[A]fter the failure of first the Communists and later the Social [D]emocrats to get nearer to a better society the European New Left is confronted with a task similar to yours: a new beginning with new ways of agitation and a new discovery of the old 'theory.' "[93] The conflict with the SPD thus advanced to a symptomatic test case for New Left organizations everywhere, who were trying to emancipate themselves intellectually and organizationally from their parent organizations. As German SDS President Eberhard Dähne phrased it, "We do not want to consider our conflict with the SPD a particular German, an accidental problem. We know [that] what happened to us happened to other organizations, before. It is the situation which all leftists of the labour movements in all industrial nations face when they protest the petrifaction and bureaucratization of these movements."[94]

Due to the early and drastic nature of the separation, this topic exerted a formative influence for the German SDS, and was a powerful spur to its international efforts. In the years ahead, however, and especially with the beginning of the antiwar movement, it receded into the background in favor of a more substantial international cooperation among an international New Left. The German SDS's aim was not only to include the top-level officials into such transnational cooperation, but also to reach out to its individual members. International seminars, pilot-studies, and the wide publication of results and topical bibliographies were designed to facilitate this goal. As was clear to the people in charge of the international office within the German SDS, the newly founded institutional framework could serve the purpose of creating an international New Left only if it were able to go beyond purely rhetorical forms of exchange. What was needed was to move toward more permanent and substantial structures of cooperation.[95] To facilitate this, the German SDS in 1964 developed a questionnaire that was to compile information on the various activities, working groups, experts, and publications of the respective national organizations.[96] Notwithstanding its focus on the Western European Left in this project, the German SDS was equally present in the United States through its net of personal contacts and its mutual presence, with the American SDS, on various mailing lists. Don McKelvey from the American SDS in December 1962 especially welcomed the international edition of the "SDS-information," for example, which would give people a chance to get a quick overview of the situation in Germany.[97] The German SDS both appreciated and attempted to sustain this transatlantic informational exchange, since it considered material from the American SDS very stimulating for its own work in West Germany.

Although these transatlantic networks thus worked both ways, one partner nevertheless had more influence over the other in terms of ideological orientation and political strategies in this New Left alliance at the beginning of the 1960s.[98] Notwithstanding Michael Vester's input during the drafting of the Port Huron Statement and his role in shaping the international perspective of the American SDS, his impact remained no match to the range and intensity of the American influence on the German SDS. The civil rights movement, the American SDS, and theoretical inspirations such as the writings of C. Wright Mills offered a disproportionate stimulus for an organization that had just won its institutional independence and was looking for a new theoretical position. In this internal transformation process, voices and examples from the other side of the Atlantic, whose transmission was assisted by an increasingly globalized media, as well as personal channels of communication, would prove an inspiring point of reference for young West German activists.

The American Influence in the New Left Definition of the German SDS

In its identification as part of a wider movement under the umbrella term "New Left," the German SDS especially looked toward Great Britain and to the newly established group around the journal *New Left Review* for theoretical and practical inspiration at the beginning of the decade. From 1961 onward, however, the development of the American New Left progressively evoked a greater interest among German SDS members, encouraged by Michael Vester. Hannes Friedrich reported on the American magazine *Dissent* in the journal of the German SDS, the *neue kritik*, and introduced its program to a German audience. He drew upon the socialist theories that were being developed in the United States to provide an analysis of contemporary American society. For Friedrich, the emerging concepts of the American New Left were of crucial significance to its German counterpart.[99] The German SDS empathized with an emerging New Left that was rethinking orthodox socialist concepts, and the Germans therefore closely watched its developments in the United States. This is also evidenced by advertisements for specific American magazines and listings of other American works in the "for further reading" sections in the *neue kritik*.[100] In fact, the journal itself and its editors functioned as the most prominent platform and coordination pool for New Left concepts in general and their dissemination among student activists.

The writings of American sociologist C. Wright Mills provoked the most fundamental discussions, and eventually exerted the greatest influence on the German SDS.[101] In 1962, the German-language translation of his famous book *The Power Elite* appeared. Mills's ideas, however, had already been widely received and had become very popular in the United States and among the English New Left at the beginning of the decade. In its discussions and portrayals of the United States, the German SDS now began to mirror Mills's sociological approaches and analyses of contemporary American society. As early as 1963, Michael Vester wrote a portrait of the United States, which was heavily influenced by his reading of Mills.[102] He analyzed the economic and social situation in the United States and the various strategies that the Kennedy administration and other groups offered as a reaction to it. Vester came to the conclusion that despite the good will and energy of the administration, the supremacy of the so-called "power elite," a term coined by Mills that referred to a group of influential military and industrial leaders dominating crucial decisions in society, was still dominating U.S. politics:

> The political practice of the Kennedy administration so far is not suitable to refute Mill's criticism. . . . The assertion that an accommodation of conflicting interests between the countervailing powers could guarantee social justice is untrue because it is less the social but the corporate or industrial countervailing powers which could not care less about the majority of consumers. The countervailing powers are like hyenas fighting for prey. The hegemony of the power elite remains untouched.[103]

Thus, the image of the United States, as analyzed by the German SDS at the beginning of the decade, was presented using central concepts of an important theoretician of the American Left. This trend continued so that Mills's thoughts gradually disseminated and were implemented by the German SDS, even with regard to its own position in the structure of West German society. For example, the American SDS had already adopted the idea that Mills put forth in his "Letter to the New Left," that students, intellectuals, and academics in general were a crucial force for social change; this very concept now also became commonplace in discussions within the German SDS.[104]

Unsurprisingly, it was again Michael Vester, who, in December 1963, delivered a detailed presentation of the application of C. Wright Mills's theory to the German context. In his analysis, Vester examined different phases of capitalist development from a socialist perspective in order to estimate the real potential and strategies for social change in West Germany. Acknowledging comparable capitalistic and economic situations in the United States and West Germany, Vester applied Mills's concept to political processes in the latter and, for the first time, drew practical consequences for the political work of the German SDS.[105] Facing the ultimate control by a supposed power elite, Vester refused the alternatives of reform or revolution and dismissed them as beside the point. Instead, he argued for a mobilization of the workers by the intellectuals. For him, the ultimate goal of a socialist policy had to be the breakup of the forced-consensus culture from above. As a consequence, Vester adopted Mills's ideas—particularly the role he assigned to the intellectuals—and transformed them into a theoretical tool with which to understand and strategically alter West German society.[106] In addition to Vester and others in the German SDS who subsequently implemented the ideas of Mills in their theoretical and practical work, the German-born American scholar Herbert Marcuse also stressed the role of the intellectual in social(ist) change. In both the United States and in Germany, then, Marcuse would go on to fill the void in the movement's theoretical inspiration that was created by Mills's sudden death in 1962.[107]

Drawing upon his extensive experience in the United States, Michael Vester also offered a comprehensive introduction and historical overview of the American Left itself for the German SDS. Assuming an increasing similarity between the United States and Western Europe, Vester argued that attention had to be given to the American Left, because its strategies could potentially be adopted and used in a West German political context.[108] Of special interest to him were the trade unions, the civil rights movement, leftist and socialist intellectuals, and the disarmament movement. Vester turned to a detailed description of these "single purpose movements" and their strategies, as well as the numerous student organizations on the Left. Among these student organizations, he saw striking parallels to the New Left in England—again a reminder of the perceived similarities associated with the term "New Left."[109] What is even more interesting, however, is the emphasis that Vester placed on the role of the leftist intellectuals in the United States; he believed that they argued for a realignment of powers in American society by supporting the civil rights movements, the trade unions, and the liberals in the Democratic Party in order to reshape the political party landscape. It was hard to overlook his enthusiasm for the potential of this alliance between intellectuals and single-purpose movements on the left both to change American society and to involve the population in a truly democratic process.[110] In this strategy he saw an implicit example for the German SDS.

In Vester's view, American activists had overcome political illusions by accepting the fundamental imbalance of power in society and their own relative powerlessness in the face of it. Combined with existentialist influences, this insight had eventually paved the way for a revival of methods of direct action as a more sober and effective political strategy. This approach of the American Left therefore appeared to be both a realistic assessment of the situation and a promising guideline to Vester. This is why he argued for its adoption for the political constellation in West Germany.[111] Vester thereby went beyond providing a coherent introduction to the American Left for the German SDS as early as 1963. In supplying a comprehensive framework with which to understand the situation of the contemporary protest movements in the United States, he simultaneously set the tone for any later discussion of it. As a result, his writings can be viewed as the starting point of an important awareness, although with varying degrees of significance, within the German SDS of the theoretical and practical approaches on the American side.

By providing first-hand information on the situation in Germany and rectifying it from his perspective, Michael Vester thus served as an important channel of information between the German and American SDSs and can be seen as an early precursor of the transatlantic countercultural networks and alternative news services that student activists established at the end of the 1960s. He not only transported ideas from the United States to Germany through his writings in *neue kritik*, but he also brought the German SDS's perception of Germany and the Berlin question to the early American SDS. He established the groundwork for further personal channels of communication. All of this was possible only because in the early 1960s the German SDS and its American counterpart saw themselves as part of an international movement under the umbrella term "New Left." Each could identify with the other's respective departures from established left dogmas, criticism of authoritarian tendencies, and demands for social change. Vester described the international scope of this network: "What keeps the New Left together is its common pattern: not only the common protest against the frustrations inherent in society but also a common approach, even if it becomes manifest in such various ways."[112] What is equally interesting, though, is that at that point he already saw the potential dangers of the New Left's idealism with regard to this international perspective, which in hindsight may seem a strange prophecy:

> The problematic nature of the New Left indicates that its immediate idealism is not enough for long-run survival and success which requires the qualities of patience and a time perspective which are just beginning to develop. Disillusionment with their own effectiveness, when it occurs, however, would lead again to apathy or integration into the short-sighted routine of the old organizations. This demonstrates [that] a utopia which is not based on a realistic understanding of reality is doomed to defeat its own purpose.[113]

Nevertheless, in the years to come, the German SDS would work on enhancing its internationalist outlook and connections even further, partly through an intensification of contacts with its West European and African counterparts. The link to the American scene, however, was only to deepen over time. Through a plethora of personal contacts and its main publications, (*neue kritik*, *SDS-Info*, and other leftist periodicals such as *Konkret*), the German left continued to be well-informed about the emerging American student and civil rights movements and their developments throughout the decade. This transatlantic connection was, however, not unidirectional but also included the desire for further cooperation on the side of the American SDS. In a letter and formal greeting sent to Michael Vester, Tom Hayden probably best expressed the common bond that had already been established between the two organizations:

> SDS greets SDS in its present convention. We are acquainted directly through Michael Vester whose participation at our national convention was instrumental in the adoption of our present stand on the German question. We are related fraternally in our common aim of building democracy in this revolutionary time while simultaneously attempting to end the Cold War which has been the definitive social experience for us all. We are perhaps historically bound by our common unrest with the accomplishments of our radical predecessors, and our creative conflict with them and society as a new left emerges. We wish you and, through you, ourselves, vitality and advancement.[114]

How, and to what degree, this "other" cold-war alliance composed of students could gain mutual "vitality and advancement" through the individual successes of its members, as Tom Hayden and others had hoped it would at the beginning of the decade, will be the topic of the following chapters.

Chapter 2

BETWEEN BERKELEY AND BERLIN,

FRANKFURT AND SAN FRANCISCO

THE NETWORKS AND NEXUS OF TRANSNATIONAL PROTEST

"GERMANY. OH REALLY? We have a sister organization there, also called SDS. We'll give you the names and you can go and see them over there."[1] This was the information that Douglas Blagdon received in the summer of 1964 when he told the U.S. national Students for a Democratic Society (SDS) office of his plan to spend an academic year in West Germany. What he did not know at that point was that ever since Michael Vester's visit in 1961/62 the German and the American SDS had kept in touch and continued to enjoy a loose but fraternal relationship. Members of the American SDS such as Blagdon would regularly inquire for contact addresses when traveling to Europe to meet with their German counterparts. Both organizations invited each other for conferences, received each other's publications such as the *neue kritik* or the *New Left Notes*, and included their transatlantic peers on their mailing lists and international newsletters. As a result, both groups were very much aware of their respective activities and discussions.[2]

Consequently, it was only natural that after this revelation Douglas Blagdon was looking forward to getting in touch with his German peers. As he wrote in a letter to the Frankfurt SDS, "I am very happy to have found comrades in Germany and am looking forward to learning more about your work."[3] Blagdon subsequently stayed in Frankfurt and later in Berlin and frequently visited the local German SDS chapters. In their discussions, he often illustrated the official American perspective on foreign and domestic policy issues and contrasted it with the domestic critique put forward by the American SDS or other organizations. Blagdon recalls, however, that while most of the discussions in Germany had previously concentrated on New Left politics and civil rights, in 1965 these topics were already being replaced by what was to become one of the prime topics among student organizations in both countries during the second half of the 1960s: the American involvement in Vietnam.[4]

A Truer Internationalism?
Attempts at Internationalizing the Antiwar Movement

By mid-1965, the American SDS had been swept up almost completely by the emerging antiwar movement in the United States. After Port Huron, the organization had gradually become more radical in its views on the state of society, liberalism, university reform, and the role of students as agents of social change. Three factors help illuminate this transformation: First, the massive and violent resistance against the civil rights movements in the South, which was symbolically embodied by the Birmingham police commissioner, Eugene "Bull" Connor, further stimulated the SDS's search for "new forms of insurgent politics" to actively bring about social change.[5] Moreover, the increasing militancy in the civil rights movement fostered by the refusal of the Democratic Party to grant the Mississippi Freedom Democratic Party (MFDP) equal national representation, as well as by Stokely Carmichael's call for Black Power, was a significant factor in broadening the New Left's basis. Second, the Free Speech Movement (FSM), which started in the fall of 1964 at the University of California at Berkeley and was organized to rally students for the cause of the First Amendment, the right to collect funds, and the right to be politically active on campus, politicized more and more students and inspired them to seek active political engagement.[6] For the SDS, the campus confrontations with the administration and the Berkeley police as well as Mario Savio's inspiring rhetoric provided a model for later conflicts on campus around university reform, the draft, and opposition to the war.

Third, the organizational structure and membership of the SDS was rapidly changing. In short, the SDS was on its way to becoming a mass organization. It had grown from 800 members in May 1962 to 1,500 in October 1963 to 2,500 in December 1964, and it would climb to 10,000 by October 1965. The number of its chapters had risen from nine in January 1963 to twenty-nine in June 1964, to eighty chapters a year later, and this number would climb to eighty-nine in October 1965 and to 172, thus almost doubling its size, in June 1966.[7] Newcomers were now often recruited through mass media, and so personal recruitment with its socialization process decreased. In addition, they were predominantly attracted to SDS through their opposition to the war. As a result, they felt more alienated from society, were geographically more broadly based, and also were sometimes more countercultural and angrier. They had not gone through the political and intellectual educational experience of the so-called "old guard," and were influenced more by C. Wright Mills, the French existentialists, and Herbert Marcuse than by the classics of political theory or of socialist thought.[8]

Under these conditions the opposition to the war in Vietnam was the dominant force for the shift of the SDS to a mass student movement in the years 1964–66. This transformation, however, was very controversial. Several voices in the organization feared the loss of a multi-issue movement and advocated a balanced attention to foreign issues and domestic problems such as racism and poverty, the latter being realized through the SDS's community-organizing efforts in disadvantaged neighborhoods of Cleveland and Newark. Despite these concerns, the beginning of the Vietnam War with the Tonkin Gulf Resolution in August 1964 and its escalation with operation "Rolling Thunder" in February 1965 slowly pushed other issues into the background.[9] Already in 1963, the American SDS had seen Vietnam as an example of an irresponsible U.S. foreign policy.[10] It was only in 1964 and 1965, however, that the war in Vietnam became a paradigm, used to illustrate all that was fundamentally wrong with American society and with the American system as it had developed at large. About 2,500 students discussed the war in the first major teach-in organized by SDS at the University of Michigan on March 24–25, 1965. On April 17, after the spread of the teach-in movement, SDS organized a march on Washington—during which SDS president Paul Potter delivered what was to become one of the most famous speeches against the war in Vietnam, as 20,000 to 25,000 people demonstrated in front of the Washington monument—to that point the largest peace march in American history.[11]

In the aftermath of the march, internal plans concerning the international extension of the antiwar movement and the SDS as an organization blossomed. Even before the national convention, a debate about foreign policy issues erupted in a series of working papers. In one of them, SDS member Richard Ochs suggested that the organization should expeditiously build up a transnational network of connections to other movements, particularly in Western Europe and the Third World. According to Ochs, global problems made global solutions necessary:

> If American students and intellectuals ever intend to seriously grasp the problems of world poverty, democracy, and the Cold War, they must eventually communicate with intellectuals the world over. Now is the time to start. But more than just sending SDS ideas to other students in the struggle for social justice, we have a lot to benefit and to learn from reciprocal communications from these students in the midst of world revolution.[12]

Other SDS members suggested that before reaching out to other movements, the prime task was to initiate a comprehensive internal education program on foreign student and protest organizations.[13] In another working paper, former SDS Vice President Paul Booth summed up the goals of all of these proposals for the summer of 1965 under the heading "Building bridges to students and others in the Third World," stating that ideas ranged from "including foreign consulates among the targets for demonstrations (please intervene), to setting up contacts between campuses and national student unions in the 3rd world." For Booth, the realization of these plans could lead to a "truer internationalism" within the movement and would put the SDS in a position to "trigger worldwide demonstrations" in unity with likeminded students all over the globe.[14]

In contrast, one of the most popular spokesmen for the antiwar cause at that point, SDS President Paul Potter, voiced his deep concern about the unintended consequences such an international outreach could bring. Although he saw a growing need for dealing with the national liberation movements in Latin American and Asia, he was particularly troubled by the perspective of Americans uncritically identifying with the Viet Cong without sufficient background knowledge.[15] Potter worried that the SDS might attract people who, out of naïve enthusiasm or fascination, would substitute active work for social and political change within the United States for empty revolutionary solidarity. As a consequence, he provocatively argued for a deemphasis on Vietnam and foreign policy issues. Instead, Potter maintained that the SDS should focus on domestic grievances and decisions that directly affected people's lives in the United States, as had been its guiding principle in the first half of the decade. A rather tumultuous national convention of the SDS at Kewadin, Mich. during June 9–13, 1965, was in large part a reaction to Potter's argument. Despite acknowledging that global U.S. interests were often obstructing national self-determination, the convention underlined the primacy of domestic concerns. Consequently, sympathy with other movements abroad had to be justified "within a movement-building strategy" anchored at home and preceded by sufficient research.[16]

Contrary to this formal decision, the desire to reach out to other activists overseas was becoming more tempting to a number of SDS members in the wake of an antiwar movement that was gaining more and more public attention at home and abroad. This was also due to the newly elected president and vice president, Carl Oglesby and Jeff Shero, who were examples of a new generation coming into leading positions in SDS, which by 1966 came to be known as "prairie power" due to its midwestern roots. In a letter to SNCC activist Bob Moses, the newly elected SDS president, Carl Oglesby, for example, explained that in his view "the major thrust of the anti-war movement during the coming months lies on the path of international action." For Oglesby, this in no way endangered domestic or local organizing efforts but rather lent them a global dimension:

The theme underlying our action approaches this: a union of the
people of the world demands peace. International action is of course
easier for intellectuals and students than for others because the former can think more easily in global terms and have more confidence
in long-distance communication. This means that it must become one
important function of intellectuals to help create an international
bond of the poor, the disprivileged, the quiet.[17]

The cultivation of this "international bond" slowly gained greater promi-
nence among members of the American SDS, even if it had to be pursued
on an informal level outside the established channels of the organization.

The International Days of Protest scheduled for October 15–16, 1965,
were an official attempt to combine the domestic with the international.
The initiative for this action stemmed from the Berkeley Vietnam Day
Committee (VDC) leader Jerry Rubin, who made the proposition in early
August during a gathering in Washington, D.C., of Vietnam War opponents, which was called the Assembly of Unrepresented People (AUP). In
agreement with Rubin's proposal, the participants formed the National
Coordinating Committee to End the War in Vietnam (NCC) to coordinate
the event. This quickly drew not only the attention of the national press
and government officials, but also the interest of the American SDS.[18]
Even before the NCC, a newly formed Vietnam Committee of SDS had
requested the endorsement of the International Days of Protest, arguing
that "[o]nly the strong protest of thousands of voices around the world
can end the brutality and injustice of the war in Vietnam and of the foreign
and domestic policy which is responsible for it."[19] But as the national
convention in June had exemplified, the American SDS was not in a position to find consensus either on a coherent strategy against the war in
Vietnam or on its place in the nascent antiwar movement. Similarly, a
September 7 National Council meeting in Indiana presented a plethora
of proposals ranging from civil disobedience tactics, such as the stopping
of troop trains, to antidraft organizing, to the transformation of the antiwar movement into a movement for overall domestic social change. Majorities for any one of these ideas, however, were hard to find. Nonetheless, the SDS finally agreed to support the International Days of Protest
and thereby massively benefited from the success of this largely nationwide series of protest activities in terms of public attention and the broadening of antiwar sentiment among students.

In its aftermath, the rising media coverage for the antiwar opposition
required some kind of follow-up action. Due to the internal disunity over
strategy and for lack of a program of its own, SDS thus decided to join
in with a march on Washington that the National Committee for a Sane
Nuclear Policy (SANE) had called for the Thanksgiving weekend of

1965.[20] This second march on Washington took place on November 27, 1965, and assembled 30,000 participants, surpassing even the number of people from the previous march in April. As a representative of the New Left, the new SDS president, Carl Oglesby, was asked to deliver a speech, since after his election in June of that year he had gone on a trip to Saigon to gain a first-hand impression of the local effects of the war. On his way back, he had visited groups in opposition to the war in Japan, returning with the feeling that the antiwar movement was "rapidly becoming a global force."[21] Deeply affected by this experience, Oglesby would involve himself in various international antiwar efforts in the years to come, such as the international Russell-Tribunal.[22]

During his speech at the march, Oglesby delivered a fervent attack by openly connecting the war in Vietnam to the failure of American liberalism. In his view, American liberalism was corrupted by capitalism and anticommunism. He revealed what he considered to be the blunt hypocrisy of American foreign policy and American rhetoric by not only comparing the revolution in Vietnam to the American Revolution or national revolutions in general, but also by providing a chronological list of questionable decisions in U.S. foreign policy from 1953 to 1965. Oglesby pointed out the ethical evil of "corporate liberalism," which, with the help of common ideological schemes of the cold war, was used to justify nearly any American intervention:

> Far from helping Americans to deal with this truth, the anti-Communist ideology merely tries to disguise it so that things may stay the way they are. Thus, it depicts our presence in other lands not as a coercion, but a protection. It allows us even to say that the napalm in Vietnam is only another aspect of our humanitarian love—like those exorcism[s] in the Middle Ages that so often killed the patient. So we say to the Vietnamese peasant, the Cuban intellectual, the Peruvian worker: "You are better dead than Red. If it hurts or if you don't understand why—sorry about that."[23]

Since the heritage of liberalism in general had been betrayed so severely according to Oglesby, there could only be a choice between this form of corporate liberalism and a humanist version that "in the name of simple human decency and democracy and the vision that wise and brave men saw in the time of our own Revolution" was true to its own roots. For him, the SDS was trying to build a social movement that would safeguard that "humanist reformation," rescue true American ideals, and prevent future wars with U.S. involvement.[24]

The success of the march and Oglesby's speech was phenomenal. The national press picked up the story, and students, youth organizations, and sympathizers both within the United States and abroad sent greetings in the form of solidarity telegrams and letters. With this increased public status, Oglesby further pursued his plans for an internationalization of the antiwar movement. He proposed an international picketing of the British and Soviet embassy to demand that they, as former co-chairs, reconvene the Geneva Conference to debate the war in Vietnam.[25] Moreover, he recommended the establishment of an International Citizens' Peace Brigade that should be sent to Vietnam to "actually intervene between the conflict parties, thus forcing the U.S. administration either to initiate steps toward peace or kill American and international students."[26] What he termed "A New Departure for the Peace Movement," and what was in fact the use of human beings as protective peace shields, unsurprisingly fell through, as SDS executive bodies at the end of 1965 were busy mending the organization's internal fissures.[27]

Nonetheless, throughout the year, and in particular during the summer of 1965, connections to sympathetic movements overseas had been blossoming and international contacts increased.[28] As a consequence, the American SDS was trying to reach out to international pacifist networks through their American branches, such as the War Resisters League.[29] It also launched frequent exchanges with groups such as the London-based International Confederation for Disarmament and Peace (ICDP), whose representative American affiliate was SANE. These exchanges concerned the coordination of antiwar actions and the mobilization of British students.[30] The British Campaign for Nuclear Disarmament (CND) even called for a parallel demonstration in London on November 27, 1965, in support of the second march on Washington.[31] Shortly before Christmas, Paul Booth expressed to Bill Savage, the president of the National Union of Students in London, that "American students have come 'out of apathy' into a swelling movement of opposition to the war. We look around the world now for allies—to people like us who share an intimate concern for ideas and whose intelligence guides them as it has guided us to a rejection in action of our government's policies."[32]

The reality of managing these international connections, however, looked a little different. Although SDS gladly entertained guests from foreign movements when they visited the United States, such as Gerry Hunnius from the ICDP and Peggy Duff from the British CND in January 1966, the goals of its international involvement still remained controversial. The internal debate about an International Student Strike, which originated from Carl Oglesby's international travels at the request of foreign activists, was symptomatic of the indecision and split inside the organization regarding international outreach. The SDS Vietnam Committee had put forward the idea of such a project in August 1965, and so it also came on the agenda of the National Council meeting the following month.[33] In the debate about whether to get in touch with international groups to negotiate the date and form of such a joint action, Carl Oglesby in particular defended the need to internationalize the antiwar movement. He argued that although there had not been enough political analysis of the Vietnam War as such, these "international ties are part of the education process" and it was historically important to deliver an appropriate response to international groups.[34] Oglesby also won support for the idea from Clark Kissinger, Mel McDonald, and Steve Johnson, the latter arguing that foreign groups "share moral opposition to the war" and that it was "important to establish [the] principle . . . of world student cooperation."[35] Since no consensus could be reached, however, the issue was postponed with the task of requesting the opinion of the membership in the meantime.[36]

Rhetorically, SDS by mid-1965 thus not only cautiously acknowledged the international scope of student opposition and the potential benefits of a more thorough networking; it also pledged to take "upon itself the task of building bridges to such bodies, through united action, travel, and through much increased exchange of information," arguing that "[t]hese bridges carry us not merely to Vietnam but to all fronts of the Cold War."[37] Particularly the Vietnam Committee and parts of the National Council seemed extremely enthusiastic about the prospect of what they considered the "most impressive worldwide campus demonstration ever staged." Even more, the supporters of this plan claimed that although the idea came from students in Western Europe and elsewhere, foreign students "since the March on Washington expect SDS and the American movement to lead the way in the struggle against the war."[38] Illustrating the need for a decision, National Secretary Paul Booth pointed out in January 1966 that "things are so bad that I have a folder full of unanswered foreign letters (about 40) asking simply for info on what we're doing and planning."[39] In other words, the advantages of a greater international role for the SDS seemed obvious: First, it would demonstrate the worldwide opposition to the U.S. involvement in Southeast Asia, undermining the U.S. government's claim to fight in the name of the whole "free world."[40] Second, it could help broaden the antiwar mobilization in other countries that could then be directed toward U.S. military bases overseas. And finally, it would connect the SDS to a global protest network and increase national and international publicity for the antiwar cause.

Despite all of these reasons, the proposal for an International Student Strike, as well as other plans for international outreach, eventually fell through. A majority of SDS members present at the convention and the National Council meeting in January 1966 still considered the Vietnam War an outgrowth of the American system, such as racial discrimination and poverty, and preferred to focus on the mobilization of the domestic scene.[41] With this sentiment, the SDS upheld its traditional and somewhat isolationist maxim to prevent the organization from becoming entangled in divisive discussions of foreign relations, as much of the Old Left had done.

One thing that was nonetheless initiated at the National Council meeting in January 1966 was a Radical Education Project (REP) at the University of Michigan, Ann Arbor, which was to provide, among other things, the necessary background to make better judgments about international cooperation. This "brainchild of Al Haber" was structured as a comprehensive program to supply SDS groups and members with educational bulletins and pamphlet series covering a wide range of political and philosophical issues.[42] International education was planned to be initiated by a "nations series" with annotated bibliographies as guides for further reading, alongside which international organizations and alliance systems were supposed to be investigated.[43] SDS member Richard Flacks even suggested a firm institutionalization of this international section in the academy through an "International Intelligence Network" stemming from the peace movement.[44] The actual realization of this project, however, remains uncertain and seems to have been swept aside by the course of events.

The SDS in the period after the Port Huron Statement and the beginning of the antiwar movement therefore only hesitantly opened up to international issues. The main concern for most of the SDS membership, especially for the older generation, was to remain focused on the domestic scene. The cold war, or the war in Vietnam, was of predominant significance only insofar as it aggravated internal problems and had a direct effect on people's lives and the political development of the country. Inspired by William Appleman Williams's analysis of American imperialism, many SDS activists insisted on taking a closer look at the roots of American policy.[45] To prevent factionalism from surfacing around the debates about international solidarity, the SDS was therefore only very cautiously stepping into international forms of cooperation.[46] At a time when an ever-growing faction of a new stream of people coming into SDS demanded more open and engaged international connections, the older leaders in response still pressed for the priority of the domestic agenda, afraid of unwanted diversions from the international sphere. Expressing eagerness in rooting out the underlying causes leading to the aberrations of the American system, American SDS member Richard Rothstein was quoted as saying, "SDS shouldn't focus on ending the war in Vietnam, it should focus on ending the sixth war from now."[47]

As a result, SDS as an organization refused to take an avant-garde position in mass mobilization against the war in Vietnam. It failed to live up to the role that was publicly attributed to it as the leading American antiwar force, thus leaving an institutional vacuum. Nevertheless, as the debate concerning the International Student Strike, International Peace Brigades, and further connections to movements around the world indicate, the growing international opposition to the war in Vietnam, as well as a generational leadership change within the organization, gradually increased the pressure on both the attitude and general practice of the American SDS with regard to international cooperation. In 1965–66, however, the organization was still a long way away from a "truer internationalism."

THE RISE OF WEST GERMAN OPPOSITION TO THE WAR IN VIETNAM

"MURDER. Murder through napalm bombs! Murder through gas? Murder through atomic bombs? . . . How long will we allow murder being committed in our name? AMIS GET OUT OF VIETNAM!" During the night of February 3–4, 1966, a self-declared "International Liberation Front" stuck posters containing these slogans on walls all over West Berlin and on the campus of the Free University. Five people were arrested for this illegal action, which was intended to cause a political scandal in denouncing the West German government as an accomplice of murder in Vietnam and the Third World. The posters had been drafted by a small Situationist group called "Subversive Aktion" located in Munich and Berlin, whose actions had ultimately been provoked by the renewed U.S. bombing of North Vietnam in January 1966.[48] Although the police removed most of the posters that same night, the Berlin daily newspapers carried the story on February 5, the same day that a major antiwar rally took place, sponsored by the Berlin SDS, the "Argument Club," the Liberal Student Association (Liberaler Studentenbund Deutschlands, LSD), and the Humanist Student Union (Humanistische Studentenunion, HSU). As a result of this unexpected publicity, more than 2,500 students took part in the demonstration. After blocking traffic on West Berlin's most prominent shopping street, the Kurfürstendamm, for about twenty minutes, a number of demonstrators assembled at the Amerikahaus (America House) to conduct a sit-in. Some of the demonstrators decided to pull down the American flag from the pole of this overseas U.S. cultural institution. Others tried to lift the flag back up, and eventually the group agreed to leave it at half-mast. In addition, nine eggs were hurled against the walls of the America House. All of this caused a massive public outcry in Berlin. In the cold-war atmosphere of a city that had depended on American support to survive in the decades after the war, such a performance was perceived as a clear anti-American affront. Most Berliners and a local media outlet prone to dramatization interpreted the incident as an attack on the city's most important ally, whose president only three years before had symbolically declared himself to be a citizen of Berlin, sworn to protect its freedom.[49]

This episode was by no means the first expression of West German protest against American foreign policy in Southeast Asia. Similar to the rise of domestic opposition in the United States, sentiment against the war in Vietnam had been equally mounting in parts of West Germany, in no small part due to the activities of a well-established pacifist movement with international connections.[50] Embedded in this movement were numerous members of the German SDS, who could also look back on a deeply rooted internationalist tradition that had intensified in the aftermath of their organization's split from the German SPD. The French war in Algeria, the apartheid regime in South Africa, and the situation in the Congo had spurred SDS international activism and solidarity and channeled it into various protest events.[51] In the mid-1960s, however, it was primarily the escalation of the war in Vietnam that received the growing attention of the West German students and the German SDS. Especially the internal opposition against U.S. actions in Southeast Asia significantly shaped the global perspective of West German activists and strengthened their interest in the actions of their American counterparts.

Already in September 1964, the nineteenth national convention of the German SDS had urged local chapters to host information events on Vietnam. Considering American engagement in Southeast Asia a neocolonial project, the convention asked the federal government to stop any further moral or technical support of the American war effort and the current government of South Vietnam.[52] At this point, primarily local SDS groups in Munich and in Berlin had been studying the conflict in greater detail. This was to change drastically during 1965. Due to its ongoing escalation, the war gradually came to the attention of the organization as a whole, thus emerging as the prime topic in discussions about the Third World.[53] At the beginning of 1965, a permanent informal study group on South Vietnam was instituted at the Free University (FU) in Berlin and led by SDS members Jürgen Horlemann, Peter Gäng, and Klaus Gilgenmann, who were preparing a book on Vietnam and soon became experts on this issue.[54] A demonstration of their expertise was given in a panel discussion on February 26, 1965, at the FU, in which SDS representatives, as well as a journalist from the U.S.-controlled Berlin radio station RIAS, publicly debated with two American mission officials on the war. During the discussion the mission officials proved to be largely unprepared for the arguments and evidence put forth by the SDS members, which caused them to contradict themselves frequently. As a result, this first "teach-in" in West Germany not only proved to be a public success for the student organization but also was the last time American officials accepted an invitation from the Berlin SDS.[55] Similarly, in other cities all over the Federal Repub-

Erhard und die Bonner Parteien unterstützen

MORD

Mord durch Napalmbomben!
Mord durch Giftgas!
Mord durch Atombomben?

Die US-Aggression in Vietnam verstößt nicht gegen
die Interessen des demokratischen Systems: Wer es
wagt, sich aufzulehnen gegen Ausbeutung und Unter-
drückung, wird von den Herrschenden mit Brutalität
niedergemacht.

Die Völker Asiens, Afrikas und Lateinamerikas kämpfen
gegen Hunger, Tod und Entmenschlichung. Die ehemaligen Sklaven wollen Menschen werden. Kuba, Kongo,
Vietnam - die Antwort der Kapitalisten ist Krieg.
Mit Waffengewalt wird die Herrschaft aufrechterhal-
ten. Mit Kriegswirtschaft wird die Konjunktur gesi-
chert.

Ost und West arrangieren sich immer mehr auf Kosten
der wirtschaftlich unterentwickelten Länder. Jetzt
bleibt den Unterdrückten nur noch der Griff zu den
Waffen. Für sie heißt Zukunft:

REVOLUTION

Wir sollen den Herrschenden beim Völkermord helfen.
Deshalb beschwören sie das Gespenst der gelben Ge-
fahr.

Wie lange noch lassen wir es zu, daß in unserem
Namen gemordet wird?

AMIS RAUS AUS VIETNAM !

INTERNATIONALE BEFREIUNGSFRONT

IMAGE 1. Flyer condemning the Vietnam War, unauthorized by the German SDS (February 1966) (Archive "APO und soziale Bewegungen," Free University of Berlin) lic, numerous war-related demonstrations and information activities began to take place during 1965.

The war in Vietnam seemed to become the second most-important issue that the SDS was campaigning against. It was eclipsed only by the imminent emergency laws—a legislative effort that threatened to disempower parliament in case of a vaguely defined state of emergency. German SDS president Helmut Schauer saw the organization's prime task in forming political coalitions against the ratification of these emergency bills. In May, he had already organized a congress "Demokratie vor dem Notstand" (Democracy Before the State of Emergency) in Bonn together with other university groups to initiate this campaign. His political program, however, was to come under considerable internal attack from a faction in the Berlin SDS that favored a more action-oriented line and greater engagement with the issue of Vietnam. Even more important, this group drew much of its inspiration and support from the apparent success of protest techniques practiced in the United States. Earlier in the decade, the example of their American peers had exercised a major influence on the German SDS through the first-hand reports of Michael Vester. In the mid-1960s, this inspiration and corresponding orientation toward political action was considerably advanced by the Free Speech Movement, which reached its peak in the fall semester of 1964 at the prestigious University of California, Berkeley campus. In February 1965, Günter Amendt from the Frankfurt chapter was the first to offer the German SDS a detailed account of the Berkeley events.[56] Based on an earlier visit to the United States and the national office of the American SDS in Chicago, Amendt expected a deepening of transatlantic contacts and had written the following to his American peers at the end of 1964: "I hope that there will be something like a coordination between the German SDS and the American and I think that after having been in America that we could learn a lot from you."[57] Other German SDS members had similar learning experiences and were shaped by the events in Berkeley. Wolfgang Nitsch from the Berlin SDS visited the American SDS in 1965 and even took part in its national convention at Camp Maplehurst.[58] Nitsch not only worked to deepen the relationship between the two organizations but also informed the German SDS on the transformations within its American counterpart and on the strategic discussions concerning the beginning of the antiwar movement.[59] Articles written by members of the German SDS appeared in German student newspapers and told of the student revolt in the United States. These publications further introduced new forms of political action to a broader university audience.[60]

In discussions within the German SDS, the events and protest techniques from Berkeley were thus beginning to play a prominent role. The reception of the civil rights movement had already caused a renaissance of ideas about civil disobedience.[61] The strategy of a limited but open and symbolic overstepping of rules, laws, and values in the form of direct actions such as sit-ins or teach-ins now gradually turned into a firm component of the German movement. Even critics such as the philosopher Jürgen Habermas would later praise these new forms of protest, because they took aim at the political alienation of broad segments of the population.[62] German SDS members were thus increasingly looking across the Atlantic for inspiration and through a variety of personal connections and media coverage had familiarized themselves with the actions of their American peers.

In this setting, it was again Michael Vester who provided a systematic analysis of direct-action concepts employed by the civil rights movement, the Free Speech, and the slowly building antiwar movement. In a widely read article in the *neue kritik* in the summer of 1965, Vester elaborated on the theoretical underpinnings of "direct action." For Vester, direct action was only useful in the form of nonviolent civil disobedience which targeted places and institutions that were critical for the smooth functioning of society.[63] The subjects of such an action were ideally academics and officials from trade unions and youth organizations. There were two strategies of "direct action," one being a defensive strategy, in which only *Aktivbürger* (active citizens) were mobilized and alerted to social and political wrongs. The other strategy was offensive and involved the population, who, with the help of the active citizens, would realize these wrongs and act accordingly. Particularly in the second case, the role of students and intellectuals was to lead themselves and the population out of apathy and toward greater democratic involvement. To this end, the institution of the teach-in appeared to be extremely useful, as illustrated according to Vester by the success and recognition it had achieved in the United States.

Consequently, Vester explained that "direct action" had four great advantages as a political strategy: (1) it reached out directly and could address people personally (direct contact); (2) it focused on a concretely experienced or perceived injustice (direct experience); (3) it engaged in critical discourse at the place of the injustice or at a strategically important place (direct criticism); and (4) it surpassed local limits and expanded to a broader national struggle, thereby widening its mass basis. For these reasons, Vester demanded the implementation of direct action as a vital political strategy for the German SDS in its protest against the planned emergency laws.[64] The concept of direct action as practiced in the United States appeared to him worth adopting for the action repertoire of the German SDS, which strove for substantial social change. Thereby attempting to extend the concept of citizen participation radically in political processes, he presented this strategy as a possible approach to help enforce his organization's domestic agenda. As he had already argued in the drafting process of the Port Huron Statement, the role of the intellectual was to be the catalyst rather than the sole agent of social change; and the catalyst would be someone who helped mobilize fellow citizens to become politically active. In other words, Vester now transferred ideas developed and mainly practiced in the United States by the civil rights and antiwar movements to Germany to test them in a similar political setting, aiming at analogous goals. Due to the close contact and degree of mutual information between the two student organizations, the national office of American SDS also took note of Vester's efforts in West Germany, and in September 1965 the Americans recommended his article and the *neue kritik* to its members as "required reading for the complete radical."[65]

Most important, Vester supplied a theoretical framework for the notion of nonviolent civil disobedience and teach-ins to a German audience who would soon come into contact with these new forms of protest through events at the Free University in Berlin, thereby placing these practices in a larger agenda of a New Left ideology. Vester's writings and his plea for a "participatory democracy" are thus largely responsible for the introduction of what historian Wini Breines has termed "prefigurative politics" to West Germany, meaning "the effort to create and prefigure in lived action and behavior the desired society, the emphasis on means and not ends, the spontaneous and utopian experiments that developed in the midst of action while working toward the ultimate goal of a free and democratic society."[66] In the years ahead, this understanding of politics and, more importantly, political action would become a decisive feature of the German student movement, when public conventions or rules were strategically violated or ridiculed to capture the attention of the public in preparation for a long-term, broad-based, social and cultural change. Vester earned not only applause for his demands, however, but also criticism and refusal, since his article was situated in a very serious debate within SDS between the more action-oriented wing in Munich and the realist group that gathered around German SDS president Helmut Schauer. It was this controversy, purposefully orchestrated by members of the artist group Subversive Aktion, that was to alter fundamentally the ideological direction of the German SDS and turn the opposition to the war in Vietnam into an integral part of its political agenda.

SIT-IN, TEACH-IN, GO-IN: CONFLICTS OVER
STRATEGIES OF POLITICAL ACTION IN THE GERMAN SDS

The conflict about strategies of political action within the organization originated from developments in the Munich chapter of the German SDS, where new members with an arts background had gradually taken over in the course of 1964 and pushed back the influence of the traditionalist trade union wing. Specifically, a group of Situationists loosely affiliated under the name of "Subversive Aktion" slowly tried to combine traditional Marxist positions with their ideas for provocative action.[67] The most prominent of these was Dieter Kunzelmann, who came to be considered the "prototype of the anti-authoritarian movement."[68] Kunzelmann, who was born in 1939, the son of a bank director from Bamberg, had left his provincial environment at the age of nineteen and traveled to Paris, where he lived the life of a *clochard* for eight months, at the same time studying French literature and theory. After his return in the summer of 1960, he joined the Munich-based artist group SPUR, which considered itself the German branch of the Situationist International (SI).

The SI emerged in 1957 out of various artist groups inspired by Dadaism, Surrealism, and the Lettristic International. It was led by the Frenchman Guy Debord and the Dane Asger Jorn, among others.[69] Their aim was to formulate a comprehensive criticism of modern society transcending traditional Marxist theory by encompassing all aspects of human life. The modes and routine of social relations were to be disturbed through the creation of provocative "situations" devised to alter the conventional meaning of social interactions and to allow for new perspectives and experiences. In other words, common actions or procedures should be deprived of their traditionally assigned functions by placing them in a different context, thereby attributing a new significance to them. This *détournement* was designed to provoke a process of critical questioning by participants and audience alike in order to create a new consciousness. These action-oriented techniques could be utilized for political or artistic purposes, but their provocative and experimental character was always connected to the Situationists' radical critique of society.

Within the Munich group SPUR, Kunzelmann soon advanced to the position of leading theoretician. In their journal and political pamphlets, the group fervently attacked the existing culture industry and its commercialization, which was perceived to have perverted the original critical or subversive potential of art. In their view, consumer society had largely succeeded in manipulating and streamlining the individual and controlling his/her needs through social conventions. According to Situationist theory, in this context the game and playful character of action was a way to recover suppressed human passion and instincts. The "homo ludens" (as first termed by Johan Huizinga in his famous essay of the same name) became the solution to a world devastated by the catastrophes of the twentieth century and subtle authoritarian influences. Therefore, when internal differences caused the dissolution of SPUR in the fall of 1962,

Kunzelmann was determined to further develop the Situationist impetus in a group of his own.

Soon, the vehicle for this task became the newly founded Subversive Aktion, which continued to adhere to an action-oriented strategy for initiating social change. In addition to their Situationist repertoire, Kunzelmann and his co-founders, the sociology student Rodolfe Gasché and his long-time friend Rudolf May, developed a new interest in psychoanalysis and the works of Herbert Marcuse. Subversive Aktion now integrated a more complex analysis of modern society based on the critical theory of the Frankfurt School, whose ideas they sought to translate into action. The goal was to reveal the character and extent of the suppression of human faculties in modern industrial society.[70] To spread their influence, the group succeeded in establishing a local branch in Berlin in the course of 1963. They were able to recruit two new students from the Free University in the following year who would not only drastically transform the Berlin section and Subversive Aktion as a whole, but also the entire German SDS. Their names were Rudi Dutschke and Bernd Rabehl.

Both Dutschke and Rabehl had escaped from East Germany to study sociology at the FU in West Berlin and to critically assess the writings of socialist and Marxist-Leninist literature.[71] With this curiosity in and knowledge of leftist theoretical texts and the history of the labor movement, they joined the Subversive Aktion in the spring of 1964. What attracted them to this group was their shared interest in bringing together theory and action, following in particular the critical theory advanced by the Frankfurt School with an emphasis on corresponding political action. In other words, the two students and their new-found group sought an action-oriented strategy that would shape and refine the overarching theoretical legitimacy accompanying it.[72] Even before the arrival of Rabehl and Dutschke, members of the Subversive Aktion had discussed infiltrating existing political groups and organizations and exposing them to their own agenda, thereby multiplying their strength. In accordance with the group's tradition, Situationist techniques would uncover power rivalries and manipulations within these groups and organizations to parody them and exploit them as a means of agitating the membership. At the end of 1964 this idea was taken up again by Dutschke and Rabehl with respect to the German SDS in Berlin, whereas Kunzelmann attempted to gain more influence in the Munich branch of SDS.

According to Dutschke, the anti-authoritarian revolt in West Germany started with the protest against the Prime Minister of Congo, Moise Tshombe, who came to visit the Federal Republic in December 1964. Both in Munich and Berlin the Subversive Aktion tried to organize a coordinated action with the local SDS chapters.[73] On December 14, they distributed flyers denouncing the crimes committed by Tshombe in the Congo and organized a rally in Munich at which participants greeted him with stink-bombs. Four days later, he was given a similar welcome in Berlin. A demonstration called by the Berlin SDS and members of the African Student Union, the Latin American Student Association, as well as the Anschlag Gruppe (the renamed Berlin branch of the Subversive Aktion), confronted the Congolese prime minister at city hall in Schöneberg and hurled tomatoes at his car as he departed. For Dutschke, the Tshombe demonstration was the first event where participants had shown their determination to transcend established rules and even adopt illegal methods. In his opinion, this experience would lead them toward a critical questioning of current social conditions and a reflection upon their own position in society.[74] Following Subversive Aktion's strategies, the category of action had for the first time been put into practice and involved a larger group beyond itself. Dutschke therefore later considered this event as "the beginning of our cultural revolution," during which all conventions and values were being reexamined through the "actionist process."[75]

Dedicated to extending this strategy, Dutschke and Rabehl joined the Berlin SDS on January 27, 1965, together with other members of the Berlin branch of the Subversive Aktion. In Munich, Kunzelmann and Frank Böckelmann, a fellow member of the Situationist group, attempted to follow a similar, although less successful strategy to try to utilize the local SDS branch for their own ends. Their denouncement of the German Trade Union Association (DGB) as bureaucrats and "apparatchiks" and the subsequent hold that the trade union placed on funding for SDS, however, caused the national office to intervene, with SDS President Schauer demanding the suspension of Kunzelmann's and Böckelmann's memberships. Since the growing Munich chapter withstood the pressure and was reluctant to expel the perpetrators, Schauer was unable to enforce the suspension and was left with dwindling influence over a group of people both in Munich and Berlin that stood diametrically opposed to his policies and that was slowly gaining more and more strength.[76]

The conflict between Schauer and the members of the Subversive Aktion also attracted the attention of Michael Vester in May 1965. In a series of letter exchanges, he accused the SDS president of a self-complacent and bureaucratic political strategy that was largely focused on traditional alliances and far removed from the SDS membership, let alone the population at large. Schauer's strategy, he warned, could lead to a harmful lack of political discussion within the organization. Vester eventually decided to speak up to ensure that neither the diversity of opinions within SDS was suppressed nor action-oriented strategies as such denounced, since he viewed these as a more promising political strategy for the German SDS than the narrow coalition course pursued by the current leadership.[77]

Vester also felt that the acting SDS president neglected the issue of actual class divisions in society in favor of more abstract issues and policy debates. Vester claimed that SDS needed to reach out to the population directly by addressing the concerns of average people. He suggested a grassroots mobilization with the help of direct action techniques to break out of traditional political infrastructures and enlist a greater number of students and the general population.

Schauer, on the other hand, viciously defended his traditional Realpolitik and policy of forming strategic alliances, which had found their latest expression in a congress (Demokratie vor dem Notstand) opposing the impending emergency law legislation that he had put together in May 1965 in cooperation with social democratic, liberal, and progressive student organizations. He argued that in the current situation, theoretical work had to begin with what could actually be accomplished, even if the underlying socialist approach might at times be difficult to discern. SDS should therefore concentrate on the issues of coexistence, disarmament and Easter peace marches, and the impending emergency legislation. His aim was to mobilize against the growing popularity of "actionist concepts" in the German SDS, which he saw represented by the group surrounding Kunzelmann. In Schauer's view, this group practiced elitist and authoritarian manipulation, followed a short-sighted political strategy, and was no longer open for discussion.[78]

Vester was not satisfied with Schauer's response, feeling that instead of seriously discussing the issue the SDS president was only trying to disqualify his opponents' arguments.[79] As a result, the controversy between them ultimately remained unresolved.[80] In the aftermath of their letter exchange, Vester revised his aforementioned article on direct action, particularly stressing the differences between the action-oriented concepts he saw represented in the American movement and those advanced by the Kunzelmann group, whom he considered pseudo-radical and narcissistic. In his eyes, this self-elected avant-garde and its "blind activism" was far too theoretical and detached from the people they were trying to reach. Direct action, in Vester's conception, allowed for an open exchange of opinions with adversaries rather than being a closed event for like-minded intellectuals. For him, this was the main reason for the success of the "teach-ins" in the United States, as well as of the Berlin panel discussion from February 26, 1965, at the FU with American mission officials.[81] It also explained the failure of SDS President Schauer's strategy for political action, which fell short of connecting the discussions about the emergency bills to a local basis such as student groups or the population at large.

Vester consequently portrayed the German SDS as an organization torn by two opposing factions blocking each other, disinterested in a basic grassroots political engagement and completely absorbed by their respective strategies.[82] To get out of this deadlock, he advocated engaging the population directly through teach-ins, cooperation with the trade unions, and student-worker pilot projects. Heavily criticizing both followers of the action-oriented strategy in the Munich SDS and the Realpolitik of the current SDS leadership, Vester proposed a third way, which was modeled after his experience and theoretical explanation of the American protest scene. For him, a decentralization of SDS's organizational structure modeled after the American SDS with its autonomous regional projects (for example, Economic Research and Action Project (ERAP), the influence of its National Executive Council on the political direction of the leadership, greater involvement of the individual chapters in the drafting of resolutions, and the flexible affiliation and cooperation with other student groups and nonmembers as introduced by the early American SDS president, Al Haber, were seen as models to transcend the factional infighting within the German SDS.[83] Vester's contribution can therefore be interpreted both as an attempt to introduce American protest techniques into a West German context and, at the same time, as a counterpoint to the internal fissures that were dividing the German SDS at a critical juncture in its development.

This division also set the tone for the national convention from October 14–17, 1965, in Frankfurt. There SDS president Helmut Schauer had to acknowledge the growing influence of the new American and English forms of protest, but he rejected "direct action" as a guiding strategy in the opposition against the emergency laws. Although he lauded the success of the teach-ins in Berlin and elaborated on the advantages of these protest techniques, he underlined his preference for coalition politics as initiated under his auspices. For him, teach-ins still remained rather vague and unpredictable in their political consequences.[84] He thereby positioned himself not only against Vester and a majority of the Frankfurt SDS, but also against the rising action-oriented faction of the Berlin chapter. To avoid being outmaneuvered by Schauer at the convention, both groups had entered into a temporary alliance against him with the common goal of achieving a further opening toward action-oriented strategies within the organization.[85]

By the time of the convention, Rudi Dutschke had solidified his position in the Berlin SDS and become one of the national delegates of his chapter. He temporarily even ran for SDS president, but pulled out of the race at the very last minute to avoid being absorbed by organizing on a national level. This was all the more significant since Dieter Kunzelmann had also relocated to Berlin after severe internal differences in the Munich base of Subversive Aktion.[86] In this situation, Dutschke considered it more beneficial to continue the original infiltration concept devised by Subversive Aktion on a local level, where it promised to be more successful. Despite these considerations, the Frankfurt convention elected him as a member of the national advisory board, thus making him part of the leading circle of an organization that he had joined only at the beginning of the year. The confrontation between the group and the ideas that Dutschke represented and the reelected SDS President Schauer thus seemed to be almost unavoidable. In the aftermath of the national convention, the self-proclaimed anti-authoritarians from the Berlin SDS would completely succumb to an action-oriented strategy based on a characteristic blend of situationism, voluntarism, and socialist internationalism. This strategy, which would move them even further away from the American concepts outlined by Vester, spread rapidly inside the organization and came to dominate the German SDS in the following years.

THE ANTI-AUTHORITARIAN BREAKTHROUGH: THE INTERNATIONALIST FACTION OF THE BERLIN SDS

Given the prominent position of the city in the cold war, the development of political concepts favoring direct action and international perspectives did not prove too difficult in Berlin. In 1965, the atmosphere among student activists was not only affected by the war in Vietnam but also heated up due to the conflicts at the Free University. Since the beginning of the decade, SDS's long-term goal in university politics had been the democratization of the university, which was to be preceded by a fundamental structural change whereby the "Ordinarienuniversität," in which full professors continued to exercise an almost unchecked power, was to be abolished.[87] Going along with this institutional transformation was the demand to revise the role of science in general. In May 1964, Hellmut Lessing, then vice president of the German SDS, proclaimed that although scientific research was influenced by power relations in society, it had to maintain its strict independence from any kind of censorship or co-optation.[88] SDS soon adopted this view as one of its core demands and values. Nonetheless, this was problematic with regard to the Free University (FU) of Berlin, which had been established on December 4, 1948, in the highly ideologized setting of the cold war.

More specifically, the FU was explicitly set up as a political counterpart to the Humboldt University in Berlin, which was heavily supervised by the East German SED, and thus strongly urged students to follow East Berlin's party lines. A massive wave of protest over a case of political censorship in a student newspaper in April 1948 eventually led to the foundation of the Free University, strongly supported by the American general Lucius D. Clay.[89] In contrast to its Eastern opponent, the university's statute, later known as the "Berlin model," allowed for the democratic influence of students in university life, drawing on the idea of students and professors as equal partners in the scientific endeavor. With such an agenda the FU was naturally isolated from the rest of the Federal Republic and could not as easily attract professors as other universities that still offered privileges and largely rejected the notion of student participation in university politics. From its inception, the FU was therefore in an extraordinary situation: founded on an anti-totalitarian and even anticommunist understanding, it viewed itself as an institution that strongly favored and supported democracy and equality even in the academic realm. As long as this self-portrait was perceived to be consistent with reality, the FU stood as a democratic and progressive island in a hostile, communist surrounding. As soon as the first cracks in this bastion appeared, however, questions were raised as to the true nature of academic freedom at the "free" university.

Various incidents soon led the students to question precisely this foundation, lending credibility to the notion that political expression was permitted only when students followed the officially sanctioned policy of anticommunism, in other words, when they confirmed the status quo and the opinions of the university's president (Rektor).[90] Whereas the president in June 1962, for example, sanctioned a solidarity campaign for the students in East Germany, he prohibited a collection of funds for Algerian refugees on university grounds in the following December. During the summer semester of 1965, things very soon came to a head, when the president did not allow the student body to invite journalist and writer Erich Kuby to speak in its lecture halls. Kuby had publicly criticized the concept of the Free University. As a result, in May 1965 a wave of protest went through the whole student body, and the students denounced the president's actions as illegitimate political censorship. After unsuccessful negotiation attempts with the president, the student assembly, undoubtedly inspired by the Berkeley Free Speech Movement of the previous year, called for the implementation of free speech on campus and referred to the university's charter.[91] The situation escalated further with the "Krippendorff" case, which most obviously connected the frustration over domestic conditions with international issues again. Ekkehart Krippendorff, assistant professor at the Otto-Suhr-Institute for Political Science, had published incorrect information in a newspaper article in which he criticized the university president's actions and also the U.S. war in Vietnam. Although Krippendorff apologized for the incorrect information a week later, the president cancelled the usual renewal of his contract, neither informing nor consulting with the department's chair, who strongly protested against this move.[92] The combination of these events caused a growing disillusionment on the part of the student body about the true relations of power and the actual degree of freedom, academic or political, that the concept of the Free University was willing to offer them. It also shed light on the growing opposition to the war in Vietnam, which was yet another issue adding to the tense political atmosphere in the city.

In August 1965, student representatives Wolfgang Lefèvre and Peter Damerow signed a petition calling for peace in Vietnam. The petition was initiated by an organization affiliated with the ruling East German Socialist Unity Party (SED). Under mounting public pressure, they were forced to step down from their positions at the end of October.[93] A faction of Berlin students and intellectuals, however, were becoming increasingly uncomfortable with the analogy between the American intervention in Vietnam and the U.S. protection of their divided city: in other words, the notion that Berlin was also being defended in Vietnam. A "Call Concerning the Vietnam War" initiated by SDS members in October 1965 thus demanded a "voice of protest" emerging from the city, following the example of domestic opposition in the United States and questioning the legitimacy of America's presence in Southeast Asia.[94] In solidarity with the second march on Washington on November 27, 1965, by the American antiwar movement, a second and even more widely distributed "Statement on the War in Vietnam" brought more than 150 signatures of German intellectuals nationwide and about 1,300 from students at the Free University.[95] Furthermore, from December 13 through 17 in Berlin, the SDS organized an exhibition on the war in Vietnam based on the works of the study group formed around Jürgen Horlemann and Peter Gäng on South Vietnam. Other events on Vietnam (co-)sponsored by various student organizations followed, such as the screening of American and North Vietnamese propaganda movies. All of this coalesced into a comprehensive information campaign mostly originating from members of the Berlin SDS, thereby turning the winter semester 1965–66 into the "Vietnam-Semester." The action producing the most publicity and political consequences, however, was to come in early February, when members of the by-now dissolved Subversive Aktion clandestinely distributed posters denouncing American involvement in Vietnam.

Despite its public visibility, the poster action by Dutschke and other members of Subversive Aktion, as well as the subsequent attack on the America House in West Berlin, both taking place in the short period from February 3 to 5, 1966, caused internal outrage among SDS members nationwide. The Berlin SDS, equally surprised by the event, also distanced itself from it. Older SDS members demanded the immediate expulsion of the perpetrators. The SDS national office and president Schauer eventually suggested a special assembly of Berlin SDS members to debate the issue.[96] Dutschke was now forced to win over the SDS to his political strategies in order to avoid a potential expulsion similar to the Munich members of Subversive Aktion. The justifications he would provide for the independent and illegal poster action of February 3–4, 1966, were based largely on theoretical approaches that he had developed in previous years. Ever since Dutschke and Rabehl had obtained membership in the Berlin SDS their goal had been to utilize the organization for their own ideological purposes developed in the Subversive Aktion. The thinking and long-term goals of the Subversive Aktion were particularly clear in a confidential strategy paper written by Dutschke for the group's council convening on April 25, 1965, in Munich. In the paper, Dutschke outlined the major themes of the theoretical perspectives that he would later came to represent and push for in the SDS, which were as follows: 1) the interconnected and globalized framework of any revolutionary politics; 2) the acknowledgment of the "one-dimensional" character of modern industrial society (Herbert Marcuse), which only the marginalized or minorities could transcend; and 3) the intricate relationship of political theory and political action, namely theoretical consciousness-raising through direct political action.[97]

Although the SDS itself was only of marginal significance for Dutschke, it provided the well-established institutional structure that would give the faction around Dutschke "the opportunity to forge international contacts" in order to realize his ideological agenda. This was especially important since Dutschke had come to regard the international dimension of the capitalist expansion as a basis for the development of any socialist theory. In his view, the financial forces had already transcended national boundaries and were, in combination with imperialist policies, suppressing national liberation movements around the globe. The international marketplace and dependencies between industrial nations and poorer countries thus made global interconnectedness, with respect to revolutionary theory, indispensable. As Dutschke wrote in July 1964, history did not suffer from any "standstill" but was now unfolding itself on a global playing field while at the same time deeply affecting national structures.[98] The consequence of this analysis was to reach out to other revolutionary movements around the world in order to respond adequately to what was perceived as a "counterrevolutionary challenge" that could no longer be grasped within the confines of nation states. Accordingly, Dutschke argued in April 1965 that the "internationalization of the strategy of revolutionary forces seems to become more and more urgent." Following from this, "contact and cooperation with American, other European, Latin American and also Afro-Asian students and nonstudents has to be initiated."[99]

An embodiment of this international outlook was the "Third World" study group, the so-called Viva Maria Gruppe, which met weekly in Berlin during 1965. The group was named after a movie by Louis Malle released the same year about an Irish political dissident (Brigitte Bardot) and a

IMAGE 2. Louis Malle's *Viva Maria!* (1965) with Jeanne Moreau and Brigitte Bardot (Ullstein bild/The Granger Collection, New York, NY)

traveling circus performer (Jeanne Moreau) who came to lead a revolutionary uprising in Latin America. Bardot, symbolizing the anarchist strategy, joins forces with Moreau, who embodies the Marxist line, thus uniting in a new revolutionary theory that combines the best of both traditions. This romanticized version of Third World revolution mesmerized both Dutschke and Rabehl, as well as the other participants of the "Third World" study group. Among other things, it seemed to suggest a way for a revolutionary avant-garde to combine the cultivation of the "subjective factor," or individual and collective liberation, with revolutionary politics.[100] At the same time, this movie and the group itself symbolized, very much in the Situationist tradition, that fun was also an integral part of the revolution.[101]

In addition to his internationalism and in keeping with the understanding of Subversive Aktion, Dutschke also sought a way to translate the analysis of the critical theory into political action.[102] One problem that was troubling him in this respect was that of the revolutionary masses and ways to activate them. The theoretical works provided by Herbert Marcuse served as a special influence in helping to solve this issue. Together with Marcuse, Dutschke assumed that workers as revolutionary agents were manipulated and repressed in current society, and so their revolutionary potential was absorbed by the system. This outsider theory and the term "Great Refusal" had been proclaimed by Marcuse in probably his most influential book, *One-Dimensional Man*, which was published in 1964.[103] Marcuse's concept that the only potential forces for social change in a "one-dimensional" society could be found among society's minorities and marginalized persons appeared very plausible to Dutschke.[104] In Dutschke's adaptation, intellectuals could be instrumental in instigating these forces to break out of their repression and initiate a social transformation, since they were equally outside of society. As a result, the avant-gardist task of the intellectual or student would be to perform the role of mediator between these minorities and the articulation of their grievances on the one hand, and the politicization of the masses by raising awareness of their suppression on the other.

The crucial question for Dutschke was how to achieve this "emancipation," since, due to the altered historical situation, traditional Marxist models no longer provided an answer.[105] His solution to this dilemma was to redefine the subject-object relationship, first by helping to cultivate a revolutionary situation through political education and information, and second, by gaining theoretical knowledge and direction through direct political action.[106] Drawing upon the works of the Hungarian Marxist philosopher and literary critic George Lukács, Dutschke advocated a voluntaristic concept of revolution, in which revolutionary consciousness is created through action.[107] In other words, the experience of political praxis provided the necessary complement to transcend the repressive mechanisms of society and develop a revolutionary theory.[108] Dutschke differed with Lukács, however, in that his focus was no longer on the working class as a potential revolutionary agent but on the social minorities as suggested by Marcuse. In a world dominated by global forces, these minorities could now also be found on a global level, namely in the liberation movements of the Third World.

For this reason international examples occupied a central position in Dutschke's thinking, since he saw them as prime models for the process of revolutionizing oneself through action. Through the Viva Maria Gruppe and the South Vietnam study group, he was amply acquainted with the situation in the Third World and Southeast Asia. In his mind, the liberation movements formed part of an international class struggle, which, as the German writer Hans Magnus Enzensberger described in the magazine *Kursbuch*, had long replaced the cold war in its political and military intensity.[109] The shift from the bloc confrontations of East and West to the axis of the North-South divide between wealthy industrialized societies and countries stricken by poverty was one of the essential reasons why Dutschke turned his attention to the national liberation movements. Through them, he found the "guerilla" techniques to create revolutionary consciousness, which he considered transferable to his own situation in conjunction with the aforementioned theoretical premises. The theories of Frantz Fanon in particular, which began to occupy Dutschke in mid-1965, and those of Che Guevara were to become prominent ingredients further complementing these concepts.[110]

These international examples reconfirmed his theoretical approach and the role he attributed to the avant-garde, thereby spurring his urge to work for revolutionary change within the "European periphery."[111] To further the revolutionary process in the Federal Republic, Dutschke already in April 1965 viewed the transfer of demonstrations into "illegality" and "confrontations with the state authority" as a suitable tactic to change individual consciousness through protest action.[112] With this in mind, it is easy to understand how he came to consider the Tshombe demonstration of December 1964 as the beginning of the student movement's cultural revolution in West Germany. Even more so, this confrontational attitude also provided the appropriate ideological framework in which to view the poster action of February 1966 and the subsequent demonstration in front of the America House.

Outraged by the poster action, the older generation in the German SDS and the current leadership forced Dutschke to lay out his theoretical program in full, making the connection between the Third World and the situation in modern industrial societies more explicit. Referring to Frantz Fanon, Dutschke thus argued that, due to the globalized market economy and its alienating and repressing consequences, the liberation movements of colonized people were exemplary for revolutionary movements in the countries of the First World.[113] The latter's task was now to reach a similar revolutionary consciousness through the radicalization of their own actions, removed from any kind of romantic escapism or glorification of the Third World:

> The struggles of the Vietcong of the MIR in Peru are our struggles and, as a matter of fact, have to be given, through rational discussion and principally illegal demonstrations and actions, a new function of gaining conscious insights—an enormous, almost impossible task.[114]

Dutschke's first basic public policy declaration thus outlined the major theoretical foundations of his later political actions. He now cautiously formulated his arguments for an SDS audience, emphasizing (1) the global interdependence through the forces of capital and imperialism, (2) the shift of the challenges facing the world order from the cold-war confrontation to the North-South divide, and (3) the need for the avant-garde to form a coalition with the liberation movements in the "colonial periphery" in order to weaken the oppressive powers in their metropolitan centers through potentially illegal direct actions.[115]

Especially concerning the last point, Dutschke now drew on the concept of the "urban guerilla" influenced by Che Guevara's "foco theory," which supported the idea of actually creating the appropriate conditions for revolution on your own.[116] In Dutschke's application of this theoretical model as shown by his written notes, the starting point of all action was the university, from which "small homogenous guerrilla units" were to start the politicization process of the masses. Dutschke therefore already in 1966 saw foco theory as a further theoretical complement to his goal of uniting political theory and praxis through political action. Although drafted in a highly military jargon, Dutschke's primary aim was not to build up an urban guerilla force, but to implement this theory in his mobilization strategies.[117] As he wrote around the turn of 1967–68 with respect to the poster action,

> For the first time an attempt is being made to apply the foco theory by Che Guevara for political practice. . . . [T]he revolutionaries do not have to constantly wait for the revolution, but they can, through the focus, through the armed avant-garde of the people create the objective conditions for revolution by their subjective action. In its last consequence, this question also stood behind the poster action, and still stands behind every action today.[118]

Due to his only slowly strengthening position in the Berlin SDS and the controversy in the aftermath of the poster action, these ideas could not be discussed in full in February 1966 since they would have highly disturbed most of the SDS membership at that point. Furthermore, the most important reason for not revealing the full extent of his views was the significance that Dutschke himself, in keeping with his ideological amalgam, attached to the dynamic relationship between theory and political action.

Nevertheless, with the poster action the faction around Dutschke, Rabehl, and Kunzelmann for the first time successfully presented their provocative action-oriented strategies to the Berlin SDS, although only partly revealing the ideological implications they attached to them. The concept of direct action that they represented and sought to install as a core political strategy of the German SDS by now differed markedly from what Vester had proposed six months earlier, taking his cues from the American protest scene.

From Berkeley to Berlin? American Models
of Protest and the Ideological Change in the German SDS

Following the presentation of his political program and understanding of direct action, the group around Dutschke—which consisted of the participants of the poster action, former members of Berlin's Argument Club, and other students from his study groups—progressively gained more ground in the Berlin SDS. By April 1966, the Berlin SDS had largely adopted Dutschke's vision of a globally connected revolutionary movement. The small group, which at the beginning of 1965 had entered this local branch as members of the Subversive Aktion, had by now succeeded in winning over a sufficient majority for its ideological pursuits and particular contextualization of direct action as an emancipatory program. Having gained this local backing, this faction was now able to challenge SDS President Schauer on a national level.

The organizational contest that followed once again evolved around Vietnam, this time deliberately provoked by a war-related informational flyer that was published by the Berlin SDS at the beginning of May. In it, the American government was portrayed as completely inaccessible to the reasoning of antiwar protesters and willing to fabricate constant lies regarding its conduct in Southeast Asia. The authors therefore considered any opposition movement that simply called for peace and an American retreat a farce and an insult to the victims, since it based its demands on a naïve understanding of American imperialism. Instead, an active identification with the Vietcong through an international solidarity that connected one's individual fate to the situation in Vietnam was seen as the only appropriate response. As the flyer pointedly argued, "[E]very victory for the Vietcong means a victory for our democracy."[119]

Unsurprisingly, the language and implications of the flyer yet again provoked a fierce debate within the SDS national office and resulted in the threat of disciplinary measures.[120] In a special meeting on May 18, 1966, SDS president Helmut Schauer considered the flyer a mockery based on a misconception of the anticolonial revolution's realities.[121] According to Schauer, due to the aggressive nature of imperialism, authoritarian or fascist tendencies in capitalist countries had to be countered by an antiimperialist movement at home that could obstruct further capitalist and, in turn, imperialist expansion at its roots. Only this could eventually have an effect on the situation in the former colonies and make solidarity productive. In Schauer's opinion, the immature identification with the Vietcong as well as the sympathy toward violence displayed in the flyer was counterrevolutionary, since "[o]ur solidarity with Vietnam is not a solidarity with the people exercising violence but with the victims who are forced by a barbarian system to answer violence with violence."[122]

For Schauer, SDS needed to reach out to the broader community of peace activists instead of condemning its supposed naivety, which would only hinder the dissemination of a socialist analysis of the colonial conflicts. Even more importantly, he regarded the factionalizing policies and actions of the Berlin SDS as a determined attack against the SDS itself and the policies represented under his leadership.[123] Although resolved to secure the internal unity of the organization, Schauer gradually realized that he was powerless in the face of this resolute opposition against his policies. He and his vice-president thus resigned on May 23, 1966, acknowledging their inability to lead the organization in the face of the Berlin chapter's obstruction policy. Although internal pressure and a conciliatory resolution from the Berlin SDS led them to rescind their resignation shortly afterward, their coalition politics were left severely damaged.[124]

Assuming the mantle of American protest techniques, the action-oriented faction within the German SDS, led by the Berliners, had gained a first victory in the internal power rivalry and continued to undermine the policies of the SDS leadership in the following period. Despite their different ideological interpretation of the role of direct action, the Berlin chapter's references to the protest scene in the United States were, however, hardly just political tools to increase their organizational status. Contacts with the protest movement in the United States were of greatest significance, especially for the internationalist and action-oriented group around Dutschke, since they perceived the situation in the United States as a similar or more advanced stage of capitalism in comparison to the Federal Republic. Thanks to his American wife, Dutschke not only was personally connected to the United States but also had direct access to information on events in America. Gretchen Dutschke, in fact, introduced the Viva Maria Gruppe to the black nationalists and revolutionaries represented by Malcolm X in the fall of 1965. She differentiated the picture of the United States as the ultimate, imperialist enemy, by complementing the image of the "other" America held by Dutschke and his companions with the ideology of "Black Power."[125]

Following Marcuse's theoretical framework, Dutschke, as of April 1965, had already included the African Americans among potentially revolutionary social minorities.[126] Through his wife and a friend of hers, Ron Watson, he now received first-hand information about a group of black nationalists in Harlem who had formerly been associated with Malcolm X.[127] The indirect contact included an exchange of each other's writings, information on current events, and the content of respective group discussions. For Dutschke, activists in the United States were of special interest since they resided in the center of capitalist and imperialist aggression and had firsthand experience of the " 'society in abundance,' the current world society."[128]

For other German SDS members, the poster action in early February 1966 and its consequences had triggered even further curiosity about American protest techniques.[129] In its aftermath, the Berlin SDS therefore attempted to repeat the success of the teach-in with U.S. mission officials from February 26, 1965. In a letter to the American ambassador to Germany, George McGhee, they argued that their opposition to the war in Vietnam had regrettably been associated with communist causes; a connection that was only illustrative of the democratic deficiencies of West Germany. In contrast to this view, they claimed that the youthful antiwar protest as it manifested itself in Berlin was part of an international phenomenon.[130] To make this distinction explicit and refute any charges of anti-Americanism, they asked the ambassador to help facilitate another teach-in on the Vietnam War at the FU:

> We consider it necessary to stress the point that we are certainly not interested to have these activities identified with anti-Americanism. That is why we think it necessary to have a teach-in on Vietnam with well-known American critics and defendants of the US government policy on Vietnam, 'doves, hawks, and moderates'. This should prove that criticism on [sic!] the US Vietnam policy is not to be identified with anti-Americanism, as the majority of the Berlin press wishes to make believe.[131]

The illustrious list of potential participants extended from McGeorge Bundy and George Ball to Arthur Schlesinger, Henry Kissinger, Robert Kennedy, J. William Fulbright to American SDS President Paul Potter.[132] Unsurprisingly, there is no record of a response from the U.S. embassy, probably because it sensed the likely public relations difficulties such an event would pose.

The adoption of what were considered American forms of protest also took place in SDS chapters outside of Berlin. In the planning process of the Vietnam Congress in May 1966, the chairman of the SDS group from Cologne, Karl-Heinz Roth, repeatedly demanded to integrate these other forms of protest to get away from a purely academic discussion of the problem. Roth stressed the value of turning the congress into a teach-in that included representatives from various organizations and governments. Critical of the one-sided focus that these events had placed on U.S. officials, he later suggested extending an invitation to members of the American civil rights and antiwar movements, such as Mario Savio from Berkeley.[133]

The prime example of a further adoption of American forms of direct action, however, was the first sit-in that took place at the Free University of Berlin on June 22, 1966. Since February, events at the FU had taken a dramatic turn. For the first time, students published evaluations of seminars and lectures in the student newspaper, much to the dismay of professors. Furthermore, on February 16, the Academic Senate had decided to delete the paragraphs in the university constitution that allowed political student groups the use of university rooms for events they organized, so that they had to divert to the cafeteria. As a result, the student representatives submitted their resignation and a broad coalition of nearly all student organizations was formed to protest these measures. Plans to limit the duration of university education and the administration's refusal to allow a student ballot on this issue further exacerbated the situation, so that an all-party coalition of the student body decided to hold a demonstration at the next meeting of the Academic Senate.

Originally designed as a teach-in, the demonstration eventually moved into the Henry-Ford building, thus transforming the event into a sit-in, in which the participants insisted on the fulfillment of the demands that they had previously submitted to the administration. After the university president promised only to engage in further talks, the students entered into a prolonged and spontaneous discussion, which was dominated by members of the SDS. Late at night, 2,000 students ratified a resolution that placed their demands squarely into the debate on the democratization of the overall governing of the university, claiming that they were seeking a "reduction of oligarchic rule and the realization of democratic freedom in all areas of society. . . . The task is to view the freedom inside the university as a problem that points outside the borders of the university itself."[134] With this sit-in modeled after the actions of their American counterparts, the student body of the FU had therefore, just as their peers in Berkeley had done two years before, made the connection between the university's problems and the shortcomings of society at large. As a result, the successful import of this new form of protest now became a cornerstone in the German SDS's discussion about its future political strategy. Defending an action-oriented course, the Munich SDS in July 1966, for example, emphatically welcomed sit-ins as a form of protest because "[s]it-in situations separate the opportunist from other comrades within the SDS."[135]

Questions of strategy also figured prominently in the search for a new SDS president. Reimut Reiche, who was gradually emerging as a potential successor to Schauer, considered the first German sit-in as inextricably tied to the peculiar situation at the FU and was otherwise suspicious of the actual long-term effect of the mobilization in terms of the political activation of the student body.[136] He was not, however, outright dismissive of a direct-action strategy as such. Reiche was therefore an ideal candidate for the presidency, since he was neither ideologically anchored in one of the diametrically opposed groups that had emerged in the organiza-

IMAGE 3. First sit-in at the Free University of Berlin (June 22, 1966): FU rector Hans-Joachim Lieber (with microphone) stops the meeting of the Academic Senate and demands that the students cease their demonstration (Ullstein Bild/The Granger Collection, New York)

tion, nor bound by the influence of the older generation of SDS. Consequently, he was elected president of SDS at the national convention in September 1966.

Symbolically enough, Schauer urged Reiche to give an analysis of the latest student revolts at the national convention, with particular reference to the events in Berkeley and West Berlin. Accordingly, Reiche composed his speech together with the help of German SDS member Claus Offe, who had just returned from Berkeley.[137] For Reiche, these two places were the most significant for the German SDS, not least due to the comparable capitalist development in both countries.[138] Despite marked differences in terms of student organization and university structures, Reiche believed that the events at Berkeley would nonetheless serve as an inspiring model for the German SDS:

> In Berkeley a university revolt took place which remains to be witnessed in the Federal Republic. In its process and due to the training of the FSM [Free Speech Movement] leadership through the civil rights movement, political forms of struggle in civil disobedience have been developed and, above all, successfully practiced, which we have only dreamt of so far and have to learn now.[139]

When critically analyzed, the incredible success in mobilizing a large portion of the student body and the specific techniques of protest used in California would be of particular significance for the situation in Berlin, where students had already tested the "strategy of direct action" throughout the summer of 1966. The nationwide applicability of these strategies for the German SDS, however, remained unclear for Reiche, since political and university constellations in Berlin were unique and could not be easily transferred to other regions. Therefore, neither Berkeley nor Berlin could completely serve as leading examples for the future policy of the national leadership of the West German SDS, although their crucial influence remained undisputed.

By helping Reiche to become his successor, Helmut Schauer for the last time tried to contain the successful integration of direct-action techniques into the political repertoire of the German SDS as pushed for by the faction around Rudi Dutschke. Although Schauer did not know the details about the infiltration and subversion program of Dutschke and the Subversive Aktion from 1964 to 1965, he had an impression of possible things to come through a variety of sources reconfirming his fears about an ever-escalating provocation strategy.[140] Schauer was certainly aware of the consequences of this planned radicalization, of which the poster action in February 1966 and the Vietnam flyer of May 1966 were only the beginning. The old leadership under Schauer may have overestimated the concrete effects of this strategy, but there is hardly any doubt that the long-term outcome of this ideology caused a fundamental transformation of the German SDS, its mobilization strategy, and, ultimately, its political orientation as a whole.[141]

In this shift, the examples from the American scene and the growing internal opposition to the war in Vietnam that had reached West Germany through the writings of Michael Vester, the media, or the accounts of other German SDS members had a significant influence on the action-oriented group in the Berlin SDS that was attempting to lead the SDS in a different political direction. Despite the variety of intellectual sources in the faction around Dutschke, which ranged from Lukács and Marcuse to Fanon and Guevara, the methods of direct action practiced in other industrialized countries of the First World, particularly the United States, shaped their debates in fundamental ways. When the group was convening for its legendary June 1966 strategy meeting at the Kochelsee in Bavaria, these successful role models were equally part of the preparations for a new subversive group that was later to emerge as the "Kommune I." As Dieter Kunzelmann recalls,

> The Provo-movement as well as the experience of the American student and civil rights movement played a substantial role in Kochel; all of this was familiar to us not only through the texts of Michael Vester in the SDS journal 'Neue Kritik' but also from reports by SDS members who had been in the U.S. on a stipend. Certainly Rudi [Dutschke] had very direct insights through his American girl-friend Grete and absorbed all these experiences almost sensually; similar to everything that had been relayed to him about the practice of other groups which were close to us in spirit.[142]

American concepts of "direct action" and the example of the civil rights, free speech and antiwar movements were therefore a formative factor present at the creation of what can be considered the anti-authoritarian breakthrough within SDS, which was already completed when Reimut Reiche became SDS president in September 1966. At this point, the group around Dutschke, Rabehl, and Kunzelmann, which had been ideologically bonded in the Subversive Aktion, had by and large succeeded in winning over the Berlin SDS to their emancipatory program of direct action with regard to Vietnam and other issues. From now on, they would appear as the representative avant-garde in the organization and dominate the national discussions as well as the attention of the media. Berkeley had thus become a model not only for the Berlin SDS but also for the German SDS as a whole, which continued to follow events in California while discussing their implications for the political work in the Federal Republic.[143] As Rudi Dutschke noted in a strategy paper at the end of 1966, the German SDS was now having the historical chance of learning from the American SDS.[144]

Chapter 3

BUILDING THE SECOND FRONT

THE TRANSATLANTIC ANTIWAR ALLIANCE

OVERCOMING ISOLATIONISM:
THE INTERNATIONAL EFFORTS OF THE AMERICAN SDS, 1966–68

When American exchange student and SDS member Ruven Brooks enrolled himself at the University of Freiburg in Germany in the fall of 1966, he was astonished. Having just arrived from the United States and its heated domestic atmosphere, he found that the

> German political constellation has a rather frightening resemblance to the American: . . . On the left there's a pacifist element, represented by the Easter Marchers and the Campaign for Disarmament as well as the Marxist-dominated German peace party—about the same axis as SPU [and] SANE. There's a doctrinaire Marxist element, represented by uncountable splinter elements along YPSL, YSA, PL etc line. The German equivalent of the NAACP-type civil rights movement is the opposition to the "laws of necessity."[1]

Probing deeper and starting "an investigation of German left-wing groups for one which resembles the [American] SDS viewpoint," Brooks was, however, unable to identify an exact "New Left of the SDS-SNCC sort." One of the most promising candidates he found was the German SDS: "True to its initials, the latter looks like the best bet; it seems a bit doctrinaire Marxist but moving in the right (left!) direction."[2]

By the mid-sixties, the close political and ideological affinity between the German and American SDS had greatly strengthened the two groups' institutional relations. The American SDS, however, was by no means as keen on extending international connections as its German counterpart, since many in the group still considered domestic issues and the shortcomings of the U.S. system itself to be the main target of their activism. Accordingly, the organization's periodical, the *New Left Notes* (*NLN*) merely registered international New Left activities and seldom commented upon them, except to emphasize and boost the importance of participation in events taking place within the United States.[3] A similar mood reigned at national meetings. At the national convention in Ann Arbor, Mich., from June 25 to July 2, 1967, not only did the SDS decide not to withdraw from the International Union of Socialist Youth (IUSY), but it also determined that all formal relations with international student or youth groups were temporarily frozen. In order to evaluate possible candidates for cooperation, articles in the *NLN* were supposed to analyze them in greater detail, and informal relations would be established by the end of the year.[4] A similar caution led to the withdrawal of a proposal for the creation of an SDS National Coordinator for Liaison with Revolutionary and Liberation Movements and Organizations at the December 1967 National Council meeting.[5] Although the strong internationalist forces that existed within the SDS pushed in this direction, an increasing factionalism prevented the establishment of any official organizational consensus on international outreach at the beginning of 1968.

Despite these divisions, international cooperation in conjunction with the antiwar movement expanded. In the spring of 1966, Paul Booth had already argued that SDS join the International Confederation for Disarmament and Peace (ICDP) as a base for creating an international antiwar network and for encouraging further cooperation with the New Left in other countries.[6] Along with a generational leadership change in 1966/67 and a strengthening of the regional chapter's independence, the organization also experienced a greater individual opening toward international influences among its members.[7] Greg Calvert, the new National Secretary, was an apt reflection of this personal and ideological break from the older generations in SDS.[8] At the beginning of the decade, Calvert had spent over two years in Paris, where he became not only personally acquainted with French philosophers and academics such as Michel Foucault and Roland Barthes, but also associated with activists connected to the movement against the war in Algeria. Through this time and his immersion into French left-wing politics he was well aware of European socialist theories and Marxist rhetoric. Calvert was particularly inspired by the renaissance of the rhetoric of the French Resistance among French activists engaged in draft organizing. He subsequently imported this "language of resistance" into the United States and was the first to introduce the notion of "revolution" into the American SDS, causing what he considered a "strategic shift" that found its expression in the national draft resistance program that the SDS ratified in December 1966.[9] The refusal to be sent to Vietnam and the decision to actively help "organize unions of draft resisters" adopted by the SDS under its new leadership thus further contributed to its radicalization and to the move, in Calvert's phrase, from "protest to resistance."[10] Thereby departing from what was propagated by the SDS in its earlier days, Calvert set in motion the shift "from a beloved community to a revolutionary community of hope." He emphasized the need to develop a "revolutionary consciousness," which was aware of the oppressive conditions and lack of actual individual freedom in society, as a basic requirement for future political work.[11] Nevertheless, despite its striking similarities to the transformational concept of direct action advocated by Rudi Dutschke for the German SDS, which reached out to liberation movements worldwide, the strategy Calvert advocated for the American SDS still mainly targeted the United States: "For SDS, organizing people, in one sense, is detaching them from the American reality. When we break them out of that reality, that America, they begin to see their own lives, and America, in a new way. . . . The process, really, is to allow the real person to confront the real America."[12]

The organizational changes and the new leadership's increasingly Marxist rhetoric consisting of terms such as "bourgeoisie," "imperialism," and the "class divide" gradually made their way into the jargon used among SDS members, who began to consider themselves a potential "vanguard" looking around for international revolutionary peers. Along with this new avant-gardist self-confidence came an increasing identification with the Viet Cong. A sizeable group of SDS members went to Bratislava, Czechoslovakia, in September 1967, where about 40 Americans attended a summit-like conference with North Vietnamese officials and a delegation of the National Liberation Front (NLF) initiated by Tom Hayden and Dave Dellinger. According to Sol Stern, the former editor of the left-leaning *Ramparts* magazine, the American participants were "a motley combination of long-haired hippie types from the counterculture and the emerging underground press, earnest community and antiwar organizers, and a handful of New Left journalists and academics. Most were in their mid- to late twenties." They stood in marked contrast to their Vietnamese counterparts, who were "older, hardened revolutionaries, dressed in almost identical black pants and jackets, and they seemed to be under strict Communist Party discipline." The Vietnamese representatives also included Madame Nguyen Thi Binh, who would later become the principal negotiator in the Paris peace talks. As Stern recalls, Tom Hayden, in his speech at Bratislava, made a startling comparison between the war in Vietnam and the 1960 movie *Spartacus*, bringing the North Vietnamese into an analogy with the rebellious slave army. Moreover, just as each of the slaves after their lost battle against the Roman army pretended to be the revolt's leader in order to protect him, so should the American activists intervene personally to stop the war: "The United States was trying to annihilate our Vietnamese brothers and sisters in a murderous colonialist war, according to Hayden. Thus each of us in the American antiwar movement must now step forward and confront our own government, proclaiming: 'Take us, too. We are all Vietcong now.' "[13]

Meetings like these left deep impressions on the American travelers, most of whom had not been abroad before, and hardened their resolution to oppose the war by increasing the stakes at home. As Christopher Jencks wrote in the *New Republic,* "The common bond between the New Left and the NLF is not, then, a common dream or a common experience but a common enemy: the US government, the system, the Establishment. The young radicals' admiration for the NLF stems from the feeling that the NLF is resisting The Enemy successfully, whereas they are not."[14] Other journeys to Hanoi and Cambodia, a meeting of North American and NLF students in Montreal, Canada, Carl Oglesby's participation in Bertrand Russell's war crime tribunal, as well as visits to Havana for the Triconti-nental Conference in July and the Cultural Congress in December 1967 further familiarized American SDS members with Third World liberation movements. These travels did more than create a sense of being connected to an almost global revolutionary upsurge in which their own country had seemingly occupied the role of the oppressive imperialist power.[15] They also raised the stakes for the confrontations at home.

The European movements came back to the attention of the American SDS with the fatal shooting of German student Benno Ohnesorg in West Berlin during a demonstration against the Shah of Iran on June 2, 1967. In a solidarity cable to the German SDS, Greg Calvert stated his organiza-tions's "shock and horror at the blatant terrorism of the West Berlin po-lice" and declared it "important for the development of political con-sciousness among our members" to be kept informed of further consequences and actions resulting from the killing.[16] On April 11, 1968, the shooting of Rudi Dutschke again spotlighted events in Europe and the situation of the German student movement. The coverage of the shoot-ing filled the front page of the April 15, 1968, issue of the *New Left Notes* with the American SDS expressing its outrage over the attack: "We stand with you in this critical hour. An injury to one is an injury to all."[17] In light of this assassination attempt on "one of the most respected antiwar leaders in Europe," the American SDS, the Student Mobilization Commit-tee, and other groups in New York City called for rallies at Columbia and New York University in solidarity with the German SDS. Declaring that "now it is the time for the American antiwar students to protest this attack on the international antiwar movement,"[18] the coalition blamed Axel Springer's conservative publishing house and the West German govern-ment for the attack on Dutschke and proclaimed, "We of the Students for a Democratic Society in the U.S. wish to express our sympathy for Rudi Dutschke and the other victims of repression in Germany and our solidar-ity with their struggle."[19] To underline their support, they also called for a picket in front of the New York office of Axel Springer at Rockefeller Plaza on April 17, 1968. The demonstration attracted between forty and fifty participants who burned a Nazi flag in support of the student riots in West Germany. According to the *New York Times,* fistfights broke out with the police and the security officers of the building, and fourteen persons were arrested.[20] Determined to push the issue, the New York SDS demanded that "Axel Springer publications leave the United States" and called for another demonstration the week after in order to "show America that we support our German brothers and sisters in a struggle that is against the same fascist tactics that the U.S. uses to suppress black Americans and the Vietnamese people."[21] The structural comparison of American and German society and the willingness to be arrested once again for trespassing on private property was not only indicative of a growing sense of international solidarity but also of a change in militancy among American student activists, which was to translate itself in the radical occupation of Columbia University later that week.[22]

In the following month, the events of May 1968 in France deepened the perception of a common cause between the American and European movements. As long-time SDS member Robert Ross recalls, the French riots caused a feeling of solidarity and encouragement, "a sense that we are not alone," of being part of a fundamental worldwide transformation.[23] The SDS national convention in East Lansing, Mich., from June 9 to 15, 1968, was equally moved by these feelings. A proposal by Tom Bell, Bernardine Dohrn, and Steve Halliwell suggested the development of urban revolutionary centers, which were supposed to transcend SDS's campus base by forging alliances with nonstudent groups (for example, young professionals and workers) as well as students previously unaffected by the SDS. The declared goal was to transform SDS into a "professional revolutionary organization."[24] Inspired by the heated international atmosphere, the authors particularly stressed the need for a greater outreach to organizations overseas:

> SDS is part of an international force fighting an international capitalist system. We face a growing responsibility to establish working relationships with the insurgent elements in other countries that have independently developed an analysis similar to our own— groups in West Germany, France, Japan, England, Italy and others. In addition, we must develop better ties with the revolutionary movements in third world nations exploited by American imperialism. To make these ties functional and to sustain them, an organization must be developed by [SDS] that is capable of utilizing those contacts most productively for the development of the broader movement.[25]

In other words, the proposal laid out a specific program for turning the American SDS into an effective organization that was to become an integral part of a global revolutionary network.[26]

The inter-organizational secretary of the SDS, Carl Davidson, even went a step further and considered the events in West Germany and in France to be role models for the American SDS, particularly in terms of reaching nonstudent constituencies. In his view, student actions in Europe had spurred the protest and subsequent occupation at Columbia University, "giving many Columbia rebels the audacity and inspiration to go beyond what seemed possible." Davidson hoped that now "isolationist attitudes" could be overcome in favor of a greater "radical internationalism within the ranks of SDS." Since "US imperialism is an international system" and "all the oppressed peoples falling within its perimeter are our potential allies," it followed that the struggles of the American SDS were then "part of this single revolutionary process within a multinational imperialism."[27] For Davidson, it was therefore time for a "New Left internationalism to unite workers and students in a common fight on all fronts within the Empire."[28] What made such a global cooperation even more attractive was the presence of U.S. troops overseas and the entanglement of most Western countries in military alliances with the United States: "A variety of programs joining American, Japanese, and European New Left Students could be developed, co-ordinating international actions around Draft-resistance, desertion, or attacks on the CIA, NATO, and other military alliances."

In this framework for future action, Davidson particularly highlighted the striking similarities between the contexts of the West German and American student movements: a pervasive anticommunism in their societies, a lack of true parliamentary opposition, the rise of right-wing and conservative ideologies, a manipulative mass media, and a general public apathy. On an institutional level, both the German and American SDSs had emancipated themselves from their parent groups in the first half of the 1960s, shared similar protest techniques, and could look back on a history of cooperation and exchange.[29] The extent to which Davidson saw the development of his own organization mirrored in the situation and features of the German SDS is extraordinary and indicative of a substantial change in the minds of many SDS members who began to see the international scene as a reflection and reinforcement of American domestic grievances. In their attempts to reach out internationally, they felt that especially the shooting of Rudi Dutschke and the May events in Paris had shown that the neglect of the European scene by the American SDS in favor of the Third World had been a mistake.[30]

A series of reports and dossiers on the European student movements by Barbara and John Ehrenreich in *New Left Notes* in the aftermath of the convention tried to remedy these shortcomings. The authors, however, concluded that a hasty transfer of foreign protest techniques and strategies without thorough discussion was in vain, since "[i]nternational exchange of tactics and analyses will be valuable insofar as we understand the setting in which they were developed and the context in which they were applied."[31] While this was true for the American SDS, the situation was different for American activists who had been living in Europe for an extended period of time due to professional reasons or academic exchange programs. Their understanding of local conditions and willingness to involve themselves in joint protest activities differed markedly from the official ideas about international contacts on an organizational level. With their mostly local collaborations, they formed a new and more personal venue of the border-transgressing protests of the 1960s.

Colonies of American Dissent: The U.S. Campaign to End the War in Vietnam and GI-Organizing in West Germany

"We disassociate ourselves from the destruction by the United States of Vietnam. . . . We will speak for a growing number of Americans when we begin, on Saturday, on April 22 [1967], a series of weekly one-hour walks through West Berlin. One hundred loyal Americans, walking in an orderly column, will carry a sign demanding the neutralization of Vietnam." With these words the group called the U.S. Campaign to End the War in Vietnam addressed Vice President Hubert Humphrey prior to his visit to Berlin on April 6, 1967, declaring its commitment to assert publicly its opposition to the American policy in Vietnam. The group, founded by Peter Standish and Francis Fuller as a nonpartisan, nonprofit organization of U.S. citizens living in Berlin, consisted of Americans from various professions and social backgrounds, thus transcending an exclusively student membership. In their five-point program, they demanded the neutralization and withdrawal of all foreign troops from North and South Vietnam, and proclaimed their support for all politicians in favor of such a policy. Until then, they pledged to continue their public display of dissent in West Berlin, a city whose security and government was still supervised by the Allied powers.[32]

Much to the alarm of U.S. officials, who even considered banning what they viewed as an anti-American display in a city of unique symbolic value for the United States in the cold war, the U.S. Campaign hosted its demonstrations on a bi-weekly basis along with other picket-lines on the Kurfürstendamm and "read-ins" about Vietnam.[33] As Elsa Rassbach, one of the participants, recalls, "[W]e wanted to make a statement. . . . We, as Americans, also disagree."[34] The demonstrations were peaceful and restrained, since its participants were convinced of the public and political impact they would make:

> We were still filled with the belief that somehow the Americans were the good guys. If 60 or 100 Americans in Berlin, the "window of the free world," politely protested, we thought the U.S. government would certainly agree that the war has to be stopped![35]

IMAGE 4. U.S. Campaign members during an antiwar demonstration with German student organizations on Tauentzienstrasse/Wittenbergplatz, West Berlin, October 21, 1967 (Landesarchiv Berlin)

U.S. Campaign members distributed flyers at German-American events in the city, such as troop parades and the annual German-American Volksfest, conducted lectures on Black Power in the Republikanischer Club (Republican Club), an affiliate of the German SDS, and participated in SDS panel discussions on the student movement in West Germany and the United States.[36] As a visible expatriate branch of American dissent in West Berlin, the U.S. Campaign and its activities thus served as yet another source for German students to find out more about the domestic opposition in the United States.

Juan Flores, for example, a Fulbright exchange student living in Berlin in 1966/67, joined the U.S. Campaign shortly after his arrival.[37] Due to his good command of German, he became one of the mediators between the U.S. Campaign and the German SDS and was frequently in touch with influential German SDS members such as Rudi Dutschke, Bernd Rabehl, and Klaus Meschkat.[38] Despite differences in political agenda and membership, Vietnam provided the unifying issue between the two groups; although the American group was strongly aware of the fact that their protest would have greater moral legitimacy and "symbolic value" in public if it were not directly connected to the German SDS. As a result, the two antiwar networks mostly operated separately in public. As Flores recalls,

IMAGE 5. Panel discussion on "Goals and Methods of the Extra-Parliamentary Opposition in Germany and the U.S.," West Berlin, November 28, 1967: Participants include, among others, FU professor Charles Nichols (third from left), Vice Chairman of the U.S. Campaign Keith Chamberlain (sixth from left), and Rudi Dutschke (first from the right) (Landesarchiv Berlin)

It would have been easier to get hundreds of German students to join the American thing, but . . . the idea was not to do that, but was rather to keep it an American, by American citizens, who were doing it and marching—that was going to be the impact.[39]

Over time, however, the U.S. Campaign began to emulate the radicalization processes that the protest movements in the United States and West Germany were going through. The influx of new Americans arriving in Berlin slowly transformed the originally bipartisan group and eventually caused a split among its members along political lines.[40] The break occurred in March 1968 when the U.S. Campaign decided to organize an auction of paintings and sculptures of Berlin artists, whose profits were supposed to be donated to the South Vietnamese Liberation Front.[41] Through contacts in East Berlin, the group organized a meeting with delegates from the National Liberation Front in Prague in June 1968. After two days of discussion, they publicly handed over the money to the North Vietnamese during a press conference.[42] The fact that the financial support was given without any conditions (for example, purchase of medical supplies), among other issues, caused various people to leave the group. In the meantime, however, another area of cooperation between the U.S.

Campaign and German activists had already emerged and would dominate in the years to come.

GI-organizing, in which West German students played a prime role, first entered the public eye in October 1967 when a small rocket exploded over an American barracks in West Berlin and flyers advocating desertion from the U.S. army as a means to escape service in Vietnam were dispersed all over the area.[43] Similar activities took place in and around Frankfurt and other U.S. military installations in West Germany. A month earlier, American SDS member Jeff Shero had already reported on these draft resistance groups in the *New Left Notes*: "They used to whisper, 'Pssst soldier! Dirty pictures?' But times have changed. Just as likely now that long-haired kid hanging around the European train station or soldier's bar is offering a better deal—Freedom. 'Hey man, FTA [Fuck the Army], take one of these.' That's the new hustle. An elusive cobweb army of hippies, Provos, new lefties, and some GIs themselves spread the word."[44] Emulating the GI-organizing of their American peers in the United States, German activists in particular tried to foster protest and resistance within the army in a direct attempt to obstruct the war effort from within Europe. In trying to make American GIs allies for their cause, the activists tried to reverse the relationship between the U.S. army and Germans in the decades immediately following the Second World War from one of occupation and defense to one of joint rebellion and potential sabotage.

During its national convention in September 1967, the German SDS officially determined U.S. military bases in West Germany as legitimate targets of their actions.[45] With West Germany being a major site of U.S. troops, the American SDS had already supported these efforts and proclaimed "the need to bring an anti-imperialist perspective to anti-war work in Europe" as part of its own draft desertion campaign in the spring of 1967.[46] Since the mid-sixties, a European-wide network of desertion support had been developed, which guided American soldiers to France (via Amsterdam or later directly from Germany). For the successful working of this "underground railroad" European, and particularly West German, students proved to be crucial, and West German SDS and local student governments (AStAs) actively took part in these efforts.[47] At the end of 1967, German SDS President Karl-Dietrich Wolff told an East German source that through this campaign, with the support of the German trade unions, SDS was able to channel about 150 soldiers a month out of the country.[48]

More and more groups in West Germany sought contact with American soldiers now to organize them and discuss their role in the war.[49] The Republican Club at the University of Mannheim, for example, tried to reach out to African American soldiers by inviting them for discussions and distributing information on Black Power, the use of violence and their role in the U.S. military.[50] At the Vietnam Congress in West Berlin on February 17–18, 1968, U.S. Campaign member Patty Lee Parmalee offered detailed practical advice for GI-organizing based on her knowledge and experience gained in the United States. Parmalee had become involved with the American SDS in 1964 at the University of California at Irvine. She had traveled to West Berlin in December 1967 to write her doctoral dissertation on Bertolt Brecht, but was intrigued by the German SDS, of which she became a quasi-member. Working with the U.S. Campaign, she took part in actions organizing GIs and was also part of the first expatriate chapter of the American SDS in West Berlin. During the congress, Parmalee laid out a plan for the effective organization of GIs in West Germany, emphasizing that West Berlin "should have the effect on the army that San Francisco together with Berkeley has on the navy."[51] By sharing the experience she had gained in the United States with similar actions, she transferred her "know-how" to a West German context, further underlining Dutschke's call for more comprehensive and active organizing efforts all over the country.

In the course of 1968, the organizing of American soldiers became both more substantial and institutionalized. Members of the U.S. Campaign distributed flyers in bars and restaurants frequented by American GIs in West Berlin and attempted to extend their actions to the American quarters, but were, however, soon confronted by both U.S. military and Berlin police forces.[52] Despite these interventions by the authorities, the group continued its work and started the publication of its own GI newspaper, *Where It's At*, written by American civilians in West Berlin, who were students, former GIs, or professionals.[53] Their idea was to provide an alternative news source for American soldiers and bridge the gap between the military and student protestors, a cooperation that the military command and German authorities sought to prevent at all costs. During the Easter riots in April 1968 in West Berlin, for example, American soldiers were ordered not to leave their base. In case U.S. military troops were called to support Berlin police forces in confronting student unrest, the editors of *Where It's At* urged soldiers to make the right choice: "If that time comes, German students hope soldiers will realize that their interests lie not on the side of a government of old Nazis and Nazi methods, but on the side of the students, who are the main support of freedom and democracy in Germany."[54]

In the second half of the 1968, the GI-organizing group behind *Where It's At*, which was still publicly regarded as the U.S. Campaign, continued its outreach to American soldiers, opened up a shop in Charlottenburg, and gradually came to understand itself as an American SDS chapter in West Berlin.[55] Frequent correspondence with the national office of the American SDS kept it up to date with other GI-projects in the U.S. and enabled it to continue its role as a source of information for German activists on the American movement and the internal transformation that it was going through.[56] In December 1968, this affiliation to the American SDS, although very loose, gave the German authorities an argument to initiate legal proceedings against the U.S. Campaign by demanding its registration as a public club according to German laws.[57] Based on articles in *Where It's At*, the German police also repeatedly charged various members of the U.S. Campaign with solicitation of desertion. In September 1968, new Allied legislation made it illegal to advocate desertion in Berlin and enabled German courts to prosecute the perpetrators.[58] U.S. Campaign members, however, successfully rejected these charges with the help of Horst Mahler, the local New Left lawyer. They defended their paper as an alternative source of information for "news that for some reason never manages to get into print in *Stars and Stripes*, for example."[59] In their view, the work of U.S. Campaign members who were also members of the American SDS was conducted under the umbrella of the German SDS and would thus not be part of an independent political organization liable to German laws.[60] Due to the U.S. Campaign's official affiliation with the German movement, the police were finally forced to drop the case.[61]

In the years following, the work of the U.S. Campaign increasingly resonated with other GI-projects, such as the underground paper *Venceremos* in Frankfurt, and it strengthened the group's relationship to the German left as a whole.[62] Although the U.S. Campaign's antiwar character remained unaltered, the group's membership began to change. The GI paper *Up Against the Wall*, which succeeded *Where It's At* at the beginning of 1970 and whose title was both a reference to an activist group in New York City and a pun on the situation in Berlin, signaled the final departure to GI work that was mostly by and for soldiers themselves. With the publication of *Forward* in 1970/71, these American activists abroad emancipated themselves from the German student movement and almost exclusively concentrated on the burgeoning GI-movement, which marked a turning point in the history of the transatlantic cooperation of activists that had emerged in the course of the 1960s.[63]

THE INTERNATIONAL OUTREACH OF THE GERMAN SDS

For the German SDS, the attempts to connect to foreign protest movements in the second half of the decade predominantly took place within an international network of opposition against the Vietnam War. The organization's 1966 national convention finally established Vietnam as a fundamental issue on the organization's agenda. Previous SDS resolutions and congresses such as "Vietnam—Analysis of an Example" of May 1966 had already described the conflict as a model case for both colonial liberation movements and U.S. imperialism.[64] A majority of SDS activists now felt that the West German government, too, indirectly supported the war through its transatlantic alliance and shared a responsibility for what was happening in Vietnam.[65] Assuming the task of spreading the cause of the American antiwar movement to Germany and Western Europe, they demanded the transformation of German SDS into a central source for information about the war to educate students and the public at large.

To facilitate this, German SDS groups published key texts of U.S. antiwar groups in translation and frequently contacted American antiwar groups for cooperation.[66] Johanna Hoornweg from the Munich chapter of the German SDS, for example, informed the national office of the American SDS in November 1966 about the establishment of a local "Vietnam Committee for Peace and the Liberation struggle."[67] As the committee's founding declaration highlighted, its particular concern was the suppression of domestic dissent in the United States similar to that imposed during the time of McCarthyism. The committee proclaimed its solidarity with the African American liberation movement, as well antiwar and anti-imperialist groups in the United States.[68] In the committee's view, the Federal Republic, as part of the ideological and military Western alliance, was complicit in the U.S. imperialist foreign policy carried out in Southeast Asia. Any protest by Western activists was thus part of a larger internationalist effort connected to liberation movements worldwide: "By combating this system here and now by joining ranks for further struggles, we are acting at the same time in a spirit of solidarity with the democratic movements in the USA and with the people of Asia, Africa, and Latin America."[69] In his reply to Hoornweg, the National Secretary of the American SDS Greg Calvert acknowledged this transnational bond and assured his support for the committee by declaring, "Those of us here in Students for a Democratic Society who are struggling against a system which promotes genocide abroad and repression at home are encouraged by the efforts of our brothers in other countries who bear the banner of freedom in the face of the destructive power of the American giant."[70] As a result of their correspondence, the Munich chapter of German SDS and the American SDS exchanged information materials and set up regular mailings, thereby installing a permanent channel of transatlantic communication.

Institutional contacts between the two student organizations such as these took place in abundance, despite the lack of official commitment to international cooperation from the American SDS on a national level. From 1966, the German SDS frequently sought to emulate the actions of its peers in the United States and used them as a model for its own strate-

IMAGE 6. Antiwar demonstration in West Berlin, December 10, 1966 (Bildarchiv Preussischer Kulturbesitz /Art Resource, New York)

gies. In a letter to Bettina Aptheker of "Students Strike for Peace in Vietnam" in California, German SDS president Reimut Reiche, for example, noted that his organization had been inspired by the new escalation of the Berkeley revolt in 1966 and had "first applied '[A]merican' or non-traditional forms and terms of agitation and action at the universities and in the streets" in West Germany.[71] Since the American and German SDS faced similar problems, Reiche also frequently asked for other, especially "more theoretically oriented," material from the American side that could be published in the organization's journal *neue kritik*.[72] Since the German SDS possessed the same initials, buttons from the American SDS displaying the organization's acronym or famous antiwar slogans such as "Make Love Not War" were also in extremely high demand among West German activists. Their popularity and open display further nourished the perception of SDS as being one organization that was active on both sides of the Atlantic.[73]

Beyond these immediate contacts, the transatlantic networks of dissent also relied on deeper historical roots. In both Germany and the United States, a whole generation of German (r)emigrants that had found exile in America during the time of National Socialism exerted a strong influence on the emergence of the New Left. C. Wright Mills, for example, was a student of the German emigrant Hans Gerth at the University of Wisconsin, Madison.[74] In addition to American academics such as Paul

Goodman or Arnold Kaufman, emigrants such as Bruno Bettelheim, Hans Morgenthau (both at the University of Chicago), and Carl Schorske (Berkeley) played a considerable part in the foundation of the American and German student movement. Their theories on human alienation in modern society and an analysis of the early writings of Marx provoked the interest of the young generation. Through their participation in magazines such as *Dissent* and *Studies on the Left*, and through their direct support of student activists' projects, they became not only direct transmitters but also active supporters of the emerging American New Left, whose representatives such as Tom Hayden and Todd Gitlin later published in the very same journals.[75]

In the Federal Republic, the reception of the works of these emigrants started in the mid-sixties. In particular Rudi Dutschke and the antiauthoritarian faction of the German SDS opened up the space for a whole variety of almost forgotten scholars, cultural critics and socialist thinkers. Through the group Subversive Aktion, Dutschke had already encountered and discussed the writings of other German emigrants long before they were known within the German SDS.[76] Once their ideas were rediscovered and disseminated among the student activists, however, they became an important part of a critical analysis of society. As political scientist Kurt Shell argued, "When Marxist tools had largely fallen into disuse, seemed incapable of grasping the new reality or were too disgraced by their Stalinist utilization, the critical voices coming from America, dealing with a reality rawer, more dramatic than the postwar German scene, were listened to attentively."[77]

The adaptation of these analytical tools as "re-imports" provided by these thinkers thus enabled the students to embark on their critical scrutiny of society's shortcomings.[78] Along similar lines, Theodor W. Adorno and Max Horkheimer's writings in American exile, as well as their teaching in the reopened Institute for Social Research in Frankfurt after their return, similarly shaped West German activists. Although the returned members of the Frankfurt School refused to draw any practical consequences from their critical theory and questioned the possibility of the student movement to bring about social change, they, too, were an integral part of this long-term transatlantic circulation of ideas.[79] As one sociologist has pointed out, "Without the United States, there would be no critical theory."[80]

The emigrant and critical theorist who exercised the most significant influence on the New Left was Herbert Marcuse. With *Eros and Civilization* (1955), *One-Dimensional Man* (1964), and *Repressive Tolerance* (1965), he presented key texts for protest movements on both sides of the Atlantic. In addition, Marcuse was actively promoting the students' cause and tried to bring together American and West German activists. After a talk at the SDS cosponsored 1966 congress "Vietnam-Analysis of an Example," he visited Berlin and other cities in Germany several times to discuss the students' problems and his views on social change.[81] In 1967, he accepted an invitation by the Berlin SDS for a lecture series on "The End of Utopia" at the Free University, in which he demanded more transnational cooperation between the protest movements:

> Radical opposition can only be viewed today in a global framework; as an isolated phenomenon it is distorted from the very beginning. The development of relations between student opposition in the various countries is therefore one of the most important tasks of this strategy in these years. There are hardly any relations between the student opposition in the United States and the student movement here. . . . We have to work on the development of these relations— and if I discuss the topic of my presentation at the example of the USA, I am doing this to prepare for the development of these relations.[82]

Marcuse was therefore not only an important intellectual inspiration for and institutional link between the two movements, but also a personal embodiment of the impact of the "Frankfurt School" on both the American and German New Left. He and the other emigrants developed a radical critique and rethinking of capitalism under the influence of having narrowly escaped the Holocaust, which was taken up by the young generation of the 1960s in the context of the cold war. Kurt Shell described this intercultural exchange as a unique example of both a " 'Germanizing' of American youth" and an American influence on West German students because the rediscovery of these intellectual legacies took place "*via* America and loaded with a specifically American change" during the 1960s.[83]

All of this offers a clear impression of how manifold the historical connections and cooperation between the two movements already were by 1967. The rise of major antiwar sentiment in both organizations, as well as a feeling of solidarity and common cause, made frequent exchanges, such as publishing in each other's journals, appear natural. Among German SDS members, particularly the protest against the Vietnam War served as a connection to revolutionary movements abroad and a vehicle to mobilize against imperialism and capitalism, both internationally and domestically. The protest thus acquired a central role in the organization's political strategies. As a resolution of the 1967 national convention of the German SDS put it, "the battle against US-imperialism and its support by the Federal Republic becomes more and more the progressive moment of the revolutionary movement in West Germany itself."[84]

IMAGE 7. Herbert Marcuse at the Free University of Berlin, 1967 (Ullstein Bild/ The Granger Collection, New York)

A Global Revolutionary Strategy: Institutionalizing the Second Front

The most visible peak of antiwar sentiment in West Germany was the Vietnam Congress organized by the German SDS at the Technical University (TU) in Berlin on February 17–18, 1968, which attracted roughly 5,000 students and antiwar activists from Europe and overseas.[85] With the feeling of having achieved at least some of their goals (both the West Berlin police president and the mayor had resigned in August and September 1967), Berlin students displayed both their own confidence and their solidarity with the Vietnamese people. At the closing demonstration, around 12,000 people marched through the streets of West Berlin, carrying posters of Che Guevara, Rosa Luxemburg, and Leo Trotzki, chanting "Ho Ho Ho Tschi Minh" and "We are a small radical minority."

At the congress, Rudi Dutschke further underlined the internationalist and action-oriented agenda developed in previous years. In a speech on "The Historical Conditions of the International Emancipation Struggle," Dutschke argued that through the war in Vietnam the U.S. government had proven its determination to suppress any revolutionary uprisings in the Third World, which were the role models for the extension of the global revolutionary process into the capitalist countries of the First World.[86] In the face of such a threat, Dutschke believed the role of Vietnam in mobilizing for revolution to be crucial. The struggle against university bureaucracy was now fully superseded by the significance of the Vietnamese revolution.[87] In Dutschke's mind, a global alliance of revolutionary forces to defend Vietnam and, with it, the hope for a worldwide revolution, had become indispensable: "The globalization of revolutionary forces is the most important task of the whole historical period that we live in and in which we are working towards human emancipation. . . . In the world-wide demonstrations lies, in an anticipatory sense, something like a global revolutionary strategy."[88] Based on this insight, Dutschke called for a comprehensive coordination of revolutionary protest in order to counter global imperialism and liberate humankind from capitalist and bureaucratic repression.[89]

In this transformation process, the American protest scene had become a reference point for Dutschke.[90] Long before the congress, he had emphasized the need to establish contact with U.S. protest groups. On the one hand, he saw the American government and the American power elite as prime enemies in his fight against global imperialism in favor of socialist revolution. At the same time, he regarded the African American movement and the New Left in the United States as extremely useful strategic models and cooperation partners. His views on the Vietnam war and the urgency to end the atrocities committed against the Vietnamese people therefore spurred him to call not only for immediate actions in Germany but also for a coalition with what he considered to be the "true America." For Dutschke, the American counterculture and grassroots organizing tactics and techniques formed a model for a strategic attack on imperialism from within that could equally inspire German activists.[91]

Other members of the German SDS at the congress, especially those with even stronger ties to the United States, saw a similar connection between the two movements. Berlin SDS member Ekkehart Krippendorff, for example, who had spent the years 1960–63 at the universities of Harvard, Yale, and Columbia as a fellow and assistant instructor, even considered political developments in the United States as decisive for the situation in Germany as was the conflict in Vietnam. Drawing upon the German past and upon a Marxist analysis, Krippendorff interpreted the actions of the U.S. government as a gradually evolving, globally operating fascism that made cooperation between the German and American movements an existential necessity: "I believe that even and especially if the victory of the Liberation Front in Vietnam is successful . . . that the repression in the USA will be even more serious. And I believe that we have to be clear about the consequences of what it can and will mean if the American system transforms itself from a latent to an open fascism; that this is incredibly more dangerous for us than what we will be facing currently in its latent state."[92]

Both countries, Vietnam as a victim of imperialism and the United States as perpetrator, thus turned into symbols for a West German politics of solidarity that was increasingly seeking validation in transnational political action. The first step was to attack the North Atlantic Treaty Organization (NATO) as the central offspring of global imperialism in Western Europe. Mass actions, subversive attacks on NATO war material, as well as GI-organizing were to unite protest transnationally and to weaken the U.S. war effort in individual European countries.[93] At the same time, they would enable more militant actions in the Federal Republic itself. As Dutschke argued, "We dare attack American imperialism politically but have not yet the will to break with our own ruling apparatus, to conduct militant actions against the centers of manipulation, for example the inhuman machinery of the Springer-corporation, or to destroy the inhuman war machinery."[94] Through opposition against NATO, abstract solidarity with the American protest movement and the Third World could thus be transformed into a meaningful struggle against imperialism on various fronts.[95]

American participants of the Vietnam Congress in West Berlin reconfirmed this fundamental need for an international "second front," insisting that activists had to put an end to the oppression both in Vietnam and on the domestic level by any means necessary. SNCC member Ray Robinson particularly defended the legitimacy of violence associated with Black Power, claiming that African Americans were an internal colony suffering from violence similar to the Vietnamese.[96] SNCC representative Dale A. Smith was even more explicit in his call for a move from mere protest to active resistance at home: "Nobody will be able to sleep peacefully as long as they have not stopped their criminal activities, have pulled back and resigned. Resistance means: As long as parents in Vietnam are crying about their children, parents in the USA should cry about their children, too."[97] With the public burning of their draft cards in front of a cheering audience, the Americans Rogis Lader and Robert Peirce were no less impressive in their call for more international acts of protest. Accusing the United States of crimes against humanity and perverting its democratic ideals, Lader and Peirce even compared U.S. actions in Vietnam to the atrocities of National Socialism. For Lader, his draft card was "a sign for an SS of an American kind" and burning signified his resistance against it.[98] Similarly, Peirce compared the prison camps in Vietnam to concentration camps and referred to the trials of Nuremberg as a justification not to take part in this war.[99] Invoking the historical precedent of Nazi Germany, both men pleaded to the assembled congress

IMAGE 8. SNNC Representative Dale Smith speaking at the Vietnam Congress in West Berlin, February 17, 1968 (Ullstein Bild/The Granger Collection, New York)

participants to follow their example and oppose any personal cooperation or that of their respective countries with the United States in order to avoid similar guilt.[100]

For the American delegates the congress was, however, not simply a place to meet representatives from the European movements. Even more significantly, it was a chance to confer with a North Vietnamese delegation. Susan Eanet, the official representative of the American SDS, recalls her very emotional encounter with the Vietnamese representatives, some of whom had become amputees as a result of the war: "And the Vietnamese admonished us, the Vietnamese directed us to work closely with the Germans in order to tell these American soldiers to go to any place but Vietnam. Go anywhere, go to Sweden, go to France, go wherever you go. Jump in the ocean before you go, but do anything to resist. So they gave us this charge. This is your job. If you are in Germany, you are in the ideal strategic position to discourage these guys from coming over."[101] The politics of transnational solidarity were thus complemented by the practical task of organizing American soldiers stationed in Germany.

Other foreign representatives supported the framework of an institutionalized revolutionary network that transcended national borders. The Belgian Marxist Ernest Mandel called for a globally united front born out of revolutionary practice.[102] Alain Krivine from the French group Jeunesse Communist Rvolutionaire (JCR) demanded actions in urban centers

IMAGE 9. Antiwar demonstration during the Vietnam Congress, February 18, 1968: Participants include Tariq Ali, Dale Smith, Rudi Dutschke, and Gaston Salvatore (Landesarchiv Berlin)

worldwide that would make the presence of American troops impossible.[103] Similarly, the Austrian writer Erich Fried viewed the metropolis of the First World as the key basis for further development of global revolutionary interconnectedness.[104] The significance of these calls for congress participants is also reconfirmed by undercover agents of the Berlin Ministry of the Interior, who reported that "[i]n the speeches given at the conference it was continuously emphasized that the most important precondition for the success of world revolution is international cooperation, the solidarity of all revolutionary movements worldwide."[105]

To ensure the formation of such a global protest network, the institutional infrastructure to be formed for the campaign against NATO was to serve as a stepping stone. As Dutschke argued,

> The installation of an *independent revolutionary information network* is indispensable and possible. We are able to and have to create tactical centers and offices in Western and Central Europe for this campaign in the various countries, in which comrades from various countries cooperate. This means that German comrades would go to France, French comrades to Germany, English comrades to Italy and Italians to France in order to truly anchor internationalism already in the nationality.[106]

The plans outlined during the congress eventually materialized in its aftermath with the foundation of the International News and Research Institute (INFI) in West Berlin under the auspices of Berlin SDS members Rudi Dutschke, Jürgen Horlemann, and Gaston Salvatore.[107] For them, the congress had proven Europe's active role in the global imperialist order that was oppressing the Third World and opened up the opportunity of an "internationalism of a new type" among student activists worldwide. Preliminary talks at the congress had determined that the INFI, as a central institute coordinated by the SDS Berlin, was to serve as the link for these activities and feature offices in various European cities. These branches were designed to supervise conferences, newsletters, and the institution of a documentary center, as well as a variety of European-wide action programs: demonstrations and blockades of American companies producing weapons of destruction (DOW-Chemical), organization of strikes in harbors trans-shipping military goods, a Western European GI-organizing and desertion campaign, and demonstrations against selected NATO bases.[108]

The institute's prime task was to study the Third World liberation movements and provide insights that would benefit revolutionary work in Western Europe. In order to link center and periphery, a particular part of the institute's program was the training of "revolutionary socialists" who could "participate directly in the struggle and, as revolutionary experts, help set up socialism in those countries where the revolution had won."[109] By juxtaposing repressive mechanisms in the industrialized countries with their more brutal variants in the Third World, the institute sought to demonstrate that "the Third World would fight for and with us."[110] Thereby the institute sought to create revolutionary consciousness in the First World, refute reformist agendas, and initiate broad mobilization on an international scale.[111]

Organizationally, INFI operated financially independent from the Berlin SDS and on individual donations.[112] Various sections, which together formed a council of twenty to thirty members, were responsible for certain geographical regions and independently coordinated their work with other organizations. Members of INFI included activists from the Berlin SDS as well as members of the U.S. Campaign and the local branch of the American SDS, who applied the techniques of "power structure research" to their work in the Berlin institute. The INFI and its European network also opened up channels of communication to their American counterparts, which soon led to the demand for a systematic informational exchange between radical groups in West Germany and the United States.[113] In April 1969, Berlin SDS and INFI member Wolfgang Nitsch therefore proposed the establishment of a permanent transatlantic network. According to Nitsch, the plan was based on the idea of a documentation center at Berkeley that originated at the Ljubliana conference of the New Left in August 1968 at the initiative of Bernardine Dohrn, Peter Wiley (Leviathan), Keith Chamberlain (U.S. Campaign member and now director of the Communication Centers Project, Berkeley), the Liberation News Service, and the journal *The Movement*.[114] The U.S. group of the INFI, which was to become the organizational interface in this network, created an extensive German-American group inventory that was to serve as a first step to this transnational, radical nongovernment organization between the two countries.[115] The INFI can therefore be seen as an attempt to set up a permanent institutional body connecting the various protest movements as a basis for substantial transnational cooperation. The institute and its international mission, however, were not only an abstract political strategy, but they also turned into a personal reality for one of its guiding spirits in the course of 1968.

By the end of 1967, Rudi Dutschke's elevated position in the German SDS and his prominent role in the media had provoked criticism among fellow SDS members. Although Dutschke insisted on the bottom-up, decentralized structure of the German SDS, he was acutely aware of the public identification of the movement with his person.[116] To escape these dynamics and to continue his studies and political work, Dutschke considered relocating to the United States.[117] At the end of 1967, he accepted an invitation by the American SDS for a lecture tour in the United States starting in April 1968. At the same time, his wife, Gretchen Dutschke, inquired about visa options for her husband's enrollment at the University of California, San Diego, to study with Herbert Marcuse.[118] Marcuse had by then become a personal friend of Dutschke as a result of his talks at the Free University in Berlin.[119] What attracted Dutschke to these possibilities in the Unites States "for the revolutionary movement in general and me and my wife in particular" was the combination of completing his studies, working in an American university to sharpen his theoretical knowledge, and finding a new opportunity of activist work in the Americas.[120] Several of Dutschke's fellow activists had already gone to Latin America.[121] By extending the international revolutionary network coordinated by INFI, his stay was supposed to build up another base from which to disseminate his ideas from California into South America and counter American imperialism from within.

Dutschke's plans were, however, thwarted by an attempt on his life on April 11, 1968, which necessitated a long hospitalization and recuperation period in Switzerland and Italy. In addition, his emigration plans leaked to the German and American press. After coverage in the *New York Times* and *Newsweek*, a local Californian newspaper, the *San Diego*

Union, quickly began a comprehensive media campaign against Rudi Dutschke's supposed plans to enroll at the University of California, San Diego (UCSD).[122] On June 11, the paper's inflammatory editorial entitled "This Is an Order!" proclaimed the following:

> The University of California at San Diego needs no further disruptive influence such as Rudi Dutschke. This West German student and acknowledged revolutionary anarchist has caused untold chaos in his native country. He has inspired and led dangerous attacks against law and order, including physically assaulting some United States premises. He is an avowed Communist. . . . San Diego will not tolerate "Red Rudi" on its campus. And it his high time citizens demand an investigation of the persons who would bring this undesirable trouble-maker to San Diego.[123]

The university was subsequently swamped with letters, warning it not to admit "a leading Communist trouble-maker" and fearing more local student unrest. Some even anticipated harm to German-American relations should Dutschke be permitted to join the university.[124] The veteran's organization American Legion even launched a full-fledged campaign against Herbert Marcuse for his participation in student protest activities overseas and his alleged responsibility for disorder on American campuses.[125] It urged the university authorities to refuse any application of Rudi Dutschke to the University of California, offered to buy up Marcuse's contract for the academic year of 1968/69 to remove him from the UCSD faculty, and lobbied the Regents of the University of California, governor Ronald Reagan, and all state representatives for their plans.[126] The legion's activism eventually resulted in a public debate that even attracted the national press and led to personal harassments and death threats against the philosophy professor.[127] Marcuse was forced to leave his home in La Jolla and at the end of June 1968 departed to Europe.[128] Although UCSD Chancellor William McGill tried to downplay the issue and work behind closed doors in the hope that the affair would peter out over the summer break, the campus atmosphere became increasingly polarized when the American Legion carried on its activities into the fall and winter semester. By then, the campaign against the arrival of Rudi Dutschke in California had fully transformed into an attack on Marcuse himself and slowed down only after UCSD chancellor McGill announced his firm decision to renew Marcuse's contract for the academic year of 1969/70.[129]

Given the heated political atmosphere and the public pressure in California, Rudi Dutschke's immigration plans with regard to the United States were severely shattered. Furthermore, the U.S. government would not decide about his visa application of July 1968, thereby prolonging the waiting period.[130] At the beginning of September 1968, Dutschke therefore withdrew his application to increase his chances for future attempts.[131] Since neither Canada nor the Netherlands, Belgium or France granted him entry, he emigrated to England in December 1968.[132] Despite these odds, Dutschke kept on pursuing his global revolutionary strategy outlined at the Vietnam Congress and continued to push for the international network through INFI. As he wrote to a Spanish group at the end of 1968,

> The "new international" . . . is still underdeveloped and kept in suppression. . . . Under no circumstances are we allowed to continue with the national mediocrity of semi-revolutionary forces. The counter-revolution operates internationally, which is shown by the temporary crushing of the Che-foci in Bolivia, by the cooperation between US-Imperialism and Stalinism (authoritarian state socialism) in the case of the reform way of the CSSR. . . . [W]e should expand our contacts as expeditiously as possible.[133]

In May 1969, Dutschke was even confronted with plans to involve himself in the Third World liberation struggle through Gaston Salvatore's stay in Chile. Salvatore's idea was to join the revolutionary movement MIR (Movimiento de Izquierda Revolucionario) in Chile, which was oriented toward Castro. He asked Dutschke to represent the MIR at the Russell Foundation and select fifty people for a volunteer military unit, which would smuggle weapons and fight the Chilean government. After organizing sufficient financial means, Dutschke himself was to come to Chile, take up a position at the university and function as contact person.[134] Dutschke, however, declined the offer. Furthermore, Salvatore's departure from Chile only two months later caused his German friend to rethink the realities and chances of cooperation between revolutionaries of the First and Third Worlds.[135]

The efforts to "revolutionize the revolutionaries" in the First World according to the global revolutionary strategy that emerged at the Vietnam Congress thus translated itself into a comprehensive attempt of the German SDS to nurture a global protest network in 1968/69. In this endeavor, Rudi Dutschke was one of the prime intellectual forces spurring international consciousness and cooperation. The INFI in Berlin was to serve as a coordinating center, as well as another urban "focus" modeled after Che Guevara's foco theory and intended to be established worldwide.[136] Despite these far-reaching plans for international cooperation, the INFI faltered a year after the Vietnam Congress. Its demise closely followed the ideological factionalization that finally led to the dissolution of the German SDS as a national organization. The INFI was, however, not the only attempt to unite the worldwide protest of activists in the

1960s. Other projects ran parallel to the institute, which further illuminated the multitude and challenges of transnational cooperation.

THE CHALLENGES OF INTERNATIONAL COOPERATION

After the Vietnam Congress of February 1968, opportunities for international exchange increased rapidly. Aside from numerous personal visits,
a conference in Ljubljana, Yugoslavia from August 25–28, and the "International Assembly of Revolutionary Student Movements" at Columbia
University, in New York on September 18–23 were two other major international gatherings that took place in 1968.

The International Confederation for Disarmament and Peace (ICDP)
and the German SDS organized the conference in Ljubljana as a "working
meeting of leading student and youth activists who wish to cement
their links of solidarity with their comrades in other countries."[137] Feeling
that the European student movements had been largely ignored in favor
of the Third World, the interest of American SDS in the European protest
scene had peaked after the French May.[138] When the SDS National Council thus discussed the invitation to Ljubljana in mid-June, individual SDS
members had already asked about their inclusion in the official delegation.[139] Although initially hesitant about language barriers as well as the
"international rhetoric and factionalism," the council decided to participate in the event, especially since the trip included a meeting with a North
Vietnamese delegation in Prague.[140] As Bernardine Dohrn, then Inter-
Organizational Secretary of the American SDS, recalls,

> [T]hat was a very big invitation because most of the meetings with
> the Vietnamese had been a couple of people going to Hanoi to pick
> up POWs or meetings organized in Canada which were primarily
> composed of the Canadian movement but a few SDS people would
> go and meet with the Vietnamese. So, to actually have an invitation,
> to have a formal week-long meeting with delegations that would in-
> clude the NLF and the North Vietnamese was kind of a big deal.[141]

The opportunity of both a meeting with the North Vietnamese delegation
and representatives from the European New Left was considered so ap-
pealing that it even excused her absence from the planned protest activities at the 1968 Chicago Democratic National Convention.[142]

On August 25, 1968, representatives from West Germany, France, Finland, Spain, Switzerland, Canada, and the United States came together in
Ljubljana to discuss the "Anti-Imperialist and Anti-Capitalist Struggles
and Student Revolts" and draft an international action program.[143] The
Soviet invasion of Czechoslovakia four days earlier had shocked the dele-

gates and vastly overshadowed the atmosphere of the gathering. The participants nonetheless managed to continue their meeting during which particularly the German and American delegates discovered striking similarities in their political agendas and organizational problems.[144] Notwithstanding these resemblances, conversations on a coherent New Left political agenda among all delegates proved to be extremely difficult. Diverging ideological viewpoints and strategies with respect to militancy, the relationship to workers and the solidarity with the Third World, as well as the vastly different domestic conditions activists were facing made the development of a joint program simply impossible. As one of the participants, Dan Swinney from the Wisconsin Draft Resistance Union, reported about the theoretical discussions during the meeting, "It was very abstract and almost useless, not because of the effort, but because of the inability to really communicate at the conference."[145] The high level of ideological debate displayed by their European counterparts not only alienated (and challenged) the American delegates, but also affected the future of transnational cooperation among the New Left.[146] Delegates could only agree on a gradualist and nonformalized form of internationalism, avoiding any kind of organized revolutionary (non-Soviet, non-Chinese dominated) "Internationale." International cooperation such as the conference itself, in fact, came under heavy criticism, since it was perceived as unfocused and cost- and time-intensive. Instead, "[i]t was felt that it was very important and necessary to increase other means of communication between the various movements. Most were very isolated and were just beginning to understand how to break down that isolation."[147] Discussions therefore concentrated on the domestic consolidation of the various movements, unity in opposition to the Vietnam War, and methods of agitation that would ensure lasting attacks on repressive structures at home.[148]

For Bernardine Dohrn, however, "the international, equivalent scene in Europe sprang to life" after the Ljubljana conference.[149] After the meeting, she and other American delegates traveled to Budapest to meet the North Vietnamese delegation before stopping briefly in occupied Prague and then continuing to Frankfurt to attend the national convention of the German SDS. Witnessing the debates in Germany further underscored the close parallels between the American and German SDS that had emerged in Yugoslavia. As Dohrn recalls, "[T]he fact that it was also called SDS, we felt very sororal, we felt very fraternal: we felt this is an organization like us. . . . W]hen we got there, politically it was clear that it was very much like us."[150] Particularly the emerging women's movement and the "tension between internationalism and local issues" struck Dohrn as similar to the debates in the United States.[151]

The direct exposure to European activists and the experience of this summer was to change her future work in the American SDS in a signifi-

cant way. The meetings in Ljublijana and with the Vietnamese illustrated
the urgency of her political activism and raised the stakes in terms of
personal determination to the extent that both the idea and necessity of
going underground began to enter her mind. Particularly stirring were the
encounters "with people who had experience, particularly the Spaniards,
who had been part of an underground. I don't know why that was appeal-
ing to us even this early on: the experience of those who had been jailed
and who had been fighting a fascist government and who were very facile
with crossing borders and with doing things on multiple levels."[152] The
contact and attraction to European models thus played a vital role in her
growing militancy, which would eventually lead to the radicalization of
the American SDS and the formation of the Weathermen.

For her German counterparts, the personal affiliation to the American
New Left was an equally vital part of the international experience of
1968, whether it was in Ljublijana or during the World Youth Festival in
Sofia three weeks earlier.[153] When the American SDS organized a North
American pendant to the Ljubljana conference with the International Assembly of Revolutionary Student Movements at Columbia University in
the fall of 1968, German delegates also played an important role. The
assembly, which was organized by the Columbia Strike Co-Ordinating
Committee and the American SDS, attempted to bring together representatives from various international protest movements on American soil to
overcome the isolation of the U.S. antiwar movement and "to learn from
each other and about each other, and to talk about where we go from
here."[154] In the eyes of the organizers, the occupation of Columbia University, the Easter riots in West Germany, and the French May had pointed
toward the necessity of "a dialogue leading to the creation of a coherent
revolutionary theory . . . if we wish to insure the growth of an international movement." To this end, the assembly sought to discuss "the stage
of class struggle in the individual countries and the potential of new revolutionary agents, and the prospects and possible forms of an international
revolutionary movement."[155]

As a result, international participation was diverse and abundant. From
the German SDS, Barbara Schneider-Reilly, sister of the German writer
Peter Schneider, had already been present in New York City and established contacts with the Columbia SDS over the summer. Together with
her husband, Robert Reilly, she had founded the guerilla street theater
in West Germany and subsequently exported it to the American protest
scene.[156] Through her work with the Columbia SDS, she served as a direct
and visible connection between the two movements.[157] Other delegates
from the German SDS at the conference included Dietrich Wetzel and
Sigrid Fronius. Wetzel had arrived in New York after his visit to a Latin
American student conference in Merida, Venezuela, and was able to bring

the conference "to its feet with his reading of a message from the MIR Guerrilleros in Venezuela. The crowd stood for several minutes, with arms raised chanting 'Che! Che!' "[158] He and Fronius outlined the political development and agenda of the German SDS, and, similar to the organizers, advocated a tighter international socialist movement.[159]

The first reports on the assembly were thus marked by an unparalleled optimism toward the creation of a truly internationalist protest movement. As one U.S. student commentator phrased it, "All left the hall with a greater sense of internationalism than the U.S. Revolutionary Movement has ever seen. Linking arms with brothers from France, Germany, Italy, and Mexico, students chanted the 'Internationale' in French, marched around the campus and then headed into the streets. *Viva la lucha armada*!"[160] This revolutionary enthusiasm was, however, soon crushed by factionalist bickering. During the last assembly meeting, the conflict came to a head after a Mexican delegate called for a gesture of solidarity with Mexican students. Chaotic debate, aggressive rhetoric, and an "internationalist exchange of epithets" ensued. The *New York Times* reported that the meeting ended "in confusion, shouting, rhetorical speeches, factional disputes and a steady exodus of young people whose patience did not match their revolutionary zeal."[161] The German delegation itself seemed to suffer from internal divisions about the relationship to the working class and even admonished the American students to reflect upon their own actions more critically.[162] In short, the International Assembly of Revolutionary Student Movements at Columbia very much followed the lines of the Ljublijana conference the month before in its factionalism and inability to unite on a coherent international agenda. In the fall of 1968, the New Left and the various protest movements across the globe could therefore succeed only in establishing a powerful emotional and spiritual bond, but were unable to translate their solidarity into concrete forms of transnational institutions or actions.

The continuing connections among the various dissenting student groups worldwide remained, however, unharmed by this fact. The bonds among them comprised a loosely similar ideology of anti-imperialism and opposition to the war in Vietnam, common action repertoires, and most of all, a shared counterculture and emotional disposition that was by then able to withstand these minor setbacks. After the Columbia conference, the German delegate Sigrid Fronius went on to the annual convention of the American National Student Association (NSA) in Manhattan, Kans., where she conducted a teach-in on the German SDS and attended a National Council Meeting of the American SDS to contribute to their discussions on the development of a greater international perspective.[163] Dietrich Wetzel equally extended his travels in the United States and visited universities on the East Coast with Columbia SDS member Mark Rudd and other international delegates.[164] Contacts like these often deepened transnational ties during the years 1968/69 and beyond, rather than underlining their known limits. A visit that stands out in this regard and further amplified the transatlantic protest network by including Black Power solidarity and the Black Panther Party was the lecture tour by the former German SDS president Karl-Dietrich Wolff through the United States and Canada which took place in February and March of 1969.

Wolff had spent an exchange year at a high school in Marshall, Mich., in 1959/60, where daily life in the democratic environment of a small-town community left him enthusiastic about the potentials of democracy. During his time in the United States, Wolff witnessed the beginnings of the civil rights movement, the first freedom rides, and the student sit-ins in Greensboro, N.C. Through a Quaker youth group that had contact with participants of the first Freedom Rides, he was able to obtain extensive information on the aims and strategies of these activists. As he later recalled, "My political development is unthinkable without the year in the USA. . . . The lived civil society impressed me tremendously as well as ways of discussing nonviolent action and civil disobedience."[165]

After his return to Germany, Wolff closely followed the emergence of the New Left in the United States. Although he joined the German SDS only in the mid-sixties, he soon achieved a leading position in the organization, being elected president at the national convention in September 1967. Due to the ideological isolation of the German SDS in the political landscape of 1960s West Germany, the awareness of a similar and fraternal organization in the United States always retained a special significance for Wolff.[166] Consequently, the publications of the American SDS such as *New Left Notes* and *Monthly Review* formed an important part of the theoretical discussions in the German SDS groups that he was involved in.[167] The first personal contact he established with members from the American SDS was at the Vietnam Congress in West Berlin in February 1968, which further intensified in its aftermath. During the conference in Ljubljana, Bernardine Dohrn invited him to do a lecture tour through the United States.[168] Wolff visited about twenty cities, giving talks on the situation in Germany and stressing the need for international cooperation to help foster an "International Revolutionary Alliance."[169]

After a speech at George Washington University, Wolff entered the public limelight when he was subpoenaed to a hearing of the Senate Subcommittee on Internal Security, the official explanation having to do with a visa irregularity. Reminiscent of Bertolt Brecht's appearance before the House Committee on Un-American Activities in 1947, Wolff viewed the hearing as part of a tactical repression against him and the international student movement and seized the opportunity to turn it into a public happening.[170] Directly attacking the committee chairman Sen. Strom Thurmond, Wolff accused the committee of scapegoating him as an outside agitator and of conspiring against liberation movements worldwide.[171] He detected the "emergence of a new institutional fascism both in West Germany and the United States" and put the official relationship between the two nations on trial: "They show us who is allying with whom when they speak of American-German friendship in West Berlin or in Washington. In West Berlin their brand of German-American friendship consists of the news that the Secret Service might shoot unpredictably when the President of the United States sneaks in and out of the city like a thief. In West Germany this kind of German-American friendship consists of the Springer Press having a total blackout of news about the situation in the U.S. ghettos."[172]

Wolff purposely extended the reference to fascism to include the American system, indicating the close similarities between the German past and current U.S. politics in the German New Left's interpretation of global power relations. What is even more interesting is that Wolff strongly underlined the alliance of the German and American protest movements against this perceived repression conducted by the governments of both countries:

> But you see, Mr. Senator, our movements do not give in to harassment any more. . . . The least thing I could do here—I have tried to do—is bring the message that the victories of the movement in the United States are considered our victories, that the repression against the radical movement in the United States which is being stepped up is repression against us. The economic and political interdependence of our societies has made international solidarity more than just a moral duty to speak up for the oppressed anywhere. You, Mr. Senator, and your like, are just a bunch of criminal bandits. . . . We know that we are not alone.[173]

With these words, Wolff aptly described the web of transatlantic links that had been developed between the German and American SDS throughout the 1960s. By elevating the domestic opposition in both countries to the transnational level, he gave voice to a different kind of transatlantic partnership, namely the "other" alliance between the protest movements of the 1960s, formed in reaction to the cold-war politics and their global consequences. Lashing out against what in his view was the imperialist complicity of the U.S. and West German governments, Wolff made it very clear that he saw the protest movements of the 1960s as unrestrained by national borders and thus beyond the reach of respective governments: "As I said before, you do not see that there are problems in our society which are the same in West Germany and in the United States or at least very similar and you do not see that we are up to debate about

IMAGE 10. Karl Dietrich Wolff's appearance before the Senate Subcommittee on
March 14, 1969, together with his lawyer Michael Tigar and a policeman who
was positioned between Wolff and the audience (Stroemfeld Verlag)

them now and that we are up to realize that our interests are the same.
You see, you have been conspiring for a long time. We do not need to
conspire. And our efforts to create an internationalist consciousness
[have] only started."[174]

The U.S. government officials conducting the hearing were mostly
stunned by Wolff's searing condemnation. Whenever the chairman tried
to establish any direct evidence for links between the two movements,
Wolff refused to answer and involved him in technicalities, while alluding
to the common agenda: sympathy and solidarity between the German
and American SDS.[175] Finally, he caused the biggest surprise when he
simply got up and walked out of the session, denouncing the committee,
and leaving its members speechless over his unceremonious departure.[176]
As the *Washington Post* wrote, "*Der Zirkus*, which is German for
circus, played briefly before the Senate Internal Security Subcommittee
yesterday, but closed abruptly when its star performer stalked out of his
act and into the Capitol's long history of showbiz. The sudden exit . . .
made him the first witness ever to walk out of an open session of the
subcommittee."[177] Wolff's spectacular appearance before the subcommittee subsequently provoked an intense media reaction in the American and
German press but did not stop him from continuing his trip throughout
the United States.

In San Francisco, Wolff met American SDS members Tom Hayden and
Todd Gitlin, who took him to San Francisco State University during the

local student strike. Even more importantly, Hayden introduced him to Bobby Seale from the Black Panther Party.[178] This meeting and the relationship that the former German SDS president forged with Seale and other Black Panther members in the following years opened up a new chapter in the transatlantic relations between the protest movements of the 1960/70s. After his return, Wolff helped build an extensive Black Panther solidarity network in Europe and West Germany. This new connection not only brought the category of race into the German debate but also resulted into an even closer relationship between the American and West German protest movements that continued well into the 1970s. Solidarity campaigns with African American GIs stationed in West Germany, visits by representatives of the Black Panther Party to the Federal Republic, and a rapid increase of German literature on Black Power further challenged the official transatlantic relationship between the Federal Republic and the United States, as well as America's image in West Germany. At the same time, a small minority of the West German student movement used the example of the Black Panthers and associated theories of colonial liberation to justify a greater militancy and escalation of violence that ultimately led to the emergence of terrorism in the Federal Republic in the form of the Rote Armee Fraktion (Red Army Faction, RAF).

Chapter 4

BLACK AND RED PANTHERS

"As I listened to Stokely's words, cutting like a switch-blade, accusing the enemy as I had never heard him accused before, I admit that I felt the cathartic power of his speech. But I also wanted to know where to go from there."[1] With these words, Angela Davis remembers the speech of one of the leading figures of the Black Power movement in the United States, Stokely Carmichael, during the two-week congress "Dialectics of Liberation" in London in July 1967. For Davis, who later became an icon of the African American protest movement, this encounter proved to be formative for her political development. Together with Angela Davis, a delegation of the German SDS from Frankfurt had also arrived in London. The German representatives were equally impressed by Carmichael's appearance. As the German publisher Bernward Vesper reflects in his autobiographical novel fragment *The Journey*, "Berlin, and June 2 [the killing of the German student Benno Ohnesorg by a policeman] are nothing but sandbox games next to the manifestation of the colored races, for which the question of violence is not a question, since they have been living under the violence of racist whites for centuries.... How much does one dead person count for the liberation movements in the Third World, where they count hundreds and thousands of deaths each day?"[2]

The influence of the African American Black Power struggle on the West German protest movement not only consisted in the creation of a transnational protest identity, but also substantially shaped the formation and dynamics of the student activists' ideological position. For parts of the West German movement, Black Power appeared to be fulfilling Che Guevara's foco theory as much as Herbert Marcuse's minority theory and epitomized the liberation from imperialism and capitalism from within the First World. In this context, the model of colonial conflicts developed by Frantz Fanon and adapted under this perspective was of great consequence: West German activists adopted the Black Panthers' interpretation that viewed the black population as an "internal colony" of the United States, which could liberate itself from oppression only through the use of violence. This interpretation was strengthened by an anti-imperialism accelerated by the escalation of the war in Vietnam, which, for parts of the West German movement, linked the United States and its foreign policy semiotically to the crimes of National Socialism. In a reversal of the official doctrine that the freedom of Berlin was defended in Saigon, West German activists frequently invoked the analogy between Vietnam and Auschwitz. The close transatlantic partnership between the countries was thus regarded as one of complicity in the crimes committed in Southeast Asia and elsewhere, which were perceived through the lens of Germany's past. In their eyes, the Federal Republic had been transformed into an "external colony" of the United States, bearing at least part of the responsibility for crimes committed on behalf of imperialist suppression.

Against this background, solidarity with the African American struggle significantly changed the ways in which members of the West German student movement viewed their country's history after 1945. The counter-cultural practices that they adopted from the United States and the attraction to the provocative militancy of the Black Panthers became an integral part of defining their own identity. Solidarity with the Black Power movement and transformations in the image of the United States were thus fatefully combined and utilized as yet another vehicle for coming to terms with the past. Interpreting the transatlantic alliance as a colonial relationship also helped justify even violent resistance against it and contributed to the rise of terrorist groups such as the Rote Armee Fraktion (Red Army Faction, or RAF), who framed their attacks as part of a liberation struggle. The transatlantic activist networks of the New Left and their turn to the African American struggle in the United States therefore had a significant impact on the radicalization of the German student movement and its turn to violence.

The Early Reception of Black Power in West Germany

The civil rights movement in the United States during the late fifties and, in particular, the early sixties, received the attention of people worldwide. Due to the spectacular nature and imagery of its actions and its moral implications set in the propaganda battles of the cold war, it transcended national borders and was formative for a variety of people outside the United States. In addition, it forced representatives of the American political system to react to its assertions so that these domestic struggles would not undermine America's claim to uphold democracy around the globe.[3]

The iconography and content of the African American struggle also seized the attention of many Germans, East and West.[4] Although the mainstream press broadly followed its different stages, the coverage of the civil rights movement in the left-leaning media provided detailed and critical comments on its development from the very start.[5] The leaders themselves, such as Martin Luther King, Jr., were given a voice in these periodicals, and their strategies were both discussed and applied to the

West German situation.[6] Already in September of 1963, about 100 West German students demonstrated for the equality of African Americans in the United States and handed over a petition signed by 450 people addressed to John F. Kennedy at the U.S. Consulate General in Frankfurt, protesting discrimination against blacks. A coalition of the SDS, the Sozialistischer Hochschulbund (SHB), and the conservative student association Ring Christlich-Demokratischer Studenten (RCDS) organized this march, a clear sign that the issue transcended traditional party lines.[7] In February 1965, SDS member Günter Amendt was the first to offer a detailed account of the events of Freedom Summer and the Free Speech Movement (FSM) in Berkeley. He noted that the involvement of the young students in the civil rights movement through such strategies as voter registration drives in the summer of 1964 was a decisive moment for their protest on behalf of free speech at the university: "The physical and psychological terror the young people have experienced in the South in their confrontations with white racists has transformed itself into a political consciousness that is able to see political problems beyond the negro question. . . . The events in California are an embodiment of this politicization. But here, too, the students see the larger social dimensions beyond the local event. One of the slogans of the Free Speech Movement demands 'A free University in a free society!' which brings back the connection to the demands of the Negro movement full circle."[8]

Already at that point, the African American struggle for equality was seen as strongly connected to university protest—a connection that, in the American and German perception of it, was to deepen by the end of the decade. Moreover, Amendt also mentioned SNCC's vow of nonviolence, which was being questioned at that time, and its call for "direct action." For him, the civil rights movement had already made the transition from a protest movement focused on issues of race to one advocating change for American society at large; it had made the connection between the legal status and daily discrimination of African Americans and the economic situation that also affected the white working class.[9] This class component, and the emphasis it would receive in the following years from within the African American community itself, proved to be a particular point of attraction for some West German student activists.

Rudi Dutschke, for example, was not only personally connected to the United States from a very early stage but also had direct access to information on events in America through his American wife, Gretchen Klotz, as previously mentioned. During the summer of 1966, she had introduced a new picture of the United States to the Viva Maria Gruppe (the Third World study group to which Dutschke belonged), namely that of the black nationalists and revolutionaries represented by Malcolm X. Klotz thereby corrected the picture of the United States as the ultimate, imperialist

IMAGE 11. Silent march for African American rights, Frankfurt, 1963 (Institut für Stadtgeschichte, Frankfurt/Main)

enemy and pointed to an aspect that was later to gain even more ground among Dutschke and his companions, the image of the "other" America. Through her views and the letters of a friend of hers in New York City, Ron Watson, Dutschke was kept informed about the situation of the Left in America and could indirectly get in touch with a group of black nationalists in New York's Harlem district who had formerly been associated with Malcolm X.[10] During his only visit to the United States in September 1966, Dutschke had the chance to visit the slums of New York and Chicago, an experience which made a lasting impression on him. This first-hand acquaintance with the poverty of the African American communities and the movement for black revolution in Harlem left him deeply stirred and bewildered: "[B]ringing along the book by Malcolm X, read a lot in it on the plane. Not all the words are within grasp, not even for the white female American. Or maybe because of it?"[11]

   With the growth of antiwar sentiment and protest actions in West Germany, the German SDS also began to focus its attention on the increasingly vocal Black Power movement.[12] A turning point in this process involved the Detroit riots in July 1967, which erupted among black residents after the police raided a blind pig and arrested more than eighty people on the city's west side. The riots that swept through the neighborhood in the following five days forced President Lyndon Johnson to call in troops from the U.S. army and National Guard. The escalation of violence during the conflict resulted in more than 40 deaths, over 450 injuries, and about 7,200 arrests. In addition, 2,000 houses burned down.[13]

The major civil disturbance in Detroit prompted the German SDS to declare its solidarity with Black Power at the 22nd national convention during September 4–8, 1967 in Frankfurt. The attention given to these riots came about partly because individual SDS members had witnessed first hand the living conditions of African Americans in various urban neighborhoods during their visits to the United States. SDS member Gerhardt Amendt, for example, had spent the summer of 1967 in Harlem and reported about the situation in African American ghettos.[14] In their support of Black Power, West German student activists now saw the leaders of the civil rights movement of the early 1960s as part of the "bourgeois" class of African Americans who had been corrupted by co-optation attempts of the "ruling class."[15] The black masses, in turn, had been manipulated by their "bourgeois leaders," such as Martin Luther King, Jr., to believe in the supposed successes of the movement in the judicial realm in 1964/65, but gradually began to realize that no appropriate remedy had been found against the continuance of both white racism and black poverty. In the eyes of the German SDS, Malcolm X emerged in this situation as a "revolutionary leader and national spokesman" who placed the African American struggle in the international context of class struggles, making the connection to the national liberation movements in Asia, Africa, and South America. The German SDS thus interpreted the aims of "black nationalism" in terms of an international class struggle demanding revolutionary counterviolence, which, since Malcolm X's death, had been taken up by the Student Nonviolent Coordinating Committee (SNCC).[16]

From this angle, SNCC, which by then had moved from a civil rights organization to a revolutionary agenda dominated by Black Power, was understood as an additional contributor to the emancipation of African Americans from capitalism. As such, it emerged as an important ally for West German activists in their fight against global imperialism, helping to dismantle the "American empire" from within. Through SNCC's work and particularly its exclusion of whites, African Americans would gain the self-confidence necessary for a fundamental transformation of U.S. society, for which the cooperation with white revolutionary organizations would eventually become indispensable. Similar to the American New Left, the German SDS therefore considered its main task the creation of its own revolutionary organizations to show solidarity and support to their African American peers: "The 22nd national convention of the [German] SDS therefore decides: 1. The groups of [the German] SDS will conduct information events on the revolutionary struggle of blacks in the U.S. 2. The national council [Bundesvorstand] will initiate organizational contacts with SNCC. 3. If an SNCC member is murdered or SNCC is declared illegal, direct actions against the branches of U.S. imperialism in the FRG [Federal Republic of Germany] and West Berlin will take place."[17]

This direct link to the Black Power movement and the stated willingness to respond in its own country to attacks against SNCC in the United States illustrate how strongly the German SDS identified with SNCC's cause, an identification that paralleled its members' solidarity with the Vietnamese people. For German activists, the character of Black Power served as a far more suitable model since it was a case of an anti-imperialist movement in a highly industrialized country that was seen as the motherland of imperialist aggression.[18] Accordingly, in a conversation with Hans Magnus Enzensberger from October 1967, Rudi Dutschke portrayed the development of the situation of African Americans in the United States as an indicator for a future revolution and radical change in society: "In America we can recognize a guide toward the future. We already have radical negation there in the form of the national minorities, the negroes. That is, already in the present, a radical negation with the most extreme consequences. It means the creation of new human relationships through struggle, organization of poor negroes, perhaps even the organization of poor whites. Out of this, in turn, specific organizational forms are being developed which are more humane, and which are perhaps already being pushed aside here [in Germany]."[19]

In the eyes of Dutschke, the hippie movement in the United States was shaped by and gained its momentum from the Black Power movement, a dynamic that could not easily be transferred to a German context. The Federal Republic lacked ethnic minorities or ghettos similar to those in the United States. Although there was already a sizable community of Italian, Yugoslavian, and Turkish "guest workers" who had been invited due to the labor shortages of the 1950s and 1960s, their treatment within West German society would emerge as an issue of public debate only in the following decades.[20] As a result, Dutschke argued that, alternatively, the conditions for such a negation of the existing system would have to be created through conflict with the state and the emergence of a countermilieu, which could then serve as a basis for radical social change.[21]

Another means of overcoming merely rhetorical solidarity and support for black nationalism from the students' side was to approach the "internal American colony" abroad, namely the black American GIs stationed in West Germany. The involvement of black GIs in the general GI-organizing efforts by the German SDS was illustrated by the Vietnam Congress in Berlin during February 17–18, 1968, where one of the American SDS delegates, Patty Lee Parmalee, elaborated on the connection between the antiwar movement and the Black Power movement. For Parmalee, the situation in the United States was more conducive to revolutionary change because of the existence of an oppressed black minority that demanded the attention of the American student movement: "Because anybody who is black, anybody who does not find a job, anybody who does not serve the war effort is able to understand that the system is oppressing him. . . . In the United States militant demonstrations still play an important role, because there are still many liberals who can be convinced of the oppressive nature of the regimes and because the black Left sees that the white Left are as serious as they are."[22]

Emphasizing the significance of the Black Power movement for the student activists' strategies, Parmalee's ultimate goal overlapped with that of the German SDS at that point, namely the abolition of imperialism after the model of, and with the help of, the national liberation movements. In this context, the student movements, in synergetic alliance with the Black Power movement, could occupy a vital role: "If one day it gets to the point where the exploited countries of the Third World will smash the imperialist U.S., an uprising of African Americans and a resistance movement of the American Left could make an important contribution."[23]

In the case of the West German student movement's relationship to the African American struggle, two aspects were therefore most important: first, a close observation of the strategies and tactics of the pacifist civil rights movement in an early phase and its transformation into a Black Power ideology with a slowly developing focus on class; and second, the students' involvement in GI-work and desertion campaigns all over Europe. All of this, however, was turned into a much more intense transatlantic association with the visit of the former chairman of the German SDS, Karl-Dietrich Wolff, to the United States in February/March of 1969.

Beginning in 1967, the left-leaning West German press directed its attention more intensely to the radicalization of the African American movement. The race riots in Newark and Detroit in the summer of 1967 received intensive coverage, and leading representatives of the Black Power movement gradually began to obtain space in the general print media and the various publications of the German Left to lay out their ideas.[24] With the growing radicalization of the student movements in Germany and the United States in 1968/69, the leftist media's interest in U.S. race relations and the radical approaches by Black Power activists to confront them deepened.[25]

In West Germany, the publisher Bernward Vesper in particular developed a fascination with Black Power and vastly increased the dissemination of related material through his publishing house.[26] Ever since his attendance at the congress "Dialectics of Liberation" in London during July

15–30, 1967, as part of a West German delegation, Vesper published translated versions of articles, speeches, and programs relating to Black Power and black nationalism, initially with the help of his girlfriend, the later RAF terrorist Gudrun Ensslin. In his first booklet on Black Power from 1967, Vesper also interpreted the race conflict in the United States as a class conflict and advocated the destruction of the oppressive, white capitalist society. Very much in line with Dutschke's ideas, he regarded the black nationalist movement as a possible path even for white people to change society. What is striking in his argumentation is the absoluteness that he employed for this transition process. The only way out for white people would be nothing less than the destruction of their own culture: "The destruction of this culture, which in reality is more horrific than anything preceding it, opens up the opportunity for humankind that its history has not yet come to an end. . . . The freedom struggle of the colored people across the world is therefore at the same time the hope for the white people who are cut off from their future."[27]

The fate of revolutionary change was inextricably tied to the progress of the African American movement, which served as a guide, source of inspiration, and partner for the student movement. Although West German students recognized the different quality between their own movement and the "black liberation struggle," it gave them even greater incentive to close the gap by raising their own aims and ambitions. While Vesper, for example, underlined the relatively harmless nature of one's own situation in the face of worldwide, life-threatening oppression, the example of the Black Power movement only spurred his readiness for radical solutions on the home front, which appeared morally corrupt and beyond all reform efforts.[28] From the very beginning, this double-binding to the black nationalist movement thus pushed West German activists into a spiral of continually escalating demands to resort to even more radical strategies, such as the complete renunciation of their own culture that Vesper demanded. The emergence and popularity of the Black Panther Party only intensified this and made an escape from this circle of radicalization even more difficult.

Telling in this regard was the publication by Volkhard Brandes and Joyce Burke, a Black Power activist from Harlem who temporarily lived in West Germany. In their introduction to a German collection of texts by James Forman and H. Rap Brown, they also acknowledged the deep interconnectedness between the student movements and the struggle for black emancipation: "In the annually intensifying struggles of black America we see the hope for an end to oppression and exploitation—also for us! Because as international as the oppression is, equally international is the fight against it."[29] Brandes even further illustrates this transatlantic connection in his memoirs. When describing the move with his African

American girlfriend to Germany in the summer of 1967 and her lecture tours in Munich and the Bavarian provinces, where he accompanied her as a translator, he raises serious questions about his motives: "Whenever we spent time in Bavarian villages for recreation, I enjoyed the provocation: to walk around with a black woman in the bulwark of reactionism. Whether that was equally enjoyable for J., I dare to question today. . . . For me, J. was often a means to an end: to play the rigid establishment its own tune—even in the guise of the black skin. Provoking them was a passion, even if it was at the expense of our best friends."[30]

The utilization of the black nationalist movement and its early integration into a local ideological agenda was also obvious in Brandes's admiration of the clenched fists of the two Olympic champions John Carlos and Tommie Smith, who, in October of 1968, with black gloves on their right hands, performed the Black Power salute during their award ceremony. Despite public outrage in the world of sports, Brandes and a lot of others saw it as a gesture "which spoke from our heart: to raise the fist self-confidently in the face of the system."[31]

Others in the German student movement shared these feelings, and general public interest in Black Power increased tremendously in 1967 and 1968.[32] The German press closely observed the gradual emergence and media dominance of the Black Power movement and the alliance between black and white revolutionaries in the United States, often viewing it as the main difference from the student movement in the Federal Republic.[33] In his epilogue on the German translation of Elridge Cleaver's *Soul on Ice*, for example, journalist Kai Hermann from *Die Zeit* underlined the different quality of the African American struggle: "This is a black book. A black American wrote about himself and his world. Not for white people, but for blacks. And Watts is not Berlin, the prison of [San] Quentin no university, life in the ghetto not a life in the affluent society."[34] This was precisely the distinction that parts of the German student movement were beginning to ignore.

THE FOUNDING OF BLACK PANTHER
SOLIDARITY COMMITTEES IN WEST GERMANY

The murder of Martin Luther King, Jr., on April 4, 1968, gave rise to shock and grief worldwide. In West Germany, people were equally traumatized by this seemingly senseless incident. Solidarity demonstrations and marches of mourning took place in various German cities. In Berlin and Frankfurt, German students gathered to share their grief and articulate their misgivings about the racial divisions in the United States. Their complaints often troubled West German officials, who were trying to prevent their ceremonial expressions of mourning from being disturbed by voices critical of the United States. In Frankfurt, conflicts arose between security guards and various participants of a silent march led by mayor Willi Brundert on April 9, because demonstrators had brought banners saying "To mourn the death of Martin Luther King means to oppose Bonn's support of the U.S. war in Vietnam" or "Long live the Vietnamese Liberation Army."[35] In West Berlin, members of the U.S. mission joined a march alongside Mayor Schütz and the acting president of the city's House of Representatives, which was met by a student demonstration at the JFK Square in front of city hall in Schöneberg. As U.S. officials reported, the student group was "carrying red banners and such slogans as 'Memphis is burning—when will the Pentagon burn?' and 'Race warfare equals class warfare.' " During the march and upon arrival at city hall, according to the report, this group repeatedly chanted "Black Power now!" After the official ceremony had ended and before the mayor's microphone was removed, Republican Club member Ekkehart Krippendorff spoke to the group, followed by U.S. Black Power spokesman Ray Robinson. "This demonstration," the officials noted, "ended with the singing of the 'Internationale.' "[36]

In a remarkable turn of interpretation, West German student activists now also began to appropriate King's legacy for their own political agenda. Krippendorff, for example, underlined King's significance for student movements worldwide as the "first great leader, spokesman and organizer of the extra-parliamentary opposition." In Krippendorff's view, the black leader's quest for justice, as well as his emphasis on the power of moral conscience and nonviolence, had been formative for the West German student movement. King's memory therefore now obliged them to "continue his social-revolutionary struggle with his, but also with our own, methods here in our own country."[37] In other words, Krippendorff appropriated the iconic character of Martin Luther King, Jr., from the American background and recontextualized it in a West German setting, where it could be used as a further inspiration for one own's political activism.[38]

Another solidarity demonstration, this time by the Berlin Komitee Black Power, announced for April 12, 1968, caused even greater alarm at the U.S. mission. The organizers planned an assembly at Lehniner Platz in the American zone and distributed flyers calling for a collection of money under the heading "Guns for Black Power": "The Black Power struggle is part of the struggle of all suppressed and exploited people," the flyer said. "Their resistance struggle is also our resistance. This is why the American negroes do not need words, but guns. Only this language . . . Burn, Baby, Burn can be understood by the white *Herrenmensch*."[39] In light of the shooting of Rudi Dutschke the day before, local U.S. officials were naturally nervous and contacted both the Berlin Senate and the mayor to ensure an adequate police force to monitor the demonstration.[40] These incidents illustrate, however, that by now leading elements of the German student movement had completely integrated Black Power ideology into their political agenda of anti-imperialism. In contrast to solidarity with other Third World liberation movements, Black Power became a very concrete reference point and chance for practiced solidarity in the West German student movement. Representatives of the fast-growing Black Power movement were present in places such as Berlin and Frankfurt or circulated among African American GIs across the country, and they frequently participated in protest activities of West German students.

This level of solidarity with the Black Power movement reached a new height with the visit of Karl-Dietrich Wolff to the United States in February/March of 1969.[41] During his lecture trip around the country, Wolff met Tom Hayden and Todd Gitlin in San Francisco, Calif., where the former introduced him to Bobby Seale from the Black Panther Party.[42] This somewhat incidental meeting turned out to be the beginning of a long-lasting connection between the German student movement and the Panthers and the jump start for Black Panther Solidarity committees in West Germany. Before that encounter, the Black Panther Party had only been vaguely aware of student protest in West Germany.[43] As a result of Wolff's visit, however, the former German SDS president started publishing articles in the Black Panther's newspaper, the *The Black Panther: Black Community News Service*, in which he elaborated on the situation in West Germany, underlining that "West German S.D.S. supports Black Panthers and Black Liberation."[44] After his return to West Germany, Wolff actively gathered support for the Black Panther Party among a German Left that had become even more interested in this organization, which was, unlike SNCC, open for alliances with white groups and represented an ideology of worldwide revolution.[45]

Starting with the exile of Elridge Cleaver and the establishment of an international branch of the Black Panther Party in Algiers, Algeria, in the summer of 1969, the party had begun to enjoy a greater international presence and popularity with other radical organizations worldwide.[46] In May 1969, Constance (Connie) Matthews, a Jamaican working for UNESCO in Copenhagen, became the representative of the party in Scandinavia and was "authorized to mobilize to carry out demonstrations of support, raise funds, and inform the peoples of Scandinavia about poor black and oppressed peoples' revolutionary struggle from the Panthers' vanguard position."[47] As a result of her work, throughout 1969 a number of European left-wing organizations became aware of the party's international presence and intensified their support.

The so-called "Senghor Trial" against SDS members Günter Amendt, Hans-Jürgen Krahl, and Karl Dietrich-Wolff in October 1969 in Frankfurt offered the first opportunity to bring awareness of the group's solidarity with the Black Panthers to a larger German public. The court accused the defendants of disturbing the ceremonies for the awarding of the peace prize to Senegalese President Léopold Sédar Senghor at the Frankfurt book fair. In what the *Frankfurter Rundschau* called the "most serious clashes since the Easter riots," about 2,000 demonstrators had tried to cross police barricades in front of Frankfurt's St. Paul's Church on September 22, 1968, and prompted a confrontation with the police that resulted in the demolition of cars, the erection of barricades, as well as numerous injuries. In addition, the demonstration closed down the book fair for several hours.[48] The students' objections against the award winner were based on his brutal treatment of domestic opposition. Instead, they proposed that an alternative award be given to a revolutionary from the African or American liberation movements, such as Stokeley Carmichael, Frantz Fanon, Patrice Lumumba, Amilcar Cabral, or Malcolm X.[49]

During the fifth day of their trial, Wolff underlined this sentiment by rising from his seat and raising a clenched fist to show his solidarity with Bobby Seale, who was made to stand trial in Chicago gagged and tied to a chair. Wolff's gesture provoked the majority of the audience to stand up in his support, likewise saluting in Black Power fashion, much to the dismay of the presiding judge, who ordered the room cleared. In an article for *The Black Panther: Black Community News Service*, Wolff later argued that he saw striking parallels between the "Chicago 8" trials and the Frankfurt conspiracy trial: "The same scene in Frankfurt and Chicago; the right of the people to assemble suppressed, 'impartial' courts establishing 'evidence' through pig informers, agents, and infiltrators. There were differences though: we were still allowed to argue politically in front of the court."[50] Despite these distinctions, he described his continued participation in the trial as mainly geared toward a campaign to "help create solidarity with the Black Panther Party." "Till the next day in court," he recalled, "the information reached us about Bobby Seale being sentenced to four years in jail for contempt of court. The first response was an attack of more than 150 people against the Frankfurt U.S. Consulate General; 28 huge windows were painted with 'Free Bobby Seale'; when the pigs arrived, no one was there any more. [At] the next session of the court, with immense coverage by the press, we had almost every one in the audience bring posters with Bobby Seale's picture. When the court entered, all of a sudden the whole court was full of banderoles, posters, clenched fists and slogans. The photograph of the bench with Bobby Seale went through the whole German press."[51]

Similar attacks and clashes with the police continued during the "Anti-imperialist Week" in the following month. In the aftermath of a demonstration on November 15, 1969, which brought together more than 2,500 participants—including Karl-Dietrich Wolff, Daniel Cohn-Bendit, and representatives from the National Liberation Front (NLF) and the El Fatah—activists smashed windows in various parts of the city and in the American shopping area.[52] In his open letter to the Black Panthers, Wolff described the situation as follows: "On November 15 besides slogans of support for the revolutionary struggle of the Vietnamese people, agitation against repression in the U.S., and the U.S. Army in West Germany were important. The first block of demonstration carried white flags with a Black Panther, there were more than 50 pickets with 'Free Bobby Seale' posters. The police tried to break up the demonstration, but small groups went all over town to agitate and to attack: Chase Manhattan, USIS, American Express, Consulate General, and the court were the main targets. Altogether, the police announced, some 50,000 dollar damage was created against the imperialist institutions. More important: for the first time, American GIs participated in the demonstration (even though many had been restricted to the base), and when a part of the demonstration reached the American Gutleut Kaserne, GIs were waving out of their windows, giving the clenched fist salute, responding to the 'Free! Free Bobby Seale!' slogans. Soon the officers would order the GIs to close the windows."[53]

With the foundation of a Black Panther Solidarity Committee by Wolff and others on November 23, 1969, solidarity became institutionalized in West Germany. The committee was set up after a meeting among the Black Panther Party's Minister of Information, Albert Howard, its European representative Connie Matthews, representatives of the German New Left, and the Berlin branch of the American SDS, as well as African American GIs in West Berlin.[54] Declaring the formation of this committee a new form of international solidarity, the founders saw its aims in the following areas: "1) Education about the struggle of the Black Panther Party and the fascist terror of the ruling class in the U.S., 2) Agitation and propaganda among the GIs stationed in West Germany, 3) Material support for the Black Panthers."[55]

In other words, the committee's purpose was twofold: to show support with the antiwar groups that were setting up "a second front in the core land of imperialism," and, more practically, to generate financial contributions for the Black Panthers.[56] Underlying these activities was the belief that the efforts of activists in Western Europe were of utmost significance to their American counterparts. As SDS member Reimut Reiche expressed it during a teach-in on December 12, 1969, "At this stage of oppression of any opposition in the motherland of imperialism, our anti-imperialism-

IMAGE 12. Anti-Imperialist Week, Frankfurt, November 15, 1969: German SDS President Karl-Dietrich Wolff (center) is leading the demonstration (Harald Meisert)

actions in West Germany do not only have the external significance of 'abstract solidarity' with the NLF and the American people. These actions are literally existential for the American opposition in its phase of creating an anti-imperialist nucleus."[57]

This transatlantic link that was fostered through alternative channels of information and media networks thus created a close-knit feeling of a shared identity that stretched beyond different national borders and conditions. To correct the public image of the Black Panthers in West Germany, one of the first actions of the committee was an information and solidarity campaign from December 12 to 22, 1969, which was later continued with the help of the newly founded publishing house Verlag Roter Stern (Red Star) by Karl-Dietrich Wolff.[58] At the end of February 1970, Wolff drew a first balance sheet and presented the Black Panther Solidarity Committee as a model for practical international solidarity that could even be useful for organizing in educational settings, for example at vocational/regular high schools. He even formed a study group for trainees and high school students with the name "Red Panthers" in Frankfurt.[59] Interestingly enough, in the years ahead, Wolff's suggestions and portraits of the United States were partially incorporated in teaching material and school curricula.[60] Nonetheless, Wolff was aware of the problematic tendency of a "total identification without any moral compromise" and the difficulties in mediating knowledge about the Black

Panthers, which could be overcome only by a firm knowledge of the facts and their context.[61]

Johannes Weinrich, a member of the solidarity committee who would later cofound the terrorist group Revolutionäre Zellen (Revolutionary Cells) and become a supporter of international top terrorist "Carlos" (Ilich Ramírez Sánchez), expressed a similar sentiment after a conference of European Black Power Solidarity Committees in Frankfurt on April 18–19, 1970. Surveying the development of internationalist actions in Germany, beginning with the start of the student revolt, Weinrich concluded that previous methods of emancipation and consciousness raising, namely anti-imperialist street demonstrations, had become insufficient. Instead, the goal of current actions had to be a "push for the defeat of imperialism itself."[62] As a consequence, Weinrich, just like Wolff, highlighted the value of overcoming an uncritical identification with national liberation movements and proposed a critical and contentious form of solidarity to keep up the pressure in the highly industrialized countries. For him, the practical use of solidarity lay in the mutually reinforcing cross-over between the impact of the committee's anti-imperialist actions for the worldwide liberation struggle on the one hand, and revolutionary developments in Germany on the other.[63] With that, Weinrich took up the demand of Frankfurt SDS member Detlev Claussen not to treat "the international conflicts as the moment of our movement," but to understand "our movement as one of the moments of these international conflicts"; in other words, as part of a potentially global revolutionary uprising.[64] By declaring West Germany as yet another arena for this worldwide revolt, the solidarity committee opened the country to foreign revolutionary groups, in this case the Black Panthers.

THE RAMSTEIN 2 AND BLACK PANTHERS IN WEST GERMANY

On July 4, 1970, about 700 African American GIs filled the halls of the Neue Aula of the venerable University of Heidelberg following an invitation by students from the English Department for a "Call for Justice Day." Participating groups included the Unsatisfied Black Soldier, Black Defense Group, and Black Action Group, who, in between music and poetry recitations, were given the opportunity to voice their grievances and demands, as in the following: the creation of a civil committee to hear their complaints, better accommodations, more career opportunities and education in black studies, the withdrawal of all troops from Indochina, the abolition of U.S. bases in Africa, and a commission on the treatment of black inmates in military prisons. The local press even predicted that this event might be only the beginning of an issue that would have repercussions on German society as a whole: "Perhaps people realized that although there are 'only' 700 colored U.S. soldiers in the Federal Republic, they confront this country's citizens with a problem that up to now seemed to be far away. Perhaps people realized that problems such as oppression, discrimination and injustice cannot be pushed away—to the far away America. The meeting of American negroes in Heidelberg also posed a question for German society: Would it behave differently?"[65]

The relationship between West German society and the American troops stationed in West Germany was also at the center of a debate involving the West German army and two black GIs, which emerged after a shooting incident at the Ramstein base on November 19, 1970. On that day four people who appeared to be of African American descent tried to enter the U.S. Airbase at Ramstein. After they refused to show the German guards their identification or to get out of the car, they were involved in a shooting incident at the gate, in which the guard was injured and they fled from the scene. A few hours later, William Burrell and Lawrence Jackson, former GIs who had chosen to remain in Germany after they were released from the army, were arrested as suspects by the German police. Burrell and Jackson had been touring American bases in southwest Germany to distribute information on the Black Power movement and an upcoming rally with Black Panther Party representative Kathleen Cleaver.[66] Their arrest received widespread news coverage and the Black Panther Solidarity committee in Frankfurt launched an information campaign and extensive coverage of their trial, which started on June 16, 1971, in Zweibrücken.

Reports on deteriorating morale and discipline within the U.S. army in West Germany had already appeared in the *New York Times*, which was told by a senior military officer in November 1970 that "[o]utside influences such as the Black Panthers and German student radicals are responsible for the protests."[67] The relationship between the two was also on display in the small town of Zweibrücken on March 6, 1971, when the Black Panther Solidarity Committee called for a demonstration in front of the local prison where Burrell and Jackson were held. The committee argued that "the baiting against the Black Panther Party concerns all of us. They are our natural allies. Every attack on them is also directed against us."[68] About 1,200 demonstrators followed this call and poured into town chanting, "Free the Ramstein 2" or "Revolution in America and West Germany." Although major conflicts with the locals and police were avoided, the "Ramstein 2" remained a reference point for Black Panther solidarity in the Federal Republic even after a district court on July 12, 1971, acquitted Burrell but sentenced Lawrence to six years in prison, which was later reduced to four years. Similar processes of solidarity went into effect after the arrest of Larry Barnes, the co-editor of the

GI-underground paper *Voice of the Lumpen*, which considered itself the "Black Panther Task Squad" in Germany.[69]

The committee also tried several times to invite prominent representatives of the Black Panther Party for its events in West Germany. In December 1969, plans for a lecture tour by Albert Howard, the party's minister of information, were thwarted by Hans-Dietrich Genscher, West Germany's minister of the interior.[70] After consulting with the foreign ministry and the U.S. embassy, Genscher advised the border police to refuse entry to Howard fearing a serious threat to internal security and calls for desertion directed at American soldiers in the Federal Republic.[71] Almost a year later, the committee attempted to invite one of the most prominent representatives of the Black Power movement, Elridge Cleaver, to West Germany. In August 1969, Cleaver had already discussed West European support for the Black Panther Party in an interview, encouraging activists to engage in urban guerilla warfare in Europe and to send over weapons and explosives to the United States.[72] In September 1970, the Black Panther Solidarity Committee, in an open letter to the government, asked for diplomatic immunity for Cleaver in the Federal Republic arguing that he was persecuted in the United States for political reasons and that the reach of the American FBI and other agencies would naturally extend to West German territory.[73] In response, Minister of the Interior Hans-Dietrich Genscher labeled Cleaver an "ordinary criminal" during a television interview.[74] Meanwhile, various organizations and student bodies had followed up on the committee's initiative and also invited Cleaver for a lecture or seminar with the help of ready-made invitation forms prepared by the solidarity committee. When the federal government refused to issue an official response, the committee angrily changed plans and instead announced the arrival of Elridge Cleaver's wife, Kathleen Cleaver, the communications secretary of the Black Panther Party, for November 24, 1970, in Frankfurt.[75] Although paying tribute to the growing role of women in the movement and the nexus between ethnic and women's liberation, Cleaver's visit was to coincide with a demonstration on November 28, 1970, in Frankfurt against U.S. imperialism and the beginning of Bobby Seale's trial in Connecticut.[76] Nevertheless, Kathleen Cleaver, traveling to Frankfurt from Algiers via Paris, was equally refused entry into the Federal Republic by the border police. Although she tried to circumvent her unspoken ban to enter the country by changing passports with another black passenger, her plan was discovered and she was immediately placed on a return flight to Paris.[77]

The repeated exclusion of Black Panther leaders did not sit well with West German activists. The news of Cleaver's refused entry caused anger and frustration, which translated itself in clashes between demonstrators and the police at Frankfurt airport and during the subsequent solidarity

(a)   (b)

IMAGE 13. Covers of the Berlin underground journal *Agit 883*. (a) Announcement (November 27, 1969) of a visit by Black Panther Party representatives in Berlin. (b) Call for a counterdemonstration (May 22, 1970) against a U.S. military parade in West Berlin. This cover features a Black Panther quote in the center: "We believe in armed revolution, a permanent revolution, and the creation of as many Vietnams as are necessary to defeat U.S. racism and imperialism all over the world."

demonstration for Bobby Seale, in which 3,000 people participated.[78] The increased militancy both in rhetoric and physical confrontations was palpable. Already in the days preceding the demonstration, the Black Panther Solidarity Committee had pointed to the United States as the center of the international imperialist network, which, faced with domestic threats like the Weathermen and the Black Panthers as well as Third World liberation, needed to firmly tighten the strings of its allies, such as the Federal Republic. In defiant rhetoric, the committee argued that "As is generally known, capitalism seeks his escape in imperialism, fascism and racism. Ok, we will be prepared for that."[79] Such a change in tone did not go unnoticed by the German press, which, in turn, also did not hold back with their estimation of the solidarity committee, claiming that "the American cars set on fire in Frankfurt and the splintered windows in US-office buildings are the work of the German-American 'Panther-Solidarity' which directly endangers the security of our country."[80] The spread of black nationalism into the country, subsequent racial tensions among U.S. military personnel stationed in the Federal Republic, as well as the increasing fascination

IMAGE 14. Kathleen Cleaver speaks at the University of Frankfurt, July 7, 1971 (Barbara Klemm)

on the part of activists toward the Black Panthers thus served as additional factors deepening the confrontation between the West German state and members of its young generation.[81]

Despite her previous entry ban, and after a wave of public protest and an official invitation by the university's academic senate, Kathleen Cleaver eventually gave a talk at the University of Frankfurt, on July 7, 1971, in which she demanded the solidarity of the German Left with the African American struggle and called for further support of the "Ramstein 2."[82] The Black Panther Solidarity committees remained active in Europe throughout 1970 and 1971 and organized solidarity actions on behalf of prominent leaders of the party in the United States, such as Bobby Seale or Ericka Huggins, or on behalf of Black Panther activists in their own countries.[83] With the splintering of the Black Panther Party, the committees slowly dissolved during 1971/72. In Germany, this demise was intertwined with an intense discussion about the question of violence, which emerged as a result of the first actions of terrorist groups in the Federal Republic.[84]

BLACK POWER AND 1970S' TERRORISM IN THE FEDERAL REPUBLIC

The identification with the Black Power movement by terrorist groups in West Germany at the beginning of the 1970s was motivated by a variety of factors and often connected to individual experience. Nonetheless, there are indications that a collective mindset concerning images of the United States and processes of cultural transfer already existed within the student movement. This could be seen particularly in the adaptation of countercultural forms in such areas as music and clothing styles, the cultivation of a radical and potentially violent anti-imperialism, as well as an integration of the Black Power movement as a role model for one's own "armed struggle" in the Federal Republic. All of these factors entered into a particular terrorist's self-stylization. They also illustrate the catalytic role that the Black Power movement played in the emergence of the West German terrorism of the 1970s, even with regard to the utilization of the National Socialist past.

One of the most important symbolic appropriations among terrorist groups such as the Rote Armee Fraktion (RAF) and the Bewegung 2. Juni (Movement June 2) were the cultural signs that the Black Panthers embodied. Michael Baumann, a member of Bewegung 2. Juni, for example, ascribed an enormous significance to cultural factors such as black music for an understanding of his own political and spiritual situation: "Well, in my case, I mean, at the beginning in Berlin, you were suddenly being treated as a negro because of your long hair, you know. They kicked us out of the bars, spat at us in the streets, cursed and followed us. . . . In my case it was also this blues music, the problems that come out of it, the situation of the negroes, you suddenly see the connections. All of a sudden you are also some kind of Jew or negro or outcast, in any case, you are somehow left outside, completely unconsciously."[85] For Baumann, the same was also true for clothing, which changed accordingly, and for political alignments in other areas.[86] Particularly the carrying of weapons as a sign of an increasing militancy in imitation of the Black Panthers came to symbolize greater determination and confrontation.[87] Despite this symbolic orientation, a transfer of very real weaponry from Black Panther groups in West Germany to groups such as the RAF also lies within the realms of possibility.[88]

The influence of the Black Power movement on the RAF also took place on other levels. Even the founding manifesto of the RAF, "Die Rote Armee aufbauen," was published in *Agit 883* with a black panther next to the soon-to-be-iconic Russian Kalashnikov.[89] According to RAF member Margrit Schiller, the Black Panthers' ideology and strategies also played a vital role in the discussions leading to the first lengthy theoretical piece explaining the group's philosophy, "Das Konzept Stadtguerilla" (The Concept of the Urban Guerilla") in April 1971. Schiller explains that Gudrun Ensslin, who was one of the leading figures of the RAF along with Andreas Baader and Ulrike Meinhof, had not only worked on early Black Power publications at Bernward Vesper's Voltaire Verlag, but had also been actively involved in the desertion campaign for GIs in the 1960s,

IMAGE 15. The founding manifesto of the RAF: "Die Rote Armee aufbauen!" (To build up the Red Army!), on the cover of *Agit 883*, June 5, 1970

when she had extensively studied the history of the black movement. Black guerrilla groups stemming from this movement, such as the Black Liberation Army, were considered by Ensslin to be particularly helpful examples, since they would operate under conditions similar to the RAF.[90] As a result, there are numerous references to the Black Panthers in the theoretical writings of the RAF, especially concerning its relationship to the masses and transition to illegality, as well as its use of violence.

Similar to the founding manifesto, "The Concept of the Urban Guerilla," for example, declared the awareness of being part of an international movement as the strategic basis for RAF's revolutionary actions. The "combination of national issues with international ones, of traditional forms of struggle with internationalist ones" in the tradition of the student movement thus formed the basis for the urban guerilla and the anti-imperialist struggle in the metropolis. The previous, mainly rhetorically declared solidarity with international groups now translated itself into the concrete "acquisition of weapons and money."[91] The awareness of the global dimension of the revolt and the example of the South American liberation movements thereby served as a guiding model for political actions in the Federal Republic. In this context, the Black Panthers and their interpretation of individual de-/oppression as a result of the capitalist system played an important role in the ideological self-definition of the RAF.[92] When confronted with accounts of the intensified persecution of the Black Panthers in the United States, the RAF, however, tried to avoid a similar fate and voluntarily chose "illegality as an offensive position" and a strategy of escalating militancy to prevent the destruction of its own organizational network.[93]

The National Socialist past likewise underlay the reception of the Black Panther movement by the RAF, which is particularly evident in "Über den bewaffneten Kampf in Westeuropa" (On Armed Struggle in Western Europe) from May 1971. Early on, the student movement, under the influence of spiritual mentors such as Herbert Marcuse, had drawn upon interpretations that evoked a semiotic proximity between Vietnam and Auschwitz.[94] The *Konkret* columns by Ulrike Meinhof already had used a plethora of Nazi references and analogies, which can be taken as an indicator of a gradual frustration and feeling of powerlessness among activists. Furthermore, a discursive positioning to a "second resistance" and the urge to avoid any complicity in crimes similar to the Nazi past as a result of the Federal Republic's transatlantic partnership led the RAF to a justification of illegal actions as a "progressive moment."[95] Particularly after June 2 and the killing of Benno Ohnesorg, the state and the protest movements entangled themselves in an escalating spiral of Manichean significations of the "other," which, against the backdrop of increased violence on both sides, was further cultivated by activists in their use of the Nazi past as a discursive weapon.[96] This dynamic is already visible in Gudrun Ensslin's alleged reaction toward Benno Ohnesorg's death: "This fascist state wants to kill all of us. We have to organize the resistance. Violence can only be answered by violence. This is the generation of Auschwitz—you cannot argue with them."[97]

During the reception of the Black Panther movement by the RAF, however, Frantz Fanon's theories and the burden of a fascist past entered a strange symbiosis. Fanon had developed his concept of violence in colonial situations based on the example of Algeria. In his most popular book, *Les Damnés de la Terre* (1961; *The Wretched of the Earth*), he analyzed the various kinds of violence that exist in a colonial relationship. Not only direct physical violence, but also structural violence that manifested itself in social and legal inequalities, were characteristic of the inequities experienced by the colonized. Any transition out of this state could be neither democratic nor nonviolent, because the essence of colonialism was to exclude the colonized from equal political participation. Decolonization was thus always connected to violence, since it needed to break the grip of both physical and structural violence that constricted the colonized. To reclaim their natural rights, native culture, and identity, the colonized were forced to break out of their suppression by using a physical violence that was both reactive and cleansing with regard to the dehumanizing influence of the colonizer. In order to regain their heritage and create a new future for themselves, they needed to liberate themselves completely from their former oppressors.[98]

Although Fanon never intended an application of his ideas to Westerm societies, his theories on decolonization and on the breakup of repressive power discourses had already played a vital role in the development of anti-authoritarian provocation strategies at the beginning of the German student movement. When Rudi Dutschke introduced Fanon's work to the Berlin SDS in 1966, he did so to strengthen solidarity with the Third World and to seek a partial application of these colonial theories in legal and illegal protest actions.[99] At the beginning of the 1970s, however, these models of postcolonial redefinitions of national and cultural identity gained a new quality in their transfer to a West German context, especially concerning the question of violence.[100] Within the student movement, the will to separate themselves from Nazi crimes had already been fostered by a supposed complicity of the Federal Republic in the worldwide system of capitalist imperialism, which was suppressing liberation movements in Algeria, the Congo, Iran, and Vietnam. The creation of an identity disconnected from a society that seemed to be latently fascist thus became one of the main aspirations of the extra-parliamentary opposition. Violence, as defined by Fanon, now appeared to be, and this is most obvious in the theoretical writings of the RAF, the only way out of imperialist repression domestically and abroad without retreating to reformism or opportunism. It was seen as a powerful approach to combat the "new fascism."[101] As the founding members of the RAF later proclaimed during their trial in Stammheim after their capture, "[W]hat Frantz Fanon discovered at the beginning of the 1960s in the experience of insurrections of the people of the Third World, namely that anger, hatred and a spontaneous movement does 'not enable one to succeed in a national war, to drive back the horrible war machinery of the enemy'; this found its counterpart in the metropoli in the fundamental experience of the student movement: that spontaneity and revolt can be absorbed unless it is armed."[102]

From this angle, the Black Panthers developed into a role model for the application of Fanon's theory of violence in the First World for groups preparing for armed struggle. For the RAF, the eruption of riots in African

American ghettos provided a convincing example of how to set off a revolution by a "revolutionary act of violence by the masses": "The Afro-Americans and their allies did neither calculate the balance of power between the classes nor the divisions of the counterrevolution in advance. They did not calculate their chances. They simply turned away from themselves and directed their violence against their oppressors. They lit the fire of revolution in the streets of Watts, which will not die down until their final victory."[103]

This way, together with Che Guevara's foco theory, the avant-gardist role of students and the intelligentsia was combined with the function of violence postulated by Fanon as a compass for revolution. Any change of direction with regard to violence displayed in the black ghettos could be used as a basis to create a revolutionary situation. The role of the avant-garde in the Federal Republic was now, even through the use of violence, to "carry along other segments of the proletariat into the revolutionary confrontation with the state powers" and, in the long run, gradually to take over the government itself.[104] Because the Black Panthers were situated in the center of imperialism, their ideology and work, as well as their focus on the African American community, lent themselves as an ideal model for West German terrorists, who considered the Federal Republic part of the very same international system of exploitation.

The adaptation of Fanon's theories also massively shaped the RAF's image of the United States, in which African Americans were of prominent significance. Considering the development of events in the United States as a prototypical process from capitalism to fascism, the RAF saw the situation in African American ghettos as particularly threatening because the unrest could spark a conservative public backlash further preparing the ground for an emergence of fascist structures.[105] Since the political-economic development in West Germany was viewed as analogous to that of the United States, the Federal Republic likewise became the target of a potentially violent anti-imperialism. The fear of a potential relapse into fascism due to an insufficient coming to terms with West Germany's National Socialist past only intensified these attacks. The idea of the Federal Republic being an "external colony" of the United States, and hence compromising its integrity, as well as the protesters' appropriation of Fanon's philosophy of violence, gave the domestic opposition its particular fervor.[106] The fear of a return to fascism under these auspices served as a unifier among diverging factions within the West German movement, and it offered the legitimacy to sabotage the seemingly imperialist foreign policy of the United States and its allies through terrorist actions from within, if only to prevent worse things from happening. The proof of international solidarity and the synergetic coordination of anti-imperialist actions in the Third and First World thus gained a new profile in the ideology of the urban guerrilla as "connection between national and international class struggle."[107] Any objections to this strategy with reference to the highly different local environment of each of these movements were disregarded by the RAF and dismissed as only minor tactical differences.[108]

What started out as GI-organizing and transnational cooperation during the 1960s was now escalating into a series of terrorist acts in the name of a global revolutionary alliance. From the very beginning, the war in Vietnam and the resulting shattered image of the United States had been a key motive for radical actions surrounding the urban guerrilla.[109] The continuation of this ever-escalating war and the rapidly growing confrontations with the state resulted in attacks on U.S. military installations in West Germany that produced an increasing number of casualties. As the RAF declared in its statement on the attack of the U.S. military headquarters in Frankfurt on May 11, 1972, "West Germany and West Berlin must not be a secure hinterland for the extermination strategists of Vietnam anymore."[110] In the ideology of the RAF, these assaults were not only "bombs in the consciousness of the masses" but were designed to shake society out of its apathy by connecting the U.S. involvement in Vietnam to the atrocities of National Socialism during the Second World War. American deliberations as to whether to expand the war in Vietnam were interpreted as follows in the RAF's statement on the bombing attack on the headquarters of the U.S. Army in Heidelberg on May 25, 1972: "This is genocide, the killing of a people, that would be the 'final solution', that is Auschwitz. The people in the Federal Republic do not support the law enforcement agencies in their search for the perpetrators of the bombing attack, because they do not want to be part of the crimes of American imperialism and their approval by the ruling class. Because they have not forgotten Auschwitz, Dresden and Hamburg, because they know that bombing attacks against the mass murderers of Vietnam are justified."[111]

The RAF thus employed a constructed parallel to Nazi war crimes not only in its battle against a supposed domestic fascism, but also in its interventions against new German entanglements in war crimes abroad, as a justification for its actions and as a source of legitimacy. Transformations in the image of the United States, in which the Black Power movement played a central role, as well as the shadows of a past insufficiently overcome, entered into a tragic union. Most telling, this also included references to a German victimhood in the Second World War, which are implicit in the sequence of "*Auschwitz, Hamburg und Dresden.*"

African American political prisoners, in particular the Attica prison riots and the case of George Jackson, were of similar interest to the RAF. Jackson, who was convicted of armed robbery at the age of eighteen, was accused of murdering a prison guard in the Soledad prison in 1970 with the help of two other inmates (Fleeta Drumgo and John Clutchette) to take revenge for the death of three black activists in the Californian prison of San Quentin. The case of the "Soledad Brothers" provoked international attention, in large part because of the support of Angela Davis, who led their defense committee. When Jackson was shot in San Quentin in August 1971 while supposedly trying to escape, the questionable circumstances surrounding his death, as well as his prison letters made him popular among the left in West Germany, where the Black Panther Solidarity Committee had been campaigning on his behalf.[112] The Attica prison riots in New York during September 9-13, which caused over forty casualties when police stormed the building where the inmates had taken hostages, only brought the intolerable conditions of the American penitentiary system further into the spotlight.

Particularly after the first wave of arrests, RAF members began to take note of the U.S. prison movement in connection with Black Power.[113] The reception of George Jackson's writings, which were often employed by RAF inmates as an inspiration for their own struggle, is striking in this context. By citing Jackson in one of her secret messages, Gudrun Ensslin, for example, called for strength and endurance to admonish fellow imprisoned RAF members Irmgard Möller and Ilse Stachowiak: "Defend our cause with toes and claws and cunningness, etc.: Violence, guerilla . . . imprisoned free. Or if you do not listen anymore, let Jackson teach you the whole thing—his joy in doing this job, for example here: 'If you ask me generally how this struggle will end, I answer: With a victory. If you ask me specifically, I answer: With death.' Or do you perhaps have anything to lose anymore?"[114]

George Jackson thus became a symbol for an uncompromising stance in the RAF's clash with the West German state. Furthermore, the lessons of the Attica riots were also transferred to the situation in German prisons and the treatment of political inmates. As Margrit Schiller stated before the district court in Hamburg on November 15, 1972, "Attica and San Quentin are also in the Federal Republic of Germany—a little piece of that just trickled through the walls here in Hamburg—where guards, prison directors, doctors, psychologists take out their sadisms and their inhumanity on defenseless prisoners."[115]

In the same way, during the RAF members' second hunger strike in prison, Gudrun Ensslin did not shy away from using Attica as a reference point for the severity of their confrontation with the state and the radical continuation of their struggle in prison.[116] The escalation of violence and the acceptance of casualties as a liberating gesture toward a system of oppression were thus again translated into a West German context. Plans to kidnap the U.S. Allied Commander of the city of Berlin by a coalition of urban guerrilla groups in the Federal Republic to exchange him for the Soledad Brothers in 1971/72, as well as the so-called "Kommando George

Jackson," for which the GI Edward Pimental was killed in August 1985, indicate the high degree of importance attributed to George Jackson.[117] It is even more illuminating, however, that the debate concerning the relationship of the West German Left with urban guerilla groups coincided with an event that also focused on solidarity with the Black Power movement: the Angela Davis Congress from June 3–4, 1972.

THE ANGELA DAVIS SOLIDARITY COMMITTEE AND CONGRESS

Angela Davis was born in 1944 in Birmingham, Ala., a child of an African American middle-class family. Before moving into the international limelight, Davis studied philosophy at Brandeis University, where she met Herbert Marcuse, who encouraged her to continue her studies with Theodor W. Adorno in Frankfurt from 1965–67. During her time in Germany, she also became active in the Frankfurt SDS, participated in demonstrations against the Vietnam War, listened to speeches by Rudi Dutschke in Frankfurt, and was generally impressed by the international outlook of the emerging German student movement. Although her studies with Adorno, Jürgen Habermas, and Oskar Negt progressed well, and she was even offered to pursue her doctoral dissertation, she returned to the United States in the summer of 1967 to join forces with the emerging Black Power movement, which she had learned about during her stay in Frankfurt.[118]

Davis continued her studies with Herbert Marcuse in San Diego, Calif., as a doctoral candidate, actively involving herself in civil rights work for African Americans and antiwar activities. She eventually joined SNCC, the Che Lumumba Club, and the black section of the Communist Party in Los Angeles in July of 1968, as well as the Black Panther Party soon afterward.[119] In June of 1969, Davis accepted a position as an Acting Assistant Professor in the Philosophy Department at the University of California at Los Angeles, but soon ran into difficulties with the University Board of Regents because of her activism. After a regents' vote of dismissal, which was overturned by a court decision, Davis, however, continued to teach at UCLA, now having emerged as a public figure and representative of the Black Power movement. Starting in 1970, she became active on behalf of the Soledad Brothers and publicly lectured about the conditions in the California penitentiary system. When another Soledad inmate had to stand trial on August 3, 1970, for the murder of a prison guard, Jonathan George Jackson (the younger brother of George Jackson) entered the courtroom armed in an attempt to free him and other prisoners who were present by taking members of the jury and the presiding judge as hostages. The police hindered their escape, and both hostages and kidnappers died in the shooting. On August 13 and 14,

IMAGE 16. Demonstration against the Vietnam War at the Opernplatz in Frankfurt, February 1967: On the right, holding the Viet Cong flag, is Angela Davis (Bildarchiv Preussischer Kulturbesitz /Art Resource, New York)

the authorities ascertained that three of the guns used in the kidnapping attempt were registered in the name of Angela Davis, and prosecution against her started immediately. The FBI issued a fugitive warrant for her arrest and put her on the list of Ten Most Wanted criminals, indicating that she was armed and dangerous. On October 13, Davis was arrested in New York City and extradited to California on December 22. Her trial began on February 23, 1972, after she had already spent about sixteen months in prison.[120]

In West Germany, Davis's case was closely watched and frequently caused anger and agitation.[121] As a student in Frankfurt stated, "Until now I have not taken part in any direct actions against the [U.S.] consulate, but if they kill Angela, all hell will break loose for the Americans here in Frankfurt."[122] The Black Panther Party Solidarity Committee and a variety of other organizations hosted solidarity events for Davis. On March 13, 1971, for example, women groups in Frankfurt organized a women and children's demonstration in support of Angela Davis, which led about 200 participants to the doors of the U.S. General Consulate to deliver a petition.[123] Soon after her arrest in November 1970, Herbert Marcuse himself had called for international solidarity declaring that only "a protest that arises in every country . . . and cannot be extinguished can save her life."[124]

IMAGE 17. "Women's Demonstration" for Angela Davis, Frankfurt, March 13, 1971 (Manfred A. Tripp)

Increasingly, Davis came to represent the African American struggle in the United States for German activists, and her imprisonment the emblematic state it was in.[125] As Detlev Claussen, Frankfurt SDS member and former peer of Angela Davis, argued, Davis's case was symptomatic for the criminalization of black political activities in the United States and of the failure to integrate the fight against racism into the class struggle of the Marxist labor movement. In his view, capitalism itself tended to encourage racism similar to antisemitism. Emphasizing structural similarities such as an anticommunist working class, co-opted labor unions, and a militant but repressed student left, Claussen thus perceived the development of the United States as a projection of the future of the Federal Republic.[126]

As an expression of this sentiment and to coordinate protest on Davis's behalf in West Germany, an Angela Davis Solidarity Committee was founded in May 1971.[127] The climax of its work was the congress entitled "Am Beispiel Angela Davis" (The Example of Angela Davis), which it conducted during June 3–4, 1972, in Frankfurt. The congress's significance for the German Left manifested itself already at the opening rally held at the Opernplatz in Frankfurt, which drew an audience of more than 10,000 people.[128] Messages of greeting arrived from Angela Davis herself, as well as from Marxist theoretician Ernest Mandel and the philosopher Ernst Bloch, and speakers included leading representatives of the left such as Herbert Marcuse, Oskar Negt, and Wolfgang Abendroth, among others.[129] Originally, the congress sought to analyze Davis's persecution and the movement that she stood for in its political, historical, economical, and international contexts, using her case as an example.[130] During May 1972, however, the RAF had intensified its terrorist acts with attacks on the U.S. Corps in Frankfurt on May 11, the police headquarters in Augsburg, and the State Criminal Police Office (Landeskriminalamt, LKA) in Munich the day after; as well as with an assassination attempt on a federal judge on May 15, a bomb attack on the Axel Springer building on May 19, and car bombs in front of the European headquarters of the U.S. Army on May 24. These actions had caused a massive, nationwide response by the police, a harsh reaction by the media, and an extremely difficult situation for the left as a whole. Naturally, the capture of Andreas Baader and Holger Meins, two of the founding members of the RAF, only two days before the conference overshadowed the event even more.

Accordingly, many speakers during the congress, while talking about Angela Davis and the situation in the United States, took a stand on the bombing campaigns of the Red Army Faction and its understanding of international solidarity. The person who took the opportunity to most drastically condemn the philosophy of this terrorist group during the Angela Davis congress was Oskar Negt, a former student of Theodor Adorno and assistant to Jürgen Habermas in Frankfurt. Already at the opening rally, Negt voiced his concerns that the congress would be dominated by the events of the previous months. In his view, a pogrom-like persecution and media terror directed toward the German left had set in, and the congress needed to come to terms with the question of violence in connection with solidarity and the status of the left in West Germany. Regarding the war in Vietnam as the critical symbol of violence in his times, Negt viewed the indifference toward the atrocities of war as telling for the state of West German society, which only served as the environment for the "desperados of the Baader-Meinhof group."[131] For Negt, the rest of the narrative was as follows: A young generation, drawing analogies from Vietnam to the war actions of National Socialist Germany, was disillusioned by this apathy and had came to the forefront in the late 1960s, spurred by the urge not to repeat the mistakes of their parents. This refusal to be "good Germans" and their public protest was, however, often answered by manifest state violence that fundamentally shaped the political consciousness of this generation. For them, the killing of Benno Ohnesorg had become emblematic for the state response to protesters and dissidents.

Although acknowledging this dynamic, Negt strongly opposed answering state violence with more violence, and he rejected any form of solidarity with the terrorist acts of the Red Army Faction. For him, their deeds were "apolitical" and a "mixture of romance with illegality, a wrong interpretation of the sociopolitical situation as open fascism, and an illegitimate transfer of urban guerilla practices to conditions that could be compared to Latin America only out of desperation."[132] Negt characterized their call for solidarity as a form of "blackmailing solidarity," which in its mechanical reflex was not based on mutual consent and discredited the daily grassroots efforts of the vast majority of the left. The RAF's complete detachment from any external criticism and self-reflection, and its separation from the experience of the majority of the population were the central points of his contention.[133] For Negt, the RAF had missed the lessons of their North American counterparts, the Weathermen, who had changed their strategies after three of their own members were killed while preparing explosives in March 1970.[134] In his eyes, the RAF's comparison of the Federal Republic, which was a somewhat stable political system with a semi-functioning democratic government, with dictatorships in other parts of the world had disastrous consequences: namely, innocent casualties and the almost complete limitation the left's ability to act in general.

Negt thus concluded that the left as a whole should not let itself be pushed into the constraints of choosing between the false alternatives of conformism or terrorist attacks. Most of the conference participants, who were active in various kinds of grassroots efforts, had come to the congress for more meaningful forms of international solidarity: "What brings them together to this congress is the need to cooperate supraregionally and the determination to bring their concrete work in the context of international solidarity with those who are leading a similar struggle in other parts of the world and under different conditions. We do not have a better way of demonstrating our solidarity with Angela Davis, with all political prisoners of racial terror and oppression, than by transcending our own factionalization, by combining our forces with the goal of creating sociopolitical conditions so that these congresses do not have to be dominated by the question of violence anymore."[135] A united front of forces on the left and a refusal of terrorist acts was, according to Negt, the most appropriate and effective demonstration of solidarity with Angela Davis.

The congress pointedly illustrates how the West German New Left used the case of this African American leader with ties to the West German scene to come to a deeper understanding of its own situation. Closely examining the conditions in the United States, it reflected upon them as a way to redefine its own position in society. Especially the terrorism of one of its splinter groups, the Red Army Faction, prompted the participants of the Angela Davis congress to a heated discussion about the use of political violence in the Federal Republic. While prominent speakers denounced the terror of this group, others—for example, a member of the Frankfurt Sponti group Revolutionärer Kampf (Revolutionary Struggle) named Joschka Fischer—opposed a disassociation from the RAF, fearing an even greater factionalizing of the left.[136] Interestingly enough though, the discussions about solidarity with Angela Davis and the Black Panthers were not only used to gain new insights and strategies for the West German political scene, but were also frequently affected by assumed obligations stemming from the legacy of National Socialism. Both the young generation of students and emigrants such as Herbert Marcuse applied these semiotic strategies. As a consequence, the German past was manipulated to understand, though not condone, the motives for domestic political violence and to justify and demand solidarity with revolutionary violence in other parts of the world. Solidarity with African Americans was therefore once more to a vast degree part of a process of self-definition and positioning in its own society.

Angela Davis was finally acquitted of all charges on June 4, 1972. Even in the reunified Germany, she has remained an icon for Black Power and international solidarity, despite her visit and close affiliation with the East German Communist Party (SED), her appearance at the 10th World Festival of Youth and Students in East Berlin in 1973, and her refusal to speak out against oppression in East European socialist states (much to the disappointment of her mentor Herbert Marcuse).[137]

The Black Power movement thus played a vital role in the West German student movement and in the emergence of terrorism in the early 1970s. Several aspects were important in this context: First was the observation of strategies and protest techniques of the early, pacifist phase of the American civil rights movement, which went along with a discussion on the adaptation of these social practices in the Federal Republic. Second, in the course of an increasing antiwar sentiment, support emerged for a Black Power ideology emphasizing class, which, in its international compatibility with colonial liberation movements, served as a model for the "fight in the metropolis" in accordance with an adaptation of Che Guevara's foco theory. Black Power representatives such as Elridge Cleaver, George Jackson, and, first and foremost, due to her personal connections to the German SDS, Angela Davis, were transformed into icons of African American protest. They were known among the left all over West Germany, not least as a result of the activities of the Black Panther Solidarity Committee. Third, the transatlantic connections and activist networks were influential and abundant, including the GI-organizing in the Federal Republic. All of this was accompanied by a mounting aggression toward American installations in West Germany, which were seen as supporting the Vietnam War effort or which served as symbols of American imperialism.

IMAGE 18. Angela Davis arrives in East Berlin, where she is enthusiastically welcomed by Erika Havemann (née Berthold), daughter-in-law of renowned East German dissident Robert Havemann, September 11, 1972 (Archiv/Berliner Verlag)

Among supporters of the Black Power movement, the variety of personal and ideological perspectives demonstrated by everyone from student activists to terrorists is particularly interesting.[138] Johannes Weinrich, Hans-Joachim Klein, and Winfried Böse represent personal continuities stretching from membership in the Black Panther Solidarity Committee to terrorism groups, which cannot, however, be taken as direct or inevitable lines.[139] Admittedly, common phrases and ideas of solidarity were intentionally integrated into the ideology of West German terrorist groups. Given the conceptual evolution from the student movement and the Black Panther Solidarity Committee to the terrorism of the 1970s, the so-called armed struggle can thus be considered a byproduct, although not the only one, of Black Power solidarity in the Federal Republic.[140] Nonetheless, the terrorist groups went far beyond mere rhetoric in their resolution to resort to violence and their acceptance of casualties. Rather, it seems as if the RAF, for example, strategically utilized the reputation and aura of closeness to the Black Power Solidarity Committee in West Germany for its own ends, such as renting a secure house that was supposed to be part of the desertion campaign for black GIs.[141]

What was even more important, especially for the development of the RAF, was the inspiration of the West German protest movement and the

Black Panther Solidarity Committee derived from Black Power on an ideological level. Through a synthesis of a voluntarism shaped by George Lukácz and a minority theory represented by Herbert Marcuse, the Third World liberation movements occupied a prominent place in the German student movement from the very beginning. Embodying the new revolutionary proletariat, these movements, according to an application of Che Guevara's foco theory, also provided a model and ignited a spark for the First World. From this internationalist perspective, the relationship to and solidarity with the Third World proved to be crucial.

The fundamental change in the image of the United States caused by the escalation of the war in Vietnam, together with an increasing adaptation of Frantz Fanon's model of colonial conflicts and an emphasis on the liberating features of violence, also had far-reaching consequences for solidarity with Black Power in a West German context. To the same degree that the Federal Republic was regarded as an external colony of the United States, the Black Power movement was seen as an internal one, which was already on the way to gaining its independence and shaping its identity, while simultaneously battling imperialism from within.

In the case of the West German protest movements, solidarity with the Black Power movement therefore also became an integral part of renegotiating one's own identity. The coming to terms with the West German past through the help of the "other" as a substratum of one's own oppression grew into a symbol of a belated resistance, and served as the background in front of which the solidarity with the Black Power movement played out. Through this discourse, the history of the Federal Republic after 1945 was continuously being renegotiated and terrorist actions legitimized. This also explains the fascination with Black Power, a militant movement in the country that was one of Germany's liberators from National Socialism. The following passage from RAF member Astrid Proll's piece on Mao's treatise on the Main Contradiction succinctly illustrates this mindset with reference to George Jackson:

> George Jackson's prison letters are the melody of the main contradiction in the metropolis—condensed in the sentence "I feel as old as a paper target must feel like after an hour of shooting practice. Used. Many greetings from Dachau. George." His poem is 'die Massnahme' by Bertolt Brecht. The decision of the 4 agitators was wrong; it did not provide for what Brecht demanded from the party in 1932 and what he had left to his readers to judge upon: Neither Auschwitz nor the destruction of the German labor movement, nor the Second World War—which would have justified it. The Red Army Faction (RAF) is the return of the young comrade from the limepit, its histori-

cal identity is the uprising of the Jews in the Warsaw Ghetto against the death squadrons of the world finance system: the SS.[142]

Evident here are the RAF's efforts to compare conditions in the United States to the rise of National Socialism based on the example of the treatment of prisoners, as well as the self-stylization of its members as potential victims trying to escape a similar repetition of the past in West Germany through the use of violence. It represents the final point in the development of a generation that could become aware of its own identity only by an undoubtedly extremely questionable appropriation of its country's past.[143] In its provocative display of militancy and in the transformative impact this had for West German images of the United States, the Black Power movement thus played the role of a mediated "self-perception from a distance" for parts of the student movement and groups such as the RAF. For West German activists, this "other" alliance brought once more into focus the burden of the National Socialist past and the split within West German society, this time in a dramatic manner.[144] By making the question of race and ethnic identity in American society a much more pressing one than the civil rights movement had done, Black Power played an almost parallel role for the New Left in the United States, which also drew much of its revolutionary inspiration from groups like the Black Panthers and sought to establish similar revolutionary alliances with them. In both cases, however, cooperation had its limits, since the nationalism and internationalism of black radicals was ultimately more focused on liberation movements in Africa and other colonial settings.

Chapter 5

THE OTHER ALLIANCE

AND THE TRANSATLANTIC PARTNERSHIP

On May 21, 1968, George McGhee left his post as U.S. ambassador to the Federal Republic to take on the job of ambassador-at-large in Washington. Throughout his diplomatic career, McGhee had shown interest in the situation of international youth. When the Department of State formed a "Student Unrest Study Group" to come to terms with the events of the "French May" in mid-1968, McGhee was the natural candidate for the chairmanship. In his first report to President Lyndon B. Johnson on "World Student Unrest," McGhee wrote that across the globe students had "toppled prime ministers, changed governments, ruined universities and in some cases harmed the economy of the country." More important, their protest transcended traditional notions of patriotism and nationalism. For McGhee, these students were not "interested in their country" anymore but would "basically feel a camaraderie with other students around the world who are doing the same thing."[1] Instead of a formal, hierarchical organization, mutual visits and the opportunities of international communication had enabled them to spur each other through mutual emulation. Much to the disadvantage of the American image abroad, the opposition to the war in Vietnam was unifying them internationally: "They see us with all of our wealth and military bases around the world as a relic of imperialism. They know, whether we like it or not, that we have . . . influence everywhere in the world, and are inclined to view us as imperialists along with the old European models."[2]

In this scenario, McGhee attributed a particular role to student protest in West Germany, his former country of duty: "I first encountered the problem of student unrest while serving as United States Ambassador to Germany—in connection with the Free University of Berlin. The three allies are responsible for Berlin. We are the government so we could not ignore it. The Free University became, perhaps, the most troublesome university in the world for a year or two, as a direct result of what happened at Berkeley."[3] Other American officials assigned to the Federal Republic shared McGhee's assessment. Witnessing dramatic changes in the prevailing images of the United States, they confronted a growing antiwar movement in West Germany, particularly in Berlin. As a former U.S. Information Services (USIS) lecturer recalled his experience of trying to give a talk about Vietnam at the Free University, "When I arrived, there were the police. There were police dogs. There was a huge banner of the Viet Cong. And there was a rowdy group of students who did not want to let me speak. . . . Eggs were thrown. Objects were thrown. I was ultimately rescued by the police and their dogs and went back to my hotel."[4] His colleague, USIS Public Affairs Officer Hans Tuch, remembers how "[l]ife in Berlin took on a definite anti-American tone" and how protesters even targeted U.S. representations in the city: "Our America House in Berlin was sacked, completely sacked, two weekends in a row. Every window was broken. In the second incident 60 policemen were hurt by students who were throwing rocks and Molotov cocktails."[5]

Due to the divided status of the city and the special bond it enjoyed with the U.S., citizens of Berlin reacted with outrage to any public criticism of their country's transatlantic partner. American diplomats therefore had to assess the danger of student disorder and supposedly "anti-American" protest in terms of an even greater problem, namely a violent public response against it. As Ambassador McGhee argued, "In Berlin, the students got out 12,000 members to demonstrate against us in Viet Nam. . . . It didn't hurt anybody very much. The next day, 125,000 workers came out to demonstrate against the students. Everybody who looked like a student, that is, who had long hair, [was] roughed up."[6] Hence, the United States faced a twofold problem in confronting student unrest in West Germany. On the one hand, the students posed a security problem to the American presence in the country. Far more seriously, however, they challenged the transatlantic partner ideologically and could not, as the country's future elite who would soon occupy positions of influence in West German society, be disregarded. On the other hand, student disruptions also caused a substantial change in the political landscape and exposed generational fissures in the Federal Republic that the American government was hard pressed to influence. This chapter explores how West German students contested several areas of traditional U.S. cultural diplomacy and German-American cooperation in the cold war with their protest during the 1960s. It traces how the U.S. government came to terms with this challenge and how its response was embedded in a larger political framework responding to youthful unrest worldwide that had been instituted under the Kennedy administration.

Confronting Youthful Unrest:
The State Department's Inter-Agency Youth Committee

With its discovery as a powerful economic and consumer force, youth became a major concern of the U.S. government at the beginning of the

1960s.[7] The election of John F. Kennedy and the image of a youthful president embodying the generational change he proclaimed in his inaugural address evoked hopes and fueled the activism of young people.[8] For Kennedy, the cold war demanded a united country that could serve as an example of the superiority of the Western democratic model and confront the communist challenge worldwide. Domestically, the new administration sought to channel youthful activism into efforts benefiting the American image abroad with the establishment of organizations such as the Peace Corps.[9] In his foreign policy, Kennedy also placed a firm emphasis on foreign youth by relying on the tools of cultural diplomacy established by his predecessors.

American cultural policy after the Second World War was part of a larger strategic endeavor to win the ensuing propaganda competition with the Soviet Union. The policy of promoting American ideas and values became part of a comprehensive diplomatic strategy for projecting political influence and power.[10] The Smith-Mund Act of 1948 gave the U.S. government the permission to entertain a worldwide information and culture program even in times of peace, which, together with the goal of reeducating the German population and countering Soviet propaganda surrounding the Korean War, eventually led to the establishment of the United States Information Agency (USIA) in 1953. Its representation overseas, the United States Information Service (USIS), tried to spread American concepts of democracy and the American way of life. Liberty, individualism, and tolerance, but also the high standard of living and an abundant consumer culture were supposed to foster the image of a society with equal opportunities for all.[11]

In this framework of U.S. cultural diplomacy, the problem of connecting to international youth had already emerged at the beginning of the 1960s. In January 1962, a letter by George McGhee, then undersecretary for political affairs, to Philip Coombs, assistant secretary of state for the Bureau of Educational and Cultural Affairs (CU), sparked a discussion in the Department of State (DOS) about how to reach out to the young generation. McGhee argued that "we are not adequately attuned to the needs and desires of youth (ages 6–20) and youth groups in the free world and that we have no specific program directed toward capturing the minds of these individuals." He proposed the creation of a mission statement for the youth of "free-world countries" that would include a commitment to individual freedom and the role of youth for the peace of nations. An organizational embodiment of the "free world youth" should see to the distribution of this statement and counter communist infiltration in youth organizations worldwide. Demanding a stronger integration of youth as a prime target group in U.S. cultural diplomacy efforts, McGhee argued that in order to create "a community of free nations," the United States had to "impart to the youth of this country and the rest of the world in clear, concise and simple terms what it is we are trying to achieve, the urgency of our task and the part youth, who will be the prime movers in the next decade, must play in this great enterprise."[12]

His request met, however, with a very mixed response within the bureau. His colleague Francis Miller, special assistant to the CU, wrote that "it is not the function of the United States government to perform either of the above tasks" and that doing so would be "equivalent to denying the assumptions of the free world and adopting the assumptions of totalitarian regimes regarding the relationship of the individual and society as a whole to the State."[13] Striking a somewhat softer tone, Philip Coombs argued that current government programs were already focusing on the political significance of youth and that such an endeavor might prove counterproductive, especially with regard to an age group that could be considered future voters.[14]

Despite this initial skepticism, the issue of influencing youth abroad was pursued further within the department. A youth task force composed of members from various agencies met in mid-March 1962 to compile an inventory of existing activities concerning youth abroad, to draft a presidential statement, as well as to elaborate new organizational avenues.[15] Soon thereafter a policy statement summed up the objectives for the role of the U.S. government in youth affairs abroad as follows: "We seek to expand U.S. Government interest in this area because we are concerned that the apparent hostility of the young people of the world to the U.S. results from our failure to convey to them an understanding of our national goals and the nature of our society, as well as from communist success in capitalizing on the aspirations of young people in order to achieve communist objectives." Despite the natural resistance of youth toward any government interference in their activities, the statement was nonetheless confident that the young generation would "welcome increased official interest in and support for their efforts, better means of bringing their ideas and programs to bear on government policy, and, in general, broader government cooperation with them in programming and planning ways to communicate the story of freedom to youths and students of other nations."[16] Along these lines, the department planned to overhaul existing youth programs and schedule meetings with American youth and student organizations, and it also suggested the appointment of a special assistant for youth affairs by the president.

Motivating these developments was the fact that Attorney General Robert F. Kennedy had returned from his trips to Latin America and Asia in 1962 highly disillusioned and concerned about the attitude of the countries' youth toward the United States. Their ignorance of Western institutions and traditions and the hostility particularly among students had left him deeply bewildered. Feeling that the United States was out of touch with tomorrow's foreign elites, he turned to the Department of State and suggested a massive expansion of exchange programs.[17] In particular, Kennedy was struck by the lack of available American books in these countries and the presence of books published in the Soviet Union and translated into English. He voiced his concern in a speech before the American Booksellers' Association in April 1962, which resulted in the establishment of the Government Advisory Commission on International Book Programs in October that year. Under the Fulbright-Hays Act, the task of the commission was to help supervise the policies and operations of the various overseas book and library programs.[18]

Robert Kennedy's experience also reinforced the youth initiatives already underway in the Department of State and led to the establishment of the Inter-Agency Committee on Youth Affairs (IAYC) on April 11, 1962, during a meeting convened by George McGhee.[19] A later report described it as "the culmination of a series of discussions and proposals in the Department of State and other interested agencies, following on the attorney general's experience with critical student audiences in Japan and Indonesia."[20] Only two weeks later, the committee presented a survey of all U.S. government programs affecting foreign youth and suggestions for further youth initiatives to representatives from the U.S. Information Agency (USIA), the Peace Corps, the White House, the Agency for International Development (AID), and the CIA, including Attorney General Robert Kennedy and USIA director Edward Murrow.[21] The committee argued that in the time of the cold war, foreign opinion of the United States would be crucial for American leadership of the free world:

> [F]aced with the task of leading half the peoples of the world, we find that we are misunderstood, misinterpreted, misrepresent[ed] and maligned in many areas. If we are to lead, we must have allies whose allegiance is firmly anchored in common aims and mutual understanding. . . . The youth of the world can identify our common goals if they are given the opportunity to know our philosophy and the policies that stem from that philosophy.[22]

The solution to this "communication problem" lay, on the one hand, in a propaganda effort to counter similar Soviet methods of influence. On the other hand, American officials needed to build a deep understanding of the United States among educated foreign leaders, whose knowledge and opinions would multiply and ensure long-term benefits for American foreign policy objectives. Although these efforts had already begun, they would have greater chances of succeeding if centrally coordinated. The committee therefore recommended that the assistant secretary of state for educational and cultural affairs take on the role of special representative to the secretary of state with regard to international youth: "In this capacity he would coordinate government youth activities, serve as the focal point for contact with private organizations concerned with international youth matters, and be responsible for stimulating the maximum possible program for winning the world's youth to the side of Western democracies."[23] In addition, various government agencies should name their own youth officers who would serve on a standing committee convened and chaired by the assistant secretary.

Following these recommendations, Assistant Secretary of State Lucius Battle became chairman of the "Inter-Agency Youth Committee" (IAYC). On June 22, 1962, he appointed Martin McLaughlin as the CU's full-time special assistant for youth affairs. McLaughlin, as Executive Secretary of the youth committee, was to serve as the main link for information and coordination of government activities aimed at reaching foreign youth.[24] In the years 1962 and 1963, the IAYC gradually expanded its efforts and began to include the U.S. posts overseas in its efforts. Already in April 1962, Secretary of State Dean Rusk had informed the U.S. chiefs of mission about his discussions with the president on "the importance of youth in world affairs." He argued that, due to the often distorted image of the United States abroad, the administration felt that "a greater and more effective effort in the youth and student field must be made if we are to be successful in our total mission." Fully aware of the sensitive nature of this task, he asked the posts to reach out to young leaders by encouraging open and intelligent dialogue and leaving simplistic cold-war rhetoric or useless "lectures on the evils of Communism" behind.[25] Further circulars to the posts detailed the nature and work of the IAYC and the administration's "new emphasis on youth." In November 1962, the Department of State also requested the designation of "a senior officer as coordinator of all US programs affecting youth in his country" together with an outline of his local duties.[26]

By April 1963, the IAYC reported the appointment of ninety-nine youth coordinators and many forthcoming country studies.[27] With the establishment of an office and staff dedicated to its tasks, the committee had firmly institutionalized itself in Washington.[28] Attendance at the committee meetings was high and, next to the president and the secretary of state, Robert Kennedy became an especially avid supporter of the committee's work, not even shying away from the occasional desk pounding needed to enforce the administration's and IAYC's demands from reluctant member agencies.[29] Shortly before his death, President Kennedy, in a memorandum to the secretary of state, also underlined once more his support for reaching out to the young generation abroad:

I want to emphasize again how important I consider our efforts directed toward young people throughout the world, and therefore the

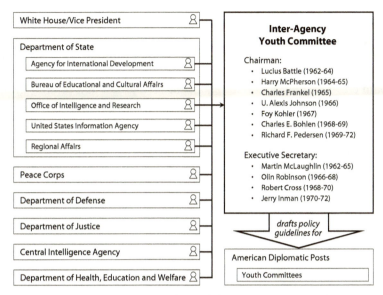

FIGURE I. Figure 1. Organization chart of the Inter-Agency Youth Committee, 1962–72

particular significance I attach to the work of the Interagency Youth Committee. It is essential to the successful conduct of our foreign affairs that we reach young people abroad to obtain their under-standing and support.[30]

Kennedy made clear that the emphasis should be on potential young leaders or capable persons from all parts of society, especially those whose behavior might be harmful to U.S. foreign policy objectives.[31] For him, this was "a priority activity both in the field and in Washington." Abroad, the ambassador, supported by his country team and youth coordinator, was responsible for this task in combination with the various American informational, educational, and cultural services. In Washington, the IAYC would be in charge of coordinating the overseas youth programs entertained by the various departments and government agencies. Thereby, existing government resources would be centralized and used to synchronize operations. Kennedy emphasized that he looked to the IAYC for leadership in this area and wanted to be kept personally informed about progress and problems.[32] In the years that followed Kennedy's death, the IAYC continued to meet regularly. It became a permanent body seeking to evaluate and improve the country's programs aimed at foreign youth.

Cooperation with posts abroad, however, often came along slowly and with great reluctance. Survey teams and other IAYC representatives who were sent out to the field found that coordination and initiative were frequently lacking on a local level. In July 1964, this negligence prompted Secretary of State Dean Rusk to send out a personal address to American ambassadors worldwide, in which he underlined the significance of the youth effort and left no doubt about the seriousness and priority of the issue for the administration: "Young leaders have risen and are rising to power, political change is occurring, and the events with which the traditional arts of diplomacy must deal are moving with a breath-taking speed. We must broaden our horizon if we wish to gain the initiative against a resourceful and ruthless competitor in the Communist bloc and in the face of considerable disarray in our own ranks."[33] In order to succeed in this competition for the hearts and minds of foreign youth, Rusk argued that the United States had to make "a much more concerted effort to identify and exercise decisive influence on the attitudes and actions of the rising young leaders, those who are coming to power now and those who will lead the 'government after the next.' " For him, this was the central aspect of the "Emphasis on Youth" program and "a great deal more important than some of our traditional diplomacy."[34]

As a result of Rusk's intervention, working relationships with the field improved in the following years, and issues dealing with such matters as the situation of youth in developing countries, foreign students in the United States and American scholars abroad, the training of foreign military personnel, the initiation of supplementary country studies, and the establishment of an international infrastructure to secure the committee's objectives locally, became the main points on the IAYC's agenda. A report from 1964 described these efforts as "a new dimension in diplomacy . . . initiated by the Interagency Youth Committee," in which the embassies would be at the "front line."[35] The purpose of the embassies' local youth committees would thus be "first to determine priority target groups, such as university and labor unions, and then to organize a systematic approach to identifying the individuals with leadership potential from among those groups. After that, a coordinated program must be undertaken, and other resources applied."[36] Although in the first half of the decade the IAYC still focused mostly on developing countries and their student movements, the committee's activities already illustrated the critical attention given to youth in U.S. foreign policy. The IAYC provided a coordinated attempt to centralize U.S. efforts targeting foreign youth. Enjoying the support of key political figures such as Dean Rusk, Robert McNamara, David Bell, Edward Murrow, Carl Rowan, and Sargent Shriver, the committee was able to make Kennedy's "emphasis on youth" a task that already in the first half of the 1960s reached across the various branches of government.[37]

THE U.S. GOVERNMENT'S INTEREST IN EUROPEAN YOUTH

In March 1967, the 22nd Report of the U.S. Advisory Commission on Information revealed an alarming new condition concerning the coming of age of international youth:

> A new generation has come to maturity. Memories of war have faded, if they have been experienced at all. To increasing millions, the cataclysmic events of 1939–45 appear unreal. . . . The new generation is skeptical, and is not confined to the Western world. From the need for "a cultural revolution" in Communist China to warnings against Western ideological blandishments in East Europe, there is evidence that the new generation is restless, asking questions and determined to make up its own mind about the important issues of its time.[38]

According to the advisory commission, this was the new framework, "complicated and compounded by the burdens of the Vietnam war," in which the USIA and other agencies had to perform their tasks from now on. For Western European youth, where information programs had suffered massive budget cuts, the consequences of this development were particularly obvious, and the commission urged that it was therefore "indispensable to our own best interests not to appear to withdraw from this strategically important continent."[39]

Aware of these generational transformations, the Department of State and the IAYC had watched the European youth scene for some time. Originally concerned with the youth of the Third World, the focus of the IAYC shifted markedly to European youth organizations in the mid-1960s.[40] Indicative of this transition was the conducting of a country survey on European youth suggested by Harry McPherson, former chairman of the IAYC and now special assistant and counsel to President Johnson, in May 1966.[41] The need for such a study emerged when a variety of voices returning from Europe independently observed "a growing problem involving relationships with young European leaders," the foundering of "serious dialogue," and a general tendency of " 'organized estrangement' and cultural alienation."[42] Especially troubling was the fact, that, going along with this, there seemed to be a rich flow of transnational exchange among international youth groups: "The young Berkeley radicals are said to have been discussing the Provos of Amsterdam even before the general public here had heard of them; they had their own informal contacts. University students in Japan were found by a visiting Berkeley professor to be at least as well informed as he about the unrest at Berkeley *while it was going on*."[43] The underlying concern was that American events might replicate themselves on a European scene to the disadvantage of the United States: "If there is in fact an international network of contacts that embraces the New Left, SNCC, . . . what does it mean, what function does it serve, in overall relationships with European youth?"[44] Or, as Foy Kohler, former U.S. ambassador to Moscow and now chairman of the IAYC, phrased it, "[D]o contacts between America's New Left and European youth help or hurt, as far as the national interest is concerned?"[45]

The survey on European youth sought to analyze the nature of these transatlantic connections and illuminate the attitudes of Europe's future elite, as well as the efficacy of U.S. government-sponsored programs targeting them. To discuss its results, Kohler hosted a special conference on "European Youth and Young Leaders" at Airlie House in Virginia during May 14–15, 1967, bringing together representatives from the White House, various branches of the State Department (CU, Office of Intelligence and Research [INR], Bureau of European Affairs [EUR], and Undersecretary of Political Affairs [G/Y]), as well as members from the USIA, the Department of Health, Education and Welfare (HEW), and nongovernment affiliates from the Ford Foundation and academia. Since most participants were also active members of the regular IAYC meetings, the conference was also supposed to serve as a general review of cultural exchange programs with Western Europe.[46]

Based on reports about the young generation in England, France, and West Germany, conference participants generally agreed that the young generation of Europe did not share the postwar experience of their elders and "how the U.S. came to be so greatly involved in European life."[47] Times had changed considerably since the rebuilding of Europe, and the spirit of cooperation had given way to a feeling of growing skepticism toward the transatlantic partnership. Furthermore, the current image of the United States in Europe was dominated either by Hollywood or military and business associations. U.S. propaganda efforts were hardly helpful in this regard, and the common ways of "influencing" or "working on" youth had largely proven counterproductive, since the young generation did not buy into Manichean cold-war rhetoric anymore and was subjected to far more powerful media influences. What could be done instead was to increase the influx of Europeans to the United States, although this had the disadvantage of exposing them to a country shattered by campus disorders and racial conflicts. This would give European students a more comprehensive picture of the diversity of the country, even at the risk of further alienating them from the current administration's policies. Moreover, multinational programs, work on common problems through venues such as the Salzburg Seminar on American Studies, and the encouragement of institutional cooperation could help alleviate the magnitude of transatlantic estrangement. In general, the conference concluded, the approach in existing youth efforts should be differentiated enough also to include the young technocratic or professional elites. To this end, CU should revamp the exchange programs altogether. As one participant remarked, "If we want to gain insight into the kind of world in which our foreign policy will operate in the future, I don't think we should close our eyes to the serious, youthful critic."[48]

Conference participants continued to view the youth effort as an integral part of U.S. cultural diplomacy with Europe, since it provided a sound informational basis that could be relied upon in the future, despite the fact that the outcome of increased cultural and educational activities abroad could neither be predicted nor guaranteed.[49] In the case of West Germany, one of America's strongest allies in the cold-war era, this strategy seemed particularly important. The youth of the country that the United States had helped rebuild after the Second World War was now turning against its protective power, openly criticizing its involvement in Vietnam, and showing indications of a profound estrangement that, if persistent, could lead to substantial changes in the transatlantic partnership.

THE DISCOVERY OF A WEST GERMAN NEW LEFT

In the years of the Johnson administration, student unrest and West German opposition to the war in Vietnam were only secondary issues in German-American relations. Although President Johnson was eager to secure West German assistance to the war effort from Chancellor Ludwig Erhard, there were other, far more pressing, problems that greatly overshadowed any evaluation of domestic unrest in the Federal Republic. These issues included the Multilateral Force and the Non-Proliferation Treaty, offsets for military costs and the balance of payment, American troop reductions in West Germany, East German threats toward Berlin, as well as the Soviet invasion of Czechoslovakia in August 1968.[50] All the while, American officials continued to evaluate internal dissent in West Germany precisely in terms of its effect on these more far-reaching foreign policy considerations, and the overall concern for the future of transatlantic relations and the efforts of détente with the Soviet Union.

In August 1966, a USIA opinion research paper had already grasped the division of public opinion in the Federal Republic with regard to Vietnam, detecting that "a noisy left-wing minority opposes everything we do and is impervious to any explanation of U.S. policy."[51] Although discernable throughout the whole country, the most vocal expression of antiwar sentiment prevailed in West Berlin, where a growing number of people began to reject the analogy between Berlin and Saigon, an analogy prominently propagated by Chancellor Erhard and by U.S. officials.[52] From the USIA's perspective, a small student minority in the city who regarded the Viet Cong as resistance fighters against American imperialists, would spread "Communist clichés and slogans."[53]

In November of 1966, historian Fritz Stern went to West Germany to survey West German youth, their attitude toward the United States, and the extent of their communications with Americans for the IAYC report on European youth.[54] Contracted by the State Department, the German-born professor from Columbia University spent two weeks talking to more than one hundred people, including academics, journalists, university students, and representatives from various youth and student organizations in major German cities.[55] In his report from January 1967, Stern concluded, "The United States has become marginal to German students; their curiosity about us has notably declined; . . . we are no longer the bright hope of a new era such as President Kennedy once more exemplified."[56] Stern was struck by the general resemblance of adult and student attitudes on this issue, although he admitted that there is "a tiny minority of radical left-wing dissenters among German students who are violently critical of existing institutions and skeptical of all adult authority."[57]

In contrast to the cliché of an apolitical and apathetic youth, he found this particular segment of West German students a very vocal and public example of political activism. He argued that "[b]y virtue of their organization and superior tactics, these left-wing groups exercise a disproportionate influence on student governments and university life."[58] The publicity they had gained through their provocative actions could, however, not hide the fact that groups such as the German SDS were very much factionalized along ideological lines. Although SDS members viewed themselves as "the spearhead of the radical democrats in the struggle for a new university and a new society," their actions were only a reflection of the fact that German youth in general had, according to Stern, lost interest in the United States, and a feeling of growing apart had set in.[59] Stern saw the rise of this sentiment as independent from the war in Vietnam, although the opposition against it drove and united criticism of the United States across political lines: "The left condemns it as an extreme example of American neo-colonialism, and the right, as an example of America's irresolute pursuit of its own ends. . . . [T]here is no doubt that the vast majority of students, which is not yet anti-American, is deeply disturbed by the brutality of the war and unpersuaded of its necessity."[60] Allegations of CIA activities targeting Free University students actively involved in the antiwar movement were further evidence for Stern that youthful opposition against the war in Vietnam was only a symptom of a much larger estrangement, which included a "widespread German suspicion that McCarthyism in its widest sense has not yet disappeared from the American scene."[61]

In January 1967, the U.S. mission in West Berlin reported more extensively on these "Red Guards of Berlin," as this group had been labeled by the press. In a lengthy assessment, it discerned a new quality of protest among them: "The Berlin Maoists do not limit themselves to protests against the FU administration or US Vietnam policy. Instead, they call for violent opposition to all forms of authority now existing in the West."[62] The mission ironically pointed out that the student group from the Free University (FU) supposedly followed a loose Maoist philosophy and embraced Marxism while rejecting the East German and Soviet variants of it. Its members were, however, "deadly serious when they talk of revolution," and numbered about two to three hundred supporters dissatisfied with current conditions. To oppose the society they lived in and counter its authoritarianism, they drew on "Viet Cong tactics" and revolutionary actions inspired by the Amsterdam "Provos," and proposed the founding of a commune and an alternative university.

The mission characterized the student left's apparent leader, Rudi Dutschke, as "chief ideologist of the SDS 'terror group'" and as "the citizens' terror incarnate," mainly agreeing with the image of Dutschke painted by the Berlin tabloid *BZ*.[63] Even his outward appearance underlined his radical posture: "He is short, thin and extremely unkempt; his voice is loud and hoarse, and he seems to go into [a] trance when speaking. Dutschke's harangues often contain factual errors and logical inconsistencies. His admirers, however, seem to feel that his passion and audacity more than compensate for these shortcomings."[64] In the mission's estimate, his group dominated the SDS, although they did not enjoy unwavering support for their actions from all parts of the leftist movement. Despite the fact that most of the protesters were students at the Free University, their provocations, according to the mission, should rather be considered "a determined attempt by a very small group of fanatics to initiate a political movement against authority in general," their objectives being the Berlin and West German government. Because of the American engagement in Vietnam, the United States simply happened to be "a natural whipping boy."[65] Although university and city authorities had previously exercised restraint in dealing with student demonstrations, mission officials saw an overreaction on the part of these authorities as the greatest threat posed by the student actions.

The "Pudding" assassination and student demonstrations during the visit of Vice President Hubert Humphrey to West Berlin in April 1967 confirmed this judgment. The night before Humphrey's visit, West Berlin police arrested eleven students, eight of whom were members of the Kommune I, for a planned conspiracy with the intent of assassinating the vice president. The next morning, the Berlin tabloid newspapers' front-page headlines reported the successful police operation that had thwarted the supposed attempt on Humphrey's life, an assassination that reportedly was to be accomplished with the help of bombs and other material from East Berlin or Peking.[66] Only one day later, the students had to be set free after pudding, yogurt, and ingredients for butter tart were found among them instead of the suspected explosives. At a press conference, the members of the Kommune I explained their intention of throwing baked goods at the vice president, referring to similar provocation techniques used by the Provos in Amsterdam.

Whereas the whole incident led only to a small article in the *New York Times*, the so-called "Pudding-Attentat" was the final wake-up call for the Department of State that the opposition to the war in Vietnam in the Federal Republic had reached a level that mandated further action.[67] Disillusioned by his reception in Europe, Vice President Humphrey himself was concerned by the profound alienation and possible total loss of support from European youth because of the war in Vietnam. As he wrote in his report to President Johnson, "At the heart of our effort must be a special outreach to the younger generation of Europeans. From all indications, the younger generation of Europe—just as our own younger generation—is idealistic, restless, outward-looking, and willing to give far more than it takes. We must increase our contacts with this younger generation and do a far better communication job than we have done thus far. As in our country, the postwar baby crop is coming to political influence at the ballot box."[68] Humphrey therefore recommended a strengthening of youth exchange programs; a view that he underlined during the next meeting of the National Security Council.[69]

By mid-1967, the West German New Left and its loud opposition to American policy had thus jumped to the attention of various U.S. agencies and was, not least because of the Pudding-Attentat, seen as a political force to be reckoned with in West German society. Fritz Stern had already predicted at the beginning of 1967 the unlikelihood of a fast nationwide university reform and noted that the current form of student unrest was only in its infancy and was a "spreading condition."[70] This estimate was soon reconfirmed by local American missions, who began to report extensively on local student disruptions and protest activities. In the second half of 1967, U.S. officials in the state of Baden-Württemberg, for example, registered visits of Vietnamese representatives to Heidelberg, protests concerning the Nazi past of State Premier Hans Filbinger at the inauguration of the new rector of Mannheim University, and general efforts at university reform.[71] As one report concluded, student unrest "is a real factor in the day to day affairs of the universities and student politics in Baden-Wuerttemberg."[72] American diplomatic posts in other parts of the country similarly observed student discontent, such as the fare increases in public transportation in Kiel and Bremen, which led to militant demonstrations

IMAGE 19. Headline in one of Berlin's leading daily tabloids, the *BILD-Zeitung* (April 6, 1967): "Berlin: Bomb-Attack on US Vice President" (Axel Springer Verlag)

in both cities at the beginning of 1968.[73] In Bremen, Senator of the Interior Loebert even inquired of American Consul General Goodman about the equipment, techniques, and strategies used to confront riots and demonstrations in the United States, eager to benefit from the experience gained by American police departments.[74]

By the spring of 1968, American officials dedicated more time and resources to an extensive monitoring of the West German student movement, whose reverberations reached into various areas of American interest. As a consequence, the reporting efforts of the local youth committees increased rapidly. Dennis Kux, political officer in Bonn during 1966–69, for example, was specifically assigned the task of monitoring the political attitudes of students from the American embassy: "I spent time on university campuses trying to understand the student movement. However, dealing with the student 'Left' was rather a specialized thing. . . . I went to some of the conventions and the offices of the student movement. I met with the leaders; I sought out what their ideas were—very much as a newspaperman would do. Then I would come back to the Embassy and write up a report."[75] That these investigations were not always painless is illustrated by an example from Hamburg, where Foreign Service Officer Ronald Humphrey joined an anti-Vietnam demonstration on March 21, 1968, in order to give a first-hand account of the demonstrators' tactics and strategy, as well as police reaction.[76] While dashing through the streets, he was nearly swept into the Springer House by the demonstrating masses and suffered bruises to his arms and legs. But despite these surveillance and information efforts on the part of American officials, there often remained a personal inability to understand the students' motives. As Kux recalled, "The whole student viewpoint seemed strange to me. . . . I read their writings, and it just went right by me. I could report on it because I knew what the people were saying, but for the life of me, I never really understood it."[77]

THE EFFECT OF STUDENT MILITANCY
ON THE INTERNAL STABILITY OF WEST GERMANY

After American posts had gained detailed knowledge of the West German student movement, the impact of its growing militancy on the Federal Republic and the possible repercussions it might have on transatlantic relations became one of their major concerns. In the aftermath of the shooting of Rudi Dutschke on April 11, 1968, when severe demonstrations and clashes with the police occurred all over the country, American officials stepped up their surveillance. Attempting to put this new level of unrest into perspective, the American embassy in Bonn argued that only a limited number of people (about 10,000) were involved in these "Easter riots" and that they did not seem to reach other segments of society. The large-scale mobilization of the "masses" proclaimed by the demonstrators had therefore turned out to be a failure. The embassy also rejected any comparison of the events with the street violence during the Weimar Republic. In contrast to Weimar, 1960s West Germany did not experience a combination of economic crisis, general desperation, and revolutionary atmosphere: "At present, student unrest takes place against a background of placid social climate and this contrast contributes to the general bewilderment about the SDS' resort to violence."[78] Based on this assessment, the embassy predicted that student militancy would gradually fade away, also due to the relatively modest response by the security forces.

Somewhat relieved, the American posts noted that as a result of the riots the focus of attention had shifted from the U.S. involvement in Vietnam toward the West German authorities, the Springer press, and the upcoming emergency legislation.[79] This change of focus and the riots themselves alienated a large part of the population, whose initial sympathy with the students after the shooting now turned into firm antipathy. According to the embassy, the student actions had turned Springer into a martyr.[80] This loss of public favor and their increasing use of violence were the reasons why the students had not been able to enlist the support of the workers and trade unions.[81]

The eruption of student protest in Paris in May 1968 changed the picture. American diplomats feared that West German students could imitate their French counterparts in an outreach to workers as the former campaigned against the planned ratification of the emergency law bill in parliament. According to a report from the U.S. embassy, "The radical left and the extra-parliamentary opposition are clearly exhilarated by the French example of parallel, if not necessarily joint, student-worker activities which is also their goal. The current debate on emergency legislation provides a tailor-made issue on which to test the extent to which workers can be mobilized here."[82] Although U.S. officials considered the odds for mobilizing large segments of the population rather small, they watched the opposition against the emergency laws very closely, keeping in mind the element of surprise exhibited by the French example. But despite the fact that students at the FU Berlin and across the country were "apparently trying hard to emulate their French colleagues"[83] in their protest against the emergency laws, their actions were often more colorful than militant and could not quite reach the same intensity. The U.S. mission in Berlin, for example, described a nationwide student strike and boycott of classes on May 15 more like a campus happening: "Red Flags flew from several vantage points, one even being used as a goal for a soccer match between commune members Langhans, Teufel, Kunzelmann, and co." In the mission's estimate, students were not prepared to cross the line from verbal to militant protest since "the emotional element so often necessary for violent action was lacking."[84] Even the visit of French student leader Daniel Cohn-Bendit to the FU Berlin on May 22 was surprisingly tepid. Mission officials described the audience as relatively unemotional and lukewarm. The differences between French and West German student activists and the extent of revolutionary enthusiasm in the city was clearly reflected in the unwillingness of students even to serve as guards for the by-then student-occupied Japan Institute at the Free University. This prompted the moderator to ask during Cohn-Bendit's visit "what good it did to applaud stories of barricades in Paris if Berlin students would not defend even one small villa in Dahlem."[85]

Witnessing these discussions, American posts realized that the "permanent revolt" proclaimed by German SDS in the remaining time before the ratification of the emergency legislation in parliament fell far short of its rhetoric. Students across the country were unable to broaden their protest to include the general public. Even worse, they often ran into outright hostility. An SDS demonstration in Wedding, for example, erupted into fists fights with local construction workers.[86] At the end of May, the American embassy in Bonn could therefore assure Washington that, despite the turbulent domestic situation, "the balance in Germany is likely to remain on the side of stability."[87] In the embassy's view, protest activities launched by West German students had already reached "serious proportions" before the outbreak in France, but did not operate in the same environment.[88] Historically, revolutions from below had never succeeded in Germany, and, although this could certainly change, the social peace was by and large undisturbed in comparison to France, with the federal political system functioning in a "satisfactory manner." German workers, the embassy argued, tended to be conservative and mostly hostile to the students, apart from local exceptions such as Frankfurt, where the left-wing of the SPD and the trade unions cooperated with them. Furthermore, the embassy considered the division of Germany another reason for a suppression of violence, since "major weaknesses in the Fedrep could be exploited by the other side."[89]

In consequence, American officials determined that student unrest in the Federal Republic would not reach the same magnitude as in neighboring France and that the negative impact on American interests remained manageable. In his final report of June 1968, the departing ambassador to Germany, George McGhee, stressed that the strong domestic opposition to the war in Vietnam had not resulted in a broad-based rejection of the United States: "We still have a reservoir of good will among the German people and strong support among government and party leaders." In the face of France's internal instability, created by student unrest, McGhee considered it likely that West Germany would seek even closer ties with the United States.[90] Despite this conclusion, however, McGhee understood the similarities of student dissent in West Germany and the United States and knew that both could not be taken lightheartedly.[91] As he commented during a German-American friendship week in Bremen at the beginning of May, "While your problems and ours differ, they should unite us in a recognition of the continuing challenge of maintaining a stable democratic system—which is at the same time responsive to a changing environment."[92] The growing militancy of the West German protest movement after the Easter riots in April and the passage of the emergency laws in May, as well as the almost complete collapse of communication between students and elected officials, were extremely worrisome to American officials. For them, the sharp increase in militancy was a result of the rising frustration and helplessness on the side of the protesters, which resulted in a challenge to the democratic process. As the U.S. mission phrased it, "The principal danger at present is that the overwhelming evidence of their isolation may prompt some radicals to go all-out for a sensationally violent confrontation with the establishment."[93] And in the Federal Republic student protesters were nowhere as isolated in geographical and political terms as in West Berlin.

THE BERLIN PROBLEM

During the cold war, the city of Berlin occupied a central place in German-American relations.[94] The material aid of the airlift and the military protection during the Berlin crisis in 1948/49 strongly bonded its citizens to the United States. This bond, although dented by the American inaction toward the building of the wall in 1961, was prevalent throughout the 1960s. Americans were cheered at military parades, and their presence and cultural influence were embraced by its population, which thereby compensated for its peculiar insularity on the front line of the global bloc confrontation.

From the American perspective, Berlin was a symbol of U.S. leadership of the Western alliance in the cold war and its commitment to freedom.[95] In 1950, the International Congress for Cultural Freedom had already declared the city as an outpost of the Western struggle against communist tyranny. Embodiment of this defiance was the foundation of the Free University of Berlin (FU) in 1948 with the firm support of U.S. military governor Lucius Clay in reaction to communist censorship at the traditional Humboldt University located in East Berlin.[96] Heavily subsidized by the Ford Foundation, the Free University became a symbol for transatlantic unity and the defense of academic liberties and Western values. In contrast to its Eastern opponent, its statute allowed for the democratic participation of students in the university bodies, drawing on the idea of students and professors as equal partners in the scientific endeavor. Founded on an anti-totalitarian and anticommunist understanding, the FU viewed itself as an institution that strongly supported democracy and equality inside as well as outside the academic realm.

In the mid-1960s, students began to contest this foundational consensus. Inspired by the Free Speech Movement (FSM) in Berkeley, they claimed unrestrained political expression on campus and a political mandate of student representatives. At the same time, the international antiwar movement against the war in Vietnam took hold among students, who began to criticize the city's protector. Yet any opposition to American policies in this symbolic city did not only provoke a public outcry. Such criticism was also politically explosive for German-American relations, since it fundamentally questioned the close association of the two countries at a time when the cold war was believed to have come to a halt. Protesting students not only cast doubt on the ideological legitimacy of the protective power, but were also a factor of instability and challenged the Allied role of governing the city and ensuring its order and security. It was in this extraordinary setting that the student movement in Berlin posed a serious strategic concern for American officials.

The events surrounding the visit of Vice President Humphrey in April 1967 had laid bare the public rift in the city concerning the support of American policy in Vietnam. Mission officials identified students at the FU as the most vocal expression of antiwar sentiment and criticism of the United States and they considered these "Red Guards" part of the general New Left movement. In its first detailed dossier of May 1967, the mission interpreted the New Left in Berlin as an expression of a generational rebellion against the hierarchical and impersonal nature of society, a consequence of the German past and its lack of democratic spirit, and as a response to worsening economic conditions for students. The fact that it crystallized in Berlin was explained by the city's position between two different ideological blocs, greater political student participation, the exemption from military service, and the unmatched opportunities for getting press attention. The mission clearly rejected the idea of communist control of the movement and ascertained that the New Left would remain a political factor in the city. It also cautioned, however, that "Berlin is not on the verge of a permanent revolution of the Masses," and proposed an increase of communication with the New Left to avoid further escalation of the situation.[97]

According to the mission's assessment, the New Left in Berlin was best defined as "an attitude, a *Weltanschauung*, shared by an undetermined number of Berlin youths and characterized chiefly by a rejection of everything accepted or valued by modern society."[98] The movement was not held together by any formal organization, and its supporters were highly diverse, ranging up to the mid-thirties in age. Its core group amounted to around fifty people with 200 to 300 active participants at its events, which could draw an additional 800 to 3,000 sympathizers depending on the issue. In political terms, the New Left encompassed a "philosophical Marxism" with a romantic edge to it and included "elements of anarchism, nihilism, existentialism and a host of other 'isms,' thrown together in a hodgepodge devoid of logical structure."[99] In other words, the New Left perceived the world as inherently dehumanizing and ruled by "establishments." These governing regimes exploited and manipulated the "masses" and reduced society's values and institutions to uphold this machinery. One of the New Left's goals was to initiate a change, "awaken the masses," and "destroy the Establishments." To achieve this, its method was a calculated overstepping of society's rules: "It says, in effect, that you *can* fight city hall if you don't use city hall's rules. . . . The Establishment, ridiculed and frustrated, will finally drop its mask of tolerance and resort to force, thereby declaring the bankruptcy of its authority."[100] This insight into the underlying violent nature of their society would pave the way for a liberation of the masses and the establishment of a socialist democratic system.

The firm anti-anticommunism of the New Left was, in the eyes of mission officials, another characteristic feature. Although New Left representatives often assumed equivalence of freedoms and repressions in Eastern and Western societies, the mission affirmed that the students' contacts with East Germany were marked by skepticism and functionality. The students largely viewed democracy in either East or West as window-dressing, hiding the mechanisms of control and manipulation. American democracy, for example, *appeared* to be more democratic, although the claims of protest movements in the United States and the "genocidal" war in Vietnam provided ample evidence to the contrary. The West German New Left thus, according to the mission, viciously refused the analogy between Berlin and Saigon in terms of U.S. commitment: "They hasten to say that they are not anti-American and do not want the US to leave West Berlin. But they view the commitment to Vietnam as only a hypocritical pact made by the US with an authoritarian puppet regime. Ho Chi Minh, they add with fine irrelevance, is no Stalin."[101]

Apart from Vietnam, the New Left's call for university reform was a major reason for its wide attraction. Students claimed that the academy was still shaped by authoritarian structures at all levels and financially difficult to afford for large segments of society. Their confrontational style and provocations in pushing this issue had, however, ambiguous effects: on the one hand, it often blocked the success of viable reform efforts; on the other hand, it caused a negative reaction on the part of the professors that seemed to reconfirm the New Left's criticism of the traditional hierarchical atmosphere at West German universities.[102] Although the mission expressed admiration for the fraternal atmosphere among the New Left and the genuine character of its worries and aspirations, it also highlighted its democratic shortcomings. Especially during public discussions, New Left representatives would often voice their disagreements by making random noise or using other forms of obstruction, which could even include the physical removal of their opponents from the podium. Conversely, in more formal settings such as the FU student government, they often employed a certain double-standard with regard to adherence of legal procedures when it benefited their own aims. As the mission summed it up, "New Leftists in contact with reality are arrogant, opinionated, unfair and remarkably stuffy." This could prove to be so irritating that the "Amsterdam Provos, imported to teach the New Left that protest can be fun, reportedly soon left in disgust."[103]

In sum, the U.S. mission's analysis stands out as a perceptive and in-depth examination of the New Left as it presented itself in May 1967. Remarkable in its deep insights into the movement's ideological interior, it set the tone for later treatment of the issue by U.S. officials stationed in Berlin and provided the Department of State with an early and comprehensive picture of the emerging student movement in the city. This picture was complicated because of the diverse American presence in Berlin. Next to the occupying military force itself, a constant influx of American culture enriched the city's atmosphere in the 1960s. With the beginning of the antiwar movement in the United States, American citizens living in Berlin also started to protest openly the war in Vietnam—in a city that was of unique symbolic value for the United States in the cold war. Particularly the U.S. Campaign to End the War in Vietnam and its founders, Peter Standish and Francis Fuller, caught the attention of American officials when they approached the U.S. mission and USIS for a police permit to begin weekly protest marches in the American sector starting on April 29.[104] To generate antiwar support among other U.S. citizens living in Berlin, Standish and Fuller had used circular letters and posters, which were also distributed to U.S. military personnel. The marches they now tried to organize would be limited to U.S. citizens and banners protesting U.S. foreign policy and calling for a neutralization of Vietnam. The organizers' plan to carry an enormous American flag at the head of the demonstration, however, posed a serious problem for U.S. diplomats who were alarmed at the idea of having this national symbol exploited for supposedly "anti-American" purposes in a city where the image of American protection and determination was essential.

To prevent this, mission officials requested that the Berlin Senate grant a demonstration permit only on the condition that a U.S. flag would not be exhibited. When Fuller and Standish rejected this proposal, the senate was unable to refuse a permit on legal grounds unless U.S. authorities issued a respective order. For the mission, such an order carried even greater risks since "a US-imposed limitation on demonstrations may trigger a renewal of anti-Vietnam demonstrations by Berlin students and other young people. It may also cause some students who have hitherto opposed US policy in Vietnam to begin demonstrating against US policy in Berlin as well." In addition, the mission feared that it might have to explain "why US authorities in Berlin cannot permit US citizens to take action (carrying the flag in such a demonstration) which could not be prohibited in the United States."[105] In spite of these serious objections, the mission, in its message to the State Department, recommended such a ban, since many Berliners and Americans would question U.S. judgment and authority if they found out that such a display could have been prevented. In addition, the mission worried that the use of a U.S. flag might cause public disturbances, or that the police might not be able intervene before any desecration took place. Such a permit would therefore not be "in keeping with the city's special status and situation."[106] To prepare for a permit application in the other sectors, the mission also consulted with the other Western Allies. Surprisingly, both suggested a potential expulsion of the people in question and while the French also agreed to a ban, the British pointed to problems similar to those raised by the mission.[107] The Department of State, however, disagreed with all these deliberations feeling that any "attempts at suppression of demonstration or denial of permission to carry flags would probably get even worse and longer-lasting publicity." It therefore decided that any Allied interference should be avoided unless there was a major security threat. Only in cases of misuse or burning of the flag should the police be called upon to intervene.[108]

This, however, did not turn out to be necessary. About seventy demonstrators marched behind the U.S. flag carrying a banner which read, "Neutralize Vietnam: End the bombing and withdraw all foreign troops—let Vietnam live" on April 29, 1967, and, according to the U.S. mission, received comparatively little public attention.[109] On June 18, 1967, the U.S. Campaign organized another protest march past the American Consulate and submitted an open letter to President Johnson calling for an end to the bombing, for the withdrawal of American troops, and for peace negotiations.[110] These open displays of dissent by American citizens in Berlin continued in the following years, and their demonstrations frequently merged with the activities of West German students. The demonstrations of the U.S. campaign in the summer of 1967, however, marked the first instance where American and Allied officials seriously considered

IMAGE 20. U.S. Campaign members voice their protest against the war in Vietnam in a demonstration leading to the city hall in Steglitz, Berlin, April 29, 1967 (Landesarchiv Berlin)

prohibiting antiwar protest and thereby interfering with the civil government of Berlin. From now on, antiwar protest and student disorder, whether imported from the United States or locally developed, became political and security issues that the Allies were hard-pressed to avoid in their administration of the divided city.

The killing of Benno Ohnesorg by a Berlin policeman on June 2, 1967, and the subsequent riots increased the concerns of the Allied powers. In the monthly meeting of Allied representatives on June 9, the French official noted that the situation had reached a point where the Allied Powers should start considering possible reactions and strategies to confront continuing student unrest, especially because of obvious student contact "with the East."[111] Only two weeks later, the students addressed the Allied commanders directly. In an open letter ratified by the FU student government they demanded that, in light of the events of June 2 and the impending emergency legislation, the Allied powers should safeguard the democracy and security of the city. In the students' opinion, any extension of the emergency legislation threatened the constitution of Berlin. For them, it was not the existence of an extra-parliamentary opposition and the exercise of their constitutional rights that were harmful to the democratic order in Berlin, but the actions of the senate that suppressed the right of free assembly and permitted police brutality. The resolution contended, "West Berlin lives from its claim and its mission to be a 'show window of freedom.' The Federal Emergency Legislation has the potential of shattering this window."[112]

The U.S. mission in Berlin interpreted the letter as one of many in a history of controversial student resolutions in Berlin, the latest of which had condemned U.S. policies in Vietnam as "criminal."[113] It saw the initiative as an attempt by the SDS to create publicity and sympathy for their cause and protest against the forthcoming disciplinary actions against several of its members. American officials therefore chose to ignore the letter to prevent the opening of a dialogue between students and Allied officials: "Any Allied reply would have been useful to the extremists: if favorable, it would imply Allied agreement with student criticism of the Berlin and Federal government; if unfavorable, it would substantiate what some extremists have been saying *sotto voce*, namely that the Allies are not interested in 'real democracy' in West Berlin."[114]

In the following weeks, the Allied Kommandantura, however, discussed the student disorders in Berlin extensively with Mayor Heinrich Albertz and representatives from the senate. A draft policy paper prepared by the U.S. mission listed various means of confronting the issue, which included, among other things, "an Allied ban on demonstrations, dismissal of civil officials, expulsion of undesirable persons, and the closure of the universities."[115] While asserting their right to take any measures guaranteeing the security and maintenance of order in Berlin, the Allied powers did not yet consider these steps necessary. They rather tried to circumvent any direct Allied control or operative involvement in dealing with student unrest.[116] From their perspective, acting in the background through bilateral talks with the mayor and senate representatives was much more efficient. It also prohibited senate officials from diverting responsibilities for their actions to the Allies and would counteract already existing rumors of Allied concern over student unrest. In short, American officials concluded that the Allies "should only intervene if the dispute reaches such magnitude that it clearly endangers the future of West Berlin itself. At that point, our intervention should be clear, unequivocal and publicly justifiable."[117]

Fearful of a further escalation of the situation, the U.S. mission in Berlin intensified its reporting of events related to student unrest in the second half of 1967. After the tensions following the death of Benno Ohnesorg had somewhat calmed, the U.S. mission warned that the fundamental problem "is unchanged, and trouble could flare up again at any time."[118] A topic that, in the mission's estimate, might ignite this spark was the compromised past of the new FU rector, Ewaldt Harndt, who had been active in various National Socialist professional and party organizations. Although there had not been any public mention of his personal background in July 1967, the mission already feared student protest as well as propaganda campaigns from the East after Harndt took office. What was even more significant, U.S. officials believed that Harndt was thin-skinned and likely to respond sharply to any of the students' attacks and concerns so that his "little talent for coping with student matters, and an unsavoury political past" made him essentially unsuitable to deal with the problem.[119]

A demonstration on October 21, 1967, on Kurfürstendamm was an illustration of what the U.S. mission saw as a further radicalization of the student movement. The "Day of International Protest against the War in Vietnam" brought about not only protest activities in Berlin, but also in many other countries. Most notably it was the same day that 100,000 antiwar protesters marched on the Pentagon. In Berlin, American officials were mostly concerned about the proximity of the demonstration to the local America House and the First National Bank, as well as the involve-ment of the U.S. Campaign.[120] The demonstration attracted around 7,000 people and remained peaceful until about 1,500 demonstrators returned to the Kurfürstendamm to block major intersections after the final rally.[121] The local authorities tried to deescalate the situation by restraining the police and limiting the use of water cannons, and the crowd was even-tually dispersed.

The Berlin press viewed the mostly peaceful demonstration as a poten-tial turning point in protest behavior, since the more radical factions had suffered a defeat. American officials, however, had a different interpreta-tion of the events. They pointed to the fact that for the first time a substan-tial crowd ready to defy police orders had come back after the demonstra-tion and withstood the water cannons for several hours, turning their usage into a spectacle. The fact that the demonstrators could be forced to retreat only by newly arriving riot police was extremely worrisome, be-cause "if riot police prove to be the only convincing form of deterrent force, future demonstrations may result in more violence than occurred Oct 21."[122] For the U.S. mission, the events therefore signaled an increase in militancy. After all, Dutschke, who, according to mission reports, had by then "emerged as the leader and prophet of what he sees as a genuine revolution," had previously shown that he was very capable of utilizing crowds for his own purposes. In addition, a hardening confrontational attitude among protesters seemed to have built up after June 2, which saw the "revolution" as bound to succeed: "The SDS intention to provoke police to the maximum possible extent is based on the belief that the revolutionary movement has nothing to lose no matter how the authori-ties react. SDS leaders anticipate that a serious clash with the police would reinforce and increase student solidarity with the radicals, as occurred after June 2."[123]

(a)

(b)

IMAGE 21. Antiwar demonstration on the Kurfürstendamm in West Berlin, October 21, 1967. (a) View of Kurfürstendamm leading to the Kaiser Wilhelm Memorial Church (AP/bpk). (b) Demonstrators holding antiwar picket signs (Ullstein bild/The Granger Collection, New York)

The acquittal of Karl-Heinz Kurras in November 1967, the policeman charged with killing student Benno Ohnesorg, further aggravated the situation. The students, enraged by the verdict, interrupted the first appearance of the new Governing Mayor Klaus Schütz and his initial meeting with a student audience through shouts, the unfurling of protest banners, and rhythmic clapping. In the eyes of the mission, the verdict had the effect of reuniting the students after the semester breaks and invigorating further demonstrations, and it could, with regard to the SPD's efforts to include students in the drafting of a new university law, "negate what little progress the party had made in the past months toward stimulating a meaningful dialogue with students."[124]

At the same time, American officials also detected a growing impatience in the public reception of student actions over the summer. When about twenty-five SDS students were protesting against the Vietnam War at the annual open house of the Tempelhof Air Force Base on July 16, their placards were torn up by angry visitors. The mission concluded that "given the continuing antipathy of the broad masses of Berliners against radical students, demonstrations of this character are likely to be ill received." Visitors to American-sponsored events such as these were mostly impressed by the hospitality they received, and would consider antiwar protest to be "decidedly out of place and in bad taste."[125] Yet another incident occurred at a demonstration during a U.S. troop parade in Neukölln on August 19. Practicing a different form of "direct action," bystanders were quick to attack antiwar demonstrators, who were distributing leaflets and carrying banners that declared their solidarity with the Viet Cong. Interpreting their rally as an insult to the American troops and the Allied powers protecting Berlin, some Neukölln citizens "assisted" the police in intervening and removing the demonstrators by assaulting them. The tensions reached a point where some of the demonstrators had to call for police protection.[126] According to the mission, this physical backlash undertaken by Berliners constituted a different quality in the public reaction to student unrest that was especially troubling. Although gratifying to many Berliners and policemen who were frustrated with the protesting students, "it adds another unwelcome element to the Senate's already difficult problems with radical youth. Governing Mayor Albertz has remarked to us privately that the problem of how to control the 'honest psychological reactions' of the Berlin population causes him at least as much concern as the problem of controlling student disturbances."[127]

To deescalate the situation and defuse increasing polarization in the city early on, the U.S. mission had made extra efforts to keep in close contact with city officials and listen to the students' grievances. On May 22, 1967, for example, Ambassador McGhee hosted a dinner for fifteen students from the FU and Technical University (TU). Most of them, including the conservative factions, not only expressed strong criticism of the U.S. involvement in Vietnam but also agreed that a substantial educational reform was indispensable. Although the students differed about the ways to achieve it, mission officials were surprised by this open and rational exchange and the forum they had provided for both sides: "They [the students] clearly welcomed the opportunity to acquaint the Ambassador and US Mission officers with their thoughts on the German university. Mission officers who had attended previous US-sponsored student evenings found the students on this occasion to be unusually open and enthusiastic about discussing university problems."[128]

The mission often hosted receptions or dinners during which American officials could exchange views on student unrest with local government or university representatives.[129] This also included obtaining first-hand information from party nonconformists such as Harry Ristock from the Berlin SPD, who sympathized with the students' attitudes.[130] This form of observation of the establishment's attitudes to student protest was not limited to Berlin. Other American posts also used lunches or other meetings to keep a close watch on public reactions and political evaluations of the "student problem." The American consulate in Hamburg, for example, would constantly, even in the years to come, keep in very close touch with the mayor, party officials, as well as university professors in order to gain a more comprehensive picture of the situation and extensively monitor the opinion of government officials in the region.[131]

Student unrest in Berlin even became a topic in German-American bilateral talks. In July 1967, a Soviet note to the Allies brought the matter to the attention of the White House in conjunction with the West German emergency legislation. The Soviet Union, through its Ambassador Pyotr Abrasimov, had protested against the extension of the emergency legislation to West Berlin, since it would, in his country's view, violate the Potsdam agreement. For Abrasimov, "[t]he bloody dispersal of the peaceful demonstration of June 2" during the Shah's visit and the killing of Benno Ohnesorg were proof for the restriction of democratic rights in West Berlin.[132] When Walt Rostow, President Johnson's Special Assistant for National Security Affairs, requested further information on the matter, his staff informed him that the emergency laws were a divisive issue in West Germany that had antagonized various political circles and student groups. The Soviets wanted to capitalize on that, and their protest could be seen as "an encouragement and propaganda play directed at these groups."[133]

The issue of youthful disruptions in Berlin was therefore already present in Washington when West German Chancellor Kurt Kiesinger arrived for comprehensive talks with President Johnson in August 1967.[134] Before their meeting, both Francis Bator, Deputy Special Assistant to the President and senior National Security Council member, and Secretary of State Dean Rusk encouraged the president to elaborate on his own domestic difficulties with student protest, thereby illustrating American attentiveness to the city's tense situation.[135] As a briefing paper by, among others, the Country Director for Germany Alfred Puhan illustrated, the State Department itself was puzzled by the situation of the city: "Berlin today is a paradox. The city faces no readily apparent external threat and yet it is the scene of more internal trouble than any time in the last fifteen years."[136] The problems of the city were summed up as follows: an aging population, few things for young people to do, a feeling of economic insecurity, a lack of complete trust and reliance on the Allied powers except in times of crimes, growing isolation, and the "uninspiring leadership" of Mayor Albertz. These problems would result in "ever greater and angrier student demonstrations" comparable to those in the United States, which were possibly also funded by the East. The department particularly blamed bad leadership for the escalation of the disruptions after the killing of Benno Ohnesorg. It even predicted that a possible ousting of Mayor Albertz due to internal party rivalries as well as the "extensive Nazi background" of the new FU rector could only aggravate the situation. As a consequence, the Allies could potentially be forced to interfere with the city's government to maintain public order "if the student demonstrations become more violent or if the students attempt to bring about confrontations with Allied personnel."[137]

In his conversations with Secretary of State Dean Rusk, Willy Brandt, now West Germany's Minister of Foreign Affairs, also brought up the topic of declining morale and student unrest in Berlin. Referring to a perceived softening of the cold-war confrontation among youth, Brandt argued that "the mission which students had in earlier years, to attack the wall, to help East Germans escape, was gone." Rusk agreed that this lack of purpose might have an effect on the political climate of the city and suggested that "some psychological actions" in order to ameliorate the situation should be discussed with the mayor when he came to Washington in October.[138] In contrast to Brandt, Chancellor Kurt Georg Kiesinger, on the other hand, avoided the subject and instead referred to an opinion poll arguing that the number of Germans favoring closer cooperation with the United States had actually risen from January to June 1967.[139]

Mayor Albertz did not, however, make it to the United States in October. As the State Department had predicted, he declared his resignation on September 26, 1967. Klaus Schütz, state secretary in the foreign ministry, succeeded him the following month and planned to visit Washington in late January 1968 to meet possible American investors. Both Dean Rusk and the U.S. mission in Berlin stressed that a meeting with the president on this occasion would greatly boost the city's morale and counterbalance the impression that "the US is less interested in Berlin because of its preoccupation with Vietnam."[140]

Further student protests in Berlin soon occupied the American officials more than the mayor's visit. On Christmas Eve 1967, student leader Rudi Dutschke tried to give a speech from the pulpit of the Kaiser Wilhelm Memorial Church on the American war in Vietnam during the service but was hindered by an attack of angry churchgoers.[141] Due to detailed intelligence information from the State Office for the Protection of the Constitution (Landesamt für Verfassungsschutz), subsequent student actions scheduled for New Year's Eve against the America House (Amerikahaus), the U.S. consulate, and U.S. military installations, could be obstructed in a joint effort by local police and Allied personnel.[142] Soon thereafter, reports of a youth conference on Vietnam scheduled for mid-February in Berlin put the U.S. mission and the embassy in Bonn on alert.[143] Especially the participation of foreign delegates, such as Stokely Carmichael, Rap Brown, and representatives from socialist states, alarmed American officials.[144] As the American embassy wrote to the U.S. mission in Berlin, "We are concerned about the direction which preparations for the Viet Nam Congress are taking (ref.). Given the participation by the East German FDJ delegation and pro-Chinese groups as well as the SDS inclination to violence, it seems to us that this situation might well get out of hand." In particular, the embassy feared that the German SDS saw the congress as "a welcome opportunity to inflict humiliation [up]on the U[nited] S[tates] in Berlin and to indulge in violent action against American installations."[145] Given the likelihood of foreign participants and the use of the city as a platform for "anti-American" propaganda, the embassy asked the mission to assess the potential danger and the possible banning of such an event with the local authorities and Allied partners.

After consulting with the French and the British, the mission concluded that a ban on the congress would be counterproductive. Comprehensive enforcement and subsequent prosecution was problematic and could only create a forum for an even greater propaganda campaign. Although the public reaction would undoubtedly be favorable in Berlin, such a ban might still shake public confidence in the Allied powers in the long run. What was even more significant, it might unnecessarily antagonize people who had previously been indifferent to the U.S. Vietnam policy and direct the criticism away from the students toward the U.S. presence in Berlin. The United States would thereby lose the respect earned among students for their restrained reaction in previous months. The students were, according to the mission, already surprised by the tough stance of the city officials and had interpreted the firm position against their plans as the senate's way of pleasing the Allies: "SDS chairman Rabehl said that it was known that the Allies did not like the way police behaved on June 2, and that for this reason the Senat[e] had reverted to a softer policy for several months. Now, Rabehl said, it is known that the Americans would like to prevent the February 17–18 Vietnam Congress. The Senat[e] has again taken a hard line in the belief that this time the Americans will give their full support to strong action. The Senat[e] is now waiting for a chance to crush the student movement, and this chance must not be given."[146] Given this reasoning, the mission and the Department of State found that, as long as the security of the city would not be endangered, the control of the congress by local authorities by far outweighed the negative public repercussions of an Allied ban.[147]

In preparation for the congress, the senate continuously briefed the Allies, and American officials continued to gather more information about the final program. The Allies even reached a tripartite agreement on their press comments for various scenarios during the congress, especially the one that was most dreaded, namely a demonstration in the American military and housing area in Dahlem.[148] Although the senate had explicitly prohibited the outdoor demonstration due to the chances of disruption and riots, the American mission and the U.S. army advised their staff to avoid the area.[149] When an appellative court repealed the senate's decision and allowed the demonstration under the condition that it would not come close to the U.S. headquarters, the Allies continued to monitor the compliance with the court order, noting that the route of the demonstration needed to be more than a kilometer away.

Despite these legal quarrels, the congress took place, much to the satisfaction of the U.S. mission, and was mostly peaceful without any attacks on U.S. installations. Fully aware of the congress's ideological message of backing revolutionary North Vietnam against U.S.-supported South Vietnam, the mission especially took note of international participation and the presence of American representatives from the SNCC, the American SDS, and the U.S. Campaign.[150] Although the CIA observed that Rudi Dutschke "urged participants to wear raincoats and protective headgear and to use flagstaff and placards as weapons against the police," all parties involved behaved calmly.[151] In adherence to the court's restrictions, Dutschke decided not to lead the demonstration to Dahlem for "discussions with Americans" and resorted to merely rhetorical admonitions by saying: "[L]et the Americans know that the day will come when we'll drive them out if they don't begin to abandon their imperialism."[152] In its report to the State Department, the U.S. mission therefore praised the response by the local police forces and considered the outcome a confirmation of the U.S. and Allied policy of avoiding any kind of interference in protest activities. Only the security issues raised by the demonstration continued to occupy Allied officials and the U.S. embassy in the congress's aftermath.[153] The enormous amount of American communication preceding the congress illustrates the degree to which U.S. officials were careful to avoid not only physical danger to their own military and cultural installations, but also the use of the city of Berlin as an international forum for criticism of American foreign policy.

The same was true for the city's new mayor, Klaus Schütz. In his first talk with U.S. Ambassador McGhee, Schütz pledged to solve the problem of student unrest, which, in his view, had given the city a "bad reputation."[154] McGhee shared these concerns about the long-term effects of students' protest activities on Berlin's image. The U.S. mission had already registered the adverse effects of student demonstrations on the deteriorating Berlin economy in the context of the longer opening hours for businesses on Saturdays, when merchants had to weigh their commercial interests against "physical and psychological harassment by radical protest groups."[155] The ambassador feared that ongoing unrest could result in the withdrawal of American companies from the city, citing the example of a merchandising outlet that had recently determined not to set up a branch in Berlin due to students' threats of a boycott.

To prevent further loss of business, Schütz also assured Secretary of State Dean Rusk and U.S. investors in Washington that he was determined to improve the situation.[156] In response to the Vietnam Congress, a rally under the motto "Berlin Stands for Peace and Freedom" was called by the Berlin Senate, the House of Representatives and local party, trade union, and youth organizations. The rally was intended to send a symbolic message and reconfirm transatlantic unity. On February 21, 1968, about 150,000 demonstrators marched to the John F. Kennedy Square in front of the Schöneberg city hall to listen to speeches by Mayor Schütz and various party representatives, who expressed their confidence in the United States and argued for a political solution to the conflict in Vietnam, while distancing themselves from the recent student unrest in the city. Venting their anger at the students, participants of the rally also began to assault supposed counter-demonstrators and people who looked like students during and after the event. More than thirty people were injured and twenty-six had to be taken into protective custody by the police. One man, whom pro-American demonstrators had mistakenly identified as Rudi Dutschke, was even chased through the streets by a mob calling for his lynching before he finally found refuge in a police car.[157]

The U.S. mission welcomed the pro-American "Peace and Freedom" rally as a reconfirmation of transatlantic unity in the face of the growing criticism of the United States by local student activists. The mission considered it an event "in keeping with Berlin tradition" and an opportunity for Berliners frustrated by the students' actions and upset by the Vietnam Congress "to stand up for more positive and traditional political val-

IMAGE 22. Pro-American rally "Berlin Stands for Peace and Freedom" in response to the SDS's Vietnam Congress in West Berlin, February 21, 1968 (Bildarchiv Preussischer Kulturbesitz/Art Resource, New York)

ues."[158] In a congratulatory message, Ambassador McGhee thanked the Berliners for their expression of "confidence in the United States and of their determination to stand with us in defense of freedom." Arguing that Mayor Schütz had persuasively illustrated that "your government and Berliners will prevent an extremist minority, many from outside of the city, from conveying to the world a false and dangerous impression about Berlin," McGhee intentionally linked the pro-American rally to past efforts to resist communist threats to the city, such as the Berlin crises at the beginning of the decade.[159] By portraying the student movement as yet another attack of external forces on the "joint pledge to maintain freedom in Berlin" by the United States and the citizens of Berlin, the American ambassador only fueled the tense atmosphere in the city.

For American officials, who were otherwise very concerned about the physical backlash against student protesters, the costs of the militant public's overreaction in reconfirming pro-American attitudes were clearly outweighed by its benefits: a necessary lift of public morale, an "opportunity to let off steam," and, most of all, "showing all concerned—students, senate, and populace—that a danger of violence is not far below the surface."[160] Even though the local Republican Club formed its own security squad as a result of the attacks, U.S. diplomats were surprised when the national press criticized the event, likening it to mass rallies of National

Socialism and decrying the fact that public employees were granted a day off to attend.[161] In the American diplomats' view, these critics "fail to realize the delicate situation that would result if an impression is created that Berlin opposes the U.S. This could have incalculable effects on the moral position of the U.S. as an occupying power in Berlin."[162] American officials thus interpreted the solidarity display of Berlin citizens as a means to re-create the city as a symbol for transatlantic unity after student unrest and the Vietnam Congress had seriously undermined it.

In light of the Easter riots, which followed the assassination attempt on Rudi Dutschke, the U.S. mission in Berlin, however, recognized a new quality in the protests as far as militancy was concerned.[163] Although there were no criminal activities such as looting, the difference in the Easter riots compared to previous ones lay in the demonstrators' resort to arson, namely the burning of Springer trucks or police cars. Despite the restrained response by the local authorities, the gap between the students and the population widened continuously. Since no American institutions were targeted during the riots, apart from the smashing of windows at the America House and the RIAS, the mission decided to adhere to its policy of noninterference during the riots.[164] In fact, mission officials viewed one of the main student goals, the expropriation of Springer, with a limited degree of sympathy and implicitly voiced concern over the effects of monopolistic press concentration and the coverage of Springer's leading tabloid "Bild Zeitung," which was "strongly and sometimes unfairly critical of students."[165] What the mission considered more problematic though, was the immeasurable harm done to Berlin's reputation and the effect on possible investors as a result of the renewed unrest. Acknowledging that the situation could have escalated even more in case of Dutschke's or another demonstrator's death, the mission, while maintaining its noninterference doctrine, continued to monitor student actions, convinced that "[t]he problem of unrest has by no means been overcome."[166]

One issue that particularly concerned American officials was the suspected support given to the demonstrators by East Germany. Contacts between East Berlin and the student movement—for example, the visit of the Kommune I to the Chinese embassy in East Berlin in September 1967—were addressed by American diplomats in almost every one of their in-depth reports on student disorders.[167] During the Easter riots, the CIA even reported that student unrest was "being influenced to a limited degree by the East German Communist Party." The agency was particularly concerned that "[t]he undisguised assistance provided to demonstrators last week by East Germany and the Communist party in West Berlin suggests that future student activity in Berlin may be accompanied by increasing Communist involvement."[168] Due to this plethora of circumstantial evidence, a Department of State intelligence note to Dean Rusk

IMAGE 23. Confrontations between demonstrators and the police during riots in the aftermath of the shooting of Rudi Dutschke in West Berlin, April 12, 1968 (Ullstein Bild/The Granger Collection, New York)

after the Easter riots elaborated on this alleged cooperation in greater detail. It concluded that the students were fully aware of these attempts by East Berlin and were utilizing them for their own ends.[169] In some instances the student and communist causes overlapped, in others they would be so disparate as to cause embarrassment for the communists, particularly when associated with Mao, Che Guevara, and the infamous Kommune I. As a result, East Berlin had largely kept its support low-key, which, in the Department of State's view, seemed to have altered slightly with the shooting of Dutschke, when protesting students were given free rides on the East German-run tram (S-Bahn) and when tightly rolled copies of *Neues Deutschland* were used as torches in the attacks of the Springer building. In any case, the Department of State concluded that East German efforts for greater influence on student leaders and exploitation of the students' causes had chiefly been in vain: "The SED does not as yet appear, however, to have captured anything resembling control of the student movement, or of its leaders. Working against them, among other factors, is the simple but devastating fact that most German students simply regard the East German and Soviet brands of communism as an anachronism."[170]

Due to the close proximity to the ideological enemy, student protesters were tempted to challenge the West Berlin government and the Allies by interfering in larger political processes of East-West tensions over the city. Such a chance presented itself during the Berlin access crisis in the spring and summer of 1968, when the GDR once more sought to capitalize polit- ically from its control of the city's transit system by denying access to members of the right-wing Nationaldemokratische Partei Deutschlands (National Democratic Party of Germany, NPD), high officials of the West German government, and, in April 1968, even Mayor Klaus Schütz.[171] American diplomats believed that these incidents purposely coincided with the student riots, which were exploited by East Berlin to once again question the status of the divided city.[172] In this context, the U.S. mission received intelligence that a blockade of the Autobahn under East German control providing access to West Berlin was discussed within the SDS, which had supposedly already ensured the goodwill of the East German authorities.[173] The Allied powers were even further troubled by the estab- lishment of a new SDS committee whose specific goal was to provoke Allied involvement. The committee's task was to develop action programs in order to challenge the Allied powers to intervene in future student dem- onstrations in order to "create public unrest and find public support." The U.S. mission saw this strategy in keeping with "the long range SDS goal to force the allies to assume a more direct day to day responsibility for city operations, thus lending strength to their claim that the senate is bankrupt and incapable of governing the city." In the view of mission officials, this strategy was "the logical source of any student plans to in- volve Berlin access routes in demonstrations."[174]

In light of this new development, American officials instructed the Ber- lin Senate and police to devise plans for the rerouting of traffic.[175] Since existing laws did not provide sufficient legal basis to prosecute demonstra- tors for such blockades, mission officials drafted an Allied legislative amendment as well as strategies to prevent and confront possible student blockades, the latter involving the clearing away of any obstacles to free up transit by American military convoys.[176] The Department of State, however, was alerted to the students' strategy of openly eliciting an Allied response to their actions in an area where the department had no jurisdic- tion, and it insisted on a passive policy of patient observation and did not allow "contact between blockaders and Allied authority outside of the Berlin city limits."[177] The dilemma that the U.S. administration faced was that American or Allied operations on East German territory would have serious political consequences that Washington was not prepared to risk. As Edward Fried, senior staff member of the National Security Council, summed up the situation in a memo to Walt Rostow, in the case of student protesters setting up a barricade in the area in question, "it would not be possible for West Berlin or allied authorities to remove students without going into East Germany or obtaining Soviet help." The U.S. mission could hence be authorized only to offer logistic and intelligence support to deal with possible blockades within the boundaries of West Berlin, since the demonstration was interpreted by the State Department to be specifically designed "to embarrass the West Berlin authorities." The department feared, however, that this could be the first time that the United States as one of the Allied Powers would have to give up its policy of restraint toward student unrest and interfere directly in opposing student demonstrations, which, in this case, could yield unforeseeable diplomatic problems as well as negative consequences for the overall image of the United States in West Germany.[178]

American officials therefore studied the legal situation, prepared traffic regulations in cooperation with the police, and monitored student actions together with the CIA until the very last day before the event.[179] The expected blockade did not, however, take place. Instead, students concentrated their energy on the May 1 demonstrations in Kreuzberg and Neukölln. The Allies nonetheless drew their lessons from this incident. In September 1968, they introduced legislation that made any disturbance of Western traffic to the city of Berlin illegal.[180] Having thus ensured an adequate legal framework in which to confront future student actions, the Allies could continue to exercise restraint in the face of mounting student disorder, since a similar direct challenge of their power did not occur. Student provocations in Berlin now for the most part shifted toward domestic issues that only indirectly affected Allied concerns.

At the same time, student protest continued to be a factor in American strategies involving Berlin, since the mission believed that only "one misstep by university authorities could ag[a]in give the radicals a basis for attracting wider support."[181] Although American officials were acutely aware of a gradual loss of support for the New Left by the fall of 1968, the "Battle at Tegeler Weg" in Berlin on November 4, 1968, in response to the trial of movement lawyer Horst Mahler, temporarily turned this tide. In what the mission considered the "worst demonstration in Berlin since [the] Easter riots, and, in terms of weapons used by both sides, perhaps most bitter since [the] beginning of [the] student protest movement," demonstrators threw cobblestones to break police lines so they could storm the court building, whereupon riot police resorted to water cannons, truncheons, and tear gas.[182] For American officials, this tactical use of violence only showed the mounting frustration within the student movement. In contrast to previous student actions, violence had now become a mobilization strategy and "radicals accepted [the] onus of striking [the] first blow."[183]

IMAGE 24. Demonstrators in hard hats face the police during the "Battle at Tegeler Weg" in West Berlin, November 4, 1968 (Landesarchiv Berlin)

Since the police did not respond to these provocations, the mission predicted that this wave of violence was merely the final "gasp" of the movement. When the FU experienced a series of disturbances and riots at the beginning of 1969 with students occupying university buildings and attacking U.S. consulates, mission officials considered these actions to be no longer deliberately planned or the product of a strategic discussion.[184] Rather, "any exciting suggestion for action made in student meetings [was] likely to be taken up and carried out in a matter of minutes."[185] In this situation, American institutions and officials again became the frequent target of protest activities and/or attacks.[186] When President Nixon visited Berlin in February 1969, for example, about 1,000 protesters were able to hurl paint bags and stones toward the presidential car convoy before police could push them aside; all of this despite comprehensive police preparations and a general ban on demonstrations. Members of the left-wing urban guerilla group Umherschweifende Haschrebellen (Rambling Hashish Rebels) even deposited a bomb along the route, which, although it did not detonate, illustrates the increasing militarization of the conflict.[187]

Apart from attacks against U.S. symbols and representatives, American officials believed that by the summer of 1969 protesting students were increasingly factionalized and "lacked meaty issues in which to sink their teeth."[188] The time when a single group like the SDS could organize a large antiwar demonstration and rely on a solid number of unified supporters was almost over. In the future, bomb threats, the development of clandestine groups, and a very active youth subculture in the city would generate a very different response among government officials.[189] The Berlin of the 1970s was not devoid of challenges from youthful protests, but their character and appearance changed, as did Allied obligations and the formal status of the divided city. The direct attacks on the American presence were, however, not only felt in Berlin in the late 1960s, but also posed a challenge all over the country; in particular to those who were seen as representatives of the American war in Vietnam: the troops of the U.S. army stationed in the Federal Republic.

DESERTION CAMPAIGNS AND GI-ORGANIZING:
THE U.S. ARMY AS TARGET OF STUDENT PROTEST

American troops in West Germany increased to about 250,000–300,000 in the years following the Second World War, which made them a significant segment in the structure of German postwar society.[190] Friendly relations between German civilians and the U.S. military were a common feature of postwar West Germany and were welcomed by American authorities as an opportunity to exercise additional influence on the ideological reorientation of the population.[191] Military bases were located in West Berlin, Bremen, Hesse, Bavaria, parts of Baden-Württemberg, and eventually also in Rhineland-Palatinate. Although at first more wealthy than the population, U.S. military personnel were soon outpaced by the German economic miracle of the 1950s and had, by the late 1960s, lost this privileged position. These changes were accompanied by transformations in the image of the occupying forces. The situation was further aggravated by the war in Vietnam, which demanded increasing deployments to Southeast Asia and a fundamental restructuring of the military forces in Europe.

American soldiers now became visible symbols of U.S. engagement in Southeast Asia and obvious targets for protest in the second half of the 1960s. In the eyes of student activists, their role shifted from protectors of West German freedom to representatives of an imperialist army. As an American GI remembered, "Before the Vietnam War ended, Americans had become targets all over the world. But particularly in Berlin, the reaction was at high pitch. It was very clear that you were an American, and that you were always visible. That was what you were supposed to be. On the one hand, the Americans had to show the flag as the defenders of Berlin in the Cold War. On the other hand, that made you the perfect target for anti-Vietnam sentiment and anti-Vietnam demonstrations. You couldn't go in some hole and hide."[192] Across the Federal Republic, American officials became increasingly worried by the increase of student actions aimed at U.S. forces. Since mid-1967, students had attempted to involve American GIs in their demonstrations and aided them in their desertion attempts. In Berlin, the U.S. Campaign tried to involve soldiers in their demonstrations and had deliberated helping U.S. deserters escape via East Berlin, but then rejected the plan as too risky. Students at the FU, however, announced that they would find other ways to aid Americans GIs who wished to avoid being shipped to Vietnam. An assembly at the FU on October 20, 1967, supposedly collected funds to set up an apartment in the British sector to serve as a refuge for deserters. At the "International Day of Protest" on October 21, 1967, English-language flyers appeared in Berlin and contained Danish phone numbers that potential deserters could call for help.[193] In Frankfurt, similar overtures were made to reach out to American GIs, in particular black soldiers, and involve them in student actions.[194] In January 1968, English-language posters even turned up on billboards near local American military installations, encouraging GIs to desert and providing contact addresses in Paris. Although the people responsible for putting up the posters could not be identified, the American consulate in Frankfurt commented that SDS Chairman Karl-Dietrich Wolff had previously announced the production of 20,000 leaflets offering U.S. soldiers support and work opportunities in case they deserted.[195]

In May 1968, even the *Washington Post* reported that West German students were resorting to unorthodox methods in their campaign to dissuade American GIs from service in Vietnam: "Action groups operating in cities with a large population of U.S. troops like Frankfurt rely heavily on the charm of the fairer sex to get their message home. Nicknamed the 'Brides of the Revolution,' girl members of such groups go to bars, where they dance with U.S. soldiers and later involve them in discussions about the Vietnam war, distribute leaflets and occasionally shelter deserters until they can leave the country."[196] The newspaper described the women as equally convinced of the rightness of their actions as their male colleagues. As a female activist from Frankfurt argued, "[T]his war in Vietnam is dirty, and so is the American Army and what it stands for. American soldiers should be told how things are and what they can do to get out of that army."[197]

Ambassador George McGhee, in his report to the State Department, also stressed the fact that student protest had begun to take advantage of existing civilian-military relations for their political goals and feared that "[a]s long as student opinion remains strongly opposed to US policy in Vietnam, we must continue to expect pinpricks."[198] Slightly more worried about these various GI-organizing and "seduction" strategies on the part

of German activists, the U.S. Army headquarters in West Germany demanded that the embassy remind the federal government of its legal responsibility "to insure by appropriate legislation the security and protection of the forces within its territory, which includes protection against
inducement or facilitations of desertion."[199] Despite this request, American posts considered the damaging effects of student actions and the desertion network on the operational fitness and morale of U.S. troops to
be rather small. The American embassy at The Hague had already established in July 1967 that, although there were several contacts and people
sympathetic to helping American deserters, there was no formal organization dedicated to this task and not more than twenty cases could be unearthed.[200] The State Department's Office of Research and Intelligence
came to a similar conclusion. Although acknowledging the increase of
deserters en route to Sweden, up until April 1968, it saw any large-scale
attempts at desertion support as having principally failed. In the first two
months of 1968, over half of the deserters came from U.S. troops in West
Germany, but their total number leveled off at about 100 soldiers: "While
Swedish pacifist and communist-front organizations have collected funds
and are trying to entice more into the country, the charm of Sweden is
apparently palling on those deserters already there and few have recently
returned to their units. Also anti-US organizations are finding the deserters less profitable for propaganda purposes than they had anticipated."[201]
Even so, the department admitted as late as April 1968 that "[t]here is
no clear picture of the organizations involved in getting the deserters
to Sweden."[202]

Preparations by the German SDS for an "International Desertion Day"
on May 8, however, forced the American embassy to put the issue on the
agenda with the West German Foreign Office. As a result, the federal
government instructed state authorities to investigate and prosecute any
solicitations to desert, no matter whether "such offense has been committed or an attempt to commit it has been made."[203] Despite these precautions, American posts reported leaflet distributions and attempted approaches on American soldiers in various parts of the country during the
event. In Frankfurt, cards and leaflets were placed around consular and
military installations and cars with army license plates, providing contact
addresses for desertions, such as local SDS branches of student unions, as
well as the Comité National Vietnam in Paris.[204] In Munich, former GI
and U.S. Campaign member Fran Fuller helped set up an "information
center" near a campsite close to the Warner barracks, but with the exception of a drunken GI who got lost and was eventually pulled back by his
comrades, the effort did not yield any major response.[205] Only about
1,500 people participated in the final rally at the University of Munich to
protest the war in Vietnam, partially to coincide with the European Cup

game of the local soccer club Bayern Munich, which drew about 40,000 spectators and was shown live in the university's central hall.[206]

The now-minimal response in Munich and across the country was indicative of the somewhat decreasing importance of GI-organizing among students in comparison to other issues, such as the upcoming emergency laws. This is not to say that West German students had lost interest in the U.S. army stationed in the country. Especially on a local level, U.S. military installations frequently offered them the chance to address their criticism of American foreign policy directly to its executing arms. In Bremen, for example, participants of the annual Easter march for peace and disarmament stopped at the U.S. army headquarters and tried to deliver a signed petition against the war in Vietnam. When the officer on duty refused to accept it, demonstrators went for the flag pole, provoking a scuffle with local police forces and military police, who could eventually secure the American flag. After another unsuccessful attempt to initiate a discussion on Vietnam after the march, demonstrators threw eggs and painted slogans and swastikas on the barrack walls before the arrival of local police reinforcement caused them to retreat.[207]

Incidents like these drove the U.S. army and the American embassy to continue negotiations with the West German Foreign Office to secure adequate protection for American military installations and personnel. In April 1968, the embassy, for example, requested that demonstrators were not to be allowed in any streets within U.S. military housing areas that were exclusively used and maintained by American forces and considered part of U.S. military territory. Overwhelmed by the disorder during the Easter riots, German officials could only acknowledge that "recognition of the pertinent laws and treaty obligations was a different problem from their enforcement."[208] The problem also came to the attention of American congress members and began to impact German-American relations. The same month, Sen. Jennings Randolph complained to Dean Rusk that a son of one of his staff members serving in the Federal Republic was frequently apprehended by German youth and spat at. Randolph argued that in the light of American balance of payments, incidents such as these "merit thorough reevaluation of why our forces are there and how much longer they must remain under such conditions. How much respect can our boys have for their uniform and their mission if both are to be defiled while they must submit to such incidents without retaliation, which they know, of course, would create an international incident?"[209]

The Department of State maintained that these incidents were exceptions and that U.S. troops continued to enjoy an excellent relationship with the West German population. A USIA study on Western European public opinion toward the United States and its impact on American forces, however, admitted that due to a growing gap of common interests "the 1970s will be an era of increasing resistance to and constraints upon the presence of U.S. military bases abroad."[210] Army intelligence also meticulously monitored and chronicled local student activities nationwide and provided specific instructions to its personnel on how to deal with demonstrators.[211] A guidance sheet from the U.S. Army in Heidelberg for the "International Desertion Day" detailed how military installations and housing areas were to be protected in case of an intrusion by demonstrators: "Remember—keep cool. These demonstrators thrive on publicity and are trying to get Americans involved. Don't put yourself or the command in an embarrassing position by careless words or reckless actions."[212]

Furthermore, calls for desertion and opposition within the army by West German student activists or GI underground newspapers equally troubled U.S. officials during the course of 1968. One problem was that the calls for desertion were often so carefully worded as to be completely within the realms of the legally admissible, which made prosecution almost impossible.[213] In Berlin, the laws declaring the solicitation of desertion an offense in the Federal Republic had not even been adopted for legislation; a circumstance, which made these activities largely unpunishable, unless some Allied provision was unduly stretched.[214] Drafting new Allied legislation, however, posed a political problem. Since desertion encouragement mostly concerned antiwar activities directed against U.S. soldiers, British officials were worried that a new legal provision against it could provoke a left-wing reaction in parliament. Along the same lines, the French referred to their official position on Vietnam and also delayed the issue, partially due to their own reception of American deserters.[215] By September 1968, however, both had given up their resistance and new Allied legislation was eventually ratified, making it illegal to advocate desertion in Berlin and ordering West German courts to prosecute the perpetrators. From then on, anyone who solicited or supported desertion could be sentenced to up to five years' imprisonment and a fine of $6,250.[216]

Confronting the issue legally, however, remained largely unsuccessful from the American point of view. In one of the first trials of a student accused of soliciting desertion of American soldiers in Bremen, a German court ruled that "the mere act of distributing leaflets could not be construed as an inducement to desert or as an attempt to do so in violation of the statute."[217] In addition, the court argued that German law would cover desertion efforts affecting only NATO defense and would not be applicable to the Vietnam War. In communication with the U.S. Consulate General, the local prosecutor therefore suggested that "extreme selectivity be exercised in bringing such cases to trial in the future, since acquittals of this type only lend encouragement to APO provocateurs."[218]

In the years following, the desertion campaign and GI-organizing in the Federal Republic remained a key focus of the Department of State's response to the West German student movement, although the department considered its actual impact on U.S. troops negligible. As an army study on the subversion of military personnel abroad from 1969 concluded, the efforts by the U.S. Campaign and the SDS had—despite their international connections to the American National Mobilization Committee to End the War in Vietnam (MOBE), American SDS, and the French Resistance Inside the Army (RITA)—only little significance and posed no imminent danger.[219] West German students were drawn to other issues in the 1970s, although their contact with the U.S. military never fully came to a halt, which is illustrated by the campaigns for the "Ramstein 2" or demonstrations against general racial discrimination in the U.S. armed forces.[220] From that angle, American GIs continued to play a role in social activism and protest in the Federal Republic, whether ideologically or in close personal contact with German groups.

What drastically changed, however, was that in the following decade the U.S. Army also became a major target for terrorist operations in West Germany. Within the ideology of these terrorist groups, the American military was interpreted as the executive arm of imperialism worldwide that could legitimately be attacked as an act of war, regardless of casualties. What began as West German student protests against the U.S. military presence in conjunction with the war in Vietnam now turned from contestation to armed conflict. How the U.S. government reacted to this, a far more dangerous security threat than the student movement ever posed, remains an untold story.

CULTURAL DIPLOMACY UNDER SIEGE: THE AMERIKAHÄUSER AND YOUTHFUL UNREST

American cultural policy toward West Germany after 1945 was shaped by three distinct factors: reeducation efforts to create a democratic society, the division of the country as a result of the bloc confrontation of the cold war, and a plethora of personal contacts and networks among Americans and West Germans in the postwar years.[221] The goal was to showcase the attractiveness of the "American model" of Western democracy to integrate the Federal Republic ideologically into the system of the Northern Atlantic Alliance.[222] Until 1955, the High Commission for Germany (HICOG) coordinated a comprehensive American cultural offensive that included various exhibitions, music and theater shows, as well as the engagement of returning émigrés, independent organizations, and private

American citizens, all of which contributed to the establishment of West Germany as a firm and reliable partner of the United States.

In the mid-1950s, bilateral cultural relations and a stronger German share in the mutual exchange efforts replaced the one-sided character of the program and resulted in a certain reduction of American cultural policy. Institutions that, due to German initiatives on their behalf, survived this transition were the America Houses (*Amerikahäuser*) in the Federal Republic. The first fully equipped America House had been established in Frankfurt in 1946 after the transfer of a reading room of the Allied Psychological Warfare Division to the city. Only half a decade later, twenty-seven America Houses and 135 reading rooms were instituted in West Germany and Berlin, which served as cultural meeting points for German people of various backgrounds.[223] Their extensive library collections were eagerly received by a German audience that had been denied access to various books during National Socialism and could now become reacquainted with a wide range of contemporary literature. The America Houses and the variety of the events that they hosted became a crucial factor in the American presence in the country and the permanent German-American dialogue.

Beginning in the mid-1960s, the USIA also started to use these institutions for information campaigns about the American war effort in Vietnam. With its infamous propaganda movie *The Night of the Dragon*, as well as panel discussions with Fulbright exchange professors and American officials, and translated information material such as William Bundy's speech "The Path to Vietnam," the agency meant to illustrate the moral and political integrity of American involvement in Southeast Asia and boost West German public opinion on the war.[224] This strategy, however, provoked disagreement among the New Left in the Federal Republic and led to open criticism and contestation of this area of U.S. public diplomacy. As Fritz Stern discovered in his talks with West German students at the end of 1966, U.S. information campaigns on Vietnam were received very unfavorably and seen as "a continued barrage of American propaganda."[225]

As a result, the America Houses soon became the focus of antiwar actions by West German students. An attack on the America House in Berlin after an antiwar demonstration on February 5, 1966, gained particular notoriety. A small group of protesters hosted a sit-in against the war in front of the America House and lowered the U.S. flag to half-mast. The lowering of the flag and the several eggs that SDS members subsequently flung against the façade of the America House crossed a line that had previously protected American institutions from open displays of criticism, especially in Berlin. The fierce public reaction about this incident and its condemnation as "anti-American excess" were therefore hardly surprising.[226] For the majority of Berliners, the America House symbolized the German-American bond as well as American protection from the communist threat, which deserved almost indivisible gratitude. In comparison to the West German public, American officials were not only more used to this antiwar opposition but also considered it negligible, assuring Berlin representatives that it would in no way harm the deep German-American friendship.[227] For the student demonstrators, in contrast, the American actions in Vietnam massively overshadowed the legitimacy of this protection, and the America Houses were the natural places to voice disappointment with and criticism of their protective power.

Accordingly, the incident in Berlin provoked similar events in other parts of the country. In September 1967, for example, several hundred participants of the national convention of the German SDS in Frankfurt, under the guidance of Rudi Dutschke and Kommune I members Fritz Teufel and Rainer Langhans, invaded the America House just before the beginning of a panel discussion on the U.S. involvement in Vietnam. As the consulate reported, "Students 'captured' platform, raised Viet Cong flag, led in singing of international[e] and chanting slogans 'Ho Chi Minh', Amis, CIA—go home'. . . . Rowdy atmosphere reigned for about an hour and efforts by consular officer and German director of Amerika Haus to restore order [were] unsuccessful."[228] Although the protesters had to be evicted by the local police and continued their demonstration outside, the American consulate still interpreted the event as a harmless "combination of a 'happening,' a political demonstration against establishment and an evening of free entertainment" that actually benefited the standing of the America House as a place of open debate.[229]

This assessment changed with the spread of militant demonstrations against American institutions all over the Federal Republic in the fall of 1967. Sit-ins, blockades, and other demonstrations were now often accompanied by protesters smashing windows and painting antiwar slogans on American buildings. In Bremen, an antiwar rally before Christmas ended with the hurling of tomatoes and eggs against the local consulate.[230] In Munich, demonstrators shattered the windows of the Consulate General on January 9, 1968, and pulled a life-size effigy of Lyndon B. Johnson up the flag pole, chanting slogans such as "Hey, LBJ, how many kids did you kill today?"[231] In Frankfurt, Rudi Dutschke reportedly urged a crowd of about 2,000 people during a teach-in in February to occupy the U.S. Consulate General. Although their plan was thwarted by the police's water cannons, demonstrators broke several windows of the America House and the U.S. Trade Center and exchanged the German flag on the roof of the trade center for the North Vietnamese flag and a picture of Che Guevara.[232]

IMAGE 25. Demonstration and sit-in against the Vietnam War in front of the U.S. Consulate General in Frankfurt, February 1967 (Bildarchiv Preussischer Kulturbesitz/Art Resource, New York)

In light of these events, American officials reconsidered and began to regard these incidents as an imminent security threat to U.S. cultural representations. Particularly the American Consul in Frankfurt expressed his concern that due to the existence of classified material in U.S. buildings in Frankfurt, "any invasion by demonstrators could have very serious and unpleasant aspects."[233] Alarmed by these nationwide incidents, American Ambassador George McGhee reported the following to Washington in February 1968: "In various parts of Germany, America Houses have again become one of the targets of an accelerated student protest movement against the US presence in Asia and Europe. This has taken the form of demonstrations, 'teach-ins,' and physical damage or defacement. The Socialist German Student Association (SDS) is the prime mover behind these events, and its chief ideologue, Rudi Dutschke, set the tone in Frankfurt recently when he exhorted his followers to 'increase political pressure on American imperialism.' "[234] McGhee concluded that similar attacks should be expected in the future and initiated a countrywide review of the physical security of U.S. installations and the impact that student unrest had on their program activities. American posts mostly recounted that the relations with local officials, who showed serious concern about demonstrations potentially erupting into disorder, were excellent and police protection adequate. Despite the attacks, the posts considered neither a reduction nor revision of present cultural or trade programs and anticipated further demonstrations as long as the war in Vietnam carried on. But as the consulate in Frankfurt suggested, the best way to deal with them was to respond calmly and let the local security forces proceed: "As of the present, our policy should be to play it cool, unless there is serious deterioration which prevents normal operations of our consulate and installations."[235]

The embassy largely concurred but recommended avoiding potentially provocative themes or events, such as public Vietnam debates. Although it regarded the small circle of movement leaders as "violently and vociferously anti-U.S.," it did not see the security of U.S. military personnel seriously endangered and considered the damage to U.S. installations relatively minor.[236] With regard to compensation for the attacks, the West German Foreign Office also proved to be very forthcoming. Although not acknowledging any legal obligation, the payments were treated as "ex gratia," and it was understood that in the event of damages to cultural installations of the Federal Republic in the United States, a similar agreement could be reached. In general, the affected U.S. consulate was to come to a solution with the local authorities and only in the event of a problem would the case be turned over to the embassy and the Foreign Office.[237]

As a result of these incidents, police protection for local America Houses was also heightened all over the Federal Republic. The U.S. mission in Berlin, in cooperation with local officials, even devised a general security checklist that could be used to prepare for demonstrations against America Houses. It suggested, for example, that the defense perimeter, including barrier gates and policemen, be situated "*more* than a 'stone's throw' from the building—even if passing vehicle traffic must be detoured." The regular business activities of the America House should be enabled to continue through the use of appropriate screening methods, and the American flag, although the frequent target of demonstrators, "should not be 'struck' until order is restored—even if the sun has set." Furthermore, policemen in civilian attire could discreetly check for possible explosive devices left in the buildings. This reflects both a hardening, and at the same time more flexible, attitude of American officials, who increasingly adjusted to the harassment by student protest and were no longer willing to grant demonstrators "the satisfaction of having stopped U.S. Government operations."[238]

Despite these comprehensive preparations and action plans, student attacks on America Houses persisted in the second half of 1968. At the end of November, the new Ambassador Henry Cabot Lodge, noticeably frustrated, informed Washington of a renewed upsurge of the assaults. After SDS leaflets had advocated to "finally to begin to smash the America Houses" in Tübingen, for example, books were stolen from the local German-American Institute, a lecture disrupted, two fires discovered, an American flag thrown out of the window and "Ami Go Home" crayoned on the walls. Similar events took place all over the country.[239] Although America Houses and German-American institutes often sought to appease students by taking up their claims and integrating them into their programs, the series of nationwide attacks did not come to a halt. As a result, the American embassy eventually prepared a sample format for the local posts on how to report these incidents, which listed categories such as advance warnings, the status of local police protection, witnesses of the assault, the theme of the protest, the extent of damages, the source for compensation, as well as the cooperation with local authorities. When paint was thrown at the American consulate façade in Hamburg on Christmas morning of 1968, for example, the process of registering, reporting, and removing traces of the incident by the local fire brigade had already become a standardized procedure.[240]

The America Houses as places of transatlantic cultural exchange remained markedly disturbed by West German student unrest until well into the 1970s. The fundamental opposition against the war in Vietnam turned out to be a challenge that even the most dedicated efforts of American officials were unable to reverse. During a German-American Friendship week in Frankfurt in May 1967, a speech in the local America House by Max Horkheimer on "America in the German Consciousness" and on the problems of mutual understanding was also interrupted by demonstrators. Directly addressing the protesters, Horkheimer countered by reminding them of the historical credit that the United States deserved for its fight against National Socialism and the liberation of Europe: "If it is necessary for the U.S. to fight a war . . . then it is not so much for the defense of the fatherland, but essentially for the defense of the constitution, the defense of human rights . . . the person who judges should at least pay attention to these things; he should also at least, when talking about Vietnam, think about the fact that we would not be sitting here together and talking freely if America had not intervened and ultimately saved Germany and Europe from the most abominable totalitarian terror."[241]

Although Horkheimer's words earned applause from the audience and subsequently caused the protesters to leave, his line of argument was not persuasive enough to silence the protest of the young generation in West Germany. In the view of the demonstrators, America's actions betrayed past historical merits and accomplishments. The image of the United States that students had become acquainted with over the years clashed vehemently with the experience of a culturally offensive America. In this sense, the attacks on the America Houses in the late 1960s were an apt mirror of the generational divide in representations of the United States in West Germany. As such, the militancy and disorder were a serious challenge to American foreign policy, posed by the West German students and other protest movements worldwide.

In the case of the Federal Republic, student unrest led to a contestation of the very transatlantic alliance that had emerged after the Second World War. West German activists scrutinized almost all areas of German-American cooperation during the cold war and fundamentally questioned the political and moral values that they were based on. In doing so, they not only posed a threat to future U.S. interests and the transatlantic partnership but could potentially throw off balance the existing geopolitical order. Confronted with these odds, the U.S. government decided to respond more actively to the youth of one of its most important allies in the cold war.

Chapter 6

STUDENT PROTEST

AND INTERNATIONAL RELATIONS

STUDENT PROTEST in the second half of the 1960s did not have an immediate influence on the course of U.S. foreign policy, but the efforts of activists on both sides of the Atlantic did play an important part in its institutional conceptualization. The impact of youthful dissent continued to occupy American policymakers in the Johnson and Nixon administrations, who sought to analyze this worldwide phenomenon most effectively and minimize its damage to U.S. interests. To that end, the role of the Inter-Agency Youth Committee (IAYC), which served as the center of all government efforts directed at foreign youth, had grown in significance since the mid-1960s. In addition, the Department of State initiated further study groups on student unrest and implemented structural changes in the training and selection of its diplomatic personnel to make them better equipped to deal with the challenge of student protest. Other agencies, such as the CIA, conducted lengthy reviews of the international dimension of youthful unrest that even provoked heated discussions in the Johnson cabinet.

On the local level, and with respect to the Federal Republic, U.S. diplomats began to pay more attention to the concerns of foreign students and tried to integrate their interests into American cultural diplomacy efforts. To cater toward this future generation of leaders more effectively, the Department of State altered its country programming and made youth its primary target group. It also adjusted its cultural exchange programs in response to the increasing influence of youth and used former West German grantees, who had participated in transatlantic exchanges during the 1950s, to counter unfavorable opinions about the United States in the Federal Republic. Sensing a growing political alienation from the transatlantic alliance and a transformation of West German society as a possible result of the student movement, U.S. officials restructured their attempts to recapture the hearts and minds of the young on various levels.

U.S. GOVERNMENT REACTIONS TO
STUDENT UNREST AFTER THE "FRENCH MAY"

The reactions of the U.S. government to the West German student movement reflected a much larger effort to come to terms with the international dimension of student unrest. The May events of 1968 in France took the Johnson administration and the Department of State completely by surprise and dramatically confirmed the significance that the Inter-Agency Youth Committee had placed on European youth since the mid-1960s. Recognizing student protest as a crucial factor in international relations, the administration now felt the need to guard its foreign political interests against the challenge of the young generation worldwide and began to devise adequate political responses with the help of the IAYC.

In the aftermath of the French May, inquiries into the Western European and international youth scene became a priority on the agenda of the Department of State. In a circular to all American overseas posts, dated May 30, 1968, U.S. Secretary of State Dean Rusk described the events in Paris as a "sobering lesson" that illustrated "how successful a handful of university students in France were in precipitating a crisis which has potentially very serious overtones for our foreign policy interests."[1] Since similar discontent might still be "somewhat masked elsewhere," Rusk urged U.S. officials to look for national trends toward similar incidents: "[O]ur concern cannot be solely with the crises such disaffection may generate. We must be concerned with the very existence of such undercurrents before they coalesce to force action on long-standing social problems. They are a part of the ambiance in which we operate today and, more importantly, may foreshadow future national policies. As such, they must be evaluated and reported."[2]

The response from diplomatic posts worldwide was overwhelming. In a memorandum to the president, Special Assistant for National Security Affairs Walt Rostow summed it up as follows: "So far 1968 has witnessed outbreaks of student violence in about 25 nations—including ours. . . . Quantitative data and factual indicators are few in the face of assertions, value judgments and speculations—many of the latter support contrary conclusions."[3] Trying to come to terms with this phenomenon analytically, Rostow pinpointed the following factors for this revolt: advances in modern technology, the need for institutional reforms, tensions from an "oligarchic to [a] more broadly based rule of society," a progressively militant urge to have a say in one's own destiny, as well as a striving for wealth among socially disadvantaged groups. More specifically, Rostow saw in these simultaneous eruptions of protest a larger tendency of geopolitical change: "For over a decade the nations of the world have undergone a diffusion of power simply from East-West power blocs to a more complex polylithic set of arrangements. In many respects, this diffusion of power phenomenon is now percolating within national societies." He assured Johnson that the U.S. was monitoring this gradual erosion of the bipolar order of the cold war and would now pay "more attention to observing—hopefully, anticipating; and ideally, influencing—these phenomena."[4]

Echoing this sentiment, Charles Bohlen, former U.S. ambassador to France and now chairman of the IAYC, also declared the recent wave of student and youth activism to be "a new, potentially powerful factor" for U.S. foreign policy.[5] To come to terms with this challenge, Bohlen suggested the development of better regional strategies to evaluate local youth movements, as well as a review of existing cultural exchange programs. Following Bohlen's suggestions, the Department of State established a special "Student Unrest Study Group" in the aftermath of the French May. The group was chaired by George McGhee, and composed of various regional officers, including Robert Cross, the department's youth advisor and staff director of the IAYC.[6]

In its first report of September 1968, the Student Unrest Study Group defined student protest as only one expression of a general worldwide unrest among all age groups that was "a result of international and domestic upheavals taking place in an era of transition." In contradiction to earlier assessments, it particularly stressed the positive effects of student protest as a stimulus for change and reform. According to the group's findings, student unrest became harmful only when it led to premature change, fed generational mistrust, or contributed to the success of prejudiced viewpoints. Especially problematic in this context was an attack on "the objectives of U.S. foreign policy, our relations with the country concerned or the worldwide functioning of our business interests and our free enterprise economic system."[7] The greatest risk in the eyes of the study group, however, lay in a division of the Western alliance, "a possible weakening of the whole fabric, so painfully constructed over the years, which holds together the Community of Free World Nations."[8]

The group treated unrest in developing countries as a separate matter, which was, in contrast to the more ethical and social concerns of the so-called "post-modern generation" in the Western world, often about "bread and butter" issues.[9] In the Third World, students usually did not aim at taking power but at improving the existing order or toppling certain regimes. Furthermore, the group categorized objectives of unrest according to local (university reform), national (race in the United States, press concentration in West Germany), or international matters (decolonization). These issues could easily overlap, for example, in the case of the Vietnam War, which was "a major catalytic factor for all types of unrest." The United States and its image abroad were also one of the main targets of protest activities, since students frequently sympathized with left-wing or socialist ideas that ran counter to the economic system proclaimed by the United States. Pointing to its worldwide economic interests and military bases, students frequently accused America of using its power solely for its own ends and neglecting other nations. In addition, America's troubled domestic scene contributed to its negative perception among students overseas.[10]

For the Student Unrest Study Group, the only way to deal with the problem was to protect U.S. national interests by trying to exploit student unrest for America's own objectives, thereby "seek[ing] to take advantage of the inevitable and to accelerate the desirable."[11] Since the topic of student unrest belonged to each country's internal affairs, any intervention or propaganda effort by the U.S. government might prove counterproductive. Instead, the first step had to be a thorough analysis of the local causes and consequences of student unrest to predict potentially negative effects on U.S. interests: internal disorder, the "replacement of a friendly with a hostile government," a change in U.S. military presence, or the "harassment or nationalization of our business interests in the country."[12] In a second step, the likely benefits of student unrest should be evaluated, since the dissent might present a welcome opportunity to foster U.S. goals by reforming societies from within. In these cases, American posts could assume the role of mediator among the parties involved.[13] In general, the study concluded, the way to confront student unrest should be to create "positive and constructive outlets for the pent-up idealism and energies of youth."[14] These vents, such as the Peace Corps in the United States and, for European students, a greater immersion in their continent's unification process, could serve as channels for the creation of a more stable world order, based on the U.S. concept of the "free world": "In varying degrees, depending on the issues in question, reform is a necessary step toward the development of that kind of world community in which U.S. interests will be best safeguarded—a community of strong and independent nations, whose governments are responsive to the needs of their people by being willing to work in concert with us and other Free World nations. Students can help bring about such a world community."[15]

The findings of the study group therefore offered a range of proposals to deal with international student unrest and its potential threat to U.S. interests. They initiated a worldwide reporting effort by U.S. diplomats and led the Department of State's Office of Research and Intelligence to categorize the problem of future leaders as a fundamental challenge to U.S. foreign policy.[16] In the process of assessing the likelihood of student unrest similar to that of France in other countries, the IAYC functioned as the center for debate and exchange among the various branches of the U.S. government. The IAYC was the place where U.S. officials evaluated the aforementioned studies and memos and drafted plans for further action. In effect, the committee served as an institutionalized forum on how to confront overseas student revolts on a very high level in the administration.

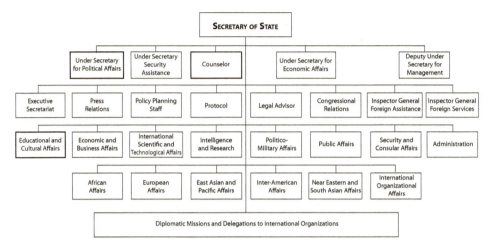

FIGURE 2. Institutional affiliation (in bold frame) of the Inter-Agency Youth Committee in the Department of State : 1962–66 the committee was under the Assistant Secretary for Educational and Cultural Affairs; 1966–69, under the Deputy Undersecretary for Political Affairs; and 1969–72, under the Counselor (based on U.S. Government Manual 1974–75, Washington, D.C.: U.S. Government Printing Office, 1974, 374)

In the second half of the decade, the IAYC effort was reorganized and its significance increased. This new formation of the IAYC in the mid-1960s had an important impact on how it reacted in 1968. In 1966, the committee was transferred from the supervision of the assistant secretary for educational and cultural affairs to the deputy undersecretary of state for political affairs (G/Y), who now also served as chairman of the IAYC. With this move, a new position of special assistant for youth and executive secretary of the IAYC was established within the Department of State, designed as the administrative center for all activities aimed at foreign youth.[17]

This heightened emphasis on youth was also reflected in new guidelines by the Department of State for its foreign-service personnel. Local officers and the posts' youth committees were now asked to report extensively on future leaders or "comers" from various sectors of society: "Officers should devote an appropriate proportion of their representational activities to persons who are not yet in positions of power and influence, but who have been identified as of potential future significance. To the greatest extent feasible, consistent with other U.S. interests in the country, they should cultivate the primary and secondary leaders of student unions, of the youth wings of political parties, trade unions, and other mass organizations, of opposition and dissident groups, nationalist movements, the military and other sectors."[18] The local mission's youth committee was supposed to entertain these contacts under the guidance of a political officer. The purpose of this attention was the department's vital interest in cultivating a long-term relationship with the country's future elite: "They are (1) to come to know and to help contribute to the democratic formation of the future leaders; (2) to correct misconceptions about the United States; and (3) to ally this country with the young leaders' nationalistic, idealistic aspirations for social justice and constructive change."[19]

By the end of 1966, almost two years before the worldwide eruption of student protest, the IAYC and its goals had therefore been further institutionalized and elevated to a higher administrative level in Washington. Throughout the committee's existence three former ambassadors and a special assistant to the president, among others, served as chairmen, which illustrates the significance that was attached to it.[20] Due to the sensitivity of the issues that the IAYC dealt with, committee membership was difficult for certain agencies. The Peace Corps, for example, was very concerned that its participation could jeopardize its independent status and the distance it sought to maintain from official U.S. foreign policy initiatives. Accordingly, Peace Corps Director Sargent Shriver advised his posts in 1965 that in order to disarm potential attacks against them, "no responsibility for Emphasis on Youth programs in your country should be undertaken by the Peace Corps. Furthermore, neither you, members of your staff, Peace Corps Volunteers or Peace Corps contractor personnel should ever be used as a means of obtaining information on potential leaders or as a means of contacting or influencing them."[21] As Shriver's successor Jack Vaughn underscored, the only way the Peace Corps could contribute to the youth effort without unduly compromising its own mission was by participating in the local embassy's youth committee meetings.[22]

Despite these concerns, the IAYC maintained its central role in assessing the U.S. government's performance with regard to foreign youth. In 1967, for example, the committee advised the secretary of state on how to react to the political repercussions stemming from the revelations of CIA's extensive funding of private and international organizations.[23] In this context, the question of the international connections of the various student movements soon emerged as the major issue. Vice President Hubert Humphrey was especially receptive to the committee's work in this area. Humphrey had been approached by the IAYC as early as 1965 to take over the role of Robert Kennedy as a "catalyst whose personal interest in the subject is widely known," and who, supplied with a presidential mandate, could be the "occasional 'muscle'" to support the committee's proposals.[24] Especially after his visit to Europe in March/April 1967 and the wide-spread demonstrations that accompanied it, Humphrey energetically defended increased attention to youth. In an IAYC meeting of February 1968, Humphrey argued that embassies should review their efforts in the field of youth activities and that young Americans abroad should overcome their "guilt complex" and speak more about "the great experiences of America."[25] Considering universities as the key in influencing foreign youth, he suggested the formation of discussion groups with young leaders at local posts, encouraged intensified contacts with communications industry leaders, and demanded an increase in quality of American cultural activities abroad, arguing that "the best doesn't cost that much more."[26]

Humphrey's appearance before the committee and the events of the French May gave the IAYC greater legitimacy and a new sense of urgency. Trying to keep pace with the rapid spread of student protest worldwide, the IAYC reviewed the status of local youth programs and incoming reports of the U.S. posts abroad, recruited external speakers, and vividly discussed the consequences of international student unrest for U.S. foreign policy. As one member suggested, the fact that the U.S. image abroad was dominated by the country's internal fissures, which were disseminated instantaneously by the international media whenever tensions erupted, actually offered a chance to rejuvenate programming policies. To prevent a monolithic image of the United States as an imperialist power, youth programs could try to incorporate the full range of domestic political voices, both critical and affirmative. This reflection of free speech in cultural diplomacy efforts would not only make a very favorable impression on foreign youth interested in these opinions, but would also showcase U.S. commitment to political diversity and individual liberties, even in the case of dissent.

The courage to permit and confront contrary viewpoints would paint a much more complex picture of the United States, one that was harder to distort or to analyze within the narrow theoretical frameworks of Marxism and imperialism. At the same time, it would lead to a more fitting contemporary approach to youth overseas: "Instead of emphasizing a one-way flow of ideas we should concentrate on establishing a dialogue in which we listen and learn as well as influence and impress.... We will make progress, I believe, in influencing modern youth only to the extent that we can develop emotional rapport with the groups in society which are anti-status quo."[27] Others agreed that it was necessary to realize the significance of students as future leaders and highlighted that "our concern at the moment is youth as a factor in protest, as a spark that sets off a chain of events."[28] To make reporting efforts and youth programs in the field more effective, the IAYC had already tried to improve channels of information within the government. In March 1968, it established a subcommittee that developed two official guidelines on "Youth as a Factor in Politics and Society" and "Means of Tapping Sources Available but Hitherto Insufficiently Used," which proposed, among other things, closer cooperation with the Peace Corps as a means to obtain steady critical and reliable information on foreign youth.[29]

The challenge before the IAYC was how to respond to youth as a new political force and how to differentiate between various youth groups. Based on the results of the Student Unrest Study Group, George McGhee argued that student unrest was, on balance, a positive trend. IAYC chairman Charles Bohlen, in contrast, replied that "it has been discovered that freedom of speech and association and other principles on which democratic nations have operated can be perverted in a deliberate attempt at confrontation and physical clash with police in the presence of TV cameras." The outcome of this, according to Bohlen, could be a right-wing counter-reaction in society with severe consequences for U.S. foreign relations.[30] Special Counsel to the President Harry McPherson suggested supporting moderate elements within the student protest movement, the feasibility of which Bohlen seriously questioned by referring to the Vietnam War as the "biggest psychological factor in anti-US attitudes." These different opinions notwithstanding, all committee members argued for a more active role of the IAYC and its member agencies in gathering information on students' attitudes and policies.[31] IAYC's Executive Secretary Robert Cross even went a step further and urged long-term adjustments of U.S. foreign policy strategies in the face of youthful unrest: "Whenever we discuss changing U.S. policy to reflect this student opinion, however, we are told, 'But U.S. policy is made on more important grounds and more relative factors than simply the need to accommodate students.' This is certainly so and really needs not be said. Yet, if the grievances now voiced by students are in fact basic, underlying problems, they may some day come to fuller fruition. If they do, they may then not only embarrass the United States but may force fundamental changes in policy under widespread popular pressure." Or, as Cross rephrased it, "I'm not saying we change *any* U.S. policy *because students* or anyone else attack[s] it. But might it not be prudent to examine any policy that comes under such attack to weigh objectively the long range risks involved if today's student attacks should become tomorrow's mass dissent?"[32]

The committee turned to external expertise to learn more about the phenomenon from a scientific perspective. For this purpose, it drew on a RAND Corporation study produced by the American sociologist Seymour Lipset on "Possible Effects of Student Activism on International Relations," which was distributed to IAYC members, within the State Department, and to the field. In this study, Lipset discussed the effect of worldwide student protest on international relations. He argued that although the structural shortcomings of today's universities as well as local factors played a certain role, the magnitude of the phenomenon could be grasped only by the emergence of a larger political ideology transcending the nation-state. Student protesters were part of a new political generation that lacked the formative experiences of their elders in terms of bloc confrontation and cold-war ideology and came of age at a time when the "end of ideology" had gained wider currency. Young people in the Western world had not lived through the ideological conflicts posed by fascism and communism and the need to develop and justify a counterposition to totalitarian threats. In consequence, they saw no reason to restrain their criticism of what they considered a society that was not living up to its democratic promises.[33]

The war in Vietnam had brought these two opposing, generational views back to the domestic arena in a fierce clash of ideologies. Whereas the generation in power still adhered to the creed of containing communist influence, the young no longer accepted the view of a monolithic communist expansionism and regarded the older generation's strategies as antiquated. As a result, they questioned the whole alliance system, including NATO and the since-disbanded SEATO.[34] According to Lipset, the student movements and their opposition to the war in Vietnam, whether located in the East or West, should therefore primarily be viewed as a domestic power struggle: "These are the revolts of activist youth against the older generation in power in their own country. They have the effect, however, of also being a revolt against the system of international alliances and against America's role in the world." For Lipset, it was "the fact that the basis for the system of alliances is no longer as strong as it once was, that has made a new international youth movement possible."[35] Whereas youth in the Western world were "post-reformist" in their efforts, they largely favored altering the existing system in the bloc and developing countries.

With regard to foreign relations, Lipset pointed to a possible rise of right-wing tendencies, which might actually strengthen American alliances. On the other hand, governments could also give in to domestic trouble caused by international alignments, eventually resulting in increased isolationist policies.[36] In general, Lipset predicted that the generation of students now involved in or affected by the protest activities would remain a highly important political force over time, and would most likely continue to be absorbed by the ideas and values of their formative political experiences. The generational conflict, in his view, thus presented itself equally as a conflict over politics, which any foreign policy strategy would be hard-pressed to disregard: "Any efforts to analyze the future of politics, whether on the domestic or international scene, will ignore the students at the peril of being in error."[37] As the future elites that were about to shape their countries' politics and societies, the protesters of the 1960s had thus become an important factor in U.S. foreign policy considerations.

Their significance was further illustrated by "Restless Youth," CIA director Richard Helms's report on the global dimension of student unrest, which was presented during President Johnson's cabinet meeting on September 18, 1968. This was the most extensive single study produced on the issue for the president. The CIA analyzed in great detail the student movements in nineteen countries. Over two hundred pages in length, the report asserts that "Youthful dissidence, involving students and non-students alike, is a world-wide phenomenon. It is shaped in every instance by local conditions, but nonetheless there are striking similarities, especially in the more advanced countries. As the underdeveloped countries progress, these similarities are likely to become even more widespread."[38] In addition to the extensive country studies, the CIA also provided a more general interpretation of the problem. Historically, it stated, student unrest was a well-known phenomenon, which had, over the course of the centuries, largely lost its political legitimacy. Although the political activism of students was currently not considered part of the political decision-making process in the United States, it had become an integral part of political life in countries such as Argentina and Japan.[39]

Concerning the general mechanisms of student protest, the report introduced a classification used by the American political scientist Zbigniew Brzezinski called "expedient escalationism," which described the gradual broadening of original student demands due to specific dynamics. After a refusal on the part of the university administration to listen or adhere to the students' grievances, students would, according to Brzezinski, turn more vocal and look for allies, whom they often found among faculty members. A so-called series of "dress rehearsals" would then ensue, in which students disrupted official procedures or willingly overstepped certain regulations. The next phase would commence with "a spontaneous incident, perhaps the arrest of a student away from university, [which] electrifies the community. A picket line or sit-in follows, and the students seek to negotiate with the authorities." Instead of direct negotiations, however, some faculty members might serve as intermediaries between the two parties. Pressure on the protesters would build up from various sides forcing them to increase their demands, especially when only minor concessions were offered by the authorities, who would be perceived as having lost control of the situation. Frustrated over this stalemate, the authorities would consequently deem any compromise solution unattainable and escalate the situation further by using force, which also affected other participants not directly involved and in turn cause public opinion to swing even more against them and in favor of the students.[40]

On a more general level, the CIA argued that this shift in public support aligning with a small minority could furthermore be explained by the fact that a certain "gulf between society's institutions and the people those institutions are designed to serve" had become apparent in modern societies. Hence, students often attracted a following because their references to shortcomings in modern society—such as impersonality, excessive bureaucracy, and so forth—rang true for a large audience: "These attitudes, particularly in Europe, are a consequence of the failure of social and political institutions to accommodate themselves to the remarkable economic strides of the postwar period, the absence of compelling ideological issues . . . and the diminution everywhere of moral authority. . . . A younger generation finds the government bureaucracy . . . antiquated, cumbersome, and in the hands of a generation that came to power twenty-five years ago and remains committed more to preserving its authority than to utilizing political power to renovate society."[41] For most students, politics had thus become a zero-sum game in which any meaningful participation was futile and the slogans of the cold war sounded anachronistic. On the other hand, certain issues could still mobilize their interest and arouse their passion. These ranged from U.S. involvement in the war in Vietnam to NATO, from supposed American participation in a "Zionist conspiracy" at the expense of Arab nations in the Middle East to the U.S. backing of unpopular military regimes in South America.[42]

As the CIA stressed, however, the major issue for student unrest was the numeric explosion of the student body, which had almost doubled in the past decade, and which the universities were unable to handle administratively and ideologically. Faculties were often ill-equipped to deal with these masses of students. Professors still remained the "autocrats of the academic world," who, because of external contracts, political careers, or other interests, had become even more distanced from the students. In Europe, these "absentee autocrats" would generally be unapproachable "mandarins." In the CIA's opinion, it was no coincidence that the students who were most active in protest were often particularly gifted students of the liberal arts, such as Daniel-Cohn Bendit in France, as well as Rudi Dutschke and Karl-Dietrich Wolff in West Germany, whose disillusionment had led them to greater social involvement.[43]

The agency estimated that the emergence of a New Left ideology at the beginning of the 1960s and the actions of the civil rights movement had provided the basis for the unrest in the second half of the decade.[44] From the African American movement, students had borrowed "the conviction that *only* confrontation works," which profoundly affected their protest techniques: "Student demonstrations are expressive, rather than directed; they are calculated to dramatize an issue and attract public notice. The demonstration itself becomes the focal point of action."[45] Based on the insight that peaceful protest was only absorbed by society's goodwill, however, the use of violence had caught the attention of an increasing number of students. Progressively, its legitimacy had then been reconfirmed in the students' minds by the actions of their respective counterparts abroad. This militancy could thus, according to the CIA, cause governments to use even more forceful measures in confronting student unrest, thereby potentially eroding the democratic basis of society.[46]

Naturally, the international connections of the various national eruptions were another focal point of the study. The findings of the CIA in September 1968 were, however, the result of a longer history of CIA reports on communist infiltration of the 1960s protest movements that had been prepared for the administration. Since the mid-sixties, President Johnson saw the control of domestic unrest by communist forces almost as a given.[47] Alarmed by the possible international extent of this subversion, the White House had already requested a study of the "International Connections of the U.S. Peace Movement" from the CIA in 1967. Although in almost any other case during the cold war the CIA had blamed communist interference for domestic dissent, it now differed substantially with the president. The CIA portrayed the U.S. peace movement in November 1967 as highly diverse and under no central control.[48] In the eyes of the agency, "joint action on an international scale is possible only because coordination is handled by a small group of dedicated men, most of them radically oriented, who have volunteered themselves for active leadership in the key organizations."[49] People such as Dave Dellinger and Tom Hayden stood out as main organizers and international intermediaries, the latter especially because of his visit and contacts to Hanoi. The "National Mobilization Committee" was the main link between them and had, next to the "War Crimes Tribunal" organized by Bertrand Russell, succeeded in rallying internationally coordinated opposition against U.S. actions in Vietnam.[50] Within this network, American students living abroad also served a crucial purpose as "an important channel for coordinating US activity with foreign activity." Organizations such as the "Stop It Committee" at the London School of Economics or the "Paris American Committee to Stop War," among others, thus functioned as "subsidiaries" of the American movement.[51]

Already at the end of 1967, the CIA took a clear stance concerning the movements' ties to foreign governments and the charges of communist interference. Although key leaders apparently entertained "close communist associations," the CIA repeatedly stressed that the movement was not under communist control but driven by the joint opposition to the war in Vietnam. Apart from extremely limited Soviet influence and funding (for example, money for airline tickets), which took place through front organizations and national parties, and apart from very minor assistance in the case of China or Cuba, the CIA concluded that "on the basis of what we now know, we see no significant evidence that would prove Communist control or direction of the US peace movement or its leaders."[52]

The only exception to this involved the contact that U.S. peace groups had established with the North Vietnamese government, which had "developed to a point where it is almost continuous" and could be regarded as "an important part in channeling anti-war activity on both sides of the world."[53] The narrow interpretation that the U.S. peace movement relied only on a limited number of key activists with close ties to North Vietnam, however, prompted the president to follow Rostow's suggestion and seek a reporter to back up his suspicions in the mass media. In Rostow's words, the plan was to "find a young, able, trusted journalist, anxious to make his reputation; making these leads available to him; and then letting him go out to earn a Pulitzer Prize."[54] This plan obviously materialized. On December 3, 1967, the *Los Angeles Times* published an article entitled "Peace Movement's Hanoi Links Grow" on the front page, using the findings of the CIA report.[55]

The White House was equally concerned that U.S. domestic protest might strengthen North Vietnamese morale and perseverance.[56] An intelligence report from December 1967 by the Military Assistance Command, Vietnam (MACV) concluded that "stated VC [Viet Cong] policy was that the longer the war continued, the stronger the US doves would become and the VC were, therefore, dedicated to fight at least until the 1968 presidential election."[57] Interpreting this as evidence of a direct influence of domestic protest in the United States, President Johnson and Rostow had Helms now report on the international connections of the U.S. peace movement on a regular basis.[58] All subsequent reports, however, corroborated what Helms reiterated during the cabinet meeting of September 1968, namely that the CIA could not substantiate any "control, manipulation, sponsorship, or significant financial support of student dissidents by any international Communist authority."[59]

Along those lines, the CIA also found no evidence supporting the view of a tight organizational, international network of activists. Rather, individual contacts of a short and irregular nature were seen as the norm, which, however, did "constitute the nucleus of what could become a source of direction."[60] Even more significant was the magnification of unrest through instantaneous global news coverage. A so-called "grapevine effect" fostered by the international media encouraged students in various places to pursue their own agendas by instilling solidarity with students elsewhere: "It seems likely that the media, by their emphasis on violence, police intervention, etc., add to the intensity and duration of a disturbance. . . . A student in the US, France, Brazil, or Japan does identify with his peers in other countries and is more likely to share their values and feel that their problems are his."[61] Easy access to foreign-language books and newspapers, a shared avant-garde culture, increasing mobility, and a growing number of foreign exchange programs had given the universities a "cosmopolitan character" leading to a high level of global interconnectedness.[62]

The CIA study concluded that the majority of students in East or West with a generally affluent background would mostly be concerned about matters of lifestyle, not in the establishment of a new revolutionary order.[63] The political effects of this value change, however, should not be underestimated: "Because of the revolution in communications, the ease of travel, and the evolution of society everywhere, student behavior never again will resemble what it was when education was reserved for the elite. . . . Increasingly, [today's students] have come to recognize what they take to be a community of interests. This view is likely to influence their future political conduct and to shape the demands they make of government."[64] The end of the war in Vietnam would most likely not solve this problem, since it was rooted in a "certain social and political malaise" stemming from the need for massive reform. Suggesting the danger of a right-wing counter-reaction, the study closed by alluding to "striking parallels between the situation today and the conditions of cynicism, despair, and disposition toward violence which existed after World War I and which later helped produce Fascism and National Socialism on the Continent."[65] It also raised the question of whether generational conflict is inherent in industrial societies, which would make a further aggravation of this phenomenon more likely, unless more constructive avenues for channeling the energies of the younger generation were found.[66]

The evaluation of the CIA report turned out to be the most time-consuming and emotionally charged item on the cabinet's agenda that day. Helms's presentation of the CIA's findings provoked a heated debate between various cabinet members and the president about the nature of communist support for student unrest worldwide:

IMAGE 26. U.S. President Lyndon B. Johnson's cabinet debating student protests, September 18, 1968 (Lyndon B. Johnson Library, Austin, Texas)

Secretary Rusk:	No support?
Director Helms:	That's right.
The President:	But there is support. There is, isn't there?
Secretary Fowler:	Aren't they giving the same kind of support that the Communists gave to the labor movement in this country?
Secretary Rusk:	Well, it is the difference between rape and seduction. . . . Let me say one thing. I was told by a trustee of an Ivy League university that he has 30 Communists on his faculty. He said that to me.
The President:	I just don't believe that business that there is no support. I've seen it in my own school. I've seen them provoke and aggravate trouble. I know that Students for a Democratic Society and the DuBois Clubs are Communist infiltrated, Communist supported and aggravated. Maybe they are not Communist led, but they are Communist agitated and aggravated.
Director Helms:	I am trying to make that distinction. The difference is there. This report deals with the world situation. I'm trying to stay away from U.S. problems and treat the world.
The Vice President:	Well, just come and travel with me. [laughter][67]

Following this brief debate, Walt Rostow delivered his interpretation of the situation, mostly concurring with Helms's analysis. For Rostow, "five general elements" could be named as contributing factors to global and U.S. dissent: the emergence of mass education, globally linked mass communications, the consequences of scientific-technological progress on the individual, the rise of so-called "soft subjects" such as sociology, which deal with "generalities and abstractions," and finally, general worldwide transition processes, in which young people wanted to find a position for themselves. Furthermore, he regarded an "impulse to traditional anarchism" as well as an unorthodox "left-wing communism," which aimed at polarizing society in order to emerge as a vital alternative after a rightward shift, as the two main characteristics of unrest across the world.[68]

Despite Rostow's nuanced analysis, a surprisingly narrow focus on communist conspiracies and a disregard for the underlying problems leading to global student unrest as spelled out by the CIA study seem to have prevailed among cabinet members as well as the president. As former Attorney General Ramsey Clarke recalled, Johnson and Rusk were especially harsh toward Helms: "I vividly remember Johnson and Rusk, in particular, giving poor old Helms hell at that [meeting]: 'What kind of idiots do you have working over there?' . . . They were contemptuous. And I thought they were pretty insulting."[69] Other members of the administration even years later concurred with the theory of communist infiltration and some sort of communist support. Former White House Press Secretary George Christian, for example, insisted, "I don't care what anybody says, some of the demonstrations were *not* spontaneous. . . . They had an efficient network of some kind. And I think one of the things that really bothered us at that time about some of the campus activities in particular [was] the people that were on the campuses stirring things up— they were *not* students." Dean Rusk later also argued that "it would be foolish to suppose that such communists as there were were not doing what they could in opposition to the war." Administration officials also voiced theories having to do with the protesters' need to prove their manhood due to their refusal to join the army, possible mental defects, as well as guilt complexes and lack of social prestige on the part of professors.[70]

Regardless, the depths and connections to underlying trends in society presented by the CIA in "Restless Youth" make this report an extraordinarily perceptive document that exhaustively informed the highest levels of the U.S. administration on details of global student protest. It furnished them with ample comparative information to gear their response, as can be seen in the charts on student figures and escalating tactics and techniques of protesters worldwide that were used at the cabinet meeting.[71]

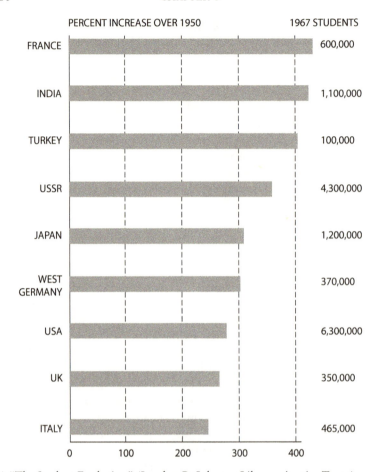

(a) "The Student Explosion" (Lyndon B. Johnson Library, Austin, Texas)

FIGURE 3. CIA charts on global student unrest used during President Johnson's Cabinet Meeting, September 18, 1968.

By the end of 1968, the State Department had thus produced various reports on student unrest worldwide and its impact on U.S. foreign policy, two of them at the request of the vice president and the president himself.[72] In January 1969, the final report of the Student Unrest Study Group of the State Department led by George McGhee dedicated itself once more to designing the most effective response to international student unrest while protecting U.S. foreign policy strategies.[73] Although it found no common denominator that could sum up motives and goals of student movements on a global level, it distinguished between international objectives and protest against local or national conditions; all of which de-

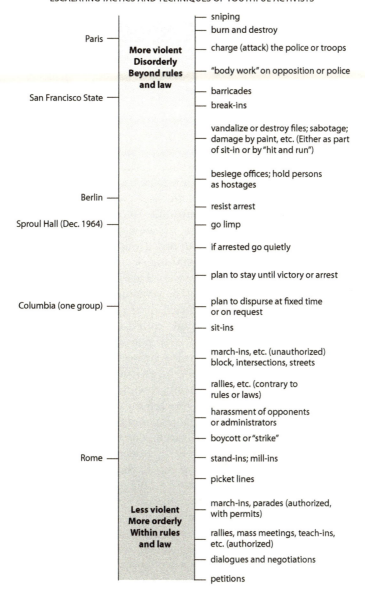

ESCALATING TACTICS AND TECHNIQUES OF YOUTHFUL ACTIVISTS

		sniping
		burn and destroy
Paris	**More violent Disorderly Beyond rules and law**	charge (attack) the police or troops
		"body work" on opposition or police
San Francisco State		barricades
		break-ins
		vandalize or destroy files; sabotage; damage by paint, etc. (Either as part of sit-in or by "hit and run")
		besiege offices; hold persons as hostages
Berlin		resist arrest
Sproul Hall (Dec. 1964)		go limp
		if arrested go quietly
		plan to stay until victory or arrest
Columbia (one group)		plan to disperse at fixed time or on request
		sit-ins
		march-ins, etc. (unauthorized) block, intersections, streets
		rallies, etc. (contrary to rules or laws)
		harassment of opponents or administrators
		boycott or "strike"
Rome		stand-ins; mill-ins
		picket lines
	Less violent More orderly Within rules and law	march-ins, parades (authorized, with permits)
		rallies, mass meetings, teach-ins, etc. (authorized)
		dialogues and negotiations
		petitions

(b) "Escalating Tactics" (Lyndon B. Johnson Library, Austin, Texas)

FIGURE 3. CIA charts on global student unrest used during President Johnson's Cabinet Meeting, September 18, 1968.

served special attention. Nonetheless, only the combination of international with local issues might lead to constraints on a government's foreign policy. If the issues remained separate, national stability or a country's foreign policy would be affected only marginally. McGhee thus urged the posts to separate, in his words, "fundamental and those more tangential issues" in order to get a better assessment of their political impact.[74]

Moreover, McGhee regarded the New Left as only one component of the whole phenomenon, which consisted of no more than a small percentage of the student body and was largely restricted to Western Europe and the United States. In its inherently transnational orientation, McGhee saw one of its most puzzling and remarkable features, which also posed the greatest challenge to foreign policy assessments: "We sense that the emergence of the attitudes associated with the New Left are indicative of a historical turning point in national attitudes. We are unable to understand the full ramifications of this intuition, but we suggest that a major contributing factor is the relative absence of broadly accepted national concerns that would foster a stronger 'nationalism' or 'patriotism,' in their traditional sense. If there is any common thread underlying the New Left, it is a marked lack of such attitudes."[75] The simultaneity of the student eruptions, according to the report, reflected three phenomena: the more advanced channels of media and communication available to the New Left, the influence of emerging national liberation movements, and, particularly in the developing countries, a new strategy of confrontation to address and improve conditions within the existing system.[76]

For McGhee, the widespread hostility toward the U.S. government obstructed any constructive dialogue between the New Left's extreme activists and U.S. officials. Likewise, he emphasized that most student activists rejected any influence or control by communist forces. Following Lipset's argument, McGhee now assumed that the students often represented only the "trigger" of long-term developments beyond their control and that their activism was more part of a power struggle than related to the proclaimed issues at stake. To confront the phenomenon, McGhee recommended a greater emphasis on cultural exchange, an increase in younger mission staff assigned to youth affairs, and more media programs and material designed for young people. He announced the initiation of advanced seminars and conferences on the topic organized by the Department of State, but also admitted that beyond these measures there was little one could do against the unfavorable consequences of student unrest.[77] Stressing the political need for observation of long-term developments and a greater understanding of the issue, he emphasized, however, that "to the extent that the disaffected student tends to articulate the concerns of the moderate masses, he provides the discerning observer with indicators of future social and political trends."[78]

By the beginning of 1969, the U.S. government had amply analyzed the potential threat posed by worldwide student unrest to its foreign policy interests. It decided to react to this challenge and increase its monitoring of youthful protest. In its attempt to incorporate these findings into individual country programming, the U.S. government sought to confront what it saw as an international problem on a local level, by addressing and possibly utilizing the idiosyncratic issues prevalent in the nation in question. In this way, student protest affected American foreign policy considerations in a remarkable way, as can be seen in the resulting adjustments taken in the relationship to West Germany.

The Reshaping of the U.S. Embassy's Youth Program

The efforts of the State Department and its overseas posts to reach the young generation in West Germany, and the protesting students in particular, were substantial, manifold, and responsive to the shifts in public opinion that became noticeable over time. An organizational center of this effort was the embassy's youth committee, which had been established in the course of the 1960s, thanks to the IAYC's efforts. The committee was chaired by the embassy's deputy chief of mission and included representatives from other branches. The embassy separated German youth as a target group into two subcategories, with high school and university students forming the first, and young people in political office and government administrative positions making up the other. The task of reaching both groups expanded in 1966/67, with the embassy's youth committee focusing mostly on the latter.

Among the various efforts directed at West German youth, the U.S. Information Service (USIS) program was the most extensive.[79] By bringing distinguished speakers, artists, and scientists to the Federal Republic, it sought to present a comprehensive picture of the positive aspects of the American way of life to a West German audience. Events were frequently held in cooperation with German youth associations and included the use of the America Houses for conferences, lectures, and panel discussions. In the second half of the 1960s, these events were categorized under the headings "Aspects of U.S. Foreign Policy" and "Aspects of American Civilizations." Especially the first category drew the largest crowds, the most pervasive topic being the war in Vietnam, and the events regularly involved high-level American officials. In the eyes of the embassy, the war in Vietnam still superseded themes such as NATO or East-West relations and lastingly tainted the image of the United States: "Among university students, young trade union people and the socialist political clubs, this subject has been and is the most controversial and damaging to American prestige. The frustration of Vietnam manifests itself in the protest rallies, the demonstrations, and the smashing of windows in the Consulates General which have been reported previously."[80]

Faced with this situation, American officials concentrated their activities on countering the detrimental effects that student protest had on the objectives of U.S. cultural diplomacy in the Federal Republic. Already in May 1967, historian Fritz Stern argued that a comprehensive overhaul of American cultural programs in West Germany was necessary, especially with regard to the treatment of the war in Vietnam. Stern advocated that the USIS should give modest American critics of the war a forum to voice their views in its program activities, thereby painting a more balanced picture of the American domestic scene: "Certainly for intelligent Germans the clash of opinions in America during this war has been the single heartening factor that they see in the whole picture. Within obvious limits of prudence we should capitalize on this opposition in order at least to strengthen German regard for the workings of American democracy."[81]

In a similar vein, many American posts favored the idea of meeting West German students halfway by conducting informal discussions in which they could present a more complex picture of the United States. When in November 1967 the U.S. Mission in Berlin, for example, reported that the ongoing student unrest contributed to lower morale and harmed the city's liberal reputation, the mission decided to change its program activities. Seeing a direct link between student unrest and the city's psychological climate, it shifted the focus of its overall activities toward youth, believing that "[w]e must do our utmost to engage and be in constant contact with those students, many of them leftist-oriented, who are politically mature and active and whose future attitudes are being shaped now in the course of their university studies. This means contacts—personal contacts—with professors and students of as many political and social views as possible."[82] This emphasis included social get-togethers in the consulate officer's home as well as the assignment of junior officers to reach out to this new, primary target group.

The American Consulate in Stuttgart was particularly creative in confronting student unrest. Arguing that "the post-war generation is becoming an increasingly important factor in German politics," which needed to be given "increased attention in U.S. foreign policy planning," the consulate in June 1967 intensified its youth efforts and introduced a "hobby" program.[83] The consulate saw junior foreign service officers as "our best sources of information on the German youth movement" and assigned each of them a city or an area of interest that they were responsible for in terms of reporting and designing new projects: "in other words, [with] the [same] range, if not the depth, of a political officer's job."[84] The hobby program, in combination with other increased efforts to address

West German youth, seemingly resulted in an increase of young audiences, more frequent visits of American diplomatic officers to many of the state's universities, a refocus of USIS efforts on the young generation, and greater contact with young leaders with political, official, and student backgrounds.[85]

All of these responses by American officials could, however, not reverse a trend in public opinion that indicated a convergence of the students' criticism with a more general dissatisfaction toward the United States. In April 1968, a study by the U.S. Information Agency (USIA) took the protest in West Germany as a starting point to analyze the validity of the claim of a "generation gap" in Western Europe that was based on long-term trends in opinion polls. It concluded that despite noticeable differences in opinion between youth and their elders, the ideas of the young generation were reflective of a larger trend in public opinion. Moreover, it was not the young people who reacted most disapprovingly to issues of relevance to U.S. interests, such as the war in Vietnam. The difference in opinions favorable or unfavorable toward the United States between younger and older people was generally below 10 percent, the largest being 14 percent.[86]

For the USIA, the greater source of concern was therefore the confluence of opinion of young and old, which indicated a "major erosion in pro-American sentiment." Among Western European nations, West Germany was leading in this downward trend. When asked about a perceived community of basic interests with the United States, USIA registered one of the largest drops in survey history from a net favorable opinion of 77 percent in January 1965 to – 9 percent in March 1967, and, after a quick rise, settling at 11 percent in December 1967.[87] Interpreting this as a striking indicator of a new phase in German-American relations, USIA decided to implement fundamental changes in its country programming, since "[p]rograms can no longer be planned on the assumption that most West Germans see a basic accord between U.S. and West German interests."[88] A similar, although not quite as drastic, negative development was noted in the other European countries. More alarming, however, was the conclusion that the popular dictum of a generation gap could not be substantiated with regard to the transatlantic partnership.[89]

As a consequence, in May 1968 the embassy in Bonn announced that "its past programs and priorities are no longer adequate."[90] Extending the definition of "youth" until the age of about 35, it declared that the embassy's programs needed a complete overhaul. In 1964 the embassy still considered youth in this country as mostly apathetic to politics, but now most segments, including even formerly nonpolitical youth organizations, had undergone some form of politicization. To be sure, only a small minority dedicated itself to political affairs, either active in the leadership of moderate youth or student organizations, or making up the core members of "radical" organizations. The latter, however, frequently earned the support of the majority of youth, which, in the embassy's view, had considerably influenced the political spectrum: "Over the past two years the radical student activists have organized numerous demonstrations against the Shah of Iran, the war in Vietnam, the Axel Springer press, the adoption of emergency legislation, NATO and the Grand Coalition. Youth have been at least partially responsible for the shift of the FDP to the left, and for the difficulties the SPD has had with its left wing. The radical student activists have obtained support from a larger group of politically involved youth, and from labor and intellectual groups on certain issues."[91]

Despite these circumstances, most U.S. officials asserted that German youth still embraced democratic beliefs and discarded political extremism from both sides. Home, school, and church remained major influences but were increasingly viewed more critically among the young generation. Moreover, American actions at home and abroad had drastically changed the previously shining image that the United States had enjoyed among young people: "Anti-Americanism is not strong among most German youth, but there is considerable opposition to American involvement in Vietnam, to the racial situation in the United States, and to 'U.S. domination' of Europe."[92]

As a consequence, American priorities in country programming for West German youth from this point on concentrated on university and advanced high school (Gymnasium) students. The embassy justified this shift by pointing out that this group had become an independent political force and was the almost exclusive pool from which the future leadership of the country would emerge: "The greatest emphasis must be placed on reaching the student leadership, both radical and moderate."[93] Organized nonstudent youth and young people in the middle of establishing their careers would come second and third in program priorities. In USIS-sponsored programs, youth therefore became the major target audience, with about 65 percent of all USIS's programming activities directed toward German youth: "USIS has selected a 'Prime Target Group' (the major audience to be reached) of approximately 263,000 Germans of all ages. Of this group, 34% are university students, 21% are secondary students and 14% are teachers and professors. Many of these are organizational leaders and activists. Of the remaining 31% of the Prime Target Group, no statistical breakdown between youth and non-youth is available, but Embassy estimates indicate that roughly half of those reached fall within the definition of youth."[94]

This change in programming was to be mirrored by similar attempts of the Military Assistance Advisory Group (MAAG) and military attaché programs, as well as embassy and consulate efforts. The latter were supposed to increase their personal contacts with youth, address their issues more effectively—for example, through a higher number of discussions with political youth organizations—and facilitate and encourage more visits to the United States. In the overall review of U.S. posts, the embassy also suggested a better utilization of the junior foreign-service officer as a valuable connection to West Germany's youth, as exemplified by Stuttgart's hobby program. Moreover, it planned to systematize contacts to youth leadership and involve private American citizens living in West Germany in the mission's efforts.

In the aftermath of the events of May 1968 in France, the American embassy in Bonn massively strengthened its efforts to reach German youth. It particularly sharpened its focus on "radical" students, arriving at a rather sober understanding of the dynamics of student unrest that had hit the country: "The leftist radicals have won positions of leadership in most of the student organizations, and even a few of the non-student organizations. For this reason, their ability to cause unrest is far greater than their number would indicate. Most of the unrest, the demonstrations and the violence over the past two years can be traced to the radical university students."[95] In response to this situation, the embassy compiled detailed lists of West German youth and student organizations in order to better adjust its youth efforts to their growing political influence.[96]

By encouraging constructive efforts in the area of university reform or a German version of the Peace Corps, U.S. officials sought to take the heat out of student protest and channel youthful activism into less controversial areas.[97] Considering student unrest to be a nationwide problem, the American embassy in Bonn also tried to ensure a greater coordination of its various posts throughout the country. In July 1968, for example, it brought together members of the various consulates concerned with youth affairs in West Germany for a joint youth officer's conference to assess the situation in the Federal Republic as a whole. Topics on the agenda included the likelihood of developments similar to those in France, the strength of the student left, its anti-American feelings, student cooperation with organized labor, as well as East Germany and Eastern European countries.[98] In the eyes of the embassy, the junior officers in particular were supposed to assume a greater role in confronting student unrest. Consequently, the embassy enlarged its youth committee by including all junior officers as ex officio members, asked that junior officers take on greater responsibility and proposed specific sets of priorities for local posts, which were supposed to examine budding student thinking and its effects on future developments in society.

To institutionalize a greater internal exchange on youth affairs among U.S. officials, the embassy also began to host annual conferences of youth

officers as part of its country programming.[99] On a European level, the
IAYC organized similar meetings that frequently took place in West Germany. European Youth Seminars in 1969 and 1972, for example, assembled embassy youth officers and respective USIS personnel from all over
Europe to discuss current trends among young people and their significance for U.S. foreign policy objectives, trying to improve the existing
government programs in individual countries.

Annual meetings about the situation in the Federal Republic painted a
comprehensive, nationwide picture with regard to the status of youth. In
November 1970, for example, the vice president of the Free University
Berlin, Uwe Wesel, and political scientist Richard Löwenthal gave a youth
officers' conference an update on the specific problems of student unrest
in Berlin. Deputy Chief of Mission Russell Fessenden from the U.S. embassy subsequently outlined his conception of the role of the youth committee as one of "potential leader identification" and constant reporting
on youth as a political force in the Federal Republic.[100] It emerged, however, during the conference that radical youth factions had by now lost
their following, causing the overall level of violence to plummet, with the
exception of an "extreme, even lunatic fringe" of the movement. American officials nonetheless decided to pay closer attention to the relationship
between students and workers, the role of left-wing students in the media,
and protest activities involving U.S. forces stationed in West Germany.
Conference participants agreed that this continued observation of youth
was crucial, since they were currently only witnessing the first years of a
generation largely unaffected by the cold war: "[T]his new generation is
less inhibited in thinking about German relations *vis-à-vis* Eastern European countries, including the Soviet Union. The Berlin Wall has not only
served to keep East Germans and East Berliners inside, but has also given
an aura of mystery and interest to events and doctrines in East Berlin
and the DDR. Previously, discussion about things East German could be
quickly resolved by a trip to East Berlin and East Germany. This is no
longer feasible for most youth."[101]

In the following years, the youth efforts of the new administration in
Washington and the directives stemming from the IAYC continued to
guide the actions of American posts in the Federal Republic.[102] As Ambassador Kenneth Rush summed up American diplomatic efforts with regard
to the West German left in December 1970, "On the whole there is ground
for optimism. In Germany today most of the left is anti-communist and
even most of the far left is non-communist. Anti-Americanism is not rampant and the far right is in severe disarray. We believe we have good and
continual contacts with most of the real decision makers as well as their
possible replacements in middle and younger generations."[103] U.S. cul-

tural diplomacy efforts in the Federal Republic therefore now increasingly focused on the country's young generation of future leaders and tried to influence them with the help of cultural exchange programs.

DRAINING THE RESERVOIR OF GOODWILL?
STUDENT PROTEST AND CULTURAL EXCHANGE PROGRAMS

German-American cultural exchange programs had a long history, which predated the 1960s.[104] Between 1948 and 1955, about 12,000 Germans had visited the United States as part of the cultural exchange program administered by the High Commission of Germany.[105] The peculiar geopolitical position of the Federal Republic in the cold war spurred incentives for initiatives on a private or university level between the two countries. The Fulbright program, which began operations in 1946, included West Germany in 1952 and brought American students to this newly established German democracy.[106]

This exchange of academic elites soon resulted in a transformation of the image of the United States in the Federal Republic. Although West German participants noticed democratic deficits such as racial discrimination, these shortcomings could not overshadow an increasing fascination with the United States. The encounter of West Germans with the American political culture and university system led to a greater acceptance of democratic values, a more positive image of the United States, as well as the impression that the American system could at least partially serve as a role model for their own country. Especially West German high school students were deeply impressed by their American experience and had difficulties readjusting to what they afterward perceived as a narrow-minded and traditionalist system at home.[107]

From the American perspective, the original reeducational purposes of German-American cultural exchange were still valid in the 1960s. As the American Consulate in Munich wrote in 1965, "A historical fact is that Germany has enjoyed a comparatively short experience in the functioning of successful democratic government. It is in the interest of the United States to do what is possible to enable a new German generation to obtain better understanding of democratic government, and of United States democracy, not always obtained by earlier German generations, subjected to subjective analysis and hostile propaganda."[108] As this new generation, which had to a very large extent taken part in these exchange programs, came of age, however, it began to take notice of the growing domestic conflicts in the United States and voiced its own protest against what it saw as tragic errors of American foreign policy in Southeast Asia. The fact that one of the early critics of the war in Vietnam, Ekkehard Krippendorff—who later played a significant role in the West German student movement—was also a former participant of academic exchange with the United States and is just one case out of many similar examples.[109]

U.S. officials equally noticed the possibility that exchange programs could help spread antiwar opposition and, in fact, be detrimental to American interests.[110] To gain a more detailed assessment of these connections, the IAYC in May 1967 analyzed the impact of exchange programs with respect to Western Europe. The participants of a respective conference, however, soon realized that in the two decades since the end of the Second World War the field of cultural exchange programs had become far too complex to get even a clear overview anymore, since "[n]ow thirty government agencies—instead of one, two or three in 1947—plus an endless number of American foundations, associations and institutes have become active in the field."[111] The problem was that most of the programs, as well as the binational commissions, predominantly served the domestic needs of the partner countries and that the "the bulk of CU's work in Europe in recent years has not really addressed itself directly to foreign policy purposes."[112] In addition, it emerged that "*no one* in the U.S. Government has a clear or full picture of exactly what is being done" and that no coordination of these various exchange activities took place.[113] As the chairman of the IAYC, Foy Kohler summed up the situation, "The most shocking thing to come out of these discussions is the revelation of how little we know about international programs run by other agencies, government and private. . . . There is no central place in the government where this is all coordinated and guided and assisted."[114]

Despite this lack of government oversight, student protest had initially only very little effect on the successful operation of the German-American exchange programs. In his annual report in 1966, Ambassador McGhee could still state that the exchange was carried out in a friendly atmosphere and that "[d]espite 'Gaullism' and student anti-Vietnam demonstrations one may still justly generalize that we enjoy the good will of the German government and people."[115] In the embassy's view, this "fund of good will" was largely the result of the exchange programs of the 1950s. Moreover, the fact that people who were now coming into positions of power and of influence in West Germany had been exposed to American ideas in the previous decade was a long-term strategic advantage: "The assumption of leadership in all sections of public affairs in Germany by a younger generation is already in process. The course of German-American relations during the next few years will test inter alia the effectiveness of what we have done in the large exchange programs of the post-war years."[116] As soon as public criticism of the United States became more widespread at the end of the 1960s, U.S. officials tried to capitalize on this supply to maintain "a sympathetic climate of informed opinion receptive to views we wish to communicate."[117] To ensure this environment, the embassy relied on the help of former German grantees in mediating its policies to the general public. Returning grantees such as the liberal politician and member of parliament Hildegard Hamm-Brücher, for example, were considered a "very good investment which has yielded immediate and impressive results" due to her political and publication activities in the field of university reform, which contributed to the popular view of the United States as an academic role model.[118]

The enthusiasm among American officials dampened with the continuing rise of strong opposition to U.S. policies by student protesters, which began to cause minor difficulties to the transatlantic exchange programs. Interestingly enough, while antiwar opposition increased among the young generation in West Germany, the interest in the exchange programs continued to be very high throughout the 1960s. Application numbers for study in the United States quadrupled between 1963 and 1972.[119] For Ulrich Littmann, who administered the Fulbright exchange program in West Germany, the colorful images of the American student movement were partly responsible for this trend: "[I]n the numerous counseling programs organized by the Fulbright Commission secretariat at universities and America Houses, students showed great interest in studying in the U.S.—often with daring expectations of alternative lifestyles, youth culture or 'counter culture' on the American campus. . . . Revolutionary fervor calmed down when students were confronted with the unexpected work load that even progressive faculties demanded from their foreign students."[120]

Growing student unrest and antiwar activities of many of its participants nonetheless started to affect the transatlantic exchange program. On July 12, 1967, thirty-seven Fulbright grantees from Berlin wrote to President Johnson and Secretary of State Rusk protesting against the U.S. involvement in Vietnam, which prompted the State Department's Bureau of Educational and Cultural Affairs (CU) to have informal discussions with future American grantees on the appropriateness of such a public display of dissent.[121] While stressing that grantees certainly enjoyed every right of American citizens, Assistant Secretary of State for Educational and Cultural Affairs Charles Frankel hinted at restrictions inherent in their grant to refrain from political activity in their host country: "[W]e believe that it is in the spirit of the Fulbright-Hays Act and of our entire cultural exchange policy that the exchange program itself retain its integrity as a non-political program." In addition, Frankel underscored that moral obligations and responsibility toward the program should be factored into any consideration of public statements.[122]

In the fall of 1967, the American embassy in West Germany also began to observe an emerging rift in public opinion toward the United States.

The issues straining German-American relations were the Nuclear Non-Proliferation Treaty, German troop reductions, as well as the war in Vietnam and domestic unrest in the United States. The embassy argued that in this situation, the actions and opinions of former grantees were crucial in maintaining a positive image of the United States in West Germany: "Returnees in the communications business—press, radio, television—have distinguished themselves from other journalists in their reporting by an objective and fair elucidation of our foreign and domestic problems and have demonstrated a sympathetic understanding of the U.S. government's difficult position."[123] The disproportionately high number of former participants of the exchange program in leading positions in the federal government (fifteen out of twenty cabinet members) was also a unique strategic advantage in these difficult times: "To find returnees in top government positions, most of them favorably disposed toward the United States and willing to cooperate, is an invaluable asset to the work of U.S. diplomatic and consular officers and to the attainment of U.S. foreign policy objectives in Germany."[124]

In the embassy's view, the *Spandauer Volksblatt*, a Berlin newspaper formerly taking a disapproving stance with regard to the war in Vietnam, for example, changed its policies after the visit of its editor, Hans Höppner, to the United States and intensive exchanges with local information officers. This was especially valuable since the newspaper's readership consisted mainly of university students and intellectuals in 1960s Berlin. It also provided the embassy with proof of the immediate effectiveness of cultural exchange programs and justified their continued funding. The embassy even hoped that these financial resources, "if used judiciously, might contribute to alleviating some aspects of the student unrest at the Free University which has been Berlin's most urgent problem this year."[125] In the face of increasing opposition to the war in Vietnam and the amount of coverage on the internal disruptions in the United States, returned West German grantees thus became crucial partners for American cultural diplomacy efforts in the Federal Republic of the late 1960s. As U.S. Ambassador Henry Cabot Lodge noted in August 1968, "The assistance of returned grantees has become indispensable to USIS Germany in programming efforts, in cooperation with the German organizations and institutions and in the co-sponsorship of cultural events."[126] Despite the fact that they would often face hostilities from antiwar demonstrators, these veterans of transatlantic exchange programs could be integrated into existing program efforts and enlisted to help explain U.S. foreign policy objectives.[127]

Although antiwar demonstrations and their attraction slowly declined during 1968–69, student unrest remained a challenge that CU had to deal with.[128] To the dismay of the embassy, however, the reservoir of good will from former participants of transatlantic exchange programs gradually diminished in relation to the annual budget cuts of the U.S. government. But now that the New Left had become a permanent factor in German political life, the embassy was especially eager to safeguard the achievements of the postwar years and prevent any further reduction of cultural exchange: "At the present time, however, it is all the more important to send young people to the U.S when many of the younger generation, influenced by leftist student groups, take a rather hostile stand toward the U.S. Government's foreign policy, U.S.-German alliance in NATO and U.S. domestic issues, especially race problems."[129] To illustrate this, the embassy detailed two incidents, one on television and the other at a public rally, in which former grantees Horst Ehmke (Federal Minister of Justice) and Günther Müller (MP) respectively were able to counter the distorted picture of the United States given by representatives of the New Left.[130] In the embassy's estimate, short-term effectiveness such as this, as well as the long-lasting gains of having former grantees at one's disposal, were "an indispensable factor in our efforts to reach overall country program objectives," particularly in times of recurring public hostilities.

American officials also strongly welcomed the new Brandt government of 1969 for the aforementioned reasons, since an even greater number of cabinet members (thirteen out of sixteen ministers) had participated in cultural or educational exchange programs with the United States.[131] In addition, 11 out of 38 state secretaries in the federal ministries, 24 percent of members of the Bundestag, 19 out of 46 regular and 28 out of 64 deputy members of the Bundesrat, and 8 out of 11 state ministers were former grantees, who, for the most part, would permanently strengthen the German-American partnership. The hope among U.S. diplomats was that especially these 1950s returnees would speak up against what the embassy at the beginning of the 1970s described as a "noticeable growth of anti-Americanism in the past two or three years, especially among German youth."[132] Scholars such as Erwin Scheuch, a sociologist from the University of Cologne, as well as more recent participants of the exchange program such as Klaus Boelling, chief correspondent of the ARD (one of the two public national television stations in West Germany) covering Washington, were, in the embassy's view, relentlessly combating a one-sided public image of the United States.[133] Former grantees also began to come out more frequently against student protest directed against American institutions. Siegfried Maruhn, chief editor of the *Westdeutsche Allgemeine*, for example, accused the people attacking America Houses in West Germany of being too young to even imagine the significance of these places where the "German war- and post-war generation became acquainted with world literature and was given access to German books banned or burned by the Nazis."[134] Regardless of these incidents, the embassy found that American universities still remained a role model for reform efforts in the Federal Republic. The ties between German and American universities were thus continually strengthened by increasing exchange numbers in spite of "anti-American" sentiments.[135] Another reason for the success of these programs was, however, the simple fact that by now West German financial support outmatched American contributions by four to one.[136]

When challenged by the West German New Left, the architects of the transatlantic exchange programs thus drew on the help of former grantees in defending America's achievements and explaining its current problems. For U.S. officials, there was "no substitute for the experience gained through direct contact with American life and institutions. The familiarity with America also increased the willingness of returnees to cooperate with USIS, and it is this cooperation of organizations, institutions, and individuals which makes it possible for USIS to carry out a really meaningful program in Germany." Despite further drastic funding cuts under the Nixon administration, CU and other American agencies continued their mission to reach out and try to win over the hearts and minds of German youth by adapting to the new challenges that they were facing in the 1970s.

THE TRANSFORMATION OF
GERMAN POLITICS BY STUDENT ACTIVISTS

In November 1967, the State Department's Policy Planning Council report concluded that the German student movement's "anti-Americanism, largely over Vietnam, coupled to that of most of the FRG's [Federal Republic's] leftist intellectuals, does present a growing problem for US policy."[137] The problem primarily consisted of the fact that despite the gradual faltering of the New Left on an organizational level, the ideological challenge it posed could not be absorbed by the dominant political forces. Only a month later, the council summed up the toll that had been taken by differences about the Nuclear Non-Proliferation Treaty, American troop reductions, and German reunification on the transatlantic partnership: "[T]he mood underlying present FRG policies is, to a much greater extent than prior to 1966, one of uncertainty, resentment, or suspicion regarding the main thrust of US policy."[138] Aware of the growing impact of student protest on society, the State Department prophesied the results of the politicization of youth for West German foreign policy: "[A] new generation of German leaders will be coming into power in the not-too-distant future. There is widespread disaffection among younger Germans with the present leadership and its policies. . . . It is somewhat easier to imagine that, when this generation assumes leadership, the FRG might, with relatively little provocation by US policies, reassess its essential interests and undertake a basic policy departure."[139] In other words, the threat of a neutralist Germany, an "all-German status" for West Berlin, massive reductions of U.S. forces, as well as the Federal Republic's withdrawal from the Common Market and NATO, could be the consequences.[140] These apprehensions of American policy planners about these potential long-term effects of student protest were only to intensify over time.

In the course of 1968, American policymakers were also concerned that the New Left would capitalize on what they considered a "serious crisis" of the SPD, which was internally torn over its participation in the Grand Coalition. They feared that a "continuation and intensification of this crisis could create a vacuum on the left and an opening for radicalism." In their view, the party was losing some of its core constituencies and its "functionaries and some of its parliamentarians are susceptible to pressures from the radical left."[141] When it therefore became apparent in mid-1969 that the Young Socialists and Young Free Democrats, the respective youth organizations of the SPD and FDP, were still very much under the radical students' influence, the American embassy in Bonn predicted the survival of New Left ideology in the established party system as a permanent legacy of the student movement: "It appears possible that the New Left will continue in the future to be a factor on the German scene. . . . As New Left youth move into the professions and places of responsibility, their more radical orientation is most likely to find political expression in a strengthened voice for the left wings of the SPD and the FDP."[142] In more concrete terms, the student movement could, in the embassy's view, yield profound consequences on the political system of the Federal Republic, namely "a right-wing backlash, a strengthening of the left among youth organizations, a new leftist ideological challenge to the Bonn political system and a connected spur to reform efforts."[143] Despite campaigns to counteract the intellectual attraction of the New Left, the ideological consequences of the student movement for the Federal Republic appeared to be hardly reversible for American officials: "As persons 'formed in the struggle' move into positions of responsibility in the decades ahead, the long-term effect will probably be as much intellectual as political."[144]

This assessment of the long-term significance of student protest echoed the analysis by sociologist Seymour Lipset and found agreement from American officials assigned to West Germany at the time. Hans Tuch, USIS Public Affairs Officer in Berlin from 1967 to 1970, conceded that the turn against the United States by the young generation was an almost natural reaction to the high degree of American information campaigns that the country had been subjected to in previous years: "[W]ith the assassinations of President Kennedy, Senator Robert Kennedy, Martin Luther King, with the Vietnam War, with our own civil rights revolution, many young Germans suddenly became very disillusioned with America. They had been over-enthusiasthic about America before that, and when they found out that we were not the perfect society, that we had our own problems and that we had major problems in our own society, the turnaround became too abrupt."[145]

Political decision-makers such as Henry Kissinger, National Security Adviser in 1969, were similarly aware of the political consequences of this transformation. At the beginning of the 1960s, Kissinger had already warned of a clash of generations when Germany's youth would be blamed for the crimes of National Socialism.[146] Furthermore, he feared that despair over West Germany's continued division could impair the transatlantic orientation of the youth. West German students were largely alienated by America's foreign policy at the end of the decade, West Germany possessed a new confidence, isolationist currents prevailed in the United States, and détente, based on the perception of a reduced Soviet threat, enjoyed a wide approval. Kissinger interpreted this development as partially resulting from a generational change, since veterans "present at the creation" of America's postwar policy in Europe had left the public scene.[147] For him, this process was part of a historical pattern that repeated itself when a change of generations severed the hitherto close emotional bond across the Atlantic.[148] Kissinger thus interpreted the ongoing political ruptures in the Federal Republic as a psychological postwar crisis, which other countries had experienced in the first decade after 1945 while West Germany was focusing on reconstruction.[149]

Official American reporting on the newly elected SPD/FDP government under Willy Brandt was marked by similar considerations about the political significance of the generation coming of age in the late 1960s. U.S. posts carefully observed and commented upon Brandt's move toward the student left and his efforts to integrate it into existing party structures. With regard to plans for an amnesty on legal prosecution for demonstrators, the embassy argued in early November 1969 that such a strategy was risky and could backfire politically.[150] In general, the embassy thought that the new government enjoyed "a honeymoon of sorts with the leftist youth." It predicted, however, that Brandt could probably not satisfy the demands of the young left; the result of which might be unrest "of more serious proportions than in the past," due to the disappointment stemming from unfulfilled expectations. In case the chancellor came to a political arrangement with the New Left or succeeded in co-opting large segments of the young generation, there "will undoubtedly arise consequences which will require a reappraisal of U.S. policy towards the FRG and Europe." These transformations were particularly significant "since they may ultimately lead to a more leftist oriented government in Bonn."[151]

This fear of leftist infiltration of the established parties and a subsequent policy change brought about by the legacy of the West German student movement was pervasive among American policymakers. In Congress, Sen. Sherman P. Lloyd argued that "we must recognize reality and unfortunately reality suggests that Chancellor Brandt's party is being influenced by a far leftist faction whose intentions do not coincide with those of the United States or our allies."[152] This transformation also had far-reaching implications for future U.S. cultural diplomacy efforts, since not only the number of loyal returnees from the transatlantic exchange programs was declining in comparison to the 1950s but also the target audience had changed: "[T]here is growing here into positions of influence a new generation of men and women whose attitudes toward the U.S., in contrast to those born before (say) 1930, have not been shaped by America's contributions to Germany's postwar recovery and the creation of a secure Western Europe. Rather, their attitudes have been shaped by the war in Viet-Nam, an America beset by serious domestic problems, the assassinations of John F. Kennedy, Martin Luther King, Malcolm X, and Robert Kennedy, and American self-doubts."[153] U.S. cultural diplomacy efforts were increasingly unable, if only due to their limited resources, to return to their "successes" of the 1950s. In the following decades, U.S. officials were thus forced to take into account the mindset of a politically influential West German generation coming of age during the 1960s.[154] As Hans Tuch remembered, "We . . . realized that these young people . . . were about to take over leadership in the German society. . . . We recognized that changes had taken place, and that we had to readdress our ideas on our association with the Germans and how to deal with the problem, how to cope with it in order to be able to maintain the relationship that we feel is necessary to maintain."[155]

The West German protest movements of the second half of the 1960s thus initiated a fundamental readjustment of American foreign policy with respect to its cultural diplomacy efforts for the Federal Republic. The protest movements, however, fell far short of achieving their declared goals of destroying NATO and provoking a disentanglement of the Federal Republic from the transatlantic alliance system in the age of the cold war. Even the nuclear crisis and the stationing of Pershing II missiles on West German soil at the beginning of the 1980s did not seriously weaken the transatlantic partnership, although it involved far greater segments of society.[156] Nonetheless, the actions of the student activists of the late 1960s caused a substantial reorientation and increasing attention on the part of American foreign-policymakers toward the students' ideology and influence in West German society, not least due to their partial integration into the two governing parties at the end of the decade. The larger framework of this shift and the role it played in the efforts of the State Department became clear in the 1970s.

A "Revolutionary Sabbatical"?
Youthful Unrest and the Nixon Administration

The Nixon administration not only continued the youth efforts instituted by its predecessors, but also completely redesigned government activities in this area. At the end of 1968, the influence of student unrest on the formulation of U.S. foreign policy strategies had been amply illustrated. During a USIA seminar in May 1968 on how to deal with protesting youth abroad, the sociologist Seymour Lipset underlined that student activists were a future political force that could not be dismissed.[157] Similarly, the State Department's Policy Planning Council held that policymakers had underestimated the political impact of student opinions. To gain more acceptance among the young generation, the council devised a guidebook to "assist in understanding the often blatant and hostile attitudes of American students toward the State Department, the present Administration, and current foreign policies."[158] For the new Special Assistant for Youth Affairs and Executive Secretary of the IAYC, Robert Cross, the events of 1968 had also illustrated that "[y]outh, regardless of its effrontery, has something new to say, a new viewpoint on the old questions of institutional and international affairs. The more we listen to the real message of change they are sending, the sooner we can move beyond their frequently unacceptable tactics to the urgent task of reform which is overdue."[159]

Based on these sentiments, Ambassador-at-Large George McGhee urged the new administration to display a strong interest in youth affairs and the work of the IAYC.[160] In 1969, however, the IAYC underwent a thorough restructuring and reassessment. Together with the department's special assistant for youth, the committee was transferred from the responsibility of the deputy undersecretary for political affairs to the counselor, at that point a position filled by Richard Pedersen. Pedersen and Cross used this change to reform the membership and goals of the committee so that the former included higher-level representatives, preferably deputy assistant secretaries of the various agencies.[161] Opinions about IAYC's future direction and purpose, however, varied considerably among the member agencies. The Peace Corps, for example, had already argued the year before that, after the revelation of the far-reaching CIA covert funding-efforts of youth organizations, its participation in the committee would compromise its mission.[162]

Other skeptical voices, such as Edward Doherty from the Policy Planning Council, claimed that the complexity of student unrest was difficult to translate into effective political responses.[163] For Doherty, the alternative to inaction was to try to understand the phenomenon "both in terms of local politics and in terms of the generalized social crisis" while concentrating efforts at a few posts and creating a network of new young reporting officers with an academic background in sociology or political science. In cooperation with experts such as Kenneth Kenniston and Seymour Lipset, State Department analysts were asked to link foreign reports to the U.S. domestic scene: "After two years of such an inquiry, we might have learned enough to begin considering what, if anything, it all has to do with the conduct of America's foreign relations."[164]

The State Department, however, continued to support the work of the IAYC and confirmed its authority to supervise all government activities aimed at foreign youth. At the beginning of 1970, it urged all posts to refocus their attention according to the guidelines revised by the IAYC after discussions with regional bureaus:

(1) To assure that we assess as accurately as possible the political and social attitudes of students and other young people and come to a sound appreciation of their likely effect on political and social structures. . . .

(2) To seek to identify and establish relationships with the rising young leaders who are most likely in future years to reach positions of national influence, particularly in economic and political fields. Wherever feasible this should include contact not only with potential future leadership within the established system but also with those among the disaffected and the 'outs.'[165]

In addition, the department suggested lowering the entry age of officers responsible for reporting on youth, recommended the designation of a special youth officer as coordinator of all the local mission's youth activities, and asked that the mission's youth committee be chaired by the ambassador or a senior official. The reactions from the field, however, were mixed. Local posts questioned the seriousness of these efforts, since Washington was demanding greater attention and increased reporting on youth and at the same time had cut back on the number of junior foreign-service officers. While the overall numbers of officers in the foreign service had declined from 3,670 in 1965 to 3,263 in 1970, the junior officer intake fell from 194 in 1967 to 44 in 1968, climbed to 123 in 1969, but was projected at 14 for 1970 due to budget cuts. As one ambassador remarked, "[I]f the U.S. interest is a really serious and long-lasting one — as I think it should be—we must be prepared to earmark some of our assets."[166] In more general terms, however, IAYC executive secretary Rob-

ert Cross concluded that many missions seemed to have failed to notice
the intended shift from a program-oriented approach of reaching youth
to an "analysis and understanding of the rapidly changing world through
youth as indicators of social dynamism."[167]

The IAYC nonetheless continued its efforts to incorporate further the
concerns of youth into the political decision-making process and to assess
the chances of further student unrest abroad. The situation in Europe
remained a particular concern for the committee. In January 1969, local
posts concluded that "European students are increasingly seeing their
problems and strategy in a common light, exchanging views and cooperating with student groups in other countries. Student unrest is thus not
a national phenomenon alone but European in character."[168] Especially
disturbing was the fact that while European students were highly critical
of both the U.S. war in Vietnam and the Soviet invasion of Czechoslovakia, thereby popularizing a concept of "two imperialisms," American officials nonetheless saw a mounting anti-Americanism among the young
generation as "one of the greatest problems for US policy in Europe and
particularly for our future relations with these countries."[169] In June 1969,
IAYC therefore convened youth officers from all the European embassies
and USIS personnel in Bonn for a seminar on "Youth and Change in Europe." The aim was to discuss current trends among European youth,
analyze their intellectual makeup and political participation, and explore
their political and social impact in national contexts and on the international system.[170]

Conference participants largely agreed that a period of reorganization
and refocusing had set in among European youth. They did not, however,
mistake the currently rather calm atmosphere for an end of youthful protest. A profound identity crisis and fundamental disaffection with the existing political system continued to spur youthful activism, which began
to occupy a firm place in the respective societies: "Armed with a sophisti-
cated knowledge of society's ills at an earlier age than ever before, more
and more European young people are becoming actively hostile towards
the prevailing values of their elders and towards the official government
ideology in both East[ern] and West[ern] Europe. Evidence in several
countries—notably France, Germany and Eastern Europe—indicates that
radicalism has taken root in secondary schools where it was never known
before."[171] The conference concluded that "present-day dissident youth
and their successors will play a significant role in the formation of foreign
policy and that this will have important implications for U.S. policies,"
especially when it came to American relations with Latin America, South
Africa, as well as the dictatorships of Portugal, Spain, and Greece.[172] U.S.
officials saw a transformation in the domestic political landscape of European countries as the natural consequence of student dissident leaders

taking influential political positions in the future. Alongside a conservative counter-reaction, they expected a "significant but not radical change in European society in the next ten years," which would make a substantial review of American foreign-policy objectives indispensable.[173]

Despite the splintering and organizational demise of the New Left, the IAYC also saw the situation in Europe as ready to explode anew at any given time, since there was "more alienation among Western European youth than ever before, and the situation is possibly a powderkeg."[174] The IAYC therefore continued to organize European-wide conferences of embassy youth officers and USIS members to gear U.S. government efforts toward addressing the situation of dissenting European youth.[175]

Of even greater concern to the State Department was, however, the first U.N. conference on world youth, the World Youth Assembly (WYA) in New York in July 1970. The fact that communist representatives dominated several commissions and were able to push through resolutions condemning American involvement in Vietnam, which were incorporated in the final message to the General Assembly, was considered a particular nuisance. Nevertheless, the U.S. mission at the U.N. came to the conclusion that while no further assemblies should be supported, the general result would not be quite as depressing. Despite frequent overlap in opinion, many youth delegates opposed the communist line and the assembly therefore succeeded, in the eyes of the State Department, in illustrating a constructive outlet for youth activism through the U.N.[176] The IAYC, on the other hand, interpreted the assembly as yet more proof of the need for a greater observation of the impact of youth on international relations, since " 'politically aware' youth, in a majority of the countries, are in basic agreement with the thrust, if not always with the stridency of language, of the reports of the Commissions on World Peace and Development that gave us so much trouble."[177]

As a further consequence of the WYA, the IAYC also took a closer look at the international youth organizations.[178] Although the significance of youth and student internationals was much reduced in comparison to the 1950s, their activities in Europe still affected U.S. interests.[179] The State Department paid particular attention to the involvement of American representatives in international youth events dedicated to détente and "East-West bridge-building." It resolved to "promote qualified American participation at selected regional and international youth meetings where we conclude our interests are involved, even discreetly seeking invitations if none are forthcoming."[180] At the beginning of the 1970s, the department and the IAYC thus continued to assess the local impact of communist-front organizations such as the International Union of Students (IUS) and the World Federation of Democratic Youth (WFDY) and developed policy guidelines for dealing with international youth.[181]

In addition, the Nixon administration increasingly looked toward the impact of international unrest on the domestic scene. In February 1971, it held a special White House Conference on Youth in which task forces composed of youth representatives from across the United States and abroad formulated reports on various issues that the White House pledged to follow up within in a year.[182] Furthermore, the administration turned to the issue of foreign students within the United States, a topic that had begun to occupy the State Department in the mid-1960s. In the course of President Johnson's task force on international education, the IAYC had already unsuccessfully attempted to devise a policy strategy for foreign students in 1965.[183] With the rise of student protest, the issue gained considerable urgency and potential for political explosiveness, and was taken up again in September 1968. Fearful of giving the impression of "brainwashing foreign students," IAYC members, however, were still hesitant to question the basic principles of cultural exchange "that by and large it is good to expose large numbers of people to the U.S., accepting some bad results with the greater good effects."[184] When it became clear in May 1969, however, that foreign-exchange students were actively participating in campus disorders in the United States, the Bureau of Educational and Cultural Affairs (CU) intervened with a guideline regulating foreign students' involvement in protest activities that was subsequently extended to all federal agencies.[185] While stating that foreign students in the United States basically enjoyed the same rights as U.S. students (with the exception of citizen rights such as voting, etc.), CU decreed that they would be subject to additional restrictions whose violation could, among other things, result in deportation. Such restrictions were the advocacy of unlawful destruction of property or crimes involving "moral turpitude." Foreign students sponsored by the U.S. government were especially reminded of their roles as ambassadors of their home countries and the high moral standard of behavior that was expected of them. Any misconduct or inconsistency with the purposes of their exchange programs could lead to a revocation of their grants.

Although foreign students comprised less than 2 percent of the U.S. student body and of these only 7.6 percent received government support, the White House initiated a comprehensive review of all government and private exchange programs in the second half of 1970.[186] Surveying U.S. government efforts since the beginning of the 1960s, IAYC secretary Geraldine Sheehan summed up the irritations as follows: "The rise in foreign student numbers has occurred simultaneously with a rise in radical thought and student dissidence on American campuses. Little is known as to what effect, if any, this has had on foreign students' attitudes toward this country, toward the organization of society, or toward international affairs."[187] Sheehan, however, argued for a moderate approach to the issue. In her view, the hope prevalent in the 1960s that foreign students would absorb American ideas and culture through their stay in the United States and present a long-term political investment for U.S. national interest abroad had been shattered by the events at the end of the decade. Sheehan's memo, together with a review of preliminary results of the government study, convinced the IAYC that the problem needed to be pursued further as part of the overall review initiated by the administration.[188] In January 1972, the IAYC submitted the final version of its study on foreign students together with policy recommendations. It argued that the spectacular rise of foreign students in the U.S. from 80,000 in 1965 to about 150,000 in 1970 demanded the attention of the Department of State as a "foreign policy opportunity of sufficient magnitude."[189] The objectives of the U.S. government were to ensure that foreign students received a "balanced understanding of the U.S." and developed permanent contacts "that may over time strengthen the links between the U.S. and other nations in key social and political sectors"—connections that could be highly beneficial to the conduct of U.S. foreign relations in the long run.[190] To facilitate this, a special office within the CU that coordinated efforts in regard to foreign students, especially the 90 percent who were non-government sponsored, was suggested. The IAYC, however, also concluded that foreign students in the United States did not have enough foreign policy importance to cause serious concern, and so the government's attention should be shifted to more promising leader groups.[191] The State Department and the White House largely followed the recommendations of the IAYC, with the president adding only that appropriate language training needed to be provided.[192]

By the end of 1972, the IAYC had, however, experienced further organizational changes. In September 1970, Robert Cross was succeeded by Jerry Inman as the Department of State's officer responsible for youth and executive secretary to the IAYC. In addition, the activities of the IAYC were revealed to the public, most likely in the wake of the revelations concerning secret CIA funding of domestic and international youth organizations. With this move, the administration attempted to assure the image of "giving adequate attention to the impact of youth on governments and in political policies around the world."[193] Under Nixon, the committee also intensified the training of local youth officers worldwide.[194] In the course of discussions with the local diplomatic posts, however, a gradual shift of focus away from university students to young professionals or recent graduates became noticeable.[195] By 1973, the tasks of the State Department's youth officer centered on the emerging leaders and national youth organizations abroad, international and U.N.-related youth activities, as well as relations to U.S. youth. Inman's role as executive secretary of the IAYC had by that time also become greatly reduced due to less frequent meetings and somewhat faltering activities of the IAYC.[196] As a consequence, the committee's remaining responsibilities and the department's youth office were transferred back to the Bureau of Education and Cultural Affairs.[197] Although ideas about possible resurrections of the IAYC occasionally resurfaced in the following years, the committee disbanded in 1973.[198]

With the end of the IAYC, U.S. government efforts directed at foreign youth did not stop, but only took on a different institutional shape. At the beginning of 1973, efforts were under way in Congress to propose a bill on the creation of a Department of Youth Affairs.[199] Similarly, National Security Advisor Henry Kissinger initiated basic research on international youth and government activities.[200] The aim of this "Policy Analysis and Resource Allocation Study on Youth" (PARAS) was to analyze the impact that various youth constituencies (political, military, labor, intellectuals, professionals, students, and so forth) had on U.S. interests. Potential goals were the improvement of U.S. prestige among moderate segments of youth by countering "activities of forces hostile to U.S. interests in order to neutralize their impact."[201] The study hoped to incorporate an analysis of the attitudes of the young generation into the political decision-making process and help the administration to react more effectively toward domestic and international dissent. One potential goal was to "improve the relative position of moderate youth vis-à-vis communist and extremist youth by strengthening and supporting the organization to which they belong and the development of democratic leadership and relationships among them."[202] The concrete effects would vary regionally, but could potentially result in "discreetly encourag[ing] counterinsurgency efforts where insurgent activities threaten U.S. interests."[203] The final outcome of this study and the ways in which the Nixon and future administrations eventually included the U.S. government's international youth efforts in the formulation of their foreign-policy objectives remains a topic for future research.

The student movements in the 1960s and early 1970s had a significant impact on the conceptualization of U.S. foreign policy. Although they never dominated its direction, the protest movements represented a major concern for high-level American officials, who viewed them as a new, constituting factor in international relations. The transatlantic alliance also changed substantially as a result of youthful protest. It is impossible to understand the development of the German-American partnership since the 1960s without taking into account the basic rupture caused by the student movements on both sides of the Atlantic during this decade.

Politically and institutionally, U.S. diplomats now had to confront the ideas and actions of West German students to minimize their detrimental effects on American geopolitical interests in the Federal Republic during the cold war. The challenge posed by this "other alliance" between West

German and American student-protesters cannot, however, be subsumed under the label of anti-Americanism, as many historians, and politicians for that matter, continue to argue. In the West German case, it was rather the result of an increased reception of American counterculture and domestic opposition critical of U.S. policy, and, as such, yet another outcome of a "grassroots Americanization" that had replaced official Americanization programs after the Second World War. At the same time, the disillusionment over America's role in Vietnam led to a far more complex and differentiated image of the United States among parts of the politically active West German student body, which was to exercise a tremendous influence on West German politics in the following decades. Coming of age during the 1960s, this younger generation was eventually able to emancipate itself from the unquestioned traditional Western alignment policy of the Federal Republic during the first half of the cold war and arrive at a more nuanced understanding of the transatlantic friendship.

It is therefore no surprise that the consequences of this paradigm shift that began in the late 1960s resurfaced in full force after the terrorist attacks on September 11, 2001, and the subsequent American decision to go to war in Iraq. Former chancellor Helmut Kohl, for example, explained the refusal of German support for the invasion in 2003 with a latent anti-Americanism of the New Left that had found its way into the highest level of the Social Democratic-Green coalition. As Kohl argued, "Many of those who today hold government offices were already demonstrating against America in the 1970s and 1980s . . . [Chancellor] Gerhard Schröder, [Federal President] Johannes Rau and [Minister of Foreign Affairs] Joschka Fischer are the most prominent representatives of this anti-Americanism."[204]

When in May of 2002, on the other hand, Germany's Minister of Foreign Affairs Joschka Fischer was asked about his perception of the United States in the 1960s, he replied that for him, with the beginning of the Vietnam war, the image of the United States as liberator of Europe had suffered a radical blow: "As a consequence of that, there now existed a two-faced America: The one that was waging a war in Vietnam as a colonial oppressor, and the other one, which was resisting this war and protesting against it. For me and other like-minded people it was never a question of being against the U.S.A. as a country. Rather, we understood ourselves as part of this protest movement that was especially powerful in the United States."[205] It was this understanding about the diversity and often contradictory voices in American politics and the significance of the country's "soft power" that emerged as a consequence of the student movement of the 1960s and continues to influence international politics to this day.[206]

CONCLUSION

IN A 1968 SPEECH on worldwide student unrest, the Executive Secretary of the Inter-Agency Youth Committee, Robert Cross, interpreted the youth of the 1960s as the "first truly international generation." For Cross, this was not the result of tight organizational networks. In his view, students in many countries shared similar political and philosophical problems and looked to their peers to solve them. This created "a great cross-fertilization, a very rapid and effective student grape-vine." As Cross summed it up, "What happens in New York is known overnight in Paris and Manila. The speeches of Rudi Dutschke are in the hands of Mark Rudd faster than you can seem to get your mail delivered."[1]

The global consciousness and interconnectedness exhibited by student activists was certainly not invented in the 1960s. The gradual evolution of an internationalism set apart from military power and national considerations can be observed throughout the twentieth century. Its various brands include economic, legal, and socialist forms of internationalism, and a cultural internationalism that was associated with the creation of a just and peaceful world order (embodied in Wilsonian concepts of international order, as in the League of Nations or the United Nations). The young generation of the 1960s and their protest were both a product and a further catalyst of this internationalism, which was perpetuated by a host of inter- and non-governmental organizations and fostered by the achievements in communication technology after the Second World War. The global dimension of their protest was thus a profound response to the cold war.[2] Through their transnational affiliations and cross-cultural borrowings, the protesting students of the 1960s were able to envision a new, albeit very vague, global order outside the constraints of cold war conformity. This alternative vision and opening of the transnational sphere contributed to the dramatic growth of INGOs (such as Amnesty International, Greenpeace, Doctors Without Borders, Human Rights Watch) concerned with the preservation of fundamental human rights, nuclear disarmament or environmental issues, which emerged during the second half of the decade and has continued ever since.[3] As Margaret Keck and Kathryn Sikkink have observed, "The new networks have depended on the creation of a new kind of global public (or civil society), which grew as a cultural legacy of the 1960s. Both the activism that swept Western Europe, the United States, and many parts of the world during that decade, and the vastly increased opportunities for international contact, contributed to this shift."[4] The protest movements of the 1960/70s therefore enhanced the cultural and institutional infrastructures that fostered the rise of the third sector and helped pave the way for the global community we live in today.

The emancipation from the rigid geopolitical system of the cold war and desire for an alternative world order was already discernible at the beginning of the 1960s in the emergence of the New Left in both West Germany and the United States; in fact, this shared vision was one of the reasons why in 1961/62 German SDS member Michael Vester was able to connect to his American counterparts and inject many of his organization's critical views on anticommunism and the cold war in Europe into the final version of the Port Huron Statement. At the same time, the personal and institutional infrastructure that Vester had created between the two organizations ultimately paved the way for their broader transatlantic cooperation in the second half of the decade, which saw a transformation of their opposition against the constraints of cold-war ideology into open resistance against the war in Vietnam.

German student leader Rudi Dutschke was most explicit in this regard, envisioning a global revolutionary strategy that was to form a "second front" against the worldwide reach of capitalism and imperialism, which for him was most visible in the U.S. involvement in Vietnam. This counteralliance included a worldwide information network and academic institutes in the urban centers of the First World. As embodiments of Che Guevara's foco theory, these institutes were supposed to organize public solidarity with the revolutionary movements of the Third World and function as links to them. The American SDS and the protest scene in the United States, regarded as a branch that operated in the center of imperialist aggression, figured prominently in this concept, which surfaced around the Vietnam Congress in Berlin in February 1968. In the course of 1968, the International News and Research Institute (INFI) in West Berlin, as well as various international conferences, attempted to put this projected transnational resistance into practice. Dutschke's plans to emigrate to the United States, as well as the activities of the U.S. Campaign and the West Berlin chapter of the American SDS, have to be seen in the context of this new type of internationalism, which sought to transcend the constraints of the cold war and derived its urgency from a fundamental opposition to U.S. involvement in Southeast Asia.

The African American civil rights movement similarly changed how student activists on both sides of the Atlantic viewed the cold war. For members of both the German and American SDSs, the African American struggle of the late 1960s came to be seen as part of an international class conflict that also manifested itself in the national liberation movements in Asia, Africa, and South America. Showing solidarity with Black Power was therefore part of resisting global capitalism and imperialism. But just as American direct-action techniques became part of a comprehensive revolutionary theory when imported to a West German context, so too was Black Power transformed in its recontextualization in the Federal Republic. At the beginning of the 1970s, it merged with West German students' increasing fascination with Frantz Fanon's theories on decolonization and the liberating features of violence. Particularly in the case of the Red Army Faction, Black Power and postcolonial redefinitions of identity merged with a coming to terms with the National Socialist past, thus developing into an especially relentless German template for terrorism in the metropolis of the First World.

Eventually, however, this "other" transatlantic alliance did not succeed in toppling the international order of the cold war. The anti-imperialist second front that it sought to build in the First World in solidarity with the national liberation movements taking place in developing countries did not materialize. The protest movements turned out to be too heterogeneous and shaped too much by national conditions for activists to reach any consensus on issues such as militancy, the relationship of the New Left to the working class, or their solidarity with the Third World, let alone a joint revolutionary agenda. As a result, they failed to implement any permanent form of a transnationally operating New Left that could seriously challenge the stability of national governments or official alliance politics.

This does not mean, however, that their efforts went unnoticed or had no effect on political decision-makers. As the present study has shown, U.S. officials were very clear about the fact that the young generation of the late 1960s was the first "post–cold war" generation who actively sought to overcome the geopolitical constraints of the antagonistic power blocs. As an internal research paper of the Department of State from 1967 suggested, "[T]he policy priorities of youth may run counter to the requirements imposed on the US by its role as a world power." For the young generation, the paper argued, "communism is neither a threat to the nation nor an answer to their problems. They seem to feel, one suspects, that for the older generation communism has come to serve as a pretext for not coming to grips with the serious problems of our society in fields like civil rights, poverty, slum clearance, and the host of other difficulties that afflict mass urban life."[5] Having come of age in the political rhetoric of détente and bridge-building in the early 1960s, student activists now challenged their governments to follow up on their promises; and their more radical ideas and actions to transform not only their own societies but also the sphere of international relations soon began to occupy political decision-makers.[6]

What was first perceived as a global imitation of the Free Speech Movement at the University of California, Berkeley, and as part of an international movement against the war in Vietnam, now came to be considered a far more serious problem for American foreign policy. In the view of U.S. diplomats, the increased communication among the young generation worldwide had by the end of the decade facilitated an international protest culture that was fundamentally opposed to American interests and policies. U.S. missions in West Germany, for example, were particularly concerned about the effect of student militancy on the internal stability and political landscape of the Federal Republic. The divided city of Berlin as one of the hot spots of the cold war naturally occupied a special place in their reporting. American diplomats, however, perceived youthful unrest as a problem affecting the whole country, since protesting students attacked American installations, consulates, military bases, and Amerika Häuser (America Houses) all over the Federal Republic, from Hamburg to Munich. Faced with growing internal unrest in the country of one of its closest allies during the cold war, the U.S. government not only stepped up its monitoring of student activities in West Germany but also decided to make the young generation the primary target group of its cultural and educational activities.

Many American officials feared that the ideology of student protesters might resonate within the established parties, thereby causing a leftist turn of the new social-liberal administration of Willy Brandt coming into office in 1969. American diplomats were concerned that this could not only help foster independent German efforts at détente but, even more worrisome, lead to a neutralist position of the country in the cold war; in other words, they were afraid that the idea of an alternative geopolitical order outside the traditional power blocs of East and West would gain ground among the political elite and future leaders in the Federal Republic.

For the U.S. government, the case of West Germany was not an isolated phenomenon. Concerned about a gradual loss of foreign youth to the Soviet Union, the Department of State, with the support of President John F. Kennedy and Attorney General Robert Kennedy, had already set up the Inter-Agency Youth Committee (IAYC) in 1962 to win over the hearts and minds of youth across the globe. The goal of bringing representatives from various branches of the State Department as well as key government agencies together in this committee was to provide a central platform to coordinate all government efforts targeting the young generation abroad. When the international antiwar movement in the mid-1960s confronted the Johnson administration with an increasing hostility toward its foreign policies, the IAYC became the natural center for devising an appropriate government response to protect American interests. Especially after the disruptions of the French May in 1968, the IAYC served as the center for policy planning and how to come to terms with student revolt overseas among high-level officials of various branches of government. The committee not only furnished the U.S. administration with the necessary background information on global student protest, but also discussed adequate local responses and possible adjustments to the U.S. government's international youth effort.

In the eyes of U.S. diplomats, this government initiative was vital, since it sought to counter international student protest as well as rescue the U.S. image around the world. Although the comprehensive cultural diplomacy efforts that the United States had launched after the Second World War had fomented a close bond between the country and its allies, this alliance system was not carved in stone. In West Germany, for example, a new generation of students coming of age in the 1960s did not share the immediate war experiences or the cold-war confrontations of earlier years. For them, any Manichean rhetoric conjuring up a Soviet threat had long been replaced by fundamental concerns over détente between the superpowers and the growing North-South divide. Their view of the United States thus differed considerably from that of their predecessors. It consisted of images of a nation divided by violence, racial disorders, a growing antiwar opposition and a vibrant youthful counterculture.

The individual reservoir of good will and sympathy that the United States enjoyed in the Federal Republic as a result of cultural exchange programs of the 1950s was still able to counter widespread attacks and criticisms by West German activists, but would not be able to safeguard America's image and interests indefinitely. Its impact was steadily undermined by more critical voices of the young generation. George McGhee, U.S. ambassador to West Germany, had to experience this backlash firsthand when, during an official ceremony at the University of Cologne, the rector had to sneak him out the back door when "a well-organized band of students used the occasion to stage a riot about U.S. involvement in Vietnam."[7] Precisely this reevaluation of American influence in the world, together with the opening toward the transnational sphere and the desire for an alternative global order outside the cold war, presented the more serious long-term challenge for American foreign policy.

In the eyes of student protesters worldwide, the U.S. role in the world had lost much of the legitimacy and positive force that it had after the Second World War on account of the war in Vietnam. Going hand in hand with this assumption was, however, not only a very often massively distorted image of the United States or simply the emergence of anti-American sentiment, but rather a much more complex perspective of the United States. As the writer Umberto Eco remarked with respect to the

Italian student movement, "Of course, for those young people America as a Power was the enemy, the world's policeman, the foe to be defeated in Vietnam as much as in Latin America. . . . But if America was an enemy as a government and as the model for a capitalist society, there was also an attitude of rediscovery and recovery of America as a people, as a melting pot of races in revolt. . . . [T]hey identified a labyrinthine camp in which there was a mixture of oppositions between old and young, black and white, recent immigrants and established ethnic groups, silent majorities and vocal minorities. They did not see any substantial difference between Kennedy and Nixon, but they identified with the Berkeley campus, Angela Davis, Joan Baez, and the early Bob Dylan."[8]

This ambivalent perception of the United States and the separation between an "official" America, which was responsible for racial suppression and the war in Vietnam, and the "other" America, consisting of countercultures and protest movements opposed to these shortcomings, became the dominating feature of the protest movements of the 1960/70s worldwide. These ambiguous notions would shape the image of the United States for generations and decades to come. Their legacy consists of a much more nuanced and diverse transnational picture of the United States, which has begun to incorporate ethnic minorities and other marginalized voices into its canon.[9] Although by no means free from gross distortions and misrepresentations, it is nonetheless a more mature and balanced perspective on the United States as a country, including its many advantages as well as shortcomings. In any case, it is also a further result of an increasing American cultural influence across the world and, as such, yet another step in the intertwinement of the forces of Americanization and globalization in the history of the twentieth century.

• • •

Jefferson Airplane cofounder Paul Kantner once remarked, "If you can remember the Sixties, you weren't really there!" Despite this verdict, we do remember this turbulent decade quite extensively. In many ways, the fortieth anniversary of the events of the metaphorical year 1968 even marked a watershed in the memorial culture surrounding the "sixties." The number of conferences, books, lecture series, and media attention given to the 1960s was unparalleled. Everywhere, the memory of "1968," which serves as the common chiffre for the "sixties" in Europe, has by now far surpassed the level of personal anecdote and public acknowledgment and (re-)entered the realms of official politics. In France, Nicolas Sarkozy made a particular point in his election campaign of 2007 to distance himself from the legacy of 1968. At his final campaign rally in front of 20,000 supporters, Sarkozy declared himself the representative of the "silent majority," who wanted to "turn the page on May 1968." As he argued, "The heirs of May '68 have imposed the idea that everything has the same worth, that there is no difference between good and evil, no difference between the true and the false, between the beautiful and the ugly, and that the victim counts for less than the delinquent."[10] Trying to recapture a sense of order and moral, Sarkozy accused the French Left and his Socialist opponent, Ségolène Royal, of being responsible for all that was wrong with contemporary France, from youthful frustration to fundamentalism and loss of national identity.

In Poland, President Lech Kaczynski also chose to address his country's heritage of "1968" in March 2008. At a ceremony marking the fortieth anniversary of the crackdown on the Polish student revolt of 1968, he vowed to restore Polish nationality to the 20,000 Polish Jews who were forced out of the country by the government's antisemitism that year. More specifically, Kaczynski called the events of March 1968 a "shame," elaborating that that "[a] stain was left on the reputation of our country, and Poland lost thousands of gifted, ambitious and entrepreneurial citizens."[11]

The most interesting drama with regard to the commemoration of the "sixties," however, unfolded in the U.S. election campaign of 2008, where one of the last politically influential representatives of the baby boomer generation, Hillary Clinton, tried to secure her bid for the White House. In many ways, Hillary Clinton is a direct product of the sixties, graduating with honors from the prestigious Wellesley College to join Yale Law School and later the legal staff of the impeachment inquiry for President Richard Nixon. For many, her husband's presidency and her time as First Lady represented the final arrival of the children of the sixties in the halls of power. It is therefore ironic that her African American opponent, Barack Obama, based much of his grassroots-style campaign on the liberating and hopeful spirit of the sixties while at the same time delivering a harsh critique of the divisiveness of the decade. As Obama said in an interview in 2007, "To some degree . . . we have seen the psychodrama of the baby boomer generation play out over the last forty years. When you watch Clinton versus Gingrich, or Gore versus Bush, or Kerry versus Bush, you feel like these are fights that were taking place back in the dorm rooms of the Sixties."[12] Interestingly enough, with John McCain, Obama faced a Republican opponent who displayed a very different narrative of the sixties and turned his time as a prisoner of war in Vietnam into one of the cornerstones of his election campaign.

Examples like these illustrate that when dealing with the public memory of "1968" or the "sixties" we are still confronted with an ongoing process that has a tremendous amount of political implications and open wounds. The existence of these memories in a number of countries also reconfirms the fact that the turbulent events of the 1960s did not stop at national borders. In fact, 1960s' protest took place in far more places than we are usually aware of, and not only in Berkeley, Berlin, Paris, and Prague. Although this process has reached different levels from country to country, sixties' icons and images have been circulating across national borders ever since the turbulent decade. They have become part of our communicative memory and are now at the threshold of being passed into our transnational cultural memory.[13]

All too often, however, the memory of the decade has been turned into a superficial story of generational rebellion, sexual liberation, and countercultural liberties that is either worshipped or ridiculed from the respective fringes of the political spectrum. A recent account of the 1960s even argued that "[a]fter the decade died, it rose again as religion. For quite a few people, the Sixties is neither memory nor myth, but faith."[14] As part of this politics of memory, the metaphorical "sixties" have become an imaginary space with which to identify or from which to distance oneself. As literary and cultural historian Kristin Ross has shown in her study of the French May, the actual historical events have long been "overtaken by subsequent representations." In other words, the "afterlives" of "1968" have developed a life their own.[15] The fierce battles about the political legacy of the sixties have even created, as historian Elizabeth Peifer has labeled it, "a discursive commemoration through contestation which kept 1968 alive in political culture."[16]

Regardless of whether their evaluation of the legacy of the sixties is positive or negative, most people would probably agree that the protest movements of the 1960/70s fundamentally changed the domestic cultural fabric of their countries and societies in terms of individual lifestyles and value systems. With their radical political demands and actions, student activists challenged social conventions, generated new forms of cultural expression and alternative spaces, and created the impression of an accelerating cultural transformation. As soon as we leave the cultural legacies of the sixties, however, and enter the strictly political sphere, assuming we can make such a distinction, the narratives became far more controversial and have, for the longest time, been organized along old battle lines drawn between former activists and their opponents. Both groups have offered numerous fictional, nonfictional, biographical, and academic accounts in which they explain, apologize, condemn, or defend the achievements and failures of the decade; in other words, they continue to battle about their own legacy.

Historians and academics are no innocent bystanders in this process and cannot be. Especially a younger generation that was born after or was still very young during the 1960s has begun to interfere in the discourse about the sixties: These new voices have broadened the picture, enabled a plurality of even contradictory narratives, and followed previously unexplored venues of research. This wave of new scholarship is essential for a further understanding of this time period. Even after the fortieth anniversary of 1968, we still know too little about, for example, the actual extent of official government reactions to domestic and international dissent. Although based on ample empirical evidence, the conclusions presented in this book remain nonetheless preliminary. With regard to the Nixon administration, for example, the bulk of documents related to the U.S. government reaction to student protest worldwide are still mostly under review. The efforts to determine the exact nature between power and protest in the 1960/70s have therefore only just begun.

At the same time, we need to diversify our traditional narratives, which are still largely dominated by the Western experience of the sixties. We still know far too little about contemporary protest movements in Asia, Africa, Eastern Europe, and Latin America to have a truly global comparative frame. This book has retraced the "long sixties" from a transnational perspective with respect to West German and U.S. student activists. It has attempted to transcend a mere comparative frame by illustrating the various ways in which ideas and cultural practices crossed national borders during the cold war and how student activists in West Germany and the United States adopted and recontextualized these ideas in their different domestic environments. Future historiography would benefit from similar transnational approaches that examine how actual cooperation or mere images of the "other," for example, the Third World, have shaped local or national political ideologies and actions of activists.[17]

Eventually, historiography needs to confront the plethora of memories and voices from all sides of the political spectrum. This includes not only an analysis of the New Right but also inquiries into other segments of society such as political parties, churches, trade unions, and other local and national government institutions.[18]

Taking a more comprehensive, multidimensional perspective on the global sixties will help us escape the traditional front lines as well as fuel further research. Regardless of whether we judge the decade's legacies as positive or negative, a thorough investigation will keep alive its philosophical, artistic, cultural, and political richness as a significant, if at times contradictory, site of memory, and not allow the sixties to be turned into a site of partisan bickering or oblivion. This will eventually contribute to a more inclusive transnational cultural memory of this time, thereby bringing us closer on our way to contextualizing the "long sixties" in the larger course of a global history of the cold war and the twentieth century.

In his address before the Irish parliament on June 28, 1963, U.S. President John F. Kennedy, borrowing a phrase from the Irish poet William Butler Yeats, admonished the audience to "let us not casually reduce 'that great past to a trouble of fools.' For we need not feel the bitterness of the past to discover its meaning for the present and future." Future historians of the sixties would do well to take his words to heart.

NOTES

For a complete bibliography, scans of original documents, as well as interview transcripts and other material related to the book, please visit http://www.otheralliance.com.

INTRODUCTION

1. CIA report, "Restless Youth," September 1968, no. 0613/68, National Security File (hereafter NSF), Files of Walt Rostow, Box 13, Folder: Youth & Student Movements, Lyndon B. Johnson Library, Austin, Texas (hereafter LBJL).

2. Carole Fink et al., eds., *1968: A World Transformed* (New York: Cambridge University Press, 1998); Martin Klimke and Joachim Scharloth, eds., *1968 in Europe: A History of Protest and Activism, 1956–1977* (New York: Palgrave Macmillan, 2008), accompanying online teaching and research guide at http://www.1968ineurope.com.

3. Eric Hobsbawm, "The Year the Prophets Failed," in Eugene Atget and Laure Beaumont-Maillet, ed., *1968 The Magnum Photographs: A Year in the World* (Paris: Magnum Photos/Editions Hazan, 1998), 8–10.

4. Daniel Cohn-Bendit, *Wir haben sie so geliebt, die Revolution* (Frankfurt: Athenaeum, 1987), 15.

5. Tariq Ali, "Where has all the rage gone?" *Guardian,* March 22, 2008.

6. Compare, for example, George Katsiaficas, *The Imagination of the New Left. A Global Analysis of 1968* (Boston: South End Press, 1987); David Caute, *The Year of the Barricades: A Journey through 1968* (New York: Harper and Row, 1988); Ronald Fraser, *1968: A Student Generation in Revolt* (New York: Pantheon, 1988); Fink et al., *The World Transformed*, 1998; Arthur Marwick, *The Sixties. Cultural Revolution in Britain, France, Italy and the United States c.1958–c.1974* (Oxford: Oxford University Press, 1998); Gerard J. DeGroot, ed., *Student Protest. The Sixties and After* (London: Longman, 1998); Wolfgang Kraushaar, "Die erste globale Rebellion," in his *1968 als Mythos, Chiffre und Zäsur* (Hamburg: Hamburger Edition, 2000), 19–52; Geneviève Dreyfus-Armand and Antoine de Baecque, *Les années 68: Le temps de la contestation* (Brussels: Ed. Complexe, 2001); Jeremi Suri, *Power and Protest: Global Revolution and the Rise of Détente* (Cambridge: Harvard University Press, 2003); Jeremi Suri, ed., *The Global Revolutions of 1968* (New York: Norton, 2007); Klimke and Scharloth, *1968 in Europe*; Norbert Frei, *1968: Jugendrevolte und globaler Protest* (Munich: Deutscher Taschenbuch Verlag, 2008); Jens Kastner und David Mayer, ed., *Weltwende 1968?: Ein Jahr aus globalgeschichtlicher Perspektive* (Vienna: Mandelbaum, 2008); Karen Dubinsky, et al., ed., *New World Coming: The Sixties and the Shaping of Global Consciousness* (Toronto: Between the Lines, 2009); Philipp Gassert and Martin Klimke, eds., *1968: Memories and Legacies of a*

Global Revolt (Washington, DC: GHI, 2009). See also the forum in American Historical Review: "The International 1968, Part I & Part II," in: idem, Volume 114, Number 1 (February 2009), 42–135; idem, Volume 114, Number 2 (April 2009), 329–404.

7. Exceptions are, for example, as follows: Ingo Juchler, *Die Studentenbewegungen in den Vereinigten Staaten und der Bundesrepublik der sechziger Jahre. Eine Untersuchung hinsichtlich ihrer Beeinflussung durch Befereiungsbewegungen und theorien aus der Dritten Welt* (Berlin: Duncker and Humblot, 1996); Belinda Davis, Martin Klimke, Carla MacDougall, and Wilfried Mausbach, eds., *Changing the World, Changing the Self: Political Protest and Collective Identities in 1960/70s West Germany and the United States* (New York: Berghahn Books, forthcoming 2010). Comparative studies have started to answer some of these questions: Donatella Della Porta, *Social Movements, Political Violence, and the State: A Comparative Analysis of Italy and Germany* (Cambridge: Cambridge University Press, 1995); Ingrid Gilcher-Holtey, *Die 68er Bewegung: Deutschland, Westeuropa, USA* (Munich: Beck, 2001); Michael Schmidtke, *Der Aufbruch der jungen Intelligenz: Die 68er Jahre in der Bundesrepublik und den USA* (Frankfurt: Campus, 2003); Jeremy Varon, *Bringing the War Home: The Weather Underground, the Red Army Faction, and the Revolutionary Violence of the 1960s and 1970s* (Berkeley: University of California Press, 2004); Axel Schildt and Detlef Siegfried, eds., *Between Marx and Coca-Cola. Youth Cultures in Changing European Societies, 1960–1980* (New York: Berghahn Books, 2006); Gerd-Rainer Horn, *The Spirit of 68: Rebellion in Western Europe and North America. 1956–1976* (Oxford: Oxford University Press, 2007); Sandra Kraft, "Vom Autoritätskonflikt zur Machtprobe: Die Studentenproteste der 60er Jahre als Herausforderung für das Establishment in Deutschland und den USA," Ph.D. diss., University of Heidelberg, 2008.

8. See Klimke and Scharloth, *1968 in Europe*, 1ff.

9. Kathrin Fahlenbrach and Joachim Scharloth can be credited with initiating a paradigm shift in historiography by analyzing the symbolic nature and performativity of sixties' protest. Please see: Kathrin Fahlenbrach, *Protestinszenierungen. Visuelle Kommunikation und kollektive Identitäten in Protestbewegungen* (Wiesbaden: Westdeutscher Verlag, 2002); Joachim Scharloth, "Ritualkritik und Rituale des Protest. Die Entdeckung des Performativen in der Studentenbewegung der 1960er Jahre," in: Martin Klimke and Joachim Scharloth, eds., *1968. Handbuch zur Kultur- und Mediengeschichte der Studentenbewegung* (Stuttgart: Metzler, 2007), 75–87; Joachim Scharloth, *1968. Eine Kommunikationsgeschichte* (Munich: Fink, forthcoming). For an analysis of these cultural processes, see, for example, the following works: Detlef Siegfried, *Time Is on My Side. Konsum und Politik in der westdeutschen Jugendkultur der 60er Jahre* (Göttingen: Wallstein Verlag, 2006); Arnold Jacobshagen and Markus Leniger, eds., *Rebellische Musik. Gesellschaftlicher Protest und kultureller Wandel um 1968* (Cologne: Verlag Dohr, 2007); Klimke and Scharloth, *1968. Handbuch zur Kultur und Mediengeschichte; Detlef Siegfried, Sound der Revolte. Studien zur Kulturrevolution um 1968* (Weinheim: Juventa, 2008); Beate Kutschke, *Musikkulturen in der Revolte. Studien zu Rock, Avantgarde und Klassik im Umfeld von "1968"* (Stuttgart:

Franz Steiner Verlag, 2008); Robert Adlington, ed., *Sound Commitments: Avant-Garde Music and the Sixties* (New York: Oxford University Press, 2009).

10. On the effect and authenticity of such imagery, see Gerhard Paul, "Die Geschichte hinter dem Foto. Authentizität, Ikonisierung und Überschreibung eines Bildes aus dem Vietnamkrieg," *Studies in Contemporary History*, online edition, 2 (2005): 2.

11. Detlef Junker et al., eds., *The United States and Germany in the Era of the Cold War, 1945–1990: A Handbook*, 2 vols. (New York: Cambridge University Press, 2004).

12. Axel Schildt, "Americanization," in Junker, *The United States and Germany*, 1:635–42.

13. Kasper Maase, "'Halbstarke' and Hegemony. Meanings of American Mass Culture in the Federal Republic of Germany during the 1950s," in Rob Kroes et al., eds., *Cultural Transmissions and Receptions: American Mass Culture in Europe* (Amsterdam: VU University Press, 1993), 153–70; Maase, "Establishing Cultural Democracy: Youth, 'Americanization', and the Irresistible Rise of Popular Culture," in Hannah Schissler, ed., *The Miracle Years. A Cultural History of West Germany, 1949–1968* (Princeton: Princeton University Press, 2001), 428–50. See also Uta Poiger, *Jazz, Rock and Rebels: Cold War Politics and American Culture in a Divided Germany* (Berkeley: University of California Press, 2000).

14. Philipp Gassert and Alan E. Steinweis, ed., *Coping with the Nazi Past: West German Debates on Nazism and Generational Conflict, 1955–1975* (New York: Berghahn Books, 2006); Jeffrey Herf, *Divided Memory: The Nazi Past in the Two Germanys* (Cambridge: Harvard University Press, 1997), 334–50.

15. Knud Krakau, "Zwischen alten Stereotypen und neuen Realitäten: Westdeutsche Bilder der USA," in Junker, *USA und Deutschland*, 1:920–31.

16. David B. Morris, "The Maturization of a Relationship: The Image of America in West German Public Opinion," in Junker, *The United States and Germany*, 2:510–18.

17. Richard Pells, *Not Like Us: How Europeans Have Loved, Hated and Transformed American Culture since World War II* (New York: Basic Books, 1997), 286.

18. Allerbeck also points to the fact that students in West Germany and the United States protested against the clash between traded and practiced values in their societies, and were thus convinced that they had to defend "true" American, that is to say, democratic, values. Klaus Allerbeck, *Soziologie radikaler Studentenbewegungen, Eine vergleichende Untersuchung in der Bundesrepublik und den Vereinigten Staaten* (Munich: Oldenbourg, 1973), 207–213. See also Krakau, "Zwischen alten Stereotypen und neuen Realitäten: Westdeutsche Bilder der USA." For the use of American mythology and traditional values in the American movement, see Dominick Cavallo, *A Fiction of the Past: The Sixties in American History* (New York: St. Martin's, 1999), here 11–13, 251–55.

19. Philipp Gassert, "With America Against America: Anti-Americanism in West Germany," in Junker, *The United States and Germany*, 2:502–9. This view is also confirmed by the recollections of former activists: see Ekkehart Krippendorff, "Die westdeutsche Linke und ihr Bild von den USA," in Willi Paul Adams and Knud Krakau, eds., *Deutschland und Amerika, Perzeption und historische*

Realität (Berlin: Colloquium Verlag, 1985), 39–46, here 43–46; Bommi Baumann and Till Meyer, eds., *Radikales Amerika. Wie die amerikanische Protestbewegung Deutschland veränderte* (Berlin: Rotbuch Verlag, 2007).

20. As has been concluded, any "Americanization" of Europe would always be accompanied by a process of "Europeanizing" American culture. See Philipp Gassert, "Amerikanismus, Antiamerikanismus, Amerikanisierung," *Archiv für Sozialgeschichte* 39 (1999): 550; Rob Kroes, *If You've Seen One You've Seen the Mall: European and American Mass Culture* (Urbana: University of Illinois Press, 1996), xi; Pells, *Not LikeUus*, xv.

21. Pells, *Not Like Us*, 107–12, 280, 290.

22. The termination of the IAYC was decided on January 11, 1973, to take place by January 1, 1974. Since significant activities of IAYC could not be established for 1973, this study considers the years from 1962 through 1972 as the main period of the committee's work.

CHAPTER 1
SDS MEETS SDS

1. For a concise and detailed overview of the history of the German SDS from 1946 to the beginning of the 1960s, see Willy Albrecht, *Der Sozialistische Deutsche Studentenbund (SDS). Vom parteikonformen Studentenverband zum Repräsentanten der Neuen Linken* (Bonn: Dietz, 1994). For an introduction, bibliography, and review of recent literature on the West German New Left, see Martin Klimke, " 'The Struggle Continues': Revisiting the German Sixties," *The Sixties* 2, (2008): 247–52; Martin Klimke, "West Germany," in Martin Klimke and Joachim Scharloth, ed., *1968 in Europe: A History of Protest and Activism, 1965–77* (New York: Palgrave Macmillan, 2008), 97–110.

2. Franz Walter, *Sozialistische Akademiker- und Intellektuellenorganisationen in der Weimarer Republik* (Bonn: Dietz, 1990), 27–87.

3. Uwe Rohwedder, *Helmut Schmidt und der SDS: die Anfänge des Sozialistischen Deutschen Studentenbundes nach dem Zweiten Weltkrieg* (Bremen: Edition Temmen, 2007).

4. Gerhardt Brandt, "Die neue Linke in England," *neue kritik* 6 (1961): 22–30. For the British New Left, see Lin Chun, *The British New Left* (Edinburgh: Edinburgh University Press, 1993); Michael Kenny, *The First New Left. British Intellectuals after Stalin* (London: Lawrence and Wishart, 1995); Madeleine Davis, "The Origins of the British New Left," in Klimke and Scharloth, *1968 in Europe*, 45–56.

5. Brandt, *Neue Linke in England*, 30.

6. Albrecht, *Der Sozialistische Deutsche Studentenbund*, 414.

7. *neue kritik*, Special Issue 1961, Presentation by E. Dähne; see also Albrecht, *Der Sozialistische Deutsche Studentenbund*, 416f.

8. Herbert Wehner, "Das Auftreten der 'Neuen Linken'," in *Die Zeit*, January 26, 1962, p. 3, cited in Ossip K. Flechtheim, ed., *Dokumente zur parteipolitischen Entwicklung in Deutschland seit 1945*, vol. 7, part 2 (Berlin: Wendler, 1969), 188. For the international argument in the hastily prepared SPD collection of

documents, which were supposed to highlight the hostile tendencies in SDS, see 172 f.

9. Albrecht, *Sozialistischer Deutscher Studentenbund*, 373–446.

10. Jürgen Seifert, "Die Neue Linke. Abgrenzungen und Selbstanalyse," *Frankfurter Hefte* 18 (1963): 30–40; Manfred Liebel, "Die Rolle der Intellektuellen in der Bundesrepublik," *neue kritik* 18 (November, 1963): 5–8, esp. 5; Albrecht, *Sozialistischer Deutscher Studentenbund*, 411–14.

11. See Kirkpatrick Sale, *SDS* (New York: Random House, 1973), 15. For major works on the student movement in the United States see, for example, the following: Wini Breines, *Community and Organization in the New Left, 1962–1968: The Great Refusal* (New York: Praeger, 1982); James Miller, *Democracy Is in the Streets. From Port Huron to the Siege of Chicago*, 2nd ed. (New York, Simon and Schuster, 1987); David Farber, *Chicago '68* (Chicago: University of Chicago Press, 1988); Terry H. Anderson, *The Movement and the Sixties. Protest in America from Greensboro to Wounded Knee* (New York: Oxford University Press, 1995); Douglas Rossinow, *The Politics of Authenticity: Liberalism, Christianity, and the New Left in America* (New York: Columbia University Press, 1998); Jennifer Frost, *An Interracial Movement of the Poor: Community Organizing and the New Left in the 1960s* (New York: New York University Press, 2001); John McMillian and Paul Buhle, eds., *The New Left Revisited* (Philadelphia: Temple University Press, 2003); Van Gosse, *Rethinking the New Left: An Interpretative History* (New York: Palgrave Macmillan, 2005); David Barber, *A Hard Rain Fell: SDS and Why It Failed* (Jackson: University Press of Mississippi, 2008). Historical accounts from former participants include the following: Todd Gitlin, *The Sixties: Years of Hope, Days of Rage* (New York: Bantam Books, 1987); Tom Hayden, *Reunion: A Memoir* (New York: Random House, 1988); Robert Pardun, *Prairie Radical: A Journey Through the Sixties* (Los Gatos, Calif.: Shire Press, 2001); Helen Garvey, ed., *Rebels With a Cause: A Collective Memoir of the Hopes, Rebellions and Repressions of the 1960s* (Los Gatos, Calif.: Shire Press, 2007); Carl Oglesby, *Ravens in the Storm: A Personal History of the 1960s Antiwar Movement* (New York: Scribner, 2008); Mark Rudd, *Underground: My Life with SDS and the Weatherman Underground* (New York: William Morrow, 2009).

12. Quoted in Sale, *SDS*, 15.

13. On the roots and origins of the New Left in the U.S. see Robert Cohen, *When the Old Left was Young: Student Radicals and America's First Mass Student Movement, 1929–1941* (New York: Oxford University Press, 1993); Maurice Isserman, *If I Had a Hammer: The Death of the Old Left and the Birth of the New Left* (Urbana: University of Illinois Press, 1993); Kevin Mattson, *Intellectuals in Action: The Origins of the New Left and Radical Liberalism, 1945–1970* (University Park: Pennsylvania State University Press, 2002).

14. See the analysis of Arnold Kaufman's thinking in Mattson, *Intellectuals in Action*, 193 ff. For Hayden's own recollections, see Hayden, *Reunion*, 1988.

15. Interview with Robert Ross, Worcester, Mass., March 21, 2000, p. 8.

16. Tom Hayden, *Reunion*, 73–102; Miller, *Democracy Is in the Streets*, 106–25. See also Tom Hayden, *The Port Huron Statement: The Visionary Call of the 1960s Revolution* (New York: Thunder's Mouth Press, 2005).

17. SDS, "Port Huron Statement," printed in Miller, *Democracy Is in the Streets*, 329.

18. Ibid., 332.

19. "Fearing vision, we justify rhetoric or myopia. Fearing hope, we reinforce despair. The first effort, then, should be to state a vision: what is the perimeter of human possibility in this epoch? This we have tried to do." SDS, "Port Huron Statement," printed in Miller, *Democracy Is in the Streets*, 367; see also Hayden, *Reunion*, 75.

20. SDS, "Port Huron Statement," printed in Miller, *Democracy Is in the Streets*, 374.

21. See also John Patrick Diggins, *The Rise and Fall of the American Left* (New York: Norton, 1992), 233. David Burner also argues that the positions of the SDS and LID were in fact quite compatible in some ways, but that sensitivity and stubbornness on both sides over issues of anticommunism and nonexclusionism ultimately opened the generational divide. See David Burner, *Making Peace with the 60s* (Princeton: Princeton University Press, 1996), 154.

22. Tom Hayden, *Student Social Action* (Chicago: SDS, 1966), 19.

23. Joel Geier, National Secretary, Young Peoples Socialist League (hereafter YPSL), letter to Michael Vester, undated; Michael Vester, letter to Joel Geier, February 11, 1962; both letters are in the private papers of Michael Vester.

24. If at all, Vester is only factually listed in the historiography of the era as the only foreign participant at the Port Huron conference, but his overall role beyond this has never been exhaustively analyzed. See Schmidtke, *Der Aufbruch der jungen Intelligenz*, 41; McAdam and Rucht, *Cross-National Diffusion*, 70; Miller, *Democracy Is in the Streets*, 107; Sale, *SDS*, 48. See also Richard Flacks et al., "Port Huron. Agenda for a Generation (Symposium)," *Socialist Review* 3/4, (1987): 195–64, here 141f. See also Martin Klimke, "Sit-in, teach-in, go-in: Zur transnationalen Zirkulation kultureller Praktiken in den Protestbewegungen der 1960/70er Jahre," in Martin Klimke and Joachim Scharloth, eds., *1968. Ein Handbuch zur Kultur- und Mediengeschichte der Studentenbewegung* (Stuttgart: Metzler Verlag, 2007), 119–133.

25. Al Haber, letter to Michael Vester, January 25, 1962; in private papers of Michael Vester.

26. Michael Vester, letter to Al Haber, April 14, 1962; in private papers of Michael Vester.

27. Michael Vester, "Berlin: Why Not Recognize the Status Quo?" article enclosed with letter from Michael Vester to Al Haber, February 6, 1962; in private papers of Michael Vester.

28. Vester asked for the addresses of Manfred Liebel, Hannes Friedrich, Peter von Oertzen, and Hellmut Lessing to be included on the American SDS mailing list. See ibid.

29. Al Haber, letter to Michael Vester, April 11, 1962, p. 2. For the positive response, see Michael Vester, letter to Al Haber, April 14, 1962; both in private papers of Michael Vester.

30. Al Haber to SDS Executive Committee, "Proposed Program: SDS National Convention 14–17 June 1962," first draft, March 13, 1962, in Paul Booth Papers,

1, Box 3, State Historical Society of Wisconsin, Madison, Wisconsin (hereafter SHSW).

31. Al Haber, letter to Michael Vester, February 13, 1962. See also Al Haber, letter to Michael Vester, February 13, 1962; both in private papers of Michael Vester.

32. Michael Vester, letter to Al Haber, April 29, 1962; Michael Vester, letter to Al Haber, May 29, 1962.

33. Michael Vester, "A Note to Tom Hayden (Manifesto)," undated, p. 1; in private papers of Michael Vester.

34. Ibid., 2.

35. Ibid.

36. John Kenneth Galbraith, *American Capitalism: The Concept of Countervailing Power* (Boston: Houghton Mifflin, 1952).

37. Michael Vester, "A Note to Tom Hayden," passim. The other sections of Hayden's draft on the economy, the military-industrial complex, as well as the colonial revolution had only minor points that drew Vester's criticism.

38. Ibid., 3. As Richard Flacks recalls, "[O]ne of the critical meetings of the New Left was to formulate a new stance on communism, anti-communism and the cold war. And so to the extent that [Vester] shared that [goal], . . . one that the German SDS had [already] formulated, . . . [this] was a very important thing. 'Cause after all, Germany was one of the, maybe the paramount, battleground of the cold war, and if . . . German youth were trying to break through the categories, that was really important to people like us." Interview with Richard Flacks, Santa Barbara, Calif., August 21, 2003, p. 10.

39. Michael Vester, "A Note to Tom Hayden (Manifesto)."

40. Ibid.

41. Ibid.

42. Ibid.

43. See, for example, Michael Vester, "A Note to Tom Hayden," 1962, in Paul Booth Papers, 12, Box 2, SHSW.

44. "Minutes of the SDS National Executive Committee," Chapel Hill, N.C., May 6–7, 1962, in Students for a Democratic Society Records (hereafter American SDS Records), 1, 3, Box 1, SHSW.

45. Interview with Richard Flacks, Santa Barbara, Calif., August 21, 2003, pp. 6f., 9.

46. Interview with Tom Hayden, Boston, Mass., October 15, 2003, p. 6.

47. Interview with Robert Ross, Worcester, Mass., March 21, 2000, p. 31.

48. Miller, *Democracy Is in the Streets*, 123.

49. Interview with Richard Flacks, Santa Barbara, Calif., August 21, 2003, pp. 7, 12.

50. Vester, "Why Not Recognize the Status Quo?" 9.

51. Ibid., 1, 6, 10.

52. American SDS, "Port Huron Statement," in Miller, *Democracy Is in the Streets*, 356 f.

53. Vester, "Berlin: Why Not Recognize the Status Quo?" 6; American SDS, "Port Huron Statement," 356.

54. The two pieces I am referring to are mentioned in Al Haber, letter to Michael Vester, February 13, 1962; in private papers of Michael Vester. One of them deals with "Authoritarians in Germany" and the other one is "Berlin: Why Not Recognize the Status Quo?"

55. Vester's article continued to circulate at least until 1965, together with another article entitled "Two European Views on the Cold War."

56. Michael Vester, letter to Al Haber, March 13, 1962, in private papers of Michael Vester.

57. Draft letter to Erich Ollenhauer, SPD, Bonn, in Michael Vester, letter to Al Haber, March 19, 1962. Since only Rebecca Adams from the American SDS seemed to have been able to read German fluently, Vester, after double-checking with the national office in Frankfurt, actually provided Haber with drafts of two protest letters with explanations and recommendations concerning their content and asked him to inform YPSL or other IUSY members as well.

58. Al Haber, American SDS, letter to Ritter, Jugendpolitisches Referat, SPD, June 6, 1962, 3, in Bundesvorstand (National Office; hereafter BV) IUSY 1963 (Oslo), Congress 1961, 1962, German SDS Papers, Archive "APO und soziale Bewegungen," Free University of Berlin (hereafter APOB).

59. See IUSY, "List of Member Organizations per March 15th, 1963," Circular 2/63, March 13, 1963, p. 5, in BV IUSY 1963 (Oslo), Congress 1961, 1962, German SDS Papers, APOB. See also Radomir Luza, *History of the International Socialist Youth Movement* (Leyden: A.W. Sijtfhoff, 1970), 289 ff.

60. Al Haber, American SDS, letter to Ritter, Jugendpolitisches Referat, SPD, June 6, 1962, 3. This letter had also been drafted by Michael Vester; see Michael Vester, letter to Al Haber, May 29, 1962; in personal papers of Michael Vester. See also IUSY, "Report of the Fact-Finding Commission on the German Socialist Student Question," Circular 17/61, June 28, 1961, in BV IUSY 1963 (Oslo), Congress 1961, 1962, German SDS Papers, APOB.

61. Already in 1956, the two organizations are listed as full members, respectively associated members (SLID, then later American SDS). See "IUSY, List of affiliated organizations of IUSY per June 1, 1956, Circular 33 / 56," in BV Ausland, IUSY-Rundschreiben ab 1/63, German SDS Papers, APOB.

62. Robert Ross, "Prospectus for an International Bulletin," December 1962, in Paul Booth Papers, 11, Box 2, SHSW.

63. Ibid., 2.

64. Robert Ross, [International Student Movement], Article draft, 1, undated [1961], 30, in American SDS Records, 1, 3, Box 3, SHSW.

65. Ibid., 32.

66. Ibid., 33.

67. Robert Ross, "Prospectus for an International Bulletin," December 1962, p. 2, in Paul Booth Papers, II, Box 2, SHSW.

68. Dieter Wunder and Reinhard Hoffman, "Auslandsbrief I/1960," Auslandsreferat, SDS Bundesvorstand, Frankfurt, 1960, 1, in German SDS Papers, BV Ausland 1962, APOB.

69. Next to a report from *Pakistan Today* and one on the Danish socialist student organization, it included, for example, a long article on the march on

Washington from the April 1959 edition of the *The American Socialist*, demanding the racial integration of American schools. Ibid., 5–8.

70. See representatively *German News*, SDS, Socialist German Student Federation, Frankfurt, March 1961, in German SDS Papers, BV Ausland 1962, APOB; Volker Mosler, SDS Bundesvorstand, ed., "Relations with the East / SDS at the Deutschlandtreffen," *German Correspondence*, 2, no. 64, July 1, 1964, in German SDS Papers, BV Ausland 1962, APOB.

71. See Michael Vester to Rainer Zoll, Auslandsreferat, "Auslandsreferat, Arbeitsbericht 1960/61," draft, SDS Bundesvorstand, 1961/1962, p. 2, in German SDS Papers, BV Referat Ausland, Oct. 64–Oct. 65, APOB.

72. "Minutes of the First Meeting of an International New Left," October 1961, p. 10, in German SDS Papers, BV Ausland 1962, APOB.

73. Ibid.

74. See *International Socialist Journal* 1, no. 1 (January/February 1964).

75. "Auslandsreferat, Arbeitsbericht 1960/61," corrected draft, SDS Bundesvorstand, 1961/1962, in German SDS Papers, BV Referat Ausland, Oct. 64–Oct. 65, APOB.

76. On the detailed plans, see Michael Vester, letter to Vagn Rasmussen, Socialistisk Ungdoms Forum, March 21, 1963, in BV IUSY 1963 (Oslo), Congress 1961, 1962, German SDS Papers, APOB.

77. In 1961/62, the leadership was divided geographically as follows: Hannes Friedrich (Auslandsreferent), Office for International Affairs itself: Irmgard Bolle (Africa), Michael Vester (United States), Wolfgang Nitsch (England), and Joachim da Silveira (Spain/Portugal). See "Sozialistischer Deutscher Studentenbund/ Anschriften WS 1961/62"; "Sozialistischer Deutscher Studentenbund/Anschriftenliste SS 1962," in German SDS Papers, BV Ausland 1962, APOB. See also "Liste der Mitarbeiter am Auslandsreferat," undated, ibid.

78. "Arbeitsbericht zum Auslandsreferat," Draft, SDS Bundesvorstand Frankfurt, 1964, undated, in German SDS Papers, BV Referat Ausland, Oct. 64–Oct. 65, APOB.

79. Hannes Friedrich, Letter, Auslandsreferat, SDS Bundesvorstand, Frankfurt, April 10, 1962, in German SDS Papers, BV Ausland 1962, APOB.

80. See representatively Tom Condit, International Secretary, YPSL, letter to the German SDS, July 7, 1961, in German SDS Papers, BV Referat Ausland, Oct. 64–Oct. 65, APOB; Don McKelvey, SDS National Office, New York, N.Y., letter to Michael Vester, October 15, 1962; Michael Vester, letter to Joe Love, Assistant for Latin American Affairs, NSA, January 5, 1963, in German SDS Papers, BV Ausland 1962, APOB.

81. See Lawrence S. Wittner, *One World or None: A History of the World Nuclear Disarmament Movement. Through 1953*, vol. 1 (Stanford: Stanford University Press, 1993); Wittner, *Resisting the Bomb: A History of the World Nuclear Disarmament Movement, 1954–1970*, vol. 2 (Stanford: Stanford University Press, 1997).

82. "With the SPU in the lead, nuclear disarmament activism among American students burgeoned dramatically in the early 1960s," according to Wittner, *Resisting the Bomb*, 254.

83. Gitlin, *The Sixties*, 92–94. See also Benjamin Ziemann, ed., *Peace Movements in Western Europe, Japan and the USA since 1945*, Mitteilungsblatt des Instituts für soziale Bewegungen, Forschungen und Forschungsberichte, 32, Bochum, 2004.

84. Interview with Todd Gitlin, New York, N.Y., May 18, 2000, p. 8.

85. See Karl Naske, letter to Todd Gitlin, printed in *Opposition und Ziel*-Redaktion (editorials), March 18, 1962; Todd Gitlin, letter to editors of *Opposition und Ziel*, August 18, 1961, in Todd Gitlin and Nanci Hollander Papers, 1, 2, Box 1, SHSW.

86. Michael Vester, Auslandsreferat, SDS Bundesvorstand, Frankfurt, letter to Student Peace Union, New York, N.Y., April 4, 1963, in German SDS Papers, BV Referat Ausland, Oct. 64–Oct. 65, APOB.

87. See Dan Elwyn Jones, International Secretary, National Youth Campaign for Nuclear Disarmament and Peace, London, letter to the German SDS, March 16, 1963, in German SDS Papers, BV Referat Ausland, Oct. 64–Oct. 65, APOB.

88. Interview with Norman Birnbaum, Washington, D.C., November 4, 2003, pp. 16–21, 26–29.

89. Michael Vester, letter to Michael Harrington, January 11, 1961, in German SDS Papers, BV Ausland 1962, APOB.

90. See Don McKelvey, letter to Michael Vester, SDS National Office, New York, N.Y., December 8, 1962, in German SDS Papers, BV Ausland 1962, APOB.

91. David Komatsu, National Council, Student Peace Union, letter to SDS, Frankfurt, July 3, 1962, in German SDS Papers, BV Referat Ausland, Verschiedenes, APOB.

92. Strecker argued that the only detailed article on the exhibition appeared in the *New York Times* on April 7, 1960. Hannes Friedrich, letter to Reinhard Strecker, July 20, 1962, in German SDS Papers, BV Referat Ausland, Verschiedenes, APOB. See also Hannes Friedrich, International Secretary, SDS, letter to David Komatsu, SPU, July 20, 1962; Reinhard Strecker, letter to Hannes Friedrich, August 16, 1962, in German SDS Papers, BV Referat Ausland, Verschiedenes, APOB. in ibid. See also Hannes Friedrich letter to Reinhard Strecker, September 18, 1962; David Komatsu, SPU, to Hannes Friedrich, International Secretary, SDS, August 6, 1962; Hannes Friedrich, letter to David Komatsu, September 18, 1962, in ibid.

93. Michael Vester, letter to Joel Geyer, *New Politics*, January 26, 1962, in German SDS Papers, BV Ausland 1962, APOB.

94. Eberhard Dähne, "Programme of the 17th post-war convention of SDS," letter, SDS president, September 1962, in German SDS Papers, BV Ausland 1962, APOB.

95. Klaus Hermann, Auslandsreferent, "Entwurf einer Konzeption der Auslandsarbeit zur 18. Delegiertenkonferenz," draft, SDS Bundesvorstand Frankfurt, 1964 [?], undated, in German SDS Papers, BV Referat Ausland, Oct. 64–Oct. 65, APOB, 3f.

96. SDS Bundesvorstand Frankfurt, "Entwurf eines Fragebogens an die genannten sozialistischen Organisationen in Westeuropa," draft, 1964 [?], undated; SDS Bundesvorstand Frankfurt, "SDS International Questionaire," August 15, 1964, in German SDS Papers, BV Referat Ausland, Oct. 64–Oct.65, APOB.

97. Don McKelvey, letter to Michael Vester, SDS National Office, New York, N.Y., December 8, 1962, in German SDS Papers, BV Ausland 1962, APOB. Tom Hayden also had *German Correspondence* and other material from the German SDS mailed to his address in Ann Arbor; see Tom Hayden, letter to Michael Vester, October 1962 [?], undated, in German SDS Papers, BV Referat Ausland, Oct.64–Oct. 65, APOB, in personal papers of Michael Vester.

98. Michael Vester, letter to SDS, New York, N.Y., March 5, 1963, in German SDS Papers, BV Referat Ausland, Oct. 64–Oct. 65, APOB.

99. Hannes Friedrich, "Voices of Dissent," *neue kritik* 9 (1962): 37–39. The collection of *Dissent* articles quoted by Friedrich, which includes articles by Herbert Marcuse, Erich Fromm, Günter Anders, and Richard Löwenthal, appears in the following: *Voices of Dissent: A Collection of Articles of Dissent Magazine* (New York: Grove Press, 1958). Interesting to note is that Friedrich gives the complete address from where the magazine can be ordered.

100. "Zeitschriftenhinweise," *neue kritik* 13 (November 1962): 22–23; Gunther Wegeleben, "Zeitschriftenhinweise," *neue kritik* 21 (February 1964): 34.

101. C. Wright Mills, *The Power Elite* (New York: Oxford University Press, 1959); C. Wright Mills, *Die Amerikanische Elite: Gesellschaft und Macht in den Vereinigten Staaten*, trans. Hans Stern, Heinz Neunes, and Bernt Engelmann (Hamburg: Holsten-Verlag, 1962).

102. Michael Vester, "Schöne neue Welt?" *neue kritik* 14 (March 1963): 3–8. During his stay in the United States, Vester was already drafting articles for German SDS periodicals, occasionally drawing on the help of Al Haber and others. See Michael Vester, letter to Al Haber, April 14, 1962; Al Haber, letter to Michael Vester, May 9, 1962; in personal papers of Michael Vester.

103. Michael Vester, *Schöne neue Welt*, 8. In his article, Vester draws heavily on models established by Mills and also uses the American magazine *Dissent* as one of his sources of information.

104. C. Wright Mills, "Letter to the New Left," *New Left Review* 5 (September/October 1960): 18–23. See also Manfred Liebel, "Die Rolle der Intellektuellen in der Bundesrepublik," *neue kritik* 18 (November 1963): 5–8, esp. 5; Dieter Rave, "Die Rolle der Intelligenz in der kapitalistischen Gesellschaft," *neue kritik* 19/20 (December 1963): 3–5.

105. "Wir können diese Entwicklung in der Bundesrepublik beobachten, die—infolge der Kriegsverheerungen—gewissermaßen die gesamte kapitalistische Entwicklung wiederholen musste"; see Michael Vester, "Falsche Alternativen," *neue kritik* 19/20 (December 1963): 5–11, esp. 8.

106. That C. Wright Mills's works were a constant foil for the German movement can be seen in various articles in *neue kritik*. See, for example, Edgar Weick, "Ostermarsch und Politik," *neue kritik* 21 (February 1963): 3–4; Karl Markus Michel, "Narrenfreiheit in der Zwangsjacke? Aufgaben und Grenzen kritischen Denkens in der Bundesrepublik," *neue kritik* 25/26 (October 1964): 23–29; Michael Vester, "Das Dilemma C. Wright Mills," *neue kritik* 27 (December 1964): 20–23.

107. Herbert Marcuse often pointed to the decisive role of the intellectual as an agent of change and transmitted these beliefs to Germans through his speeches and writings. See for example, Herbert Marcuse, "Perspektiven des Sozialismus

in der industriell entwickelten Gesellschaft," *neue kritik* 31 (August 1965): 11–15, esp. 15.

108. Michael Vester, "Die Linke in den USA," *neue kritik* 17 (July 1963): 6–14, esp. 8.

109. Ibid., 12.

110. He even uses the term "participatory democracy" put forth by the American SDS. Ibid., 13.

111. Ibid., 14.

112. Michael Vester, "A Footnote on the International New Left," unpublished article, p. 1, in private papers of Michael Vester; interview with Michael Vester, Hannover, Germany, June 8, 2001.

113. Ibid., 2.

114. Tom Hayden, letter and speech to Michael Vester, October 1962 [?], undated, in German SDS Papers, BV Referat Ausland, Oct. 64–Oc. 65, APOB, in private papers of Michael Vester.

CHAPTER 2
BETWEEN BERKELEY AND BERLIN, FRANKFURT AND SAN FRANCISCO

1. Interview with Douglas Blagdon, August 22, 2003, Valencia, Calif., p. 7.

2. See Robb Burlage, letter to Jim Monsonis, May 25, 1963, in Students for a Democratic Society Records (hereafter American SDS Records), 2, 5, Box 3, State Historical Society of Wisconsin, Madison (hereafter SHSW); Clark Kissinger, letter to Volkhard Mosler, SDS Frankfurt, August 24, 1964, in American SDS Records, 2, 5 Foreign, Box 7, SHSW; Clark Kissinger, letter to Eberhard Köhl, Berlin, August 20, 1964, in ibid.

3. Douglas Blagdon, letter to Helge Knüppel, Auslandsreferat, SDS Bundesvorstand, Frankfurt, December 13, 1964, in German SDS papers, Bundesvorstand (National Office; hereafter BV) Referat Ausland, Oct. 64–Oct.65, Archive "APO und soziale Bewegungen," Free University of Berlin (hereafter APOB).

4. Interview with Douglas Blagdon, August 22, 2003, Valencia, Calif., 11f.

5. SDS, "America and New Era," in Massimo Teodori, *The New Left: A Documentary History* (Indianapolis: Bobbs-Merrill, 1969), 181.

6. W. J. Rorabaugh, *Berkeley at War. The 1960s* (New York: Oxford University Press, 1989); Robert Cohen and Reginald Zelnik, *The Free Speech Movement: Reflections on Berkeley in the 1960s* (Berkeley: University of California Press, 2002).

7. Kirkpatrick Sale, *SDS* (New York: Random House, 1973), 663 f.

8. See Sale, *SDS*, 279 ff, for the long-term consequences of the massive influx of "middle-American activists," who were slowly outnumbering the former leading circle of mostly Eastern intellectuals in the SDS in general and at the Clear Lake convention from August 29–September 2, 1966.

9. See Robert Ross, "Primary Groups in Social Movements," in R. David Myers, *Toward a History of the New Left. Essays from within the Movement* (Brooklyn, N.Y.: Carlson Publishing, 1989), 161 f.; for SDS's involvement in organizing the poor and attempts to create an interracial movement of the poor

through the Economic Research and Action Project (ERAP), see Sale, *SDS*, chs. 7 and 9; Frost, *An Interracial Movement of the Poor*, passim.

10. SDS, "America and the New Era," in Teodori, *New Left*, 178.

11. John Patrick Diggins, *The Rise and Fall of the American Left* (New York: Norton, 1992), 240. See Paul Potter, "We Must Name the System," speech delivered at the April 17, 1965 March on Washington, in Judith Clavier Albert and Stewart Edward Albert, eds., *The Sixties Papers. Documents of a Rebellious Decade* (New York: Praeger, 1984), 219–25.

12. Richard Ochs, "Suggested SDS Projects in Foreign Policy," working paper, May 25, 1965, p. 4, in American SDS Records, 2, 8, Box 4, SHSW.

13. David Garson, "Comments on Working With Other Groups," SDS 1965 National Convention—Working Paper, May 1965, p. 2, in American SDS Records, 2, 8, Box 4, SHSW.

14. Paul Booth, "Working Papers—Summer Projects," May, 1965, p. 5, in American SDS Records, 2, 8, Box 4, SHSW.

15. Paul Potter, "SDS & Foreign Policy," working paper, May 1965, in American SDS Records, 2, 8, Box 4, SHSW.

16. "Foreign Policy Resolution Passed by the SDS National Convention 1965," SDS Work List Mailing, vol. 2, no. 14, SDS National Office, July 28, 1965, p. 3, in American SDS Records, 2, 7, Box 8, SHSW. See also "SDS 1965 National Convention: Summary," in SDS Work List Mailing, vol. 2, no. 13, SDS National Office, July 16, 1965, in American SDS Records, 2, 7, Box 8, SHSW.

17. Carl Oglesby, letter to Robert Parris Moses, July 31, 1965, in American SDS Records, 2, 14, Box 8, SHSW.

18. For an overview of the planning of the International Days of Protest and government reaction, see Tom Wells, *The War Within: America's Battle over Vietnam* (Berkeley: University of California Press, 1994), 51–58. For the antiwar movement in general see also Nancy Zaroulis and Gerald Sullivan, *Who Spoke Up? American Protest Against the War in Vietnam, 1963–1975* (Garden City, N.Y.: Doubleday, 1984); Melvin Small, *Johnson, Nixon, and the Doves* (New Brunswick, N.J.: Rutgers University Press, 1988); Charles DeBenedetti, *An American Ordeal: The Antiwar Movement of the Vietnam Era* (Syracuse, N.Y.: Syracuse University Press, 1990); Kenneth Heineman, *Campus Wars: The Peace Movement at American State Universities in the Vietnam Era* (New York: New York University Press, 1993); Adam Garfinkle, *Telltale Hearts: The Origins and Impact of the Vietnam Antiwar Movement* (New York: St. Martin's Press, 1995); Michael Foley, *Confronting the War Machine: Draft Resistance During the Vietnam War* (Chapel Hill: University of North Carolina Press, 2003); Melvin Small, *Antiwarriors: The Vietnam War and the Battle for America's Hearts and Minds* (Lanham, Md.: SR Books, 2004).

19. "Draft Call for International Days of Protest, October 15–16, 1966," National Vietnam Newsletter #3, SDS, August 26, 1965, sec. 6, 1f., in American SDS Records, 2, 11, Box 9, SHSW. See also "National Council Ballot," August 1965, p. 1, in American SDS Records, 2, 1, Box 9, SHSW. The Vietnam Committee was also active in setting up international contacts or alternative news services. See Mel McDonald, SDS Vietnam coordinator, letter to Dave Smith, Regional Office, Boston, July 15, 1965, in American SDS Records, 2, 1, Box 9, SHSW.

20. Sale, *SDS*, 240–45.

21. Carl Oglesby, *A Raven in the Storm: The Vietnam War At Home*, unpublished ms., 2005, p. 122.

22. Interview with Carl Oglesby, Cambridge, Mass., December 17, 1999 / July 30, 2000. On Oglesby's visit to Vietnam and Japan, as well as his involvment in the Russell Tribunal, see also Carl Oglesby, *Raven in the Storm: A Personal History of the 1960s Antiwar Movement* (New York: Scribner, 2008), 60–84, 128–138. See also an anthology of New Left speeches, including contributions by Rudi Dutschke and Daniel Cohn-Bendit: Carl Oglesby, ed., *The New Left Reader* (New York: Grove Press, 1969). Furthermore, see Carl Oglesby and Richard Shaull, *Containment and Change* (New York: Macmillan, 1967).

23. Carl Oglesby, "Trapped in a system" in Teodori, *New Left*, 187.

24. Ibid., 187.

25. Sale probably incorrectly attributes this plan to Todd Gitlin at the September 7 National Council meeting in Indiana. See Sale, *SDS*, 226. In 1954, the Geneva Conference ended the hostilities between the French army and the Viet Minh guerillas by a set of treaties known as the Geneva Accords, which declared the territorial integrity and sovereignty of Indochina, as well as its independence from France.

26. Carl Oglesby, "New Left or Old Rights?" in SDS Bulletin #3, "Don't Trust Anyone Over 30," 2 , no. 19, November 22, 1965, p. 1, in American SDS Records, 3, 11, Box 48, SHSW.

27. Carl Oglesby, "A New Departure for the Peace Movement," Worklist #29, December 3, 1965, p. 5, in American SDS Records, 3, 11, Box 48, SHSW. On the internal development of SDS in the second half of 1965, see James Miller, *Democracy Is in the Streets: From Port Huron to the Siege of Chicago*, 2nd ed. (New York, Simon and Schuster, 1987), 223–54.

28. One example included the intensified connections to the Canadian peace movement. See Matt Cohen, SUPA, Toronto, letter to Carl Oglesby, July 17, 1965; Carl Oglesby, letter to Matt Cohen, July 18, 1965, both in American SDS Records, 2, 14, Box 8, SHSW.

29. Mel McDonald, SDS Vietnam coordinator, letter to Dave [McReynolds], War Resistors League, summer 1965, in American SDS Records, 2, 1, Box 9, SHSW.

30. Gerry Hunnius, ICDP, London, letter to Carl Oglesby, October 20, 1965; Paul Booth, letter to Peggy Duff, General Secretary, CND, November 1, 1965; Paul Booth, letter to Gerry Hunnius, November 2, 1965; all in American SDS Records, 3, 6, Box 34, SHSW.

31. See Peggy Duff, CND, London, letter to Paul Booth, November 12, 1965, in American SDS Records, 3, 6, Box 34, SHSW.

32. Paul Booth, letter to Bill Savage, president, National Union of Students, London, December 19, 1965, in American SDS Records, 3, 8, Box 34, SHSW.

33. "National Council Ballot," August 1965, 1f., in American SDS Records, 2, 1, Box 9, SHSW. Sale mistakenly attributes the plan to Clark Kissinger. See Sale, *SDS*, 226.

34. "Minutes of the SDS National Council Meeting (handwritten notes)," September 1965, pp. 81, 87, in American SDS Records, 3, 2, Box 36, SHSW.

35. Ibid., 88. In an undated proposal, SDS member Peter Orris likewise argued, "The foreign students are waiting for the call to come from the US. SDS is the only group that is capable of making this call." See Peter Orris, "In Favor of an International Student Strike," Worklist Mailing, 1965 [undated], in American SDS Records, 3, 4, Box 35, SHSW.

36. "Minutes of the SDS National Council Meeting (handwritten notes)," September 1965, p. 93.

37. "Priorities," Minutes of the SDS National Council Meeting, September 1965, 3 f., in American SDS Records, 3, 2, Box 36, SHSW. See also Worklist Mailing "Make Love, Not War," vol. 2, no. 19, September 15, 1965, in American SDS Records, 3, 9, Box 48, SHSW.

38. "NC News—Worldwide Strike," October 1965, in American SDS Records, 3, 6, Box 48, SHSW. See also SDS National Office, "National Council Report," Indiana, October 1965 [?], p. 4, in American SDS Records, 3, 3, Box 36, SHSW.

39. Paul Booth, "NICNAC 2," Report on NAC Meeting, January 1–2, 1966, p. 5, in American SDS Records, 3, 5, Box 35, SHSW.

40. Earl Silbar and Steve Baum, "Proposal for an International Student / Faculty Strike for the International Days of Protest March 25–26," SDS, National Administrative Council, January 1–2, 1966, [undated], in American SDS Records, 3, 5, Box 35, SHSW.

41. Paul Booth, letter to International Organizations and Student Groups, January 25, 1966, in American SDS Records, 3, 5, Box 35, SHSW.

42. Sale, SDS, 251. Among these issues were the following: "I. The academic disciplines; II. Radicals in the professions; III. Political philosophy, ideology and strategy; IV. Power, politics and class; V. Agents of change; VI. International education, VII. The arts." See "Radical Education Program," Draft, March 20, 1966, p. 6, in American SDS Records, 3, 2, Box 34a, SHSW.

43. Ibid., 21.

44. Richard Flacks, letter to Al Haber, March 23, 1966, p. 2, in American SDS Records, 3, 5, Box 36, SHSW; "Radical Education Project," founding manifesto, August 1, 1966, p. 17, in American SDS Records, 3, 3, Box 48, SHSW.

45. See the description of William Appleman Williams in Kevin Mattson, *Intellectuals in Action. The Origins of the New Left and Radical Liberalism* (University Park: Pennsylvania State University Press, 2002), 167.

46. In hindsight, Richard Flacks considers SDS's policies somewhat isolationist at this point and the international aspect of REP marginal. Interview with Richard Flacks, August 21, 2003, Santa Barbara, Calif., 15f.

47. Ibid., 17.

48. See Rudi Dutschke, letter to Dieter Kunzelmann et al., January 9, 1966, in Papers of Rudi Dutschke, Bundesarchiv, K-2 / 48, 1, Archive of the Hamburger Institut für Sozialforschung (hereafter HIS), Hamburg, Germany. For the detailed planning of the poster action, see Siegward Lönnendonker, Bernd Rabehl, and Jochen Staadt, *Die antiautoritäre Revolte: der Sozialistische Deutsche Studentenbund nach der Trennung von der SPD* (Wiesbaden: Westdeutscher Verlag, 2002), 227. The chronological sequence of events is largely based on this empirically solid and rich study.

49. For the public reaction, see Siegward Lönnendonker and Tilman Fichter, eds., *Hochschule im Umbruch, vol. 4: Die Krise: 1964–1967. Dokumentation.* (Berlin: Pressestelle der FU Berlin, 1975), 263–65; Lönnendonker, Rabehl, and Staadt, *Die Antiautoritäre Revolte*, 232.

50. A comprehensive view on the research of the German peace movement can be found in Wilfried Mausbach, "The Present's Past: Recent Perspectives on Peace and Protest in Germany, 1945–1973 in Benjamin Ziemann ed., *Peace Movements in Western Europe, Japan and the USA since 1945* (Mitteilungsblatt des Instituts für soziale Bewegungen, Forschungen und Forschungsberichte, 32, Bochum, 2004), 67–98. See also Alice Holmes Cooper, *Paradoxes of Peace: German Peace Movements since 1945* (Ann Arbor: University of Michigan Press, 1996).

51. See Willy Albrecht, *Der Sozialistische Deutsche Studentenbund. SDS. Vom parteikonformen Studentenverband zum Repräsentanten der Neuen Linken* (Bonn: Dietz, 1994), 143–65, 288–308; Claus Leggewie, *Kofferträger. Das Algerien-Projekt der Linken im Adenauer-Deutschland* (Berlin: Rotbuch-Verlag, 1984); Lönnendonker, Rabehl, and Staadt, *Die Antiautoritäre Revolte*, 195–97.

52. Ibid., 209.

53. The issue is reflected in numerous articles in leftist periodicals. Especially *Konkret*, which started its reporting as early as 1963, had by 1965 at least a two-page article on the war, its victims, the worldwide opposition against it, as well as the effects that the conflict had for West Germany, in almost every issue. For a representative selection of articles, see Raimund Kaufmann, "Augenzeuge in Nordvietnam," *Konkret* 10 (October 1963): 7–10; Bertrand Russell, "Vietnam," *Konkret* 3 (March 1965): 20–27; Wilfried G. Burchett, "Im Lager der Vietkong I & II," *Konkret* 7/8 (July and August 1965): 18–23, 20–23.

54. Jürgen Horlemann and Peter Gäng, *Vietnam—Genesis eines Konflikts* (Frankfurt: Suhrkamp, 1966).

55. Ibid., 212.

56. Günter Amendt, "Die Studentenrevolte in Berkeley," *neue kritik* 28 (February 1965): 5–7.

57. "I have written about that [the FSM] for different papers and also for broadcasting co[r]porations and I will send you copies later on.... Again I ask you to put me on your list for the bulletin and other things you are printing." Günter Amendt, letter to SDS National Office, December 29, 1964, in American SDS Records, 2, 5, Foreign, Box 7, SHSW.

58. "SDS 1965 Convention Directory," 1965, p. 6; "Discussion group #1 – Carolyn Craven – University Reform," 1965, both in American SDS Records, 2, 7, Box 4, SHSW.

59. Wolfgang Nitsch to SDS Bundesvorstand, Frankfurt, Postcard, Camp Maplehurst, June 12, 1965, in German SDS papers, BV I Bundesvorstand E (Intern) 1965/66 abgeschlossen, September 66, APOB.

60. Susanne Schunter-Kleemann, "SDS-Aktivistin," in Ute Kätzel, *Die 68erinnen: Porträt einer rebellischen Frauengeneration* (Berlin: Rowohlt, 2002), 110. See also the book based on her senior thesis completed at the FU Berlin in the spring of 1968: Susanne Kleemann, *Ursachen und Formen der amerikanischen Studentenopposition* (Frankfurt: Suhrkamp, 1971).

61. Wolfgang Kraushaar, "Die transatlantische Protestkultur, Der zivile Ungehorsam als amerikanisches Exempel und als bundesdeutsche Adaption," in Heinz Bude, ed., *Westbindungen. Amerika in der Bundesrepublik* (Hamburg: Hamburger Edition, 1999), 261 f.

62. Jürgen Habermas, "Die Scheinrevolution und ihre Kinder," in idem, *Protestbewegung und Hochschulreform* (Franfurt: Suhrkamp, 1969), 191.

63. Michael Vester, "Die Strategie der direkten Aktion," *neue kritik* 30 (June 1965): 12–20, esp. 13.

64. Ibid., 15f., 17 f.

65. Worklist Mailing, "Make Love, Not War," vol. 2, no. 19, September 9, 1965, in American SDS Records, 3, 9, Box 48, SHSW.

66. Breines, *Community and Organization in the New Left,* xiv. For the role of direct action from a broader historical perspective, see Martin Klimke and Joachim Scharloth, "Utopia in Practice: The Discovery of Performativity in Sixties' Protest, Arts and Sciences," in *Historein: A Review of the Past & Other Stories* (forthcoming, 2009).

67. For background on this development, see Frank Böckelmann and Herbert Nagel, eds., *Subversive Aktion: Der Sinn der Organisation ist ihr Scheitern* (Frankfurt: Neue Kritik, 1976); Wolfgang Dressen and Eckhard Siepmann, eds., *Nilpferd des höllischen Urwalds. Situationisten, Gruppe SPUR, Kommune I* (Gießen: Schriftenreihe des Werkbundarchivs, 1991).

68. Wolfgang Kraushaar, *1968 als Mythos, Chiffre und Zäsur* (Hamburg: Hamburger Edition, 2000), 302. See also Dieter Kunzelmann, *Leisten Sie keinen Widerstand!: Bilder aus meinem Leben* (Berlin: Transit, 1998), passim.

69. Christopher Gray, *Leaving the 20th Century: The Incomplete Work of the Situationist International* (London: Rebel Press, 1998); Tom McDonough, *Guy Debord and the Situationist International: Texts and Documents* (Cambridge: MIT Press, 2002). For an introduction, see Thomas Hecken and Agata Grzenia, "Situationism," in Martin Klimke and Joachim Scharloth, eds., *1968 in Europe: A History of Protest and Activism, 1956–1977* (New York: Palgrave Macmillan, 2008), 23–32.

70. Subversive Aktion, "Unverbindliche Richtlinien 2," Munich/Berlin/Assens, December 1963, in Böckelmann/Nagel, *Subversive Aktion,* 114f.

71. For a detailed biography on Dutschke, see Gretchen Dutschke, *Wir hatten ein barbarisches, schönes Leben: Rudi Dutschke—Eine Biographie von Gretchen Dutschke.* (Cologne: Kiepenheuer and Witsch, 1996); Michaela Karl, *Rudi Dutschke: Revolutionär ohne Revolution.* (Frankfurt: Neue Kritik, 2003).

72. Bernd Rabehl, "Nachtcafé," in Kunzelmann, *Leisten Sie keinen Widerstand*, 44. See also Lönnendonker, Rabehl, and Staadt, *Die Antiautoritäre Revolte,* 412–26.

73. Lönnendonker, Rabehl, and Staadt, *Die Antiautoritäre Revolte,* 199 ff.

74. See Uwe Bergmann et al., *Rebellion der Studenten oder Die neue Opposition* (Reinbek: Rowohlt, 1968), 63.

75. Ibid.

76. SDS President Schauer had already met Kunzelmann in December 1964, when the latter and Rudolf Gramke, pretending to be SDS members, tried to go through the files of the national office in its basement to search for material they

could use for their infiltration attempts. After being confronted by Schauer, they were thrown out immediately. See Lönnendonker, Rabehl, and Staadt, *Die Anti-autoritäre Revolte*, 198f.

77. Michael Vester, letter to Helmut Schauer, May 29, 1965, in German SDS papers, BV I Bundesvorstand E (Intern) 1965/66 abgeschlossen. Sept. 66, APOB. I am indebted to Heide Berndt for pointing me to the details of this controversy. See also Heide Berndt, unpublished manuscript, November 1999, "Der Traum und die Sache—Geschichte der 68er Bewegung Berlin—Frankfurt," chapter 3.1.3.2.2, APOB. See also Lönnendonker, Rabehl, and Staadt, *Die Antiautoritäre Revolte*, 117–19.

78. Helmut Schauer, letter to Michael Vester, June 9, 1965, 4, 2f., in German SDS papers, BV I Bundesvorstand E (Intern) 1965/66 abgeschlossen. Sept. 66, APOB.

79. "Your discussion style is incomprehensible to me. As a matter of fact, you use the tactic of tackling my arguments with counterattacks by labeling them 'bureaucratic,' 'ideologically integrating,' or 'emotional.' If I accuse you of having a bureaucratic style, you counter that I am also bureaucratic. . . . Talking with you one gets the impression that you are not listening properly, that you have already made up your mind. I envy the self-confidence with which you put forward your arguments as if they were completely unproblematic or final." Michael Vester, letter to Helmut Schauer, June 24, 1965, in German SDS papers, BV I Bundesvorstand E (Intern) 1965/66 abgeschlossen. Sept. 66, APOB.

80. Michael Vester, letter to Helmut Schauer, June 24, 1965, 2, in German SDS papers, BV I Bundesvorstand E (Intern) 1965/66 abgeschlossen. Sept. 66, APOB.

81. Ibid., 14, 16f.

82. Ibid., 18f.

83. See Vester's comprehensive suggestions in this regard: Michael Vester, letter to Helmut Schauer, July 15, 1965, in German SDS papers, BV I Bundesvorstand E (Intern) 1965/66 abgeschlossen. Sept. 66, APOB.

84. Helmut Schauer, "Zur Politik des SDS, Auszüge aus dem Rechenschaftsbericht des 1. Vorsitzenden," *neue kritik* 32 (October 1965): 6 f.

85. See Lönnendonker, Rabehl, and Staadt, *Die Antiautoritäre Revolte*, 125–32; interview with Michael Vester, Hanover, September 12, 2005.

86. See Lönnendonker, Rabehl, and Staadt, *Die Antiautoritäre Revolte*, 425 f.; Kunzelmann, *Leisten Sie keinen Widerstand*, 45.

87. SDS, *Hochschule in der Demokratie. Denkschrift des Sozialistischen Deutschen Studentenbundes zur Hochschulreform* (Frankfurt: SDS Bundesvorstand, 1961). See also the new edition (Frankfurt: Verlag Neue Kritik, 1965).

88. Tilman Fichter and Siegward Lönnendonker, *Macht und Ohnmacht der Studenten. Kleine Geschichte des SDS*, 2nd ed. (Hamburg: Rotbuch, 1998), 103.

89. On the history of the Free University of Berlin, see Lönnendonker and Fichter, *Hochschule im Umbruch*, vol. 4; Bernd Rabehl, *Am Ende der Utopie: Die Politische Geschichte der Freien Universität* (Berlin: Argon, 1988); James F. Tent, *The Free University of Berlin: A Political History* (Bloomington: Indiana University Press, 1988).

90. See Jens Hager, ed., *Die Rebellen von Berlin. Studentenpolitik an der Freien Universität* (Cologne: Kiepenheuer and Witsch, 1967), 13–20; Bergmann, *Rebellion der Studenten*, 14 f.

91. See Bergmann, *Rebellion der Studenten*, 16; Hager, *Rebellen von Berlin*, 65–68.

92. For quotations and documents see Hager, *Rebellen von Berlin*, 68–71. See also See Lönnendonker, Rabehl, and Staadt, *Die Antiautoritäre Revolte*, 121–24; Ekkehart Krippendorff, "Mein Weg nach '68,'" *Neues Deutschland*, Special Feature "1968," April 26, 2008.

93. Fichter and Lönnendonker, *Macht und Ohnmacht*, 114 ff.

94. "Aufruf zum Krieg in Vietnam," October 1, 1965, in Lönnendonker and Fichter, *Hochschule im Umbruch*, 4:241 f.

95. "Erklärung über den Krieg in Vietnam," November 27, 1965, in ibid., 248 ff.; Lönnendonker, Rabehl, and Staadt, *Die Antiautoritäre Revolte*, 221.

96. For a more detailed description, see Lönnendonker, Rabehl, and Staadt, *Die Antiautoritäre Revolte*, 228–31.

97. Rudi Dutschke, "Diskussionsbeitrag," Münchner Konzil der Subversiven Aktion, April 25, 1965, in Böckelmann and Nagel, *Subversive Aktion*, 324.

98. Rudi Dutschke, "Diskussion: Das Verhältnis von Theorie und Praxis," based on a letter from July 4, 1964, subsequently edited and published in *Anschlag* 1, also printed in Böckelmann and Nagel, *Subversive Aktion*, 193 f.

99. Rudi Dutschke, *Diskussionsbeitrag*, 326. See also ibid., 309. For Dutschke's trip to Paris in 1966 and his perception of the French New Left and countercultural scene, see Rudi Dutschke, letter to Gábor Révai, September 30, 1966, in Rudi Dutschke and Gábor Révai, "Briefwechsel 1966 bis 1971," in Eurozine, April 23, 2009, http://www.eurozine.com/articles/2009-04-23-dutschke-de.html.

100. For Rabehl's reflection on the appeal of the "subjective factor" and a contemporary critique, see Lönnendonker, Rabehl, and Staadt, *Die Antiautoritäre Revolte*, 425; Bernd Rabehl, "Viva Maria und die Verknüpfung von Anarchismus und Marxismus innerhalb der neuen Linken," *Kino*, Heft 1, Cologne, 1965.

101. Kunzelmann, *Leisten Sie keinen Widerstand*, 51. See also Gretchen Dutschke, *Wir hatten ein barbarisches, schönes Leben*, 78 f.

102. See Rudi Dutschke, "Diskussion: Das Verhältnis von Theorie und Praxis," based on a letter from July 4, 1964, subsequently edited and published in *Anschlag* 1, in Böckelmann and Nagel, *Subversive Aktion*, 195.

103. See Herbert Marcuse, *One-Dimensional Man. Studies in the Ideology of Advanced Industrial Society* (Boston: Beacon Press, 1964), 256–57.

104. Dutschke took this concept from Herbert Marcuse, "Freiheit: von oder zu," *Westdeutscher Rundfunk*, December 1964, p. 6, in Rudi Dutschke, *Diskussionsbeitrag*, 323.

105. Ibid.

106. See Rudi Dutschke, "Diskussion: Das Verhältnis von Theorie und Praxis," based on a letter from July 4, 1964, subsequently edited and published in *Anschlag* 1, in Böckelmann and Nagel, *Subversive Aktion*, 191 f. See also Rudi Dutschke, "Die Widersprüche des Spätkapitalismus, die antiautoritären Studen-

ten und ihr Verhältnis zur Dritten Welt," in Bergmann, *Rebellion der Studenten*, 39 f.

107. See esp. George Lukács, "Die Verdinglichung und das Bewußtsein des Proletariats," in idem, *Geschichte und Klassenbewusstsein. Studien über marxistische Dialektik* (Neuwied: Luchterhand, 1968), 355. For a detailed analysis by Dutschke see idem, *Die Widersprüche des Spätkapitalismus*, 47f.

108. See also Rudi Dutschke, *Diskussionsbeitrag*, 321 f.

109. Hans Magnus Enzensberger, "Europäische Peripherie," in *Kursbuch* 2 (August 1965): 154–73.

110. Dutschke was able to read the unpublished manuscript of the German translation of Frantz Fanon's *The Wretched of the Earth* due to his acquaintance with SDS member Traugott König. See Frantz Fanon, "Von der Gewalt," translated by Traugott König, *Kursbuch* 2 (August 1965): 1–55; Chaussy, *Die drei Leben*, 103 ff.

111. Rudi Dutschke, *Diskussionsbeitrag*, 327.

112. Ibid., 324.

113. Lönnendonker, Rabehl, and Staadt, *Die Antiautoritäre Revolte*, 233 f.

114. Quoted in Bergmann, *Rebellion der Studenten*, 69.

115. See interview with Jürgen Horlemann, quoted in Lönnendonker, Rabehl, and Staadt, *Die Antiautoritäre Revolte*, 235.

116. See Che Guevara, "Guerillakrieg—Eine Methode," in idem, *Guerilla— Theorie und Methode* (Berlin: Wagenbach, 1968), 124–42, esp. 125.

117. His handwritten notes are printed in full in Lönnendonker, Rabehl, and Staadt, *Die Antiautoritäre Revolte*, 235–37. On this point see also the controversial interpretation by Wolfgang Kraushaar, "Rudi Dutschke und der bewaffnete Kampf," in Wolfgang Kraushaar, Jan Philipp Reemtsma, and Karin Wieland, *Rudi Dutschke, Andreas Baader und die RAF* (Hamburg: Hamburger Edition, 2005), 28–31. A further example of the integration of Che Guevara's theories in Dutschke's reception of Lukács is his presentation at the SDS seminar on the history of the labor movement, March 12–20, 1966. See Lönnendonker, Rabehl, and Staadt, *Die Antiautoritäre Revolte*, 254 f.

118. Rudi Dutschke, "Vom Antisemitismus zum Antikommunismus," in Bergmann, *Rebellion der Studenten*, 69f.

119. "Informationen über Vietnam und Länder der Dritten Welt," in Lönnendonker and Fichter, *Hochschule im Umbruch*, 4:308.

120. For a more detailed chronological sequence, see Lönnendonker, Rabehl, and Staadt, *Die Antiautoritäre Revolte*, 259–67.

121. "Referat des 1. SDS-Bundesvorsitzenden Helmut Schauer während der LVV in Berlin am 18. Mai 1966," in Lönnendonker and Fichter, *Hochschule im Umbruch*, 4:314. See also Helmut Schauer, "Einige Kernpunkte der aktuellen Diskussion im SDS," *neue kritik* 33 (December 1965): 10–12.

122. "Referat des 1. SDS-Bundesvorsitzenden Helmut Schauer," 315.

123. Ibid., 315 f.

124. LV SDS Berlin, letter to SDS BV, May 29, 1966, in Lönnendonker and Fichter, *Hochschule im Umbruch,* 4:322 f. For a comprehensive view on the sequence of events after the meeting in Berlin on May 18, 1966, see Lönnendonker, Rabehl, and Staadt, *Die Antiautoritäre Revolte*, 271–83.

125. Gretchen Dutschke, *Wir hatten ein barbarisches, schönes Leben*, 79 f.

126. Rudi Dutschke, *Diskussionsbeitrag*, 323.

127. See Ron Watson, letters to Gretchen Dutschke, May 2, 1965; Jun 18, 1965; October 22, 1965; undated, December 13, 1965 [?]; undated, December 17, 1965 [?], in Papers of Rudi Dutschke, Bundesarchiv, K-8 / 48, NL 343, Bd. 64, 5, HIS.

128. Rudi Dutschke, *Diskussionsbeitrag*, 327.

129. Jürgen Horlemann, "Referat zu Flugblatt 'Informationen über Vietnam und Länder der Dritten Welt' Nummer 1," in Lönnendonker and Fichter, *Hochschule im Umbruch*, 4:312.

130. "Contrary to the United States political opposition has not yet been recognized as part of a democratic way of life in the Federal Republic. It is a fact that a large part of the younger generation engaged in politics is becoming more and more critical of the US government policy on Vietnam, in Berlin as well as in England and France." In Reinhard Strecker and Jürgen Horlemann, SDS LV Berlin to the U.S. Ambassador to the FRG, February 26, 1966, p. 2, in German SDS papers, FU WS 1965/66, Collection Wolfgang Nitsch, APOB.

131. Ibid.

132. Ibid., 3.

133. Lönnendonker, Rabehl, and Staadt, *Die Antiautoritäre Revolte*, 251, 256.

134. "Resolution verabschiedet von der versammelten Studentenschaft der FU Berlin auf dem Sit-in am 22./23. June 1966," in Lönnendonker and Fichter, *Hochschule im Umbruch*, 4:333f. See also Hager, *Rebellen von Berlin*, 72–92; Fichter and Lönnendonker, *Macht und Ohnmacht*, 134 f; Peter Mosler, *Was wir wollten, was wir wurden. Studentenrevolte— zehn Jahre danach* (Reinbek: Rowohlt, 1977), 10–12; Bergmann, *Rebellion der Studenten*, 20–22; Lönnendonker, Rabehl, and Staadt, *Die Antiautoritäre Revolte*, 140–45.

135. SDS Munich, "Vietnam-Arbeit Winter 1965/66 und Sommer 1966," July 1966, in German SDS papers, Akte SDS Gruppe München, APOB (quoted in Lönnendonker, Rabehl, and Staadt, *Die Antiautoritäre Revolte*, 285).

136. Reimut Reiche, letter to Bernhard Blanke, August 11, 1966, in German SDS papers, Akte Briefwechsel Blanke-Reiche, APOB (quoted in Lönnendonker, Rabehl, and Staadt, *Die Antiautoritäre Revolte*, 146).

137. Interview with Reimut Reiche, January 17, 2005, Frankfurt/Main, 23 f.

138. Reimut Reiche, "Studentenrevolten in Berkeley und Berlin," *neue kritik* 38/39 (October/December 1966): 21–27, esp. 21 f.

139. Ibid., 27.

140. A statement of Ulrich Enzensberger was relayed to Schauer in mid-May, in which Enzensberger speculated about the positive implication of a ban on leftist student organizations in terms of mobilization and creating a revolutionary consciousness. See Jürgen W[erth], "Gedächtnisprotokoll vom 11.5. 1966 nach einem Gespräch mit Ulrich Enzensberger am 9.5. 1966," in German SDS papers, Berlin / Frankfurt / Munich 1966/67, APOB / SDS Korrespondenz 2, 17f. (quoted in Lönnendonker, Rabehl, and Staadt, *Die Antiautoritäre Revolte*, 263).

141. Lönnendonker and Staadt consider Schauer's fear with regard to the illegalization of protest activities to have been exaggerated and argue that the Berlin

SDS chapter was by no means willing to go into illegality. See Lönnendonker, Rabehl, and Staadt, *Die Antiautoritäre Revolte*, 263 f.

142. Kunzelmann, *Leisten Sie keinen Widerstand*, 47. For an introduction to the Amsterdam Provos see Niek Pas, "Subcultural Movements: The Provos," in Klimke and Scharloth, *1968 in Europe*, 13–21.

143. Gilgenmann and Raspe, SDS Berlin, Internal Newsletter, December 4, 1966, in personal papers of Rudi Dutschke, Bundesarchiv, K-8 / 48, NL 343, Bd. 43, 3, HIS. See also Lothar Hack, "Am Beispiel Berkeley: Rigider Funktionalismus und neue Unmittelbarkeit," *neue kritik* 41 (April 1967): 36–52; Stefan Aust, "Berkeley, Anatomie einer Straßenschlacht," *Konkret* 13 (June 1969): 34–37; Wolf Dresp, "Zur Analyse der Funktion amerikanischer Universitäten: Die Entwicklung der Studentenbewegung in Berkeley," *Sozialistische Correspondenz— Info* 9 (August 1, 1969): 16–19.

144. Rudi Dutschke, "Zu einigen Problemen der aktuellen SDS-Politik," December 1966 (?), undated, in Papers of Rudi Dutschke, Bundesarchiv, K-8 / 48, NL 343, Bd. 43, 3, HIS.

CHAPTER 3
BUILDING THE SECOND FRONT

1. Ruven Brooks, letter to SDS National Office, November 5, 1966, in Students for a Democratic Society Records (hereafter American SDS Records), 3, 18, Box 54, State Historical Society of Wisconsin, Madison, Wisconsin (hereafter SHSW). With "laws of necessity" Brooks refers to the impending emergency laws debated in the German parliament that provoked a broad opposition among various parts of the political and social spectrum. See also chapter 2.

2. Ibid.

3. The periodical started on January 21, 1966. See Kirkpatrick Sale, *SDS* (New York: Random House, 1973), 272 f.

4. "Minutes of the Plenary Session," SDS National Conference, Ann Arbor, Mich., June 28, 1967, insert #4, in American SDS Records, 3, 7, Box 35, SHSW.

5. Workshop on Liberation Movements and Oppressed People, "National Coordinator for Liason with Revolutionary and Liberation Movements and Organizations," Proposal, December 1967 [undated], in SDS Records, 3, 7, Box 36, SHSW.

6. Paul Booth, "Affiliation with International Confederation for Disarmament and Peace," Letter, March/April 1966, in American SDS Records, 3, 5, Box 36, SHSW.

7. Sale, *SDS*, 288 f.

8. See, for example, Carl Davidson's paper "A Student Syndicalist Movement: University Reform Revisited," distributed at the convention. Sale, *SDS*, 292; Immanuel Wallerstein and Paul Starr, eds., *The University Crisis Reader* (New York: Random House, 1971), 2:98–107.

9. Oral history interview with Gregory N. Calvert, July 13, 1987, p. 204 f., in Student Movements of the 1960s Project, Oral History Research Office, Columbia University, New York. As he recalled later on, his stay in Paris made him "a Euro-

pean left socialist, searching for a new left. And it was only when I returned to the States that what had happened there began to change again in the context of the emerging American New Left." See ibid., 92 f.

10. Sale, *SDS*, 309 f., 313 ff.

11. Ibid., 309, 318 f.

12. Quoted in ibid., 325.

13. Sol Stern, "From the Danube to Chicago," *City Journal* 18, no. 2 (spring 2008).

14. Quoted in Todd Gitlin, *The Sixties: Years of Hope, Days of Rage* (New York: Bantam Books, 1987), 271. For the meeting itself and its serious impact on many of the American participants, see pp. 270–74.

15. See Sale, *SDS*, 391 ff.; Gitlin, *The Sixties*, 274–82; Tom Hayden, *Reunion: A Memoir* (New York: Random House, 1988), 206–41; Carl Oglesby, *Ravens in the Storm: A Personal History of the 1960s Antiwar Movement* (New York: Scribner, 2008), 128–38.

16. SDS Frankfurt, telegram to SDS National Office, June 5, 1967; Greg Calvert, SDS National Office, letter to Berlin SDS, June 5, 1967, in American SDS Records, 3, 18, Box 54, SHSW.

17. "German SDS Tears Up Berlin: Rudi Dutschke Shot," *New Left Notes*, April 15, 1968, p. 1. See also "SDS in Germany," *New Left Notes*, April 22, 1968, p. 1.

18. Student Mobilization Committee and American SDS, "Protest the Attempted Assassination of Rudi Dutschke!" flyer, April 1968, in Protest and Activism Collection, 1963–75, 8, RC 7, 3, Columbia University Archives.

19. American SDS, "We support the German SDS," flyer, April 1968 [undated], in Protest and Activism Collection, 1963–75, 8, RC 7, 3, Columbia University Archives.

20. Martin Arnold, "Burning of a Nazi Flag in Protest Stirs Clash at Rockefeller Center," *New York Times*, April 18, 1968, p. 14.

21. SDS New York, "Old Fascists Never Die . . . They Just Change Their Style," flyer, April 1968, in Protest and Activism Collection, 1963–75, 8, RC 7, 3, Columbia University Archives.

22. Based on an interview with Jeff Jones, Ingo Juchler argued that the students who started the protest at Columbia showed their readiness for militancy at the first anti-Springer demonstration. See Ingo Juchler, *Die Studentenbewegungen in den Vereinigten Staaten und der Bundesrepublik der sechziger Jahre. Eine Untersuchung hinsichtlich ihrer Beeinflussung durch Befreiungsbewegungen und -theorien aus der Dritten Welt* (Berlin: Duncker and Humblot, 1996), 289.

23. Interview with Robert Ross, Worcester, Mass., March 21, 2000, p. 25.

24. Tom Bell, Bernardine Dohrn, and Steve Halliwell, "Program Proposal," SDS National Convention, East Lansing, Mich., June 10–15, 1968, p. 1, in American SDS Records, 3, 9, Box 35, SHSW.

25. Ibid., 5f.

26. Ibid., 7.

27. Carl Davidson, "Inter-organizational: Carl's Report," *New Left Notes*, June 10, 1968, p. 6.

28. Ibid., 11.

29. Ibid.

30. Mike Klonsky, "The State of SDS," *New Left Notes*, June 24, 1968, p. 3.

31. Barbara and John Ehrenreich, "European Student Movements: Part One—Germany," *New Left Notes*, July 29, 1968, p. 7. See also Barbara Ehrenreich and John Ehrenreich, *Long March, Short Spring: The Student Uprising at Home and Abroad* (New York. Monthly Review Press, 1969), 23–50, and F. C. Hunnius, *Student Revolts: The New Left in West Germany* (London: War Resister's International, 1968).

32. Quoted in "West Berlin's U.S. Campaign," in *New Left Notes*, May 22, 1967, p. 6.

33. See "Vietnam International," flyer, October 21, 1967, in Papers of Rudi Dutschke, K-30 / 48, 2, HIS. The planned demonstration on the Kurfürstendamm, however, was prohibited by the police. See "Amerikaner in Westberlin: Demonstration am Kudamm," *Berliner Extra-Dienst* 30, August 30, 1967, p. 4; "Amerikanische Demonstration am Kudamm: Durch Polizei verboten," in *Berliner Extra-Dienst* 31, September 2, 1967, p. 2.

34. Interview with Elsa Rassbach, Berlin, January 28, 2002, p. 8.

35. Elsa Rassbach, "Aktivistin gegen den Vietnamkrieg," in Ute Kätzel, ed., *Die 68erinnen. Portrait einer rebellischen Frauengeneration*, (Berlin: Rowohlt, 2002), 66.

36. See, for example, "US-Campaign beim Volksfest: Einladung zum Nachdenken," *Berliner Extra-Dienst* 23, August 5, 1967, p. 3; U.S. Campaign, "Hootenanny im Club Ca Ira," flyer, November 1967, in German SDS papers, USA GI's, Box Archive "APO und soziale Bewegungen", FU Berlin; "US-Mission: Vietnam-'Aufklärung' nur im 'Kleinen Kreis,'" *Berliner Extra-Dienst* 50, November 1967, p. 4.

37. Interview with Juan Flores, New York City, October 16, 2003, p. 15f.

38. Ibid., 17f.

39. Ibid., 22. See also interview with Elsa Rassbach, Berlin, January 28, 2002, p. 10.

40. Elsa Rassbach, "Aktivistin gegen den Vietnamkrieg," in Kätzel, *Die 68erinnen*, 67.

41. "US-Campaign: Bilder-Auktion für die FLN," *Berliner Extra-Dienst* 20/11, March 9, 1968, p. 3.

42. Interview with David Bathrick, Bremen, May 21, 2004, p. 40ff.

43. "Geheimgehalten: 'Raketen' gegen US-Hauptquartier in Westberlin," *Berliner Extra-Dienst* 46, p. 1; "Fluchthelfer: Raketen über West-Berlin," *Konkret* 12 (December 1967): 49 f.; Gretchen Dutschke, *Wir hatten ein barbarisches, schönes Leben: Rudi Dutschke—Eine Biographie von Gretchen Dutschke.* (Cologne: Kiepenheuer and Witsch, 1996), 167 f., 178–80.

44. Jeff Shero, "Hey Soldier, Where Ya' Goin: The Mood in Europe," *New Left Notes*, September 18, 1967.

45. "Die XXII. Ordentliche Delegiertenkonferenz des SDS (Resolutionen und Beschlüsse), 27, in Papers of Ronny Loewy, Band 1 (SDS 1966–1970), Hamburg Institute for Social Research, Hamburg (hereafter HIS).

46. "Minutes of SDS National Council Meeting, Lexington, KY," March 28–31, 1967, p. 1, in American SDS Records, 3, 6, Box 36, SHSW.

47. Only a few works to date deal with GI resistance and movements in the sixties: Max Watts, *US-Army—Europe: Von der Desertion zum Widerstand in der Kaserne oder wie die U-Bahn zur RITA fuhr* (Berlin: Harald Kater Verlag, 1989), 7–38; Dieter Brünn, ed., *Widerstand in der US-Armee. GI-Bewegung in den siebziger Jahren* (Berlin: Harald Kater Verlag, 1986); David Cortright and Max Watts, *Left Face: Soldier Unions and Resistance Movements in Modern Armies* (New York: Greenwood Press, 1991). For the general situation of the U.S. army in West Germany during the 1960s, see Alexander Vazansky, "'Army in Anguish': The United States Army, Europe, in the Early 1970s," in *GIs in Germany: The Social, Economic, Military, and Political History of the American Military Presence*, ed. Detlef Junker and Thomas Maulucci (New York: Cambridge University Press, forthcoming 2010).

48. Erich Rau, "Information über ein Gespräch mit dem Bundesvorsitzenden des SDS Westdeutschlands Karl-Dietrich Wolff," December 5, 1967, p. 5, in *Sozialistische Einheitspartei Deutschlands* (Socialist Union Party of East Germany; hereafter SED), 12/11/1967, in Attentat auf Rudi Dutschke; Vietnamkonferenz in Westberlin. 1967–1970, Box SED/006,004, RAF-Sammlung (1. Generation), HIS.

49. David Cortright and Zoltan Grossman, "Die GI-Bewegung in Deutschland," in Dieter Brünn, *Widerstand in der US-Armee*, 88–101.

50. AStA Mannheim. "The Afro-American." Booklet, 1967 [?], in USA GIs, German SDS Papers, Archive "APO und soziale Bewegungen," Free University Berlin (hereafter APOB).

51. Patty Lee Parmalee, "Vom Protest zum Widerstand," in Papers of Rudi Dutschke, K-21 / 48, 1, 4, HIS; Papers of the German SDS, 1968, "USA, SDS!, Students for a Democratic Society," in German SDS, APOB. For Parmalee's recollections of her years in Germany see idem, *SDS and SDS—Eine Amerikanerin in Ost und West*, passim.

52. "Westberliner Nächte: Agitation unter US-Soldaten," *Berliner Extra-Dienst* 25/11, March 27, 1968, p. 3; "Nervosität im US-Viertel: Massenaufgebot gegen Zettelverteiler," *Berliner Extra-Dienst* 27/11, April 3, 1968, p. 2.

53. "Murder Inc.," *Where It's At* 2, no. 1, June/July 1969 [undated], p. 1, in German SDS papers, USA GIs, APOB.

54. "Where it's at," *Where It's At* 1, no. 1, April 1968, p. 1, in German SDS papers, USA GIs, APOB. West German military forces were prohibited in Berlin due to the Allied status of the city.

55. Berlin American SDS, "Americans in West Berlin," flyer, undated, in German SDS papers, USA GI's, APOB. See also Dave Harris, "FORWARD—Geschichte eines GI-Projekts in West-Berlin," in Brünn, ed., *Widerstand in der US-Armee*, 105.

56. Interview with David Bathrick, Bremen, May 21, 2004, pp. 56–59; Elsa Rassbach, "Aktivistin gegen den Vietnamkrieg," in Kätzel, *Die 68erinnen*, p. 68 f.; Where It's At, *Die Fraktionierung des amerikanischen SDS* (Berlin: Martin Dürschlag, 1970).

57. Der Polizeipräsident in Berlin (i.V.) to German SDS, Berlin, "Betr. Anmeldung der Vereinigung," December 20, 1968, in Bestand Sozialistisches Anwaltskollektiv (hereafter SAK Records)), Box 300, 62, HIS.

58. Allied Ordinance No. 511, Art. 2, amended by Ordinance No. 534, Art. 3, passed September 5, 1968. See also: Der Polizeipräsident in Berlin (i.V.), "Vorladung von David Harris zur polizeilichen Vernehmung," May 28, 1969, in SAK Records), Box 300, 44, HIS. The articles in question were "One dead 27 wounded" (*Where It's At* 1, no. 4) and "Presidio" (*Where It's At* 1, no. 5).

59. "Military Attacks 'Where It's At,'" *Where It's At* 2, no. 1, undated, p. 1, in German SDS papers, USA GIs, APOB.

60. Horst Mahler to Polizeipräsident in Berlin, "Betr. Anmeldung der Vereinigung Students for a Democratic Society (I-B-bi 50.10/69)," May 21, 1969, in ibid.

61. Der Polizeipräsident in Berlin (i.V.) to German SDS, Berlin, "Betr. Anmeldung der Vereinigung," June 13, 1969, in ibid.

62. "GIs protestieren mit dem Schlachtruf Che Guevaras: Untergrundzeitung 'Venceremos' fordert mehr Rechte für US-Rekruten in Deutschland—deutsche Studenten helfen mit," *Sozialistische Correspondenz-Info* 28, January 1, 1970, pp. 6–7.

63. Dave Harris, *FORWARD*, 105–25.

64. For the congress's speeches and resolutions, see *neue kritik* 36 / 37 (June / August 1966): 29–40.

65. Dabrowski, *Eröffnungsrede*, in ibid., 29. See also Ulrike Marie Meinhof, "Vietnam und Deutschland," *Konkret* 1 (January 1966): 2–3.

66. For a selection of translated flyers and speeches from the American antiwar movement, which includes texts by the Vietnam Day Committee of Berkeley, SANE and the American SDS President Paul Potter, see George Mohr, ed., "Dossier I: Die amerikanische Opposition gegen den Krieg in Vietnam," *Kursbuch* 6 (July 1966): 5–39.

67. Johanna Hoornweg, letter to SDS National Office, November 20, 1966, in American SDS Records, 3, 18, Box 54, SHSW.

68. Johanna Hoornweg, "Vietnam Committee for Peace and the Liberation Struggle," Munich, November 28, 1966, in American SDS Records, 3, 18, Box 54, SHSW.

69. Ibid.

70. Greg Calvert, letter to Johanna Hoornweg, SDS Munich, SDS National Office, November 30, 1966, in American SDS Records, 3, 18, Box 54, SHSW.

71. Reimut Reiche, letter to Bettina Aptheker, "Student Strike for Peace in Vietnam," December 22, 1966, in German SDS papers, BV Referat Ausland 1966–68, SDS, APOB.

72. Reimut Reiche, letter to SDS National Office, Chicago, undated, in German SDS papers, BV Referat Ausland 1966–68, SDS, APOB.

73. Wayne Draznin, SDS National Office, letter to Reimut Reiche, February 12, 1967; Dee Jacobsen, SDS National Office, letter to Reimut Reiche, undated, both in German SDS papers, BV Referat Ausland 1966–68, SDS, APOB.

74. Jost Hermand, "Madison, Wisconsin 1959–1973: Der Einfluß der deutschen Exilanten auf die Entstehung der Neuen Linken," in Claus-Dieter Krohn, ed., *Kulturtransfer im Exil*, Exilforschung 13 (Munich: edition text & kritik, 1995), 52–67. For a detailed autobiographical account see idem, *Zuhause und anderswo. Erfahrungen im Kalten Krieg* (Cologne: Böhlau, 2001), 101–170.

75. See Krohn, *Kulturtransfer im Exil*, 35; Klaus J. Milich, "1968—Vom Widerstand zum Protest. Frankfurter Schule und New York Intellectuals zwischen Dialektik und Pragmatismus," in *Der Geist der Unruhe: 1968 im Vergleich. Wissenschaft–Literatur–Medien*, ed. Rainer Rosenberg (Berlin: Akademie Verlag, 2000), 37–60.

76. See Claus-Dieter Krohn, "Die Entdeckung des 'anderen' Deutschland in der intellektuellen Protestbewegung der 1960er Jahre in der Bundesrepublik und den Vereinigten Staaten," in idem, ed., *Kulturtransfer im Exil*, Exilforschung 13 (Munich: edition text & kritik, 1995), 26.

77. Kurt Shell, "The American Impact on the German New Left," in A.N.S. Den Hollander, ed., *Contagious Conflict: The Impact of American Dissent on European Life* (Leiden: Brill, 1973), 48.

78. See Krohn, *Die Entdeckung des 'anderen' Deutschland*, 30, 42.

79. See Wolfgang Kraushaar, ed., *Frankfurter Schule und Studentenbewegung: Von der Flaschenpost zum Molotowcocktail, 1946–1995*, 3 vols. (Frankfurt am Main: Rogner and Bernhard, 1998), passim.

80. Detlev Claussen, "The American Experience of the Critical Theorists," in John Abromeit and W. Mark Cobb, eds., *Herbert Marcuse. A Critical Reader* (New York: Routledge, 2004), 51. See also idem, "Intellectual Transfer: Theodor W. Adorno's American Experience"; John Abromeit, "The Limits of Praxis: The Social-Psychological Foundations of Theodor Adorno; and Herbert Marcuse's Interpretation of the 1960s Protest Movements," in Belinda Davis, Martin Klimke, Carla MacDougall, and Wilfried Mausbach, eds., *Changing the World, Changing the Self* (New York/Oxford: Berghahn Books, forthcoming 2010).

81. See also Wolfgang Kraushaar, "'Die Revolte der Lebenstriebe': Marcuse als Mentor gegenkultureller Bewegungen," in Peter-Erwin Jansen, ed., *Herbert Marcuse: Die Studentenbewegung und ihre Folgen, Nachgelassene Schriften* (Springe: zu Klampen, 2004), 4:15–25.

82. Herbert Marcuse, "Das Problem der Gewalt in der Opposition," in Kraushaar, *Frankfurter Schule und Studentenbewegung*, 2: 272–75, esp. 272.

83. Shell, *American impact*, 39 f.

84. Die XXII. Ordentliche Delegiertenkonferenz des SDS (Resolutionen und Beschlüsse), September 4–8, 1967, 24, in Bestand Ronny Loewy, Band 1 (SDS 1966-1970), HIS.

85. SDS Westberlin and Internationales Nachrichten- und Forschungsinstitut. INFI, eds., *Der Kampf des vietnamesischen Volkes und die Globalstrategie des Imperialismus, Internationaler Vietnam-Kongreß 17. / 18. Februar 1968, Westberlin* (Berlin: Peter von Maikowski, 1968), passim; Ingrid Gilcher-Holtey, *Die 68er Bewegung*, 7–10.

86. Rudi Dutschke, "Die geschichtlichen Bedingungen für den internationalen Emanzipationskampf," in SDS Westberlin, *Der Kampf des vietnamesischen Volkes*, 110.

87. Ibid., 121.

88. Ibid., 107, 117.

89. Ibid., 116, 121.

90. See the cross-references in his personal papers to the writing of the American SDS, for example, "Dutschke-Strategiefrage," September 5, 1967, in Papers

of Rudi Dutschke, K-21 / 48, 1, HIS; interview with Juan Flores, New York City, October 16, 2003, pp. 23, 27 f.

91. Ibid., 122. Dutschke quotes Andrew Kopkind, "Von der Gewaltlosigkeit zum Guerilla-Kampf," in *Voltaire Flugschriften* Nr.14, S. 24/25.

92. Ekkehart Krippendorff, in SDS Westberlin, *Kampf des vietnamesischen Volkes*, 155. For his experience in the United States and the influence it had on his political development, see also Krippendorff, *Die westdeutsche Linke*, 39–42; idem, "Mein Weg nach '68'," *Neues Deutschland*, Special Feature "1968," April 26, 2008. For his efforts at importing protest techniques practiced in the United States to West Germany see idem, *Anleitung zum Handeln. Taktik direkter Aktionen* (Berlin: Voltaire Verlag / Oberbaumpresse, 1967). The publication is the direct translation of a "Manual for Direct Action" as it was used in the civil rights movement.

93. Rudi Dutschke, "Die geschichtlichen Bedingungen für den internationalen Emanzipationskampf," 115 f., 122.

94. Ibid., 122 f.

95. See also Günter Amendt, in SDS Westberlin, *Kampf des vietnamesischen Volkes*, 150 f. For details about the motives and goals of the NATO campaign, see Hans-Jürgen Krahl, in ibid., 141–46.

96. Ray Robinson, in ibid., 81 f.

97. Dale A. Smith, in ibid., 140 f.

98. Till Stander, in ibid., 146 f.; Rogis Lader, in ibid., 148.

99. Robert Peirce, in ibid., 149.

100. Rogis Lader, in ibid., 148.

101. Interview with Susan Klonsky, Chicago, Ill., April 15, 2000, p. 21. Susan Eanet later married fellow American SDS activist Michael Klonsky.

102. Ernest Mandel, in SDS Westberlin, *Kampf des vietnamesischen Volkes*, p. 133.

103. Der Senator für Inneres, "Bericht über die auf der 'Internationalen Vietnam-Konferenz' am 17. Februar 1968 in West-Berlin gehaltenen Reden," undated, p. 7, in Papers of Rudi Dutschke, K-30 / 48, 3, HIS.

104. Erich Fried, in SDS Westberlin, *Kampf des vietnamesischen Volkes*, 97.

105. Senator für Inneres, *Bericht*, 5f.

106. Quoted in Senator für Inneres, *Bericht*, 9. See also Dutschke, *Internationaler Emanzipationskampf*, 124; Hans-Jürgen Krahl, in SDS Westberlin, *Kampf des vietnamesischen Volkes*, 141; Rudi Dutschke, "Internationale Arbeit," Notes, 1967/68, in Papers of Rudi Dutschke, K-21 / 48, 1, HIS.

107. Both Salvatore and Horlemann are described as leading figures in the INFI. See Internationales Nachrichten- und Forschungsinsitut (INFI), "German-American Movement Group Inventory," Preliminary Draft, SDS Westberlin, 1968, in American SDS Records, 3, 19, Box 54, SHSW.

108. SDS Westberlin/INFI, letter, February 1968, p. 1, in Papers of Rudi Dutschke, Bundesarchiv, K-21/48, 1f., HIS.Ibid., 2.

109. SDS Westberlin/INFI, letter, February 1968, p. 2.

110. "INFI Informationen," May 5, 1968, in *Papers of Rudi Dutschke*, Bundesarchiv, K-21/48, 1, HIS.

111. For the internal structure of INFI, see German SDS papers, Privatbesitz Horlemann, Vietnam & INFI, APOB.

112. See Rudi Dutschke, diary entry, April 10, 1968, in Rudi Dutschke, *Jeder hat sein Leben ganz zu leben: die Tagebücher 1963–1979*, edited by Gretchen Dutschke-Klotz (Cologne: Kiepenheuer and Witsch, 2003), 70f.

113. Maarten Abeln, letter to Jeff Shero, Amsterdam, August 12, 1968, in American SDS Records, 3, 5, Box 34a, SHSW; Jeff Shero, letter to Bernardine Dohrn, SDS National Office, 1968 [undated], in American SDS Records, 3, 2, Box 35, SHSW. See also Lois Reivich, NACLA, New York, letter to Patty Lee Parmalee, March 12, 1968, in German SDS papers, Privatbesitz Horlemann, Vietnam & INFI, APOB; Wolfgang Nitsch, letter to Bernardine Dohrn, SDS National Office, March 14, 1969, in American SDS Records, 3, 3, Box 35, SHSW.

114. Wolfgang Nitsch, letter to Bernardine Dohrn, SDS National Office, April 11, 1969, 1f., in American SDS Records, 3, 3, Box 35, SHSW. See also "Ljublijana: Treffen der 'Neuen Linken,'" *Berlin Extra-Dienst* 77/11, September 25, 1968, p. 5; Keith Chamberlain, letter to Sue Eanet, SDS National Office, November 18, 1968, in American SDS Records, 3, 2, Box 35, SHSW.

115. The inventory is more than twenty pages long and lists German and American institutions, translators, and people categorized under specific sections. See Internationales Nachrichten und Forschungsinsititut (INFI), *German-American Movement Group Inventory*.

116. On his own awareness of his public image, see Rudi Dutschke, "Vom ABC-Schützen zum Agenten," *Konkret* 1 (January 1968): 53 (quoted after Karl, *Revolutionär ohne Revolution*, 198); Dutschke, diary entry of July 15, 1967, in *Tagebücher*, 58.

117. This plan seems to have emerged already in the course of 1966. See Rudi Dutschke, letter to Gábor Révai, September 30, 1966, in Rudi Dutschke and Gábor Révai, "Briefwechsel 1966 bis 1971," in Eurozine, April 23, 2009, http://www.eurozine.com/articles/2009-04-23-dutschke-de.html.

118. Ellison, airgram to Department of State, "A Dutschke 'Happening' in Bremen," A-46, American Consulate Bremen, November 30, 1967, p. 2, in RG 59, Central Foreign Policy Files, 1967–69, EDU 9-3, GER W, 1/1/67, Box 345, U.S. National Archives II, College Park, Maryland (hereafter NA).

119. Rudi Dutschke and Horst Kurnitzky, letter to Herbert Marcuse, December 26, 1967, in Kraushaar, *Frankfurter Schule und Studentenbewegung*, 329 f.; Jansen, *Herbert Marcuse, Nachgelassene Schriften*,4:185–253; Rudi Dutschke, "Pfadfinder—Herbert Marcuse und die Neue Linke," in Gretchen Dutschke et al., eds., *Rudi Dutschke: Die Revolte* (Hamburg: Rowohlt, 1983), 134–57, 207–18.

120. Rudi Dutschke, letter draft to Herbert Marcuse, manuscript, undated [1967], in Papers of Rudi Dutschke, K-24/28, 1, HIS. See also Herbert Marcuse, letter to Rudi Dutschke, January 12, 1968, in Kraushaar, *Frankfurter Schule und Studentenbewegung*, 2:336; Herbert Marcuse, letter to Rudi Dutschke, March 11, 1968, in ibid., 347.

121. See notes on conversation with Marcuse, in Papers of Rudi Dutschke, K-13/48, 2, HIS. See also Ulrich Chaussy, *Die drei Leben des Rudi Dutschke: Eine Biographie* (Darmstadt: Luchterhand, 1983), 223 f.

122. A compilation of the articles can be found in *San Diego Union*, June 6, 1968, p. B-2.

123. "This Is an Order!" in *San Diego Union*, June 11, 1968, p. B-2. See also "Campus Leftists Termed Menace," in ibid.

124. Robert L. Allison, letter to the president of USCD, June 10, 1968; Ben B. Mathews, letter to the president of USCD, June 15, 1968, both in Office of the Chancellor Papers, RSS1, 248, 4, Mandeville Special Collections Library, UC San Diego (hereafter Special Collections, UCSD).

125. George W. Fischer, American Legion Post 6, "Resolution," June 13, 1968, in Office of the Chancellor Papers, RSS1, 248, 4, Special Collections, UCSD.

126. George W. Fischer, American Legion Post 6, letter to William McGill, UCSD chancellor, July 19, 1968, in Office of the Chancellor Papers, RSS1, 242, 15, Special Collections, UCSD.

127. Gladwin Hill, "The Marcuse Case: Conservatism Aroused by a Legionnaire in San Diego," *New York Times*, October 6, 1968, p. 86; Drew Pearson and Jack Anderson, "The Washington Merry-Go-Round: Marcuse Godfather of Student Revolt," *Washington Post*, July 6, 1968, p. D7. For a detailed outline of the Marcuse case from the university's point of view, see Walter Munk, Chairman San Diego Division of the Academic Senate, "Principal Developments in the Matter of Herbert Marcuse," bulletin, July 1968, in Office of the Chancellor Papers, RSS1, 242, 11, Special Collections, UCSD.

128. William McGill, *The Year of the Monkey. Revolt on Campus 1968-69* (New York: McGraw-Hill, 1982), 59 f.

129. William McGill, letter to Herbert Marcuse, February 14 and 17, 1969, in Office of the Chancellor Papers, RSS1, 242, 17, Special Collections, UCSD. For the administrative technicalities of the whole process, see McGill, *Year of the Monkey*, 85–112.

130. This version is narrated by his wife, who based it on information from a *Stern* journalist. See Gretchen Dutschke, *Wir hatten ein barbarisches, schönes Leben*, 212. See also Karl, *Revolutionär ohne Revolution*, 221; Miermeister, *Rudi Dutschke*, 107; Chaussy, *Die drei Leben*, 273. The complete administrative files documenting Dutschke's application procedure have, unfortunately, not yet been released by the National Archives in Washington, D.C.

131. "'Red Rudi' Ends Plans to Study at U.S. School," *San Diego Union*, September 4, 1968, pp. 1, A-2; interview with Gretchen Dutschke, Newton, Mass., November 13, 1999, p. 11.

132. See Karl, *Revolutionär ohne Revolution*, 219–22.

133. Rudi Dutschke to Spanish "Comrades," December 18, 1968, quoted in Gretchen Dutschke, *Wir hatten ein barbarisches, schönes Leben*, 220 f.

134. Ibid., 221 f.; Gaston Salvatore, letter to Rudi Dutschke, May 17, 1969, in Papers of Rudi Dutschke, K-10/48, 2, HIS. See also Bolivar Echeverria, letter to Rudi Dutschke, August 25, 1968, in ibid.

135. See Rudi Dutschke diary, entry July 8, 1969, in *Tagebücher*, 93 f.

136. With the exception of the memories of its former participants, sources detailing the work of the INFI are difficult to unearth. Wolfgang Kraushaar argues that two of its sponsors were the Italian publisher Giangiacomo Feltrinelli and the German writer Peter Weiss. See Wolfgang Kraushaar, "Rudi Dutschke und der

bewaffnete Kampf," in Wolfgang Kraushaar, Jan Philipp Reemtsma, and Karin Wieland, *Rudi Dutschke, Andreas Baader und die RAF* (Hamburg: Hamburger Edition, 2005), 27.

137. Karl-Dietrich Wolff, German SDS and Gerry Hunnius, ICDP, "I.C.D.P.-S.D.S.—Student Youth Conference," undated, p. 1, in American SDS Records, 3, 19, Box 55, SHSW.

138. Particularly Carl Oglesby suggested to "get [Daniel] Cohn-Bendit or [Tariq] Ali over here speaking to . . . our people." See "Minutes of the NIC Meeting," draft, June 15, 1968, in American SDS Records, 3, 9, Box 36, SHSW.

139. Miles Mogulescu, letter to Bernardine Dohrn, July 4, 1968, in American SDS Records, 3, 5, Box 34a, SHSW; Jeffrey Blum, Frankfurt am Main, letter to SDS National Office, July 14, 1968, in American SDS Records, 3, 18, Box 54, SHSW.

140. "Announcement of Invitation," Draft, SDS National Office, 1968 [undated], in American SDS Records, 3, 1, Box 35, SHSW, 1f.

141. Interview with Bernardine Dohrn, Chicago, Ill., June 17, 2003, p. 21f.

142. See ibid., 22.

143. Delegates from the German SDS included Frank Wolff (Frankfurt), Hans-Werner Köblitz (Tübingen), Holger Klotzbach (Tübingen), Michaela Wundzte (Frankfurt), and Klaus Behnken (Tübingen). Delegates from the American SDS were Ruth Glick (NY), Ellen Lessinger and Eric Lessinger (NY), Jeff Blum (Baltimore), Larry Blum (Oxford, UK), Miles Mogulescu (NY), Bernardine Dohrn (Chicago), Martin Kenner (NY), Brian Ilick (NY), Daniel Swinney (Madison), and Judi Bernsten (Chicago) as SDS-Guardian delegate. Other American observers were Mollje Struerer (Chicago), Paul Schollmen (Chicago), and Keith Chamberlain (Berlin, Germany). The Canadian participants from Our Generation were Dimitrios Roussopoulos and J. Girard (both Montreal). "ICDP - SDS Students Conference / List of Participants, Ljubljana 26.-28. August 1968," in American SDS Records, 3, 19, Box 55, SHSW.

144. Dan Swinney, "Letter from Ljubiljana," article [from *Connection*], August 30, 1968, in American SDS Records, 3, 1, Box 35, SHSW.

145. Ibid.

146. Interview with Bernardine Dohrn, Chicago, June 17, 2003, p. 14, 23f.

147. Dan Swinney, "Letter from Ljubiljana," Article [from *Connection*], August 30, 1968, in American SDS Records, 3, 1, Box 35, SHSW.

148. "Ljubljana: Treffen der 'Neuen Linken,'" *Berlin Extra-Dienst* 77/11, September 25, 1968, p. 4f.

149. Interview with Bernardine Dohrn, Chicago, Ill., June 17, 2003, p. 17.

150. Ibid., 25.

151. "I felt there was even more similarities with Germany than with France because it seemed to me that German SDS like SDS in the US was emerging from a period during the fifties of arid apoliticalness, of a denial of what had come before, of a kind of left pediation of history instead of continuity of history, with less strong worker organization. . . . German SDS also seemed to be trying to break out of an oppressive culture of denial and a kind of apolitical oasis and being a relatively tiny organization, but able to leverage its tinyness. Because . . .

nobody expected radical left forces to emerge there. That's what I immediately felt we had in common." In ibid., 26f.

152. Ibid., 24, 14. See also Le Phuong, Information Bureau of NFL-SV, Stockholm, letter to Bernardine Dohrn, SDS National Office, October/November 1968 [undated]; Bernardine Dohrn, letter to Le Phuong, November 15, 1968, in American SDS Records, 3, 2, Box 35, SHSW.

153. See interview with Allen Young, Orange, Mass., April 26, 2000, p. 10f.; Allen Young, "German SDS," typescript, 1968 [undated], p. 3, in American SDS Records, 3, 2, Box 47, SHSW. For a comprehensive report on the festival, see Kraushaar, *Frankfurter Schule und Studentenbewegung*, 1:350 f.

154. "International Assembly of Revolutionary Student Movements," flyer, September 1968, in Protest and Activism Collection, 1963–75, pp. 8, RC 7, 3, Columbia University Archives.

155. Columbia Strike Co-ordinating Committee and American SDS, Invitation Letter, undated, p. 1, in German SDS papers, "1968 USA SDS!, Students for a Democratic Society," APOB.

156. "Strassentheater: Jetzt auch in den USA," *Berliner Extra-Dienst* 87/11, October 30, 1968, p. 4.

157. Interview with James Williamson, Cambridge, Mass., June 12, 2003, pp. 22, 27 f.

158. Bob Cohen, "Report on the Meeting of the International Assembly," in conference booklet entitled "Venceremos", vol 1, no. 2, September 19, 1968, pp., 1, 4, in German SDS papers, "1968 USA SDS!, Students for a Democratic Society, APOB.

159. Ibid., 4.

160. Ibid., 4.

161. John Kifner, "Student Revolutionaries Seek Bigger Causes," *New York Times*, September 25, 1968, p. 31.

162. Ibid. See also Sale, *SDS*, 489.

163. Eric Van Loon, American National Student Association, letter to Sigrid Fronius et al., August 8, 1968, in German SDS papers, "1968 USA SDS!, Students for a Democratic Society," APOB. For Fronius's handwritten notes, see "Stenogrammblock USA," in German SDS papers, "1968 USA SDS!, Students for a Democratic Society," APOB; "Minutes of the NIC Meeting," draft, August 30–September 1, 1968, p. 3, in American SDS Records, 3, 9, Box 36, SHSW.

164. "Mark Rudd to Debate with Amherst Teachers," *The Amherst Student*, 97, no. 4, September 26, 1968, p. 1, in American SDS Records, 3, 6, Box 39, SHSW.

165. Interview with Karl-Dietrich Wolff, Frankfurt, Germany, April 10, 2001, 5f. See also K.-D. Wolff, " 'Amis' and 'Naner': With Americans in Hesse since 1945," in Gundula Bavendamm, ed., *Amerikaner in Hessen: Eine besondere Beziehung im Wandel der Zeit* (Hanau: Cocon-Verlag, 2008), 198–204; "Testimony of Karl Dietrich Wolff. Hearings before the Subcommittee to Investigate the Administration of the Internal Security Act and other Security Laws of the Committee on the Judiciary," U.S. Senate, 91st Congress, 1st Session, March 14 and 18, 1969 (Washington, D.C.: U.S. Government Printing Office, 1969), 21.

166. Interview with Karl-Dietrich Wolff, 7, 9.

167. Ibid., 25.

168. Ibid., 11f., 31–33.

169. "Testimony of Karl Dietrich Wolff," 28. The attached memorandum gives a detailed account of Wolff's trips, lectures, and the people he met. It is without doubt an example of a very intense government surveillance that had most likely already begun in West Germany. See also "SDS Sponsors Karl Dietrich Wolff," flyer, 1969 [undated], Protest and Activism Collection, 1963—75, 8, RC 7, 3, Columbia University Archives.

170. "Testimony of Karl Dietrich Wolff," 5 f.

171. Ibid., 6.

172. Ibid.

173. Ibid., 7.

174. "Testimony of Karl Dietrich Wolff," 22.

175. Ibid., 8–13.

176. Ibid., 24. For similar behavior of German activists in courtrooms during the 1960s, see Martin Klimke, "We are not going to defend ourselves before such a justice system! '1968' and the Courts," *German Law Journal* 10, no. 3 (March 2009): 261–74.

177. Philip D. Carter, "Thurmond Presides at Senate Circus," *Washington Post*, March 15, 1969, p. A4. See also "German Student Leader Walks Out on Thurmond," *New York Times*, March 15, 1969, p. 22; *New Left Notes*, March 20, 1969; "Go-Out," *Spiegel*, March 24, 1969, pp. 158–59.

178. Interview with Todd Gitlin, New York City, May 18, 2000, p. 14 f.; interview with Karl-Dietrich Wolff, Frankfurt, Germany, April 10, 2001, p. 45.

CHAPTER 4

BLACK AND RED PANTHERS

1. Angela Davis, *An Autobiography* (New York: Random House, 1974), 150.

2. Bernward Vesper, *Die Reise* (Reinbek: Rowohlt, 1989), 589.

3. Brenda Gayle Plummer, *Rising Wind: Black Americans and U S. Foreign Affairs, 1935–1960* (Chapel Hill: University of North Carolina Press, 1996); Mary L. Dudziak, *Cold War Civil Rights: Race and the Image of American Democracy* (Princeton: Princeton University Press, 2000); Thomas Borstelmann, *The Cold War and the Color Line: American Race Relations in the Global Arena* (Cambridge: Harvard University Press, 2001); Brenda Gayle Plummer, ed., *Window on Freedom: Race, Civil Rights and Foreign Affairs, 1945–1988* (Chapel Hill: University of North Carolina Press, 2003).

4. Research in this area has surprisingly been rather hesitant. Exceptions are David Posner, "Afro-America in West German Perspective, 1945–1966," Ph.D. diss., Yale University, 1997; Jürgen Rolf Ruckaberle, "Black Panthers and German Radicals in an Unusual Transnational Alliance for Liberation, 1968–1972," master's thesis, History Department, University of Oregon, 2001; Moritz Ege, *Schwarz werden; "Afroamerikanophilie" in den 1960er und 1970er Jahren* (Bielefeld: Transcript, 2007).

5. Martin Luther King, Jr., *Freiheit: Aufbruch der Neger Nordamerikas* (Kassel: Oncken, 1964); idem, *Kraft zum Lieben* (Konstanz: Bahn, 1964); idem, *Warum wir nicht warten können* (Düsseldorf: Econ, 1964); James Baldwin, *Hundert Jahre Freiheit ohne Gleichberechtigung oder The Fire Next Time. Eine Warnung an die Weißen* (Reinbek: Rororo, 1964).

6. For early reports on the situation of African Americans, see Henri Pavre, "Comeback in Afrika," *Konkret* 4 (April 1962): 12–13; Martin Luther King, Jr., "Onkel Tom's Snackbar," *Konkret* 6 (June 1963): 7–9, 17.

7. Wolfgang Kraushaar, ed., *Frankfurter Schule und Studentenbewegung: Von der Flaschenpost zum Molotowcocktail, 1946–1995*, 3 vols. (Frankfurt am Main: Rogner & Bernhard, 1998), 1:201.

8. Günter Amendt, "Die Studentenrevolte in Berkeley," *neue kritik* 28 (February 1965): 5–7.

9. Ibid., 7.

10. Gretchen Dutschke, *Wir hatten ein barbarisches, schönes Leben: Rudi Dutschke—Eine Biographie von Gretchen Dutschke* (Cologne: Kiepenheuer and Witsch, 1996), 79 f.

11. Quoted in Ulrich Chaussy, *Die drei Leben des Rudi Dutschke: Eine Biographie* (Darmstadt: Luchterhand, 1983), 146. See also Gretchen Dutschke, *Wir hatten ein barbarisches, schönes Leben*, 107 f.

12. For a contextualization of these developments in the United States, see Clayborne Carson, *In Struggle: SNCC and the Black Awakening of the 1960s* (Cambridge: Harvard University Press, 1995); Peniel Joseph, *Waiting 'Til the Midnight Hour: A Narrative History of Black Power in America* (New York: Herny Holt, 2006).

13. Thomas Sugrue, *The Origins of the Urban Crisis: Race and Inequality in Postwar Detroit* (Princeton: Princeton University Press, 2005); Sidney Fine, *Violence in the Model City: The Cavanagh Administration, Race Relations, and the Detroit Riot of 1967* (East Lansing: University of Michigan Press, 2007).

14. Gerhard Amendt, "Das Elend der amerikanischen Neger," *Frankfurter Rundschau*, January 27, 1968. He later also edited the popular collection *Black Power: Dokumente und Analysen* (Frankfurt: Suhrkamp, 1970).

15. "Die XXII. Ordentliche Delegiertenkonferenz des SDS (Resolutionen und Beschlüsse), 26, in Bestand Ronny Loewy, Band 1 (SDS 1966–70), Hamburg Institute for Social Research, Hamburg (hereafter HIS).

16. Ibid., 26.

17. Ibid., 26 f.; Bernardine Dohrn was later quoted as saying, "The best thing we can do for the panthers is to build a fucking white revolutionary movement!" in Ron Jacobs, *The Way the Wind Blew: A History of Weather Underground* (New York: Verso, 1997), cover. See also "You Don't Need a Weatherman to Know Which Way the Wind Blows," *New Left Notes*, June 18, 1969; Immanuel Wallerstein and Paul Starr, eds., *The University Crisis Reader*, 2 vols. (New York: Vintage Books, 1971), 2:260–93, esp. 265 f.

18. Ibid., 27.

19. "Ein Gespräch über die Zukunft mit Rudi Dutschke, Bernd Rabehl und Christian Semler," *Kursbuch* 14, August 1968, pp. 146–74, esp. 155.

20. Rita Chin, *The Guest Worker Question in Postwar Germany* (Cambridge: Cambridge University Press, 2007).

21. "Ein Gespräch über die Zukunft mit Rudi Dutschke, Bernd Rabehl und Christian Semler," *Kursbuch* 14 (August 1968): 156.

22. Patty Lee Parmalee, "Vom Protest zum Widerstand," in *Papers of Rudi Dutschke*, K-21 / 48, 1, 3, HIS; Papers of the German SDS, 1968, "USA, SDS!, Students for a Democratic Society," in SDS, Archiv " Außerparlamentarische Opposition [hereafter APO] und soziale Bewegungen," Free University, Berlin (hereafter FU).

23. Ibid., 2. On the connection between the New Left and the Third World in Germany and the United States, see also Ingo Juchler, "Trikontinentale und Studentenbewegung. Antiimperialismus als Schibboleth," in Wolfgang Kraushaar, ed., *Die RAF und der linke Terrorismus* (Hamburg: Hamburger Edition, 2006), 205–17; Cynthia Young, *Soul Power: Culture, Radicalism and the Making of a U S. Third World Left* (Durham, N.C.: Duke University Press, 2006).

24. See e.g. "Rassenkampf: Übung für Vietnam," *Konkret* 8 (August 1967): 8; "Vietnam in USA," *Konkret* 9 (September 1967): 18–21; Stokeley Carmichael, "Black Power!—Der Aufstand der Farbigen Amerikaner," *Konkret* 5 (May 1968): 24–27; Rap Brown, "Von der Revolte zur Revolution," *Konkret* 6 (June 1968): 29; Hartmut Häußermann, "Der Kampf für die Emanzipation der Schwarzen in den USA," *Das Argument*, 1968, pp. 1070–79.

25. See, for example, the coverage in the following : Michael Rot, "Trauma der Gewalt, Gewalt und Repression in Amerika," *Konkret* 11 (September 1968): 12–15; William Bradford Huie, "Kill-ins," *Konkret* 17 (December 1968): 4–43 [series of six articles based on William Bradford Huie, *Kill-in* (Vienna: Zsolnay, 1968), German edition of *The Klansman* (New York: Delacorte, 1967)]; Elridge Cleaver, "Weisse Frau, schwarzer Mann," *Konkret* 11 (May 1969): 11–17; Bobby Seale, "Rede an die Weissen," *Konkret* 11 (May 1969): 17.

26. Bernward Vesper, ed., *Black Power. Ursachen des Guerilla-Kampfes in den Vereinigten Staaten*, Voltaire Flugschriften, 14 (Berlin: Voltaire, 1967); Michael Schneider, ed., *Malcolm X: Schwarze Gewalt. Reden* (Frankfurt: Edition Voltaire, 1968); Stokeley Carmichael, *Die Dritte Welt, unsere Welt. Thesen zur Schwarzen Revolution*, Voltaire Flugschriften 29 (Berlin: Voltaire, 1969); Robert F. Williams and Robert B. Bigg, *Großstadtguerilla*, Voltaire Flugschriften 24 (Berlin: Voltaire, 1969).

27. Vesper, *Black Power*, 3.

28. Ibid., 590. See also Gerd Koenen, *Vesper, Ensslin, Baader. Urszenen des deutschen Terrorismus* (Cologne: Kiepenheuer and Witsch, 2003), 124 f.

29. Volkhard Brandes and Joyce Burke, eds., *NOW. Der Schwarze Aufstand* (Munich: Trikont-Verlag, 1968), 13.

30. Volkhard Brandes, *Wie der Stein ins Rollen kam. Vom Aufbruch in die Revolte der Sechziger Jahre* (Frankfurt: Brandes and Apsel, 1980), 155 f.

31. Ibid., 176; See also Eberhard Kögel, "1968—Sport und Politik," in Lutz Schulenburg, ed., *Das Leben ändern, die Welt verändern! 1968. Dokumente und Berichte* (Hamburg: Nautilus, 1998), 328–31.

32. For monographs on the topic, see, for example, Alex Haley, ed., *Malcolm X. Der schwarze Tribun. Eine Autobiographie* (Hamburg: Fischer, 1966); Leroi

Jones, *Ausweg in den Hass: Vom Liberalismus zur Black Power* (Darmstadt: Melzer, 1967); Stokely Carmichael and Charles V. Hamilton, *Black Power: Die Politik der Befreiung in Amerika* (Stuttgart: Günther, 1968); Martin Luther King, Jr., *Wohin Führt Unser Weg. Chaos oder Gemeinschaft* (Düsseldorf: Econ, 1968).

33. See, for example, Friedrich Graf von Westphalen, "Krise des Vertrauens: Amerikas Studenten zwischen Ordnung und Anarchie," *Rheinischer Merkur*, May 15, 1970, p. 15.

34. Kai Hermann, "Nachwort zur deutschen Ausgabe," epilogue to Elridge Cleaver, *Seele auf Eis* (Munich: Carl Hanser, 1969), 247.

35. Kraushaar, *Frankfurter Schule und Studentenbewegung*, 1:304.

36. Morris, telegram, "Martin Luther King Demonstrations," Berlin 1223, US Mission Berlin, 1968, 04/08, in POL 23-8, GER W, 4/1/68, Box 2133, RG 59, Central Foreign Policy Files, 1967–69, National Archives, College Park, Md.; see also Martin Buchholz, "Rote Fahnen am Rathaus Schöneberg," *Berliner Extra-Dienst* 29/11, April 10, 1968, p. 8 f.; "Trauermarsch für King in Berlin," *Frankfurter Rundschau*, April 8, 1968.

37. Ekkehart Krippendorff, "Über Martin Luther King," *Berliner Extra-Dienst* 29/11, April 10, 1968, p. 10.

38. Ibid.

39. Berlin Komitee Black Power, "Solidarity demonstration for Black Power," flyer, April 10(?), 1968, in USA Black Panther Party (hereafter BPP), German SDS Papers, Archive "APO und soziale Bewegungen," Free University of Berlin (hereafter APOB).

40. Morris, "Forthcoming 'Black Power' Demonstration," telegram, Berlin 1241, US Mission Berlin, 1968, 04/11, in POL 23-8, GER W, 4/1/68, Box 2133, RG 59, Central Foreign Policy Files, 1967–69, U.S. National Archives II, College Park, Md. (hereafter NA).

41. For an international history of the Black Panther Party, see Jennifer B. Smith, *An International History of the Black Panther Party* (New York: Garland Publishing, 1999); Michael L. Clemons and Charles E. Jones, "Global Solidarity: The Black Panther Party in the International Arena," pp. 20–39 in Kathleen Cleaver and George Katsiaficas, eds., *Liberation, Imagination, and the Black Panther Party: A New Look at the Panthers and their Legacy* (New York: Routledge, 2001).

42. Kraushaar, *Frankfurter Schule und Studentenbewegung*, 1:407 f.

43. "Young West Berliner Hurl Eggs and Tomatoes at U.S. Warmongers," *The Black Panther*, October 26, 1968, p. 16; "West Europe Thunders: Nixon Go Home!" *The Black Panther*, March 23, 1969, p. 14.

44. Karl-Dietrich Wolff, "West German S.D.S. Supports Black Panthers and Black Liberation Movement," *The Black Panther*, March 9, 1969, p. 3, quoted in Ruckaberle, "Black Panthers and German Radicals," 45.

45. Bobby Seale was also supposed to travel through West Germany on a lecture tour beginning at the end of March 1969 after Wolff's return, but the plan was eventually cancelled. See "'Black-Panther'-Führer kommt," *Frankfurter Rundschau*, March 21, 1969; "Bobby Seale wird fehlen," *Frankfurter Rundschau*, March 29, 1969.

46. Clemons and Jones, *Global Solidarity*, passim; Smith, *International History of the Black Panther Party*, passim. For a history of the Black Panthers, see Charles Jones, ed., *The Black Panther Party Reconsidered* (Baltimore: Black Classic Press, 1998); Cleaver and Katsiaficas, *Liberation, Imagination, and the Black Panther Party*.

47. "The Black Panther Party Authorizes Leadership in Scandinavia," *The Black Panther*, May 4, 1969, pp. 10–11, quoted in Smith, *International History of the Black Panther Party*, 75.

48. Sozialistischer Deutscher Studentenbund, "Wer ist Senghor?" in Schulenburg, *Das Leben ändern*, 313–15.

49. Kraushaar, *Frankfurter Schule und Studentenbewegung*, 1:468.

50. Karl-Dietrich Wolff, "Black Panther Solidarity Committee, Frankfurt, Germany," *The Black Panther*, December 13, 1969, p. 9. For a German version of a report of the trial by one of the defendants, see Tom Hayden, *Der Prozeß von Chicago* (Frankfurt. Suhrkamp, 1971). See also "Richter ließ den Saal räumen," *Frankfurter Rundschau*, November 1, 1969.

51. Karl-Dietrich Wolff, "Black Panther Solidarity Committee," p. 9. See also the photograph in *Frankfurter Rundschau*, November 12, 1969.

52. The results, according to the police, were six injured police men, thirty-one arrested demonstrators, countless broken windows, and a burned-out car, causing a damage of 24,000 DM. See Kraushaar, *Frankfurter Schule und Studentenbewegung*, 1:473 ff.

53. Wolff, *Black Panther Solidarity Committee*, 9.

54. Letter by the Ministry of the Interior to the Verwaltungsgericht Köln, February 26, 1969, printed in Black Panther Solidaritätskomitee, "Informationsbrief 2/71," 1971, pp. 5–7, 5f. in USA BPP, Box, German SDS Papers, APOB.

55. "Black Panther," *Agit 883*, November 27, 1969, p. 2; Black Panther Solidaritätskomitee, "Solidaritätskomitee für die Black-Panther-Partei," *Sozialistische Correspondenz-Info* 24, December 6, 1969, p. 11, HIS [my transl.].

56. Karl-Dietrich Wolff, "Black Panther Solidaritätskomitee," letter, January 6, 1970, in USA BPP, Box, German SDS Papers, APOB; Idem, "Überlegungen zur Internationalismusfrage," *Sozialistische Correspondenz-Info* 34/35, February 28, 1970, pp. 26–28, here 27.

57. Reimut Reiche, "Das Conspiracy-Eight-Trial und unsere Demonstration am 13. Dezember," *Sozialistische Correspondenz-Info* 24, December 6, 1969, p. 10.

58. Black Panther Solidaritätskomitee, "Solidarität mit der Black Panther Partei," *Sozialistische Correspondenz-Info* 24, December 13, 1969, pp. 14–15, 25; Bobby Seale, *Der Prozeß gegen Bobby Seale: Rassismus und politische Justiz in den USA* (Frankfurt: Roter Stern, 1970); Eldridge Cleaver, *Zur Klassenanalyse der Black Panther Partei: Erziehung und Revolution* (Frankfurt: Roter Stern, 1970); Michael Tabor, *Harlem: Kapitalismus & Heroin = Völkermord* (Frankfurt: Roter Stern, 1970); Huey Newton, *Selbstverteidigung* (Frankfurt: Roter Stern, 1971). See also the series of articles by Helmut Reinicke on revolutionary movements in the United States: Helmut Reinicke, "berichte aus ameriKKKa (1)," *Sozialistische Correspondenz-Info* 34/35, February 28, 1970, pp. 29–34, 37; March 14, 1970, pp. 23–25.

59. "Flugblatt: Der 1. Mai ist der internationale Kampftag der Arbeiterklasse," *Sozialistische Correspondenz-Info* 44, May 2, 1970, pp. 12–13; "Rote Panter," *Agit 883*, February 26, 1970, p. 1.

60. Winfried Förster, *Das Rassenproblem in den USA: Der Negro American. Ein Beitrag zur politischen Bildung*, Schriftenreihe der Niedersächsischen Landeszentrale für Politische Bildung, Heft 11 (Hannover, 1972); Peter Böhmer et al., eds., *Der Rassenkonflikt in den USA*, Modelle für den politischen Unterricht, Modell 14 (Frankfurt: Europäische Verlagsanstalt, 1973); see also Verlag Roter Stern, *Lernen: subversiv. AMERIKKKA*, passim.

61. Karl-Dietrich Wolff, "Überlegungen zur Internationalismusfrage," *Sozialistische Correspondenz-Info*, 34/35, February 28, 1970, 27 f.

62. Hannes Weinrich, "Überlegungen zu unseren Bemühungen beim Aufbau einer zweiten Front gegen den US-Imperialismus," *Sozialistische Correspondenz-Info* 44, February 2, 1970, pp. 3–5, esp. p. 3.

63. Ibid., 4.

64. Detlev Claussen, "Der Tod Ho Chi Minhs, die vietnamesische Revolution und die revolutionäre Bewegung in den Metropolen," *neue kritik* 54 (June 1969): 3–7, 6f.

65. Bernd Armbruster, "Schwarze GIs:'Wir wollen Freiheit jetzt,'" *Heidelberger Tageblatt*, July 6, 1970. See also "700 farbige US-Soldaten in der neuen Aula," *Rhein-Neckar-Zeitung*, July 6, 1970, p. 3.

66. Black Panther Solidaritätskomitee, "Informationsbrief 2/71," 1971, 8 ff. in USA BPP, Box, German SDS Papers, APOB. See also Maria Höhn, "The Black Panther Solidarity Committee and the Trial of the Ramstein 2," in Belinda Davis et al., eds., *Changing the World, Changing the Self: Political Protest and Collective Identities in 1960/70s West Germany and the United States* (New York: Berghahn Books, forthcoming 2010).

67. "G.I.'s in Germany: Black is Bitter, and Morale, Discipline and Efficiency Decline," *New York Times*, November 23, 1970, pp. 1, 26.

68. Black Panther Solidaritätskomitee, "Internationaler Solidaritätstag mit Bobby Seale," flyer, 1971, 03/06, in USA BPP, Box, German SDS Papers, APOB.

69. "Erklärung von Voice of the Lumpen," in Dieter Brünn, ed., *Widerstand in der US-Armee. GI-Bewegung in den siebziger Jahren* (Berlin, Harald Kater Verlag, 1986), S. 101–3; *Politische Justiz gegen farbige Genossen in der BRD*, in Black Panther Solidaritätskomitee, Informationsbrief 3/71: Antiimperialistischer Kampf 1: Materialien and Diskussion, 1971, S. 41ff., USA BPP, SDS Nachlaß, APO-Archiv.

70. "West Germany Refuses Entry to Delegates of the Black Panther Party," *The Black Panther*, December 27, 1969, p. 12. See also cover of *Sozialistische Correspondenz-Info* 26, December 20, 1969. The cities that were scheduled for a visit between December 12 and 20, 1969, were West Berlin (12th and 13th), Heidelberg (13th), Mannheim/Freiburg (14th), München/Augsburg (15th), Erlangen/Nürnberg (16th), Bochum (17th); Hanau (18th), Aschaffenburg (19th), and Frankfurt (20th). See Black Panther Solidaritätskomitee, "Die Rundreise der Black Panthers durch die BRD," in *Sozialistische Correspondenz-Info* 24, December 13, 1969, p. 25.

71. Eghard Mörbitz, "Bonn fürchtet Unruhe durch die 'Black Panther,'" *Frankfurter Rundschau*, December 15, 1969; Letter from the Ministry of the Interior to the Verwaltungsgericht Köln, February 26, 1969, printed in Black Panther Solidaritätskomitee, "Informationsbrief 2/71," 1971, pp. 5–7, p. 5 in USA BPP, Box, German SDS Papers, APOB.

72. Stefan Aust, "'Ihr könnt uns Gewehre schicken', konkret-Gespräch mit Elridge Cleaver," *Konkret* 17 (August 1969): 44–47, esp. 47.

73. Black Panther Solidaritätskomitee, "Letter to the Government of FRG," October 14, 1970, in USA BPP, German SDS Papers, APOB; "SDS: Immunität für Black Panther," *Frankfurter Rundschau*, September 22, 1970.

74. Black Panther Solidaritätskomitee, letter, October 22, 1970, in USA BPP, Box, German SDS Papers, APOB; "Einreisegenehmigung für Cleaver gefordert," *Frankfurter Rundschau*, October 20, 1970.

75. Black Panther Solidaritätskomitee, "Kathleen Cleaver in Frankfurt," poster, 1970, 11, in USA BPP, Box, German SDS Papers, APOB.

76. Ibid; see also the reprinted and translated interviews from the *The Black Panther* 3, no. 21 September 13, 1969, in "Pantheretten und die Emanzipation," *Rote Presse Korrespondenz* 33, October 3, 1969, p. 12 f.; "Solidarität mit 'Black Panther,'" *Frankfurter Rundschau*, November 24, 1970.

77. "Bonn weist 'Black Panther' aus," *Frankfurter Rundschau*, November 25, 1970.

78. "Nebelbomben auf Rhein-Main: Turbulenz um Kathleen Cleaver," *Frankfurter Rundschau*, November 25, 1970; Tyon Reney, Black Panther Party Task Squad Scandinavia and Frankfurt, Germany, "Kathleen Cleaver Denied Freedom of Speech in West Germany," *The Black Panther*, February 13, 15, 1971; Kraushaar, *Frankfurter Schule und Studentenbewegung*, 1:501 ff.; "Dreitausend riefen 'Freiheit für Bobby Seale,'" *Frankfurter Rundschau*, November 30, 1970.

79. Black Panther Solidaritätskomitee, "Elridge und Kathleen Cleaver: Botschaft an deutsche Genossen!," flyer, November 25, 1970, in USA BPP, German SDS Papers, APOB.

80. Jürgen Wahl, "Kein Freibrief für Black Panthers," *Christ und Welt* 1 (January 1971): 5.

81. Horst Szwitalski, "Ku-Klux-Klan in Deutschland," *Stern* 42, October 11, 1970, pp. 68–72. See also the interview with Elridge Cleaver "'Nixon umbringen?— Mit Vergnügen!'" *Spiegel* 51, December 14, 1970, pp. 116–24.

82. "Trotz Einreiseverbot: Uni lädt Cleaver ein," *Frankfurter Rundschau*, January 14, 1971; "Kathleen Cleaver sprach in der Uni," *Frankfurter Rundschau*, July 8, 1971; " 'Einreiseverbot besteht noch': Genscher antwortet Kiep," *Frankfurter Rundschau*, August 13, 1971. For a transcript of the speech, see "Kathleen Raps to Black GIs," *Right On!* (summer 1971[?]): S. 10–11, KD-Wolff Collection, HIS.

83. "Joint Communiqué of Solidarity," *The Black Panther*, March 27, 1971, p. 14.

84. See "Black Panther Solidarity teach-in 10.12.1970 / Referat der Schwarzen Zellen," *Agit 883*, December 24, 1970, pp. 6–11; "Die Befreiung der Arbeiter kann nur das Werk der Arbeiter selbst sein!," *Agit 883*, January 15, 1971, pp. 6–9, 11; "Die spinnen, die Panther's!" *Agit 883*, April 24, 1971, pp. 2–3.

85. Michael Baumann, *Wie alles anfing* (Frankfurt: Sozialistische Verlagsaus-lieferung, 1976), 8, see also pp. 15, 61.

86. Ibid., 58, 82. See also Bommi Baumann and Till Meyer, *Radikales Amerika: Wie die amerikanische Protestbewegung Deutschland veränderte* (Berlin: Rot-buch, 2007). For similar processes with regard to American blues music, see Detlef Siegfried, "White Negroes. Westdeutsche Faszinationen des Echten," in Michael Rauhut and Thomas Kochan, eds., *Bye bye Lübben City. Bluesfreaks, Tramps und Hippies in der DDR* (Berlin: Schwarzkopf and Schwarzkopf, 2004), 333–44.

87. Astrid Proll, *Hans und Grete: Die RAF, 1967-1977* (Göttingen: Steidl, 1998), 10; Ulrike Edschmid, *Frau mit Waffe* (Frankfurt: Büchergilde Gutenberg, 1997), 113, 115.

88. Michael Baumann reported such an episode to the East German secret po-lice. See Ministerium für Staatssicherheit, Vernehmungsprotokoll des Beschuldig-ten Michael Baumann, 14. December 1973, Akte zu Michael Baumann: Verneh-mungsprotokoll vom 14.12.1973, 1973, S. 4, Box MfS 73/039, RAF-Sammlung (1. Generation), HIS.

89. "Die Rote Armee aufbauen!" *Agit 883*, June 6, 1970, pp. 6–7.

90. Margrit Schiller and Jens Mecklenburg, *Es war ein harter Kampf um meine Erinnerung: ein Lebensbericht aus der RAF* (Hamburg: Konkret, 1999), 52f.

91. RAF, "Das Konzept Stadtguerilla," in ID-Verlag, ed., *Rote Armee Fraktion: Texte und Materialien zur Geschichte der RAF* (Berlin: ID-Verlag, 1997), 41 (here-after ID-Verlag, *RAF: Texte und Materialien*). On RAF's internationalism, see Jeremy Varon, *Bringing the War Home. The Weather Underground, the Red Army Faction, and Revolutionary Violence in the Sixties and Seventies* (Berkeley: University of California Press, 2004), 68–73; Christopher Daase, "Die RAF und der internationale Terrorismus. Zur transnationalen Kooperation klandestiner Organisationen," in Kraushaar, *Die RAF und der linke Terrorismus*, 905–29.

92. Anarchist slogans such as "Macht kaputt, was Euch kaputt macht!" are combined here with the need for spiritual harmony mentioned by Michael Bau-mann, in keeping with the motto "Trust your own experience!" See ibid., 44.

93. Ibid., 48.

94. Wilfried Mausbach, "Auschwitz and Vietnam: West German Protest Against America's War During the 1960s," in Andreas Daum, Lloyd Gardner, and Wilfried Mausbach, eds., *America, the Vietnam War and the World: Compar-ative and International Perspectives* (New York: Cambridge University Press, 2003), 279–98.

95. Ulrike Meinhof, "Warenhausbrandstiftung," *Konkret* 14 (November 1968): 5.

96. A.D. Moses, "The State and the Student Movement in West Germany," in Gerard DeGroot, ed., *Student Protest. The Sixties and After* (London: Longman, 1998), 143. For the connection between terrorism and post-fascist states, see Dor-othea Hauser, "Deutschland, Italien, Japan. Die ehemaligen Achsenmächte und der Terrorismus der 1970er Jahre," in Kraushaar, *Die RAF und der linke Terror-ismus*, 1272–98.

97. Quoted in Stefan Aust, *Der Baader Meinhof Komplex* (Munich: Gold-mann, 1998), 60.

98. Frantz Fanon, *The Wretched of the Earth* (New York: Grove Press, 1963).

99. Siegward Lönnendonker and Tilman Fichter, eds., *Hochschule im Umbruch: Vol. 4: Die Krise: 1964–1967. Dokumentation.* (Berlin: Pressestelle der FU Berlin, 1975), 71. See also chapter 2 in this book.

100. See Sabine Kebir, "Gewalt und Demokratie bei Fanon, Sartre und der RAF," in Kraushaar, *Die RAF und der linke Terrorismus*, 262–79.

101. For an excellent analysis of the role of violence in RAF's ideology until 1972, see Varon, *Bringing the War Home*, 196–215.

102. RAF, " Erklärung vom 13. Januar 1976," in ID-Verlag, *RAF: Texte und Materialien*, 238.

103. RAF, "Über den bewaffneten Kampf in Westeuropa," in ID-Verlag, *RAF: Texte und Materialien*, 71.

104. Ibid., 74–77, here 89.

105. Ibid., 106 f.

106. This idea can be found in the thinking of the Black Panther Solidarity Commitee, among individuals in the student movements, as well as in the ideology of urban guerilla groups. See for example: Black Panther Solidaritätskomitee, "Solidaritätsveranstaltung mit der Black Panther Partei: Connie Matthews," flyer, April 18, 1970, in USA BPP, APO-Archiv.

107. RAF, "Dem Volk dienen: Stadtguerilla und Klassenkampf," in ID-Verlag, *RAF: Texte und Materialien*, 116.

108. RAF, "Über den bewaffneten Kampf," 101.

109. See Schiller and Mecklenburg, *Harter Kampf um meine Erinnerung*, 55.

110. RAF, "Anschlag auf das Hauptquartier der US-Army in Frankfurt/Main," in *RAF: Texte und Materialien*, 145. See Oliver Tolmein and Irmgard Möller, *'RAF, das war für uns Befreiung': Ein Gespräch mit Irmgard Möller über bewaffneten Kampf, Knast und die Linke* (Hamburg: Konkret, 1997), 64 ff; 40 ff.

111. RAF, "Bombenanschlag auf das Hauptquartier der US-Army in Europa in Heidelberg," in ID-Verlag, *RAF: Texte und Materialien*, 148. See also Martin Klimke and Wilfried Mausbach, "Auf der äusseren Linie der Befreiungskriege. Die RAF und der Vietnamkonflikt," in Kraushaar, *Die RAF und der linke Terrorismus*, 620–643.

112. George Jackson, *In die Herzen ein Feuer* (Bern: Scherz, 1971).

113. RAF members' curiosity is evidenced by respective literature requests and material found during searches of their cells. See Irene Goergens, "Auszugsweise Abschrift aus einem Brief der Angeschuldigten Irene Goergens vom 26.10.1970 an Elmar Völker," Untersuchungsrichter beim Landgericht Berlin, I VU 10/70, October 26, 1970, Anlagen zur Strafanzeige gegen Mahler, 1970–1971, Box KOK 04/010, RAF-Sammlung (1. Generation), HIS; Eberhard Becker, "Buchbestellung für Fräulein Irmgard Möller," January 31, 1973, Schriftwechsel und Beschlüsse zur Postsperre, 1972–1973, Box Mö,Ir/002,005, RAF-Sammlung (1. Generation), HIS.

114. Gudrun Ensslin, letter, undated (May 1974?), Handakte Croissant: Beschlüsse zum Ausschluss von Croissant, u.a., 1974–1975, Box Mö,Ir/007,005, RAF-Sammlung (1. Generation), HIS.

115. Margrit Schiller, "Erklärung vor dem Landgericht Hamburg," *Rote Hilfe Dokumentation* 15, no. 4 (November 1972): 1, Prozesserklärung von Margit

Schiller am 15.11.1972, 1972, Box Gr,M/024,010, RAF-Sammlung (1. Generation), HIS.

116. See Gudrun Ensslin, "Die Wahrheit in den Tatsachen suchen Antwort auf Zellenzirkular der RH Berlin vom 13.5.1973," June 30, 1973, 5f., Zellenmaterial von der Durchsuchung am 16.07.1973, 1973, Box Me,H/004,008, RAF-Sammlung (1. Generation), HIS.

117. The plan failed for a variety of reasons. See Ministerium für Staatssicherheit, "Operativer Auskunftsbericht über anarchistische Gruppierungen in Westberlin," February 12, 1975, p. 7; "Operativer Auskunftsbericht über anarchistische Gruppierungen in Westberlin," 1975, Box MfS 75/010, RAF-Sammlung (1. Generation), HIS; Brigitte Mohnhaupt, "Gefangene der RAF in Stammheim am 22. 7.1976," 1976, pp. 1–4, Erklärung von Brigitte Mohnhaupt am 22.07.1976 in Stammheim und Presse dazu, 1973–1976, Box RA 02/064,001, RAF-Sammlung (1. Generation), HIS. For information on the "Kommando George Jackson," see RAF: Texte und Materialien, 342–60.

118. For her stay in West Germany and her trip to London, see Davis, An Autobiography, 133–51.

119. Ibid., 172 ff.

120. For a detailed description of her case, see Bettina Aptheker, "The Angela Davis Case: A Brief Summary," in Ann Fagan Ginger, ed., Angela Davis Case Collection (Berkeley: Oceana Publications, 1974), xii–xxix; Reginald Major, Justice in the Round. The Trial of Angela Davis (New York: The Third Press, 1973). For her ideological development, see also Young, Soul Power, 184–208.

121. See, for example, the solidarity declaration by professors, research assistants, and students of the University of Frankfurt: "Solidarität mit Angela Davis," Frankfurter Rundschau, December 23, 1970.

122. Quoted in Werner Bastian, "Jagd auf Angela," Konkret 19 (September 1970): 15–16, esp. 16

123. Black Panther Solidaritätskomitee, "Zum Prozeß gegen die Soledad Brothers," in "Letter to the Government of FRG,", October, 22 1970, pp. 5–8, in USA BPP, Box, German SDS Papers, APOB; "Angela Davis Women and Children Solidarity Demonstration," flyer, March 13, 1971, in USA BPP, Black Panther Party, Box, German SDS Papers, APOB; see also Kraushaar, Frankfurter Schule und Studentenbewegung, 1:506.

124. "Brief von Herbert Marcuse," Neues Forum 203 (November 1970): 1020, quoted in Kraushaar, Frankfurter Schule und Studentenbewegung, 1:501.

125. Angela Davis Solidaritätskomitee, "Freiheit für Angela Davis!," poster, 1971, p. 11 in USA BPP, Box, German SDS Papers, APOB.

126. Detlev Claussen, "Zur Verhaftung von Angela Davis," Sozialistische Correspondenz-Info 56/57, November 18, 1970, pp. 18–20, HIS.

127. Its founders were Manfred Clemenz, Lothar Menne, Oskar Negt, Claudio Pozzoli, and Klaus Vack. See Angela Davis Solidaritätskomitee, ed., Am Beispiel Angela Davis: Der Kongreß in Frankfurt (Frankfurt: Fischer, 1972), 2.

128. Kraushaar, Frankfurter Schule und Studentenbewegung, 1:521; Varon, Bringing the War Home, 214.

129. Angela Davis Solidaritätskomitee, eds., *Am Beispiel Angela Davis*, passim.

130. Angela Davis Solidaritätskomitee, "Congress 'Am Beispiel Angela Davis,' " congress program, 1972, p. 2, in USA BPP, Box, German SDS papers, APOB.

131. Angela Davis Solidaritätskomitee, eds., *Am Beispiel Angela Davis*, 17.

132. Ibid., 21.

133. Ibid., 23.

134. For details see Varon, *Bringing the War Home*, 173 ff.

135. Angela Davis Solidaritätskomitee, "Speech by Oskar Negt at the Congress, 'Am Beispiel Angela Davis'." Press Information, June 3, 1972, p. 5, in USA BPP, Box, German SDS papers, APOB. The end of this version differs slightly from the printed version in Angela Davis Solidaritätskomitee, *Am Beispiel Angela Davis*, 27.

136. See Kraushaar, *Frankfurter Schule und Studentenbewegung*, 1:522; 2.400: 761–64.

137. Surprisingly, the role of Angela Davis both in East and West Germany has not yet been sufficiently analyzed despite a wealth of especially East German sources, such as Maximilian Scheer, *Der Weg nach San Rafael. Für Angela Davis. Ein Hörspiel* (Berlin: Verlag der Nation, 1971); Klaus Steiniger, *Free Angela Davis. Hero of the Other America* (Berlin: National Council of the National Front of the GDR et al., 1972); Verlag Zeit im Bild, *Frieden, Freundschaft, Solidarität. Angela Davis in der DDR* (Dresden: Verlag Zeit im Bild, 1972); Walter Kaufmann, *Unterwegs zu Angela. Amerikanische Impressionen* (Berlin: Verlag der Nation, 1973). For a comparison of Davis with Ulrike Meinhof, see Johanna Meyer-Lenz, "Angela Davis und Ulrike Meinhof: Ein biographischer Vergleich im Kontext unterschiedlicher Protestkulturen," in Karl Christian Führer, Karen Hagemann, and Birthe Kundrus, eds., *Eliten im Wandel. Gesellschaftliche Führungsschichten im 19. und 20. Jahrhundert* (Münster: Westfälisches Dampfboot, 2004): 314–35.

138. These overlaps also concerned officials both in West and East Germany. Already in February 1971, the director of the Special Terrorism Unit at the Bundeskriminalamt (Federal Criminal Police Office; hereafter BKA), Alfred Klaus, stated the connection between *Agit 883*, respectively a teach-in organized by the Vietnam and Black Panther Solidarity committees in Berlin on December 12, 1969, and the "Baader-Meinhof" group in a report of the Sicherungsgruppe Bonn. See Alfred Klaus and Sicherungsgruppe Bonn, "Bericht der Sicherungsgruppe," February 19, 1971, pp. 13, 19, Personensachakten Band IV: Bericht von Alfred Klaus, 1971, Box En,G/004,002, RAF-Sammlung (1. Generation), HIS. For the East German secret police's monitoring, see Ministerium für Staatssicherheit, "Information über die in der BRD existierenden sog. politisch extremen Ausländergruppen Ende 1972," September 7, 1973, pp. 19–21, 41–43, Aufstellung von politisch-operativ bedeutsamen Personen, 1973, Box MfS 73/013, RAF-Sammlung (1. Generation), HIS.

139. A variety of sources, although sometimes rather doubtful in nature, indicate the closeness and personal continuities between these groups. See, for exam-

ple, BKA, "Vernehmungsprotokoll des Zeugen Gerhard Müller," April 7–14, 1976, pp. 43–48, Vernehmungen - Gerhard Müller, 1976, Box SO 01/011,003, RAF-Sammlung (1. Generation), HIS; Hauptverhandlung Stammheim Prozess, "Vernehmung des Zeugen Gerhard Müller," July 13, 1976, pp. 10293, 10298, 10310, Stammheim-Verfahren - 125. Verhandlungstag, 1976, Box St.V/019,001, RAF-Sammlung (1. Generation), HIS; Ministerium für Staatssicherheit, "Bericht Weinrich," Abteilung XXII/8, 09/09/1982, Brigitte Heinrich zu Johannes Weinrich, 1982, Box We,J/101,015, RAF-Sammlung (1. Generation), HIS.

140. See Wolfgang Kraushaar, "Die Aura der Gewalt: Die Rote Armee als Entmischungsprodukt der Studentenbewegung," in his *Fischer in Frankfurt: Karriere eines Außenseiters* (Hamburg: Hamburger Edition, 2001): 224–56.

141. The apartment in question is Inheidener Str. 69 in Frankfurt-Bornheim. See Günter Textor and LKA Baden-Württemberg, "Vernehmungsprotokoll Wolfgang Pflug," June 16, 1972, Wohnung Inheidener Straße in Frankfurt, 1972–1973, Box SO 02/020,002, RAF-Sammlung (1. Generation), HIS.

142. Astrid Proll, "Der Hauptwiderspruch in den Metropolen des Imperialismus ist der Widerspruch zwischen Produktivkräften und Produktionsverhältnissen," 1973, p. 2, Handakte Croissant - Der Hauptwiderspruch in den Metropolen des Imperialismus ist der Widerspruch zwischen Produktivkräften und Produktionsverhältnissen - Rede von Astrid Proll, 1973–1974, Box Me,U/013,002, RAF-Sammlung (1. Generation), HIS.

143. Christian Schneider, "Der Holocaust als Generationsobjekt," *Mittelweg* 36, April 2004, pp. 56–73.

144. Claus Offe, *Selbstbetrachtung aus der Ferne. Tocqueville, Weber und Adorno in den Vereinigten Staaten* (Frankfurt: Suhrkamp, 2004).

CHAPTER 5
THE OTHER ALLIANCE AND THE TRANSATLANTIC PARTNERSHIP

1. George McGhee to President Johnson, "World Student Unrest," report, George McGhee: Writings, vol. 2, 1960–1969, 1968, p. 332, in George McGhee Papers: 2001 Accession, I, 2, 1, Georgetown University Library, Special Collections, Washington, D.C. (hereafter GUL).

2. Ibid., 341.

3. Ibid.

4. Patrick E. Nieburg, oral history interview, 1988, Foreign Affairs Oral History Collection, GUL.

5. Hans N. Tuch, oral history interview, August 4, 1989, Foreign Affairs Oral History Collection, GUL.

6. George McGhee, report to President Johnson, "World Student Unrest," 339.

7. See Marwick, *Cultural Revolution*, 45–50.

8. This rise in political activity was true for youth organizations on both sides of the political spectrum. See Rebecca Klatch, *A Generation Divided: The New Left, the New Right, and the 1960s* (Berkeley: University of California Press, 1999).

9. Fritz Fischer, *Making Them Like Us. Peace Corps Volunteers in the 1960s* (Washington, D.C.: Smithsonian Institution Press, 1998); Elizabeth Cobbs Hoffman, *All You Need Is Love: The Peace Corps and the Spirit of the 1960s* (Cambridge: Harvard University Press, 1998).

10. Frank A. Ninkovich, *The Diplomacy of Ideas: U.S. Foreign Policy and Cultural Relations, 1938–1950* (Chicago: Imprint Publications, 1995).

11. Walter L. Hixson, *Parting the Curtain: Propaganda, Culture, and the Cold War* (New York: St. Martin's Press, 1996); Scott Lucas, *Freedom's War: The US Crusade Against the Soviet Union, 1945–56* (Manchester: Manchester University Press, 1999); Nicholas Cull, *The Cold War and the United States Information Agency: American Propaganda and Public Diplomacy, 1945–1989* (Cambridge: Cambridge University Press, 2008). The bulk of the literature on this topic is, however, still dominated by authors once associated with the USIA and USIS: Philip Coombs, *The Fourth Dimension of Foreign Policy: Educational and Cultural Affairs* (New York: Harper and Row, 1964); Charles Frankel, *The Neglected Aspect of Foreign Affairs: American Educational and Cultural Policy Abroad* (Washington, D.C.: Brookings Institution, 1966); Thomas Sorensen, *The Word War: The Story of American Propaganda* (New York: Harper and Row, 1968); Ronald Rubin, *The Objectives of the U S. Information Agency: Controversies and Analysis* (New York: Praeger, 1968); Hans Tuch, *Communicating with the World: U S. Public Diplomacy Overseas* (New York: St. Martin's Press, 1990).

12. George McGhee to Coombs, Bureau of Educational and Cultural Affairs, "Goals for Free World Youth," Undersecretary of State for Political Affairs, January 23, 1962, in Bureau of Educational and Cultural Affairs (hereafter CU), G IV, S4, 37: Youth Office, Early History, Box 161, University of Arkansas Libraries, Special Collections, Fayetteville, Arkansas (hereafter UASC).

13. Francis Miller, memo to Alfred Boerner, "The Under Secretary's Memorandum regarding Goals for Free World Youth," CU, January 31, 1962, in CU, G IV, S4, 37: Youth Office, Early History, Box 161, UASC.

14. Philip Coombs to George McGhee, "Goals for Free World Youth," CU, March 1, 1962, in CU, G IV, S4, 37: Youth Office, Early History, Box 161, UASC.

15. "Youth Task Force," Memo of Conversation, Department of State, March 22, 1962, in CU, G IV, S4, 37: Youth Office, Early History, Box 161, UASC.

16. Memo, "Youth and Student Affairs," undated, in CU, G IV, S4, 37: Youth Office, Early History, Box 161, UASC.

17. William Brubeck, memo to Philip Coombs, CU, "Follow-up to Attorney General's Debriefing," Deputy Executive Secretary, DOS, April 5, 1962, in RG 59, Records of the Inter-Agency Youth Committee 1962–1972, Youth Committee - 1962, Box 1, U.S. National Archives II, College Park, Maryland (hereafter NA).

18. Memo, "Government Advisory Committee on International Book Programs," January 10, 1967; James Donovan, "The Interagency Youth Committee [IAYC]," Memorandum for the File, July 25, 1980, 1; both in Thomas Bowman Papers, IAYC Memoranda and Related Materials, Nov. 1956–July 1980, Box 1, John F. Kennedy Library, Boston, Mass. (hereafter JFKL).

19. The complete records of the IAYC were declassified in March 2005 due to a Special Access / Freedom of Information Act (FOIA) request by the author.

20. Lucius Battle, "Report on Inter-Agency Committee on Youth Affairs," March 6, 1963, p. 1, in CU, G IV, S4, 37: Youth Office, Early History, Box 161, UASC.

21. Lucius Battle, memo to IAYC Members, "Organization for Youth Activities," CU, June 1, 1962, in RG 59, Records of the IAYC 1962–1972, (hereafter IAYC Records), IAYC Meetings, Box 1, NA. The list of participants at the May 25 meeting reads as follows: Robert Kennedy (Attorney General), George McGhee (State), Edward Murrow (USIA), Sargent Shriver (Peace Corps), Ralph Dungan (White House), Harry Shooshan (AID), Cord Meyer (CIA). See ibid., 1.

22. Report of the Boerner Committee on Youth Programs, in ibid., Attachment A, p. 1.

23. Ibid., 2.

24. Lucius Battle, *Report on Inter-Agency Committee on Youth Affairs*, 3.

25. All quotations from Dean Rusk, airgram to all U.S. Chiefs of Mission, "Educational Exchange: New Emphasis on Youth," CW-8513, Department of State, April 24, 1962, in RG 59, IAYC Records, Youth Committee - 1962, Box 1, NA.

26. Memo, "Summary of Circulars to the Field regarding 'New Emphasis on Youth,'" May 1, 1963, in CU, G IV, S4, 37: Youth Office, Early History, Box 161, UASC.

27. Alfred Boerner, memo, "Emphasis on Youth," April 15, 1963, in CU, G IV, S4, 37: Youth Office, Early History, Box 161, UASC. See also Averell Harriman, memo, "Coordination of Country Youth Programs," June 25, 1963, in ibid.

28. IAYC Meeting, "Responsibility for Programs in the Youth Field," memo from conversation, CU, June 18, 1963, in CU, G IV, S4, 37: Youth Office, Early History, Box 161, UASC.

29. Sorensen, *The Word War*, 194 f. As a USIA representative, Sorensen was a participant in the first IAYC meetings.

30. Dean Rusk, airgram, "Emphasis on Youth: Presidential Memorandum," CA-5966, Department of State, December 10, 1963, in CU, G IV, S4, 37: Youth Office, Early History, Box 161, UASC.

31. "[W]e are interested in young leaders and potential leaders—in the universities and intellectual circles, in labor and business, in politics and the professions, and in the armed forces. We are also interested in reaching, directly or through potential leaders, those young people who are not really leaders, but who have a capacity, in the classroom or in the streets, to frustrate the achievement of our objectives" (ibid., 1).

32. Ibid., 2.

33. "I trust that there is no misunderstanding on this subject. Political desks here in Washington will be following it closely on my behalf, and the training of all U.S. personnel taking up responsible positions abroad will reflect it. I am confident that once confusion is cleared away and the active and continuing leadership of the Ambassador (or other principal officer) is exercised, it will not be necessary for future visitors to report as critically as those words I have just read." Dean Rusk, letter to ambassadors, Secretary of State, Washington, D.C., July 8, 1964, p. 2, in Aides Files, Harry McPherson, Youth Committee, Box 18 (1415), Lyndon B. Johnson Library, Austin, Texas (hereafter LBJL). The DOS also did not

leave the designation of youth officer solely up to the chief of mission but urged the appointment of a political officer.

34. Ibid.

35. Report, "The Interagency Youth Committee," 1964 (undated), p. 1, in CU, G IV, S4, 37: Youth Office, Early History, Box 161, UASC.

36. Ibid., 3.

37. See "Emphasis on Youth: Reaching and Influencing Rising Young Leaders—What the Posts are Doing: Reports from the Field," Booklet, Department of State, 1965, p. 2, in CU, IV, pp. 5, 15, Emphasis on Youth, 1965, Box 162, UASC. Despite the mentioning of IAYC's general role by its first chairman, Lucius Battle, during Congressional hearings, most of its efforts, and especially the local programs, remained classified.

38. U.S. Advisory Commission to Committee on Foreign Affairs, report, "The 22nd Report of the United States Advisory Commission on Information," 74, 90th Congress, 1st session, House, March 6, 1967, p. 5, in RG 46, Senate Foreign Relations Committee, SEN 90A-F9, Executive Communications, Doc. #17, 3, U.S. National Archives, Washington, D.C. (hereafter NADC).

39. Ibid., 17, 18.

40. This shift is also confirmed by later reports on the IAYC. See a representative account given by Neil Boyer in a memo to Richard Roth, CU–Office of Policy and Plans (hereafter CU/OPP), "Activities of the Department's Youth Office," Department of State, August 30, 1973, p. 1, in CU, IV, 5, 5: Youth Affairs, General, Box 162, UASC.

41. "Meeting of the Inter-Agency Youth Committee," Minutes, August 31, 1966, in CU, G IV, S4, 37: Youth Office, Early History, Box 161, UASC.

42. Foy Kohler, "European Youth and Young Leaders Conference," Briefing Book, Department of State, May 1967, p. 8, in Aides Files, Harry McPherson, European Youth and Young Leaders, Box 23 (1518), LBJL.

43. Ibid., 8f.

44. Ibid., 10.

45. Ibid., 5.

46. Ibid.

47. "European Youth and Young Leaders: Notes on a Conference at Airlie House, May 14–15, 1967," Department of State, July 15, 1967, p. 3, in RG 59, IAYC Records, Airlie Conference on European Youth, Box 3, NA. Two external scholars were contracted by the Department of State for the survey: Fritz Stern, professor of history at Columbia University, for West Germany, and Paul E. Sigmund, associate professor of politics at Princeton University, for England. Anton DePorte from the Department's Bureau of Intelligence and Research conducted the country study for France.

48. Joseph Colmen, letter to Olin Robison, Special Assistant to Deputy Undersecretary of State (Political Affairs) (hereafter G/Y), Deputy Assistant Secretary for HEW, May 17, 1967, in RG 59, IAYC Records, Airlie Conference on European Youth, Box 3, NA.

49. Anton DePorte, memo to Olin Robison, G/Y, "Airlie House Conference on European Youth and Young Leaders, May 14–15," Office of Intelligence and

Research, Department of State (hereafter INR)/REU, May 22, 1967, in RG 59, IAYC Records, Airlie Conference on European Youth, Box 3, NA.

50. Wilfried Mausbach, "Defending Berlin in Saigon: The Dilemmas of West German Support for America's War," unpublished paper, Vietnam War Symposium, University of California, Santa Barbara, January 1999, p. 2; Hubert Zimmermann, *Money and Security. Troops and Monetary Policy in Germany's Relations to the United States and the United Kingdom, 1950–71* (Cambridge: Cambridge University Press, 2002). See also T. Michael Ruddy, "A Limit to Solidarity. Germany, the United States, and the Vietnam War," in Detlef Junker et al., eds., *The United States and Germany in the Era of the Cold War. A Handbook*, 2 vols. (New York: Cambridge University Press, 2004), 2:126–32; Thomas Schwartz, *Lyndon Johnson and Europe: In the Shadow of Vietnam* (Cambridge: Harvard University Press, 2003), 86 ff.

51. USIA Office of Policy and Research, "Vietnam and World Opinion," report, 000951, August 1966, p. 19, in RG 306, Records of the USIA, Office of Research, Special Reports, 1964–82, S-15-66, Box 3, NA.

52. On the history of this analogy see also Hubert Zimmermann, "The Quiet German: The Vietnam War and the Federal Republic of Germany," in Christoper Goscha and Maurice Vaïsse, eds., *La guerre du Vietnam et l'Europe, 1963–1973* (Bruxelles: Bruylant/Paris: L.G.D.J., 2003), 52.

53. USIA Office of Policy and Research, "Vietnam and World Opinion," 21.

54. Dean Rusk, telegram to American Embassy Bonn, State 089030, Department of State, November 22, 1966, in RG 59, Central Foreign Policy Files, 1967-69, EDX, GER W-US, 1/1/67, Box 363, NA. See also Fritz Stern, "Reflections on the International Student Movement," *The American Scholar* 40, no. 1 (winter 1970/71): 123–37; idem, *Five Germanies I Have Known* (New York: Farrar, Straus and Groux, 2006), 242–43, 249–261.

55. Stern was, however, not informed of the existence of a comprehensive government youth effort under the supervision of the IAYC or the local youth committees and was not cleared to receive classified information. To prevent any media attention, his trip was supposed to be labeled as a gesture to a former colleague from Columbia, Charles Frankel, who asked him to examine the operation of U.S. exchange programs he was now responsible for. See Geraldine Sheehan, letter to Fritz Stern, Department of State, November 18, 1966; idem, telegram 4371 to American Embassy Bonn, Department of State, November 22, 1966; Walter Stoessel, letter to Martin Hillenbrand, American Minister, American Embassy Bonn, Deputy Assistant Secretary for European Affairs, Department of State, 1966, November 22; both in RG 59, IAYC Records, Airlie Conference on European Youth, Box 3, NA.

56. Fritz Stern, "German Young Elites," Report for the Conference on European Youth and Young Leaders, Airlie House, May 14–15, 1967, January 9, 1967, p. 30, in Aides Files, Harry McPherson, European Youth and Young Leaders, Box 23 (1518), LBJL.

57. Ibid., 19.

58. Ibid., 22. Among others, Stern claimed to have talked to the "intellectual leader of the S.D.S." but, surprisingly, nowhere in the report spelled out his name.

59. Ibid., 30.

60. Ibid., 34.

61. Ibid.

62. Wyman, airgram to Department of State, "Radical Student Activity in West Berlin," A-321, US Mission Berlin, January 11, 1967, p. 1, in RG 59, Central Foreign Policy Files, 1967–69, POL 23-8, GER W, 6/1/67, Box 2133, NA.

63. Ibid., 3.

64. Ibid.

65. Ibid., 4.

66. See Siegward Lönnendonker and Tilman Fichter, eds., *Hochschule im Umbruch, Vol. 4: Die Krise: 1964–1967. Dokumentation.* (Berlin: Pressestelle der FU Berlin, 1975), 151 f., 409.

67. "11 Seized in Berlin in a Reported Plot to Kill Humphrey," *New York Times*, April 6, 1967, pp. 1, 5. See also Neal Ascherson, "Charges of Plot against Humphrey Unfounded," *Washington Post*, April 10, 1967, p. A16. For a detailed account, see Siegward Lönnendonker, Bernd Rabehl, and Jochen Staadt, *Die antiautoritäre Revolte: der Sozialistische Deutsche Studentenbund nach der Trennung von der SPD* (Wiesbaden: Westdeutscher Verlag, 2002), 319–24.

68. Hubert Humphrey, memo to President, "Western Europe, March–April, 1967," April 10, 1967, p. 4f., in National Security File (hereafter NSF), International Meetings / Travel File, Vice President—Visit to Europe, Report to the President, March–April 1967, Box 26, LBJL.

69. "Summary Notes of the 569th Meeting of the National Security Council," May 3, 1967, in Foreign Relations of the United States (hereafter FRUS), 1964–68, 13:572.

70. Ibid., 27.

71. Bogardus, airgram to Department of State, "Vietnamese Buddhist Monk speaks in Heidelberg," A-153, American Consulate Stuttgart, June 5, 1967; Bruce Lancaster, aigram to Department of State, "Filbinger at the Inauguration of the New Rector at Mannheim University," A-62, American Consulate Stuttgart, December 12, 1967, both in RG 59, Central Foreign Policy Files, 1967–69, EDU 9-3, GER W, 1/1/67, Box 345, NA; idem, airgram, "New University Reform Law Raises Student Cry for "Long, Hot Summer" of Protest," A-120, American Consulate Stuttgart, March 26, 1968, in RG 59, Central Foreign Policy Files, 1967–69, EDU 9-4, GER W, 1/1/67, Box 345, NA.

72. Bruce Lancaster, airgram to Department of State, "Students, Teaching Assistants, Win Seats in Tuebingen University Policy Councils; University Reform and Student Activism in Baden-Wuerttemberg Affected," A-61, American Consulate Stuttgart, December 12, 1967, p. 4, in RG 59, Central Foreign Policy Files, 1967–69, EDU 9-3, GER W, 1/1/67, Box 345, NA.

73. Kidd, airgram to Department of State, "Kiel Student Demonstrations," A-119, American Consulate Hamburg, February 7, 1968; Goodman, airgram to Department of State, "Bremen Youth Accelerate Political Activity," A-71, American Consulate Bremen, February 19, 1968; both in RG 59, Central Foreign Policy Files, 1967-69, POL 13-2, GER W, 1/1/68, Box 2125, NA. See also Olaf Dinné et al., eds., *68 - dunnemals in Bremen* (Bremen: WMIT-Verlag, 1999); Detlef Michelers, *Draufhauen, Draufhauen, Nachsetzen. Die Bremer Schülerbewegung, die*

Strassenbahndemonstrationen und ihre Folgen 1967/1968 (Bremen: Edition Temmen, 2002).

74. Goodman, telegram to Secretary of State, "Bremen Police Seek Information re Equipment and Tactics Employed by US Police Forces in Combatting Demonstrations," 172, American Consulate Bremen, February 15, 1968, in RG 59, Central Foreign Policy Files, 1967-69, POL 23-8, GER W, 1/1/68, Box 2133, NA.

75. Dennis Kux, interview, January 13, 1995, in Foreign Affairs Oral History Collection, GUL.

76. For his personal account, see Kidd, airgram to Department of State, "Anti-Viet Nam Demonstration in Hamburg, March 22, 1968," A-162, American Consulate Hamburg, 1968, 03/27, in RG 59, Central Foreign Policy Files, 1967–69, POL 23-8, GER W, 1/1/68, Box 2133, NA.

77. Dennis Kux, interview, January 13, 1995, in Foreign Affairs Oral History Collection, GUL.

78. Fessenden, telegram to Secretary of State, "The Student Riots: Initial Assessment," Bonn 10845, American Embassy Bonn, April 16, 1968, p. 2, in RG 59, Central Foreign Policy Files, 1967–69, POL 23-8, GER W, 4/1/68, Box 2133, NA.

79. Goodman, telegram to Secretary of State, "Youthful Easter Marchers Decide to Vent Their Ire Against Springer Rather Than Against ConGen," Bremen 200, American Consulate Bremen, April 15, 1968, in RG 59, Central Foreign Policy Files, 1967-69, POL 23-8, GER W, 4/1/68, Box 2133, NA. See also Hans-Peter Schwarz, *Axel Springer: Die Biografie* (Berlin: Propyläen, 2008).

80. Fessenden, telegram to Secretary of State, "Round Up of the Easter Weekend Disturbances," Bonn 10849, American Embassy Bonn, April 16, 1968, p. 4, in RG 59, Central Foreign Policy Files, 1967–69, POL 23-8, GER W, 4/1/68, Box 2133, NA.

81. George McGhee, airgram to Department of State, "DGB Reaction to Violent Student Demonstrations," A-1246, American Embassy Bonn, April 23, 1968; Kidd, airgram to Department of State, "Helmut Schmidt on Springer and Demonstrations," A-177, American Consulate Hamburg, April 23, 1968, both in RG 59, Central Foreign Policy Files, 1967–69, POL 23-8, GER W, 4/1/68, Box 2133, NA.

82. Henry Cabot Lodge, telegram to Secretary of State, "French Domestic Developments and Their Effects on the FRG," Bonn 12450, American Embassy Bonn, May 23, 1968, 2, in NSF, Files of Walt Rostow, The Likelihood of More French-style Eruptions, Box 13, LBJL.

83. Morris, telegram to Secretary of State, "Unrest at Free University," Berlin 1552, US Mission Berlin, May 25, 1968, in RG 59, Central Foreign Policy Files, 1967–69, POL 23-8, GER W, 5/1/68, Box 2133, NA.

84. Morris, telegram to Department of State, "Student Strike at Berlin Universities," Berlin 1503, US Mission Berlin, May 17, 1968, in RG 59, Central Foreign Policy Files, 1967–69, POL 23-8, GER W, 5/1/68, Box 2133, NA.

85. Morris, telegram to Secretary of State, "French Student Leader at Free University," Berlin 1538, US Mission Berlin, April 22, 1968, p. 2, in RG 59, Central Foreign Policy Files, 1967–69, POL 23-8, GER W, 5/1/68, Box 2133, NA.

86. Morris, telegram to Secretary of State, "Demonstrations Against Emergency Legislation," Berlin 1593, US Mission Berlin, April 30, 1968, in RG 59, Central Foreign Policy Files, 1967–69, POL 23-8, GER W, 5/1/68, Box 2133, NA.

87. Henry Cabot Lodge, telegram to Secretary of State, "The German 'Establishment' and its Opponents," Bonn 12722, American Embassy Bonn, May 29, 1968, p. 1, section 1 of 2, in NSF, Files of Walt Rostow, The Likelihood of More French-style Eruptions, Box 13, LBJL.

88. Ibid., 2, section 1 of 2.

89. Ibid., 2, section 2 of 2.

90. Walt Rostow, telegram to President, "George McGhee's Final Report on Germany," White House, June 3, 1968, p. 2, in NSF, Country File, Germany, cables, vol. 14, 3/68–8/68, Box 189, LBJL.

91. For the wider government response, see Fessenden, telegram to Secretary of State, "West German Authorities Determined to Control Student Disorder," Bonn 10495, American Embassy Bonn, April 18, 1968, in RG 59, Central Foreign Policy Files, 1967–69, POL 23-8, GER W, 4/1/68, Box 2133, NA.

92. George McGhee, "Remarks at the Federation of German-American Clubs," USIS Press Release, 421, George McGhee: Writings, vol. 2, 1960–1969, May 5, 1968, p. 331, in George McGhee Papers: 2001 Accession, I, 2, 1, GUL.

93. Morris, telegram to Secretary of State, "Demonstrations Against Emergency Legislation," Berlin 1593, US Mission Berlin, April 30, 1968, 2f.

94. For the special role of Berlin, see also Diethelm Prowe, "Berlin. Catalyst and Fault Line of German-American Relations in the Cold War," in Junker, *USA and Germany*, 1:165–71.

95. Andreas Daum, "America's Berlin, 1945–2000: Between Myth and Visions," pp. 49–73 in Frank Trommler, ed., *Berlin: The New Capital in the East. A Transatlantic Appraisal* (Washington, D.C.: AICGS, 2000).

96. On the history of the FU Berlin, see Siegward Lönnendonker and Tilman Fichter, eds., *Hochschule im Umbruch: Vol. 4: Die Krise: 1964–1967. Dokumentation.* (Berlin: Pressestelle der FU Berlin, 1975); Bernd Rabehl, *Am Ende der Utopie: Die Politische Geschichte der Freien Universität* (Berlin: Argon, 1988); James F. Tent, *The Free University of Berlin: A Political History* (Bloomington: Indiana University Press, 1988).

97. Morris, airgram to Department of State, "Berlin's New Left," A-527, US Mission Berlin, May 12, 1967, p. 14, in RG 59, Central Foreign Policy Files, 1967-69, POL 13-1, GER B, Box 2109, NA.

98. Ibid., 2.

99. Ibid., 3.

100. Ibid., 3, 4.

101. Ibid., 6 f.

102. Ibid., 8.

103. Ibid., 8.

104. See also chapter 3.

105. Morris, telegram to Secretary of State, "Planned Vietnam Protest By Americans in Berlin," Berlin 1447, US Mission Berlin, April 21, 1967, p. 2, in RG 59, Central Foreign Policy Files, 1967–69, POL 23-8, GER W, 6/1/67, Box 2133, NA.

106. Ibid., 3.

107. Morris, telegram to Secretary of State, "Planned Vietnam Protest By Americans in Berlin," Berlin 1464, US Mission Berlin, April 25, 1967, in RG 59, Central Foreign Policy Files, 1967–69, POL 23-8, GER W, 6/1/67, Box 2133, NA.

108. Dean Rusk, telegram to American Embassy Bonn, "Planned Vietnam Protest By US Students in Berlin, April 29," 180320, Department of State, April 21, 1967, in RG 59, Central Foreign Policy Files, 1967–69, POL 23-8, GER W, 6/1/67, Box 2133, NA.

109. Morris, telegram to Secretary of State, " 'US Campaign' Demonstration," Berlin 1498, US Mission Berlin, April 29, 1967, in RG 59, Central Foreign Policy Files, 1967–69, POL 23-8, GER W, 6/1/67, Box 2133, NA.

110. Morris, airgram to Department of State, "Vietnam Protest by American Citizens in Berlin (U.S. Campaign)," A-602, US Mission Berlin, June 22, 1967, in RG 59, Central Foreign Policy Files, 1967–69, POL 23-8, GER W, 6/1/67, Box 2133, NA.

111. Morris, telegram to Secretary of State, "Student Demonstrations," Berlin 1660, US Mission Berlin, June 14, 1967, in RG 59, Central Foreign Policy Files, 1967–69, POL 23-8, GER W, 6/1/67, Box 2133, NA.

112. Morris, airgram to Department of State, "Berlin Students' Open Letter to the Allies," A-31, US Mission Berlin, July 15, 1967, pp. 4–6, in RG 59, Central Foreign Policy Files, 1967–69, EDU 9 -3 GER B, 1/1/67, Box 344, NA. See also Siegward Lönnendonker and Tilman Fichter, eds., *Hochschule im Umbruch Vol. 5: Gewalt und Gegengewalt: 1967–1969. Dokumentation* (Berlin: Pressestelle der FU Berlin, 1983).

113. Morris, telegram to Secretary of State, "Free University Student Parliament adopts Anti-US Resolution," US Mission Berlin, May 29, 1967, in RG 59, Central Foreign Policy Files, 1967–69, POL 13-2, GER W, 1/1/67, 2125, NA. See also Lönnendonker and Fichter, *Hochschule im Umbruch*, 4:167, 444–46.

114. Morris, airgram to Department of State, "Berlin Students' Open Letter to the Allies," A-31, US Mission Berlin, July 15, 1967, p. 3. The Berlin senate had also advised the Allies not to acknowledge the letter publicly. When the letter finally arrived, only brief standard press comments were prepared.

115. Morris, airgram, to Department of State, "Allied Consideration of Berlin Student Problems," A-30, US Mission Berlin, July 15, 1967, 3, in RG 59, Central Foreign Policy Files, 1967–69, EDU 9-3, GER W, 1/1/67, Box 345, NA.

116. "We have consciously avoided assuming such a role in the past, and should continue to avoid it in the future. There are existing laws and regulations which can be used by German authorities to maintain order, and for the Allies to supplement these with specific orders would be to publicly imply that civil officials are incapable of dealing with the problem." Ibid., 3.

117. Ibid., 4.

118. Morris, telegram to Secretary of State, "Berlin Student Problem - Further Developments," Berlin 1671 June 14, US Mission Berlin, June 19, 1967, p. 3, in RG 59, Central Foreign Policy Files, 1967-69, POL 23-8, GER W, 6/1/67, Box 2133, NA.

119. Morris, airgram to Department of State, "Ewald Harndt: The Newly Designated Rector of the Free University," A-46, US Mission Berlin, July 26, 1967,

p. 2, in RG 59, Central Foreign Policy Files, 1967–69, EDU 9 -3 GER B, 1/1/67, Box 344, NA.

120. Morris, telegram to Secretary of State, "October 21 Demonstration in Berlin," Berlin 0503, US Mission Berlin, October 20, 1967, in RG 59, Central Foreign Policy Files, 1967–69, POL 23-8, GER B, 1968, Box 2109, NA.

121. Lönnendonker and Fichter, *Hochschule im Umbruch*, 5:49, 242.

122. Morris, telegram to Secretary of State, "October 21 Demonstration in Berlin," Berlin 0522, US Mission Berlin, October 25, 1967, in RG 59, Central Foreign Policy Files, 1967–69, POL 23-8, GER B, 1968, Box 2109, NA.

123. Morris, telegram to Secretary of State, "October 21 Demonstration in Berlin," Berlin 0503, US Mission Berlin, October 20, 1967, p. 3, in RG 59, Central Foreign Policy Files, 1967–69, POL 23-8, GER B, 1968, Box 2109, NA.

124. Morris, telegram to Secretary of State, "Student Disturbances," Berlin 0657, US Mission Berlin, November 25, 1967; idem, airgram, "Policeman Acquitted in Killing of Student Ohnesorg," A-277, US Mission Berlin, November 27, 1967, in RG 59, Central Foreign Policy Files, 1967–69, POL 23-8, GER B, 1968, Box 2109, NA.

125. Morris, airgram to Department of State, "Anti-Vietnam Demonstrators at Tempelhof," A-36, US Mission Berlin, July 19, 1967, in RG 59, Central Foreign Policy Files, 1967-69, POL 23-8, GER B, 1968, Box 2109, NA.

126. "In a few cases, demonstrators were struck and had their beards or hair pulled. Approximately ten demonstrators requested that the police remove them from the scene for their own protection.. . . Police had to escort those booked and the ten who had requested protection out a back door of the station because a crowd of some 200 irate Berliners were awaiting them at the front door." Wyman, airgram to Department of State, "Demonstration at US Parade August 19," A-111, US Mission Berlin, August 28, 1967, in RG 59, Central Foreign Policy Files, 1967–69, POL 23-8, GER B, 1968, Box 2109, NA. See also Lönnendonker and Fichter, *Hochschule im Umbruch*, 5:41; and the documentation in *Berliner Extra-Dienst*: see vol. 28, August 23, 1967, pp. 8–10, and vol. 29, August 26, 1967, pp. 5–8; also "Neuköllner Prügel-Opfer: Anklage gegen Vietnam-Demonstranten," *Berliner Extra-Dienst* 19/11, March 6, 1968, 2f.

127. Wyman, airgram to Department of State, Demonstration at US Parade, 3.

128. Wyman, airgram to Department of State, "Ambassador McGhee's Dinner for Berlin University Students," A-544, US Mission Berlin, May 22, 1967, in RG 59, Central Foreign Policy Files, 1967–69, EDU 9–3 GER B, 1/1/67, Box 344, NA.

129. See George McGhee, telegram to Secretary of State, "Youth Attitudes in Berlin," US Mission Berlin, April 14, 1967, in RG 59, Central Foreign Policy Files, 1967–69, POL 13-2, GER W, 1/1/67, Box 2125, NA; Morris. airgram to Department of State, "Rector's Views on Developments at Free University," A-591, US Mission Berlin, July 16, 1967, in RG 59, Central Foreign Policy Files, 1967–69, EDU 9-3, GER W, 1/1/67, Box 345, NA; idem, "The Student Problem in Berlin," A-145, US Mission Berlin, Department of State, September 25, 1967, in ibid., Box 344.

130. Morris, airgram to Department of State, "Harry Ristock Discusses Schuetz and Politics in Berlin," A-180, US Mission Berlin, October 12, 1967, in RG 59, Central Foreign Policy Files, 1967–69, POL - Political Aff. & Rel., GER B, 1-1-1967, Box 2108, NA.

131. See, for example Kidd, airgram to Department of State, "Views of North German Politicians on Student Unrest," A-171, American Consulate Hamburg, April 10, 1968, in RG 59, Central Foreign Policy Files, 1967–69, POL 13-2, GER W, 1/1/68, Box 2125, NA.

132. U.S. Mission Berlin to Secretary of State, "Ambassador Abrasimov Letter to Ambassador McGhee on Emergency Legislation in Berlin," Telegram, July 27, 1968, 2, in NSF, Country File, Germany, cables, vol. 13, 3/67–7/67, Box 188, NA.

133. Nathaniel Davis, memo to Walt Rostow, "German Emergency Legislation and Berlin," The White House, August 1, 1967, in NSF, Country File, Germany, Memos, vol. 14, 8/67–2/68, Box 188, LBJL.

134. Memorandum of conversation, "The President's August 15 Meeting with Chancellor Kiesinger," White House, August 15, 1967, 2, in NSF, Country File, Germany, Visit of Chancellor Kiesinger, 3 (8/67), Box 194, LBJL. For the general agenda of this visit see Schwartz, *Lyndon Johnson and Europe*, 183–86; Joachim Arenth, *Johnson, Vietnam und der Westen: Transatlantische Belastungen, 1963–1969* (Munich: Olzog, 1994), 204 f.

135. Dean Rusk to President, "Visit of Chancellor Kiesinger, August 1967: The President's Paper," Briefing Book, Department of State, undated, 8, in NSF, Country File, Germany, Visit of Chancellor Kiesinger, I (8/67), Box 193, LBJL; Francis Bator, memo to President, "Talking Points for Conversation with Chancellor Kiesinger," The White House, August 14, 1967, in NSF, Country File, Germany, memos, Vol. XIV, 8/67–2/68, Box 188, LBJL.

136. Department of State, "Visit of Chancellor Kiesinger, August 1967: Berlin," Briefing Book, Department of State, August 11, 1967, in NSF, Country File, Germany, Visit of Chancellor Kiesinger, I (8/67), Box 193, LBJL.

137. Ibid., 2.

138. Memorandum of Conversation, "Berlin: Part IV of IV," Department of State, August 16, 1967, in Papers of Francis Bator, Kiesinger visit, 8/14–16/67, General, Box 22, LBJL.

139. Memorandum of Conversation, "The President's August 15 Meeting with Chancellor Kiesinger," White House, August 15, 1967, p. 6, in NSF, Country File, Germany, Visit of Chancellor Kiesinger, III (8/67), Box 194, LBJL.

140. Morris, telegram to Secretary of State, "Governing Mayor's trip to the United States," U.S. Mission Berlin, November 2, 1967, in NSF, Country File, Germany, Memos, vol. 14, 8/67–2/68, Box 188, LBJL.

141. Morris, telegram, to Secretary of State, "Vietnam Protest Activities during Holiday Weekend," Berlin 776, US Mission Berlin, December 27, 1967, in RG 59, Central Foreign Policy Files, 1967–69, POL 23-8, GER B, 1968, Box 2109, NA.

142. The plans included "exploding leaflet scattering devices, inviting desertion by American troops" for the U.S. Army barracks and "anti-American slogans on the building" of the US Consulate. Morris, telegram to Secretary of State, "New Year's Eve Demonstrations in Berlin," Berlin 0775, US Mission Berlin, Jan-

uary 2, 1968, in RG 59, Central Foreign Policy Files, 1967–69, POL 23-8, GER B, 1968, Box 2109, NA.

143. Morris, telegram to Secretary of State, "Plans for International Youth Congress in Berlin," Berlin 0782, US Mission Berlin, January 4, 1968; idem to Secretary of State, telegram, "Plans for International Youth Conference on Vietnam," Berlin 0818, US Mission Berlin, January 15, 1968, both in RG 59, Central Foreign Policy Files, 1967–69, POL 13-2, 1/1/68, Box 2870, NA.

144. Although Carmichael and Brown were reportedly dropped from the guest list, Carmichael especially continued to be of major interest to the Department of State since his participation would be a criminal offense due to his revoked visa. See Morris, telegram to Secretary of State, "International Vietnam Congress," Berlin 0869, US Mission Berlin, January 31, 1968, p. 3; Dean Rusk, telegram to US Mission Berlin, "Stokely Carmichael," 115723, Department of State, February 15, 1968; idem, telegram to Secretary of State, "Non-Appearance of Stokely Carmichael at Vietnam Congress," Berlin 974, US Mission Berlin, February 19, 1968, all in RG 59, Central Foreign Policy Files, 1967–69, POL 13-2, 1/1/68, Box 2870, NA.

145. Morris, telegram to US Mission Berlin, "International Viet Nam Congress," Bonn 7886, American Embassy Bonn, February 1, 1968, in RG 59, Central Foreign Policy Files, 1967–69, POL 13-2, 1/1/68, Box 2870, NA.

146. Morris, telegram, "Student Reaction to Senat[e] and University 'Hard Line,'" February 8, 1968, p. 2, in RG 59, Central Foreign Policy Files, 1967–69, 2870, POL 13-2, 1/1/68, NA.

147. For the comprehensive elaboration of these points, see Morris, telegram to American Embassy Bonn, "Mission Views on Possible Ban of Vietnam Congress," Berlin 0911, US Mission Berlin, February 8, 1968, Section 2, 2, in RG 59, Central Foreign Policy Files, 1967–69, POL 13-2, 1/1/68, Box 2870, NA.

148. Morris, telegram to American Embassy Bonn, "Press Guidance for Vietnam Congress," Berlin 950, US Mission Berlin, February 15, 1968, in RG 59, Central Foreign Policy Files, 1967–69, POL 13-2, 1/1/68, Box 2870, NA.

149. Morris, telegram to Secretary of State, "Vietnam Congress," Berlin 965, US Mission Berlin, February 16, 1968, in RG 59, Central Foreign Policy Files, 1967–69, POL 13-2, January 1, 1968, 2870, NA. See also Lönnendonker, Rabehl, and Staadt, *Die antiautoritäre Revolte*, 500 ff.

150. Morris, telegram to Secretary of State, "Vietnam Congress," Berlin 970, US Mission Berlin, February 18, 1968, in RG 59, Central Foreign Policy Files, 1967–69, POL 13-2, 1/1/68, Box 2870, NA.

151. CIA, "Central Intelligence Bulletin," CIA-RDP79T00975A0108001 30001-7, February 17, 1968, p. 6, in CIA Records Search Tool (hereafter CREST), NA.

152. Morris, telegram to Secretary of State, "Vietnam Congress Roundup," Berlin 976, US Mission Berlin, February 19, 1968, p. 3, in RG 59, Central Foreign Policy Files, 1967–69, POL 23-8, GER W, 1/1/68, Box 2133, NA.

153. Morris, telegram to Secretary of State, "Comment on the February 17–18 International Vietnam Congress," Berlin 975, US Mission Berlin, February 19, 1968, p. 2, in RG 59, Central Foreign Policy Files, 1967–69, POL 23-8, GER W, 1/1/68, Box 2133, NA; Morris, telegram to American Embassy Bonn, "Allied

Public Security Responsibilities," 2112, US Mission Berlin, February 29, 1968, in RG 59, Central Foreign Policy Files, 1967–69, POL 23-8, GER W, 1/1/68, Box 2133, NA.

154. Morris, telegram to Secretary of State, "Ambassador's Talk with Gov Mayor Schuetz," Berlin 515, US Mission Berlin, October 23, 1967, Part 2, p. 2, in RG 59, Central Foreign Policy Files, 1967–69, POL 18, GER B, 1/1/67, Box 2109, NA.

155. Morris, airgram to Department of State, "Berlin's Long Saturday Experiment: On Again, Off Again - On Again?," A-168, US Mission Berlin, October 9, 1967, pp. 1, 3, in RG 59, Central Foreign Policy Files, 1967–69, POL 18, GER B, 1/1/67, Box 2109, NA.

156. Memorandum of conversation, "Student Unrest, Disorders in West Berlin, and Related Subjects (Part 5 of 5)," 1928, Department of State, February 1, 1968, in RG 59, Central Foreign Policy Files, 1967–69, POL 13-2, GER W, 1/1/68, Box 2125, NA; Morris, telegram to Department of State, "Governing Mayor Schuetz' US Visit," Berlin 0896, US Mission Berlin, February 7, 1968, 2, in RG 59, Central Foreign Policy Files, 1967–69, POL 7, GER B, Box 2108, NA.

157. For a detailed description see Lönnendonker and Fichter, *Hochschule im Umbruch,* 5:76. See also Dan Morgan, "150,000 Berliners Cheer for U.S.," *Washington Post,* February 22, 1968, p. A15.

158. Morris, telegram to Secretary of State, "Berlin Demonstration Planned for February 21," 979, US Mission Berlin, February 20, 1968, p. 2, RG 59, Central Foreign Policy Files, 1967–69, POL 23-8, GER W, 1/1/68, Box 2133, NA.

159. See George McGhee, telegram to Secretary of State, "Congratulatory Message to Governing Mayor Schuetz," American Embassy Bonn, February 22, 1968, in NSF, Country File, Germany, cables, vol. 14, 8/67–2/68, Box 188, LBJL.

160. Morris, telegram to Secretary of State, "Continuing Repercussions of February 21 Rally," 2149, US Mission Berlin, July 3, 1968, p. 4, in RG 59, Central Foreign Policy Files, 1967–69, POL 23-8, GER W, 1/1/68, Box 2133, NA.

161. Morris, airgram to Department of State, "Berlin New Left forms 'Militia'," A-525, US Mission Berlin, March 29, 1968, in RG 59, Central Foreign Policy Files, 1967–69, POL 13-10, GER W, 1/1/67, Box 2126, NA.

162. Johnstone, airgram to Department of State, "Local Press and Labor Officials Critical of Berlin 'Freedom Rally,' " A-247, American Consulate Frankfurt, March 1, 1968, p. 2, in RG 59, Central Foreign Policy Files, 1967–69, POL - Political Aff. & Rel., GER, 1967, Box 2107, NA.

163. Wyman, airgram to Department of State, "Berlin Demonstrations—Comments on the Easter Weekend," A-567, US Mission Berlin, April 18, 1968, in RG 59, Central Foreign Policy Files, 1967–69, POL 23-8, GER B, 1968, Box 2109, NA.

164. CIA, "Central Intelligence Bulletin," CIA-RDP79T00975A0110001 20001-5, April 13, 1968, p. 5, in CREST, NA; Wyman, airgram to Department of State, "Berlin Demonstrations - Comments on the Easter Weekend," A-567, US Mission Berlin, April 18, 1968, p, 5.

165. Ibid., 2.

166. Ibid., 5.

167. Wyman, airgram to Department of State, "Members of West Berlin *Kommune I* Visit Communist Chinese Embassy in East Berlin," A-120, US Mission Berlin, September 12, 1968, in RG 59, Central Foreign Policy Files, 1967-69, POL 13-10, GER W, 1/1/67, Box 2126, NA. See, for example, the following: Morris, airgram to Secretary of State, "West Berlin Communists Seek 'United Front' with Other Leftist Groups," A-164, US Mission Berlin, October 7, 1967, in RG 59, Central Foreign Policy Files, 1967-69, POL 13-1, GER B, 2109, NA.

168. CIA, "Central Intelligence Bulletin," CIA-RDP79T00975A0110001 80001-9, April 20, 1968, p. 5, in CREST, NA.

169. Thomas L. Hughes to Secretary of State, "SED Influence in the West German Student Demonstration: Uncomfortable Alliance," Intelligence Note, 296, Department of State, INR, April 23, 1968, p. 5, in RG 59, Central Foreign Policy Files, 1967-69, POL 23-8, GER W, 4/1/68, Box 2133, NA.

170. Ibid., 5. As a consequence, American officials would register the gradual official distancing of the GDR from the student movement in West Germany in 1969.

171. Dirk Kroegel, *Einen Anfang finden! Kurt Georg Kiesinger in der Außen und Deutschlandpolitik der Großen Koalition* (Munich: Oldenbourg, 1997), 229 f.

172. "Allies Debate Move Against Berlin Ban," *Washington Post*, April 17, 1968, p. A7.

173. The part of the Autobahn in question was the "2 ½ kilometer stretch in GDR territory between the E[a]st Berlin 'mainland' and the peninsula of West Berlin at Dreilinden (Checkpoint Bravo)." Morris, telegram to Secretary of State, "Demonstrator's Threat to Harass Berlin Access," Berlin 1270, US Mission Berlin, 16 April 1968, RG 59, Central Foreign Policy Files, 1967-69, POL 23-8, GER W, 4/1/68, Box 2133, NA.

174. Morris, telegram to Secretary of State, "SDS Committee to Involve Allies in Demonstrations," Telegram, Berlin 1325, US Mission Berlin, April 25, 1968, RG 59, Central Foreign Policy Files, 1967-69, POL 23-8, GER W, 4/1/68, Box 2133, NA.

175. Wyman, telegram to Secretary of State, "Demonstrators' Threat to Harass Berlin Access," Berlin 1283, US Mission Berlin, 18 April 1968, 2, RG 59, Central Foreign Policy Files, 1967-69, POL 23-8, GER W, 4/1/68, Box 2133, NA.

176. Morris, telegram to Secretary of State, "Demonstrator's Threat to Block Berlin Access," Berlin 1347, US Mission Berlin, April 27, 1968, RG 59, Central Foreign Policy Files, 1967-69, POL 23-8, GER W, 4/1/68, Box 2133, NA; Morris, telegram to Secretary of State, "Demonstrator's Threat to Harass Berlin Access—Proposed Reactions," Berlin 1349, US Mission Berlin, April 27, 1968, ibid.

177. Dean Rusk, telegram to US Mission Berlin, "Demonstrator's Threat to Harass Berlin Access," 154588, Department of State, April 27, 1968, RG 59, Central Foreign Policy Files, 1967-69, POL 23-8, GER W, 4/1/68, Box 2133, NA.

178. Edward Fried, memo to Walt Rostow, "Berlin," The White House, April 29, 1968, NSF, Country File Germany, Memos, vol. 15, 3/68-8/68, Box 189, LBJL.

179. Wyman, telegram to Secretary of State, "Demonstrator's Threat to Harass Berlin Access," Berlin 1357, US Mission Berlin, April 29, 1968, in RG 59,

Central Foreign Policy Files, 1967–69, POL 23-8, GER W, 4/1/68, Box 2133, NA; CIA, "Central Intelligence Bulletin," CIA-RDP79T00975A011100020001-5, April 30, 1968, p. 2–3, in CREST, NA.

180. See "Allies Impose Curbs to Deter West Berlin Leftists," *New York Times*, September 20, 1968, p. 14.

181. Wyman, telegram to Department of State, "Free University Unrest continues," Berlin 1807, US Mission Berlin, June 29, 1968, p. 2, in RG 59, Central Foreign Policy Files, 1967–69, EDU 9, GER W, 1/1/68, Box 344, NA.

182. Morris, telegram to Secretary of State, "Demonstration against 'Berlin Justice,'" Berlin 2617, US Mission Berlin, November 4, 1968, in RG 59, Central Foreign Policy Files, 1967–69, POL 23-8, GER B, 1968, Box 2109, NA.

183. Morris, telegram to Secretary of State, "Assessment of Berlin Protest Movement," Berlin 2628, US Mission Berlin, November 6, 1968, p. 2, in RG 59, Central Foreign Policy Files, 1967–69, POL 23-8, GER B, 1968, Box 2109, NA.

184. Morris, telegram to Secretary of State, "January 18 Demonstrations," Berlin 0066, US Mission Berlin, January 20, 1969; Klein, telegram to Secretary of State, "Student Unrest at Free University," Berlin 0096, US Mission Berlin, January 24, 1969, both in RG 59, Central Foreign Policy Files, 1967–69, POL 23-8, GER B, 1968, Box 2109, NA.

185. Morris, telegram to Secretary of State, "Student Unrest," Berlin 110, US Mission Berlin, January 28, 1969, p. 2, in RG 59, Central Foreign Policy Files, 1967–69, POL 23-8, GER B, 1968, Box 2109, NA.

186. See, for example, Morris, telegram to Secretary of State, "Arson Attack on American Memorial Library," Berlin 0451, US Mission Berlin, March 10, 1969, in RG 59, Central Foreign Policy Files, 1967–69, POL 23-8, GER B, 1968, Box 2109, NA.

187. Michael Baumann, *Wie alles anfing* (Frankfurt: Sozialistische Verlagsauslieferung, 1976), 47; "Vernehmungsprotokoll des Beschuldigten Michael Baumann," Ministerium für Staatssicherheit, November 26, 1973, pp. 1–5, in RAF-Sammlung (1. Generation), Akte Michael Baumann: Personenblatt und Dossier zu Baumann; Vernehmungsprotokoll vom 28.11.1973. 1973, MfS 73/028, HIS.

188. Klein, airgram to Department of State, "Student Strike at Berlin Engineering Academies," A-268, US Mission Berlin, June 6, 1969, p. 3, in RG 59, Central Foreign Policy Files, 1967–69, POL 13-2, GER W, 1/1/69, Box 2126, NA.

189. Morris, airgram to Department of State, "Bombings and Bombing Threats in West Berlin," A-551, US Mission Berlin, December 10, 1969, in RG 59, Central Foreign Policy Files, 1967–69, POL 23-8, GER W, 9/1/69, Box 2133, NA.

190. Petra Gödde, "Macht im Spiegel der Geschlechter und Rassenbeziehungen: US-Soldaten und die deutsche Bevölkerung," in Junker, *USA und Deutschland*, 1:785–94.

191. For an overview, see Detlef Junker and Thomas Maulucci, eds., *GIs in Germany: The Social, Economic, Military, and Political History of the American Military Presence* (New York: Cambridge University Press, forthcoming 2009).

192. Lt. Col. Billy Arthur, quoted in Henrik Bering, *Outpost Berlin. The History of the American Military Forces in Berlin, 1945–1994* (Chicago: Edition Q, 1995), 220.

193. Morris, telegram to American Embassy Copenhagen, "Assistance to Military Deserters," Berlin 568, US Mission Berlin, October 3, 1967 (?), in RG 59, Central Foreign Policy Files, 1967–69, DEF 9-3 US, 11/1/67, Box 1666, NA.

194. "For the first time strong racial appeals were made to negro soldiers. Also new was exhortation to all soldiers to desert rather than fight." Manbey, telegram to Department of State, "October 21 Demonstrations," Priority 2942, American Consulate Frankfurt, October 22, 1967, in RG 59, Central Foreign Policy Files, 1967-69, POL 13-2, GER W, 1/1/67, Box 2125, NA.

195. Johnstone, telegram to Secretary of State, "Anti-Vietnam Posters and Leaflets," Frankfurt 5266, American Consulate Frankfurt, January 23, 1968, in RG 59, Central Foreign Policy Files, 1967–69, POL 23-8, GER W, 1/1/68, Box 2133, NA.

196. Bernd Debusmann, "Girls Induce GIs to Desert," *Washington Post*, May 23, 1968, p. H1.

197. Ibid.

198. George McGhee, telegram to Secretary of State, "Student Demonstrations," Priority 6992, Bonn 8206, American Embassy Bonn, February 10, 1968, p. 4.

199. George McGhee, telegram to US Mission Berlin, "Solicitation to Desert," Bonn 10225, American Embassy Bonn, February 29, 1968, pp. 1, 5, in RG 59, Central Foreign Policy Files, 1967–69, DEF 9-3 US, 3/1/68, Box 1666, NA.

200. "On the basis of all the facts available to the Embassy, however, it is concluded that no significant organization or 'escape route' now exists here." In Tyler, airgram to Department of State, "Alleged Amsterdam Desertion Route," A-30, American Embassy The Hague, July 13, 1967, in RG 59, Central Foreign Policy Files, 1967–69, DEF 9-3 US, 7/1/67, Box 1666, NA.

201. Thomas Hughes to Secretary of State, "Attempts to Attract American Deserters to Sweden Relatively Ineffective," Intelligence Note, 271, Department of State, Director of Intelligence and Research, April 15, 1968, 1, in RG 59, Central Foreign Policy Files, 1967–69, DEF 9-3 US, 3/1/68, Box 1666, NA.

202. Ibid., 2.

203. George McGhee, telegram to USAREUR, "Desertion Campaign," Bonn 11698, American Embassy Bonn, May 7, 1968, p. 1, in RG 59, Central Foreign Policy Files, 1967–69, DEF 9-3 US, 5/1/68, Box 1667, NA.

204. Johnstone, telegram to Secretary of State, "Desertion Campaign," Frankfurt 8041, American Consulate Frankfurt, May 9, 1968, 2, in RG 59, Central Foreign Policy Files, 1967–69, DEF 9-3 US, 5/1/68, Box 1667, NA. For Baden-Württemberg, see Bruce Lancaster, telegram to American Embassy Bonn, "Desertion Campaign," Stuttgart 470, American Consulate Stuttgart, May 8, 1968.

205. Kraushaar, *1968*, 143 f.

206. Creel, teletram to American Embassy Bonn, "Desertion Campaign," Munich 829, American Consulate Munich, May 9, 1968, p. 2, in RG 59, Central Foreign Policy Files, 1967–69, DEF 9-3 US, 5/1/68, Box 1667, NA.

207. Goodman, telegram to Secretary of State, "Bremerhaven Easter March Marred by Disorderly Demonstrations US Army Headquarters," Bremen 198, American Consulate Bremen, April 13, 1968, p. 3, in RG 59, Central Foreign Policy Files, 1967–69, POL 23-8, GER W, 4/1/68, Box 2133, NA.

306 NOTES TO CHAPTER 5

208. Fessenden, telegram to USAREUR, "Demarche to FonOff on German Protection of US Forces Installations and Personnel," Bonn 11016, American Embassy Bonn, April 19, 1968, in RG 59, Central Foreign Policy Files, 1967–69, POL 23-8, GER W, 4/1/68, Box 2133, NA.

209. Jennings Randolph, telegram to Dean Rusk, Secretary of State, U.S. Senate, April 18, 1968, in RG 59, Central Foreign Policy Files, 1967–69, DEF 6, US, 1/1/68, Box 1613, NA.

210. United States Information Agency Office of Policy & Research, "The Psychological Environment For U.S. Bases Abroad," Report, March 26, 1968, in RG 306, Records of the U.S. Information Agency, Office of Research, Special Reports, 1964–82, S-16-68, Box 4, NA.

211. See, for example, the detailed listing of student activities in Commander-in-Chief (CINC) U.S. Army, Europe, Heidelberg, message to RUEOJFA/ DIA Washington, D.C., "USAEUR Counterintelligence Summary Cable No. 27/68 Demonstrations (U)," 1414, May 14, 1968, p. 3.

212. Jack Wagstaff, "Notice of Possible Demonstrations," USAEUR Heidelberg, Brigadier General, USA / Community Leader, May 1968, in ZA-IIa, 20.2, Archive and Special Collections, University of Heidelberg, Heidelberg.

213. Creel, telegram to American Embassy Bonn, "Desertion Campaign," Munich 824, American Consulate Munich, May 7, 1968, 2, in RG 59, Central Foreign Policy Files, 1967–69, DEF 9-3 US, 5/1/68, Box 1667, NA.

214. Morris, airgram to Department of State, "Solicitation to Desert," A-520, US Mission Berlin, March 29, 1968, in RG 59, Central Foreign Policy Files, 1967–69, DEF 9-3 US, 3/1/68, Box 1666, NA.

215. Morris, telegram to American Embassy Paris, "French Delay on Two Berlin Issues," Berlin 1791, US Mission Berlin, June 26, 1968; Henry Cabot Lodge, telegram to Secretary of State, "French Delay on Two Berlin Issues," Bonn 14039, American Embassy Bonn, July 2, 1968, both in in RG 59, Central Foreign Policy Files, 1967–69, DEF 9-3 US, 6/1/68, Box 1667, NA.

216. "Allies Impose Curbs to Deter West Berlin Leftists," *New York Times*, September 20, 1968, p. 14.

217. Goodman, airgram to Department of State, "Court Acquits Student of Attempt to Induce American Soldiers to Desert - Holds Evidence Insufficient and Law Inapplicable to Viet-Nam," A-48, American Consulate Bremen, March 26, 1969, p. 1, in RG 59, Central Foreign Policy Files, 1967–69, POL 15-3, GER W, 1/1/67, Box 2131, NA.

218. The lawyer for the defense in this trial was Heinrich Hannover. Ibid., 2.

219. Department of the Army Assistant Chief of Staff for Intelligence to Carl Wallace, Special Assistant to the Secretary of Defense, "Counterintelligence Study "Revolutionary Protest Movements", 1969, L-3 f., in Nixon Papers, White House Confidential File (hereafter WHCF), Staff Member and Office Files, John Dean: Subject File: Demonstrations and Domestic Intelligence, Army, Box 78, NA.

220. See chapter 4.

221. Jessica Gienow-Hecht, "Die amerikanische Kulturpolitik in der Bundesrepublik, 1949–1968," in Junker, *USA und Deutschland*, 1:615.

222. Frank Schumacher, *Kalter Krieg und Propaganda: Die USA, der Kampf um die Weltmeinung und die ideelle Westbindung der Bundesrepublik Deutsch-*

land, 1945–1955 (Trier: WVT, 2000); Jessica Gienow-Hecht, *Transmission Impossible. American Journalism as Cultural Diplomacy in Postwar Germany 1945–1955* (Baton Rouge: Lousiana State University Press, 1999); Michael Hochgeschwender, *Freiheit in der Offensive? Der Kongreß für kulturelle Freiheit und die Deutschen* (Munich: Oldenbourg, 1998), passim; Manuela Aguilar, *Cultural Diplomacy and Foreign Policy: German-American Relations, 1955–1968* (New York: Peter Lang, 1996). For an organizational history of the USIS in West Germany, see Thomas Klöckner, *Public Diplomacy: Auswärtige Informations und Kulturpolitik der USA. Strukturanalyse der Organisation und Strategien der USIA und USIS in Deutschland* (Baden-Baden: Nomos, 1993); see also Holger Ohmstedt, "Von der Propaganda zur Public Diplomacy: Die Selbstdarstellung der Vereinigten Staaten von Amerika im Ausland vom Ersten Weltkrieg bis zum Ende des Krieges," Ph.D. diss., University of Munich, 1993.

223. Gienow-Hecht, "Die amerikanische Kulturpolitik in der Bundesrepublik, 616 f..; Maritta Hein-Kremer, *Die Amerikanische Kulturoffensive: Gründung und Entwicklung der amerikanischen Information Centers in Westdeutschland und West-Berlin, 1945–1955* (Weimar: Böhlau, 1996); Axel Schildt, "Die USA als 'Kulturnation'. Zur Bedeutung der Amerikahäuser in den 1950er Jahren," in Alf Lüdtke et al., eds., *Amerikanisierung. Traum und Alptraum im Deutschland des 20. Jahrhunderts* (Stuttgart: Steiner, 1996), 257–69.

224. For the U.S. information campaign directed at West Germany in connection with the war in Vietnam, see Wilfried Mausbach, "'A Test Case for the Free World': Amerikanische Vietnam-Informationspolitik in Deutschland," unpublished paper, delivered at the 24th Annual Conference of the German Studies Association, Section "Constructing Identity. Cold War Policies and the Promotion of Community in German-American Relations, 1950–1970, Houston, Texas, October 5–8, 2000.

225. Fritz Stern, "German Young Elites," Report prepared for the Conference on European Youth and Young Leaders, Airlie House, May 14–15, 1967, January 9, 1967, p. 31, in Aides Files, Harry McPherson, European Youth and Young Leaders, Box 23 (1518), LBJL.

226. Tilman Fichter and Siegward Lönnendonker, *Macht und Ohnmacht der Studenten. Kleine Geschichte des SDS*, 2nd ed. (Hamburg: Rotbuch, 1998), 122.

227. See the reply of U.S. commandant in Berlin, Gen. John Franklin to FU President Hans-Joachim Lieber's letter from February 9, 1966, in ibid., 265.

228. Johnstone, telegram to Secretary of State, "SDS Demonstration against U.S. Vietnam Policy," Priority 2671, American Consulate Frankfurt, September 7, 1967, p. 2, in RG 59, Central Foreign Policy Files, 1967–69, POL 13-2, GER W, 1/1/67, Box 2125, NA. See also David Binder, "German Leftists Split on Tactics," *New York Times*, September 10, 1967, p. 30; Hans Gresmann, "Ein Hauch von Revolution -- Der 'rote' Rudi stürmte das Frankfurter Amerikahaus. Rebellen mit Sinn für Publicity," in *Die Zeit*, September 15, 1967, p. 2; Wolfgang Kraushaar, ed., *Frankfurter Schule und Studentenbewegung: Von der Flaschenpost zum Molotowcocktail, 1946–1995*, 3 vols. (Frankfurt am Main: Rogner and Bernhard, 1998), 1:270 f.

229. Ibid., 3. Johnstone, telegram to Secretary of State, "Assessment of Amerika Haus Program on Vietnam," 2677, American Consulate Frankfurt, Septem-

ber 9, 1967, in RG 59, Central Foreign Policy Files, 1967–69, POL 13-2, GER W, 1/1/67, Box 2125, NA.

230. Ellison, airgram to Department of State, "Con Gen receives Pacifist Tomatoe and Egg Shower for Christmas," A-53, American Consulate Bremen, January 3, 1968, in RG 59, Central Foreign Policy Files, 1967–69, POL 23-8, GER W, 1/1/68, Box 2133, NA.

231. Creel, telegram to Secretary of State, "Physical Damage to Con Gen Building," 489, American Consulate Munich, January 10, 1968, in RG 59, Central Foreign Policy Files, 1967–69, POL 23-8, GER W, 1/1/68, Box 2133, NA.

232. Johnstone, telegram to Secretary of State, "Anti-Vietnam Demonstrations in Frankfurt," Frankfurt 5643, American Consulate Frankfurt, February 6, 1968, 2, in RG 59, Central Foreign Policy Files, 1967–69, POL 23-8, GER W, 1/1/68, Box 2133, NA.

233. Ibid., 7.

234. George McGhee, telegram to Secretary of State, "America Houses—Targets of Student Demonstrations," 8032, American Embassy Bonn, February 6, 1968, 1, in RG 59, Central Foreign Policy Files, 1967-69, POL 23-8, GER W, 1/1/68, Box 2133, NA.

235. Johnstone to American Embassy Bonn, "Student Demonstrations," Telegram, Frankfurt 5773, American Consulate Frankfurt, February 9, 1968, 2, in RG 59, Central Foreign Policy Files, 1967–69, POL 23-8, GER W, 1/1/68, Box 2133, NA, 7f.

236. George McGhee, telegram to Secretary of State, "Student Demonstrations," Priority 6992, Bonn 8206, American Embassy Bonn, February 10, 1968, p. 3, in RG 59, Central Foreign Policy Files, 1967–69, POL 23-8, GER W, 1/1/68, Box 2133, NA.

237. George McGhee, telegram to American Consulate Frankfurt, "Compensation for Damage to US Buildings as Result of Demonstrations or Vandalism," 7598, American Embassy Bonn, March 26, 1968, p. 2, in RG 59, Central Foreign Policy Files, 1967–69, POL 23-8, GER W, 1/1/68, Box 2133, NA. George McGhee, telegram to Secretary of State, "Damage to US Buildings in the FRG," 7524, American Embassy Bonn, March 20, 1968, 1f. in RG 59, Central Foreign Policy Files, 1967–69, POL 23-8, GER W, 1/1/68, Box 2133, NA.

238. Morris, airgram to Department of State, "Security Lessons Learned During March 23 Demonstration Against *Amerika Haus*," A-521, US Mission Berlin, March 29, 1968, in RG 59, Central Foreign Policy Files, 1967-69, POL 23-8, GER W, 1/1/68, Box 2133, NA.

239. Lodge to Secretary of State, Telegram, Bonn 19822, American Embassy Bonn, November 27, 1968, in RG 59, Central Foreign Policy Files, 1967–69, POL 23-8, GER W, 5/1/68, Box 2133, NA.

240. Kidd, telegram to American Embassy Bonn, "Report of Minor Incident," Hamburg 1385, American Consulate Hamburg, December 25, 1968; idem, telegram to American Embassy Bonn, "Subsequent Report of Minor Incident," Hamburg 1387, American Consulate Hamburg, December 30, 1968, in RG 59, Central Foreign Policy Files, 1967–69, POL 23-8, GER W, 5/1/68, Box 2133, NA.

241. Max Horkheimer, "Amerika heute im Bewußtsein der Deutschen: Zum Problem der Verständigung," *Diskus - Frankfurter Studentenzeitung*, June 1967, p. 10, quoted in Kraushaar, *Frankfurter Schule und Studentenbewegung*, 1:252 f. [my translation].

CHAPTER 6
STUDENT PROTEST AND INTERNATIONAL RELATIONS

1. Dean Rusk, telegram to all diplomatic posts, 170648, Department of State, May 30, 1968, p. 2, in National Security File (hereafter NSF), Files of Walt Rostow, The Likelihood of More French-style Eruptions, Box 13, Lyndon B. Johnson Library, Austin, Texas (hereafter LBJL). For a detailed estimate of the effects stemming from the student disorders for France see "The Outlook for France," National Intelligence Estimate, 22-1-1968, Director of Central Intelligence, August 28, 1968, in NSF, National Intelligence Estimates, 22, France, Box 5, LBJL.

2. Ibid.

3. Walt Rostow, memo to President, "The Likelihood of More French-style Eruptions," The White House, June 13, 1968, 2, in NSF, Files of Walt Rostow, The Likelihood of More French-style Eruptions, Box 13, LBJL.

4. Ibid.

5. Charles Bohlen, action memo, to Undersecretary of State, "Strategy for Youth Programs," Department of State, June 14, 1968, p. 1, in Bureau of Educational and Cultural Affairs, Department of State (hereafter CU), G IV, S4, 37: Youth Office: Early History, Box 161, University of Arkansas Libraries, Special Collections, Fayetteville, Arkansas (hereafter UASC).

6. "Participants in the Student Unrest Study Group," list, undated, in NSF, Intelligence File, Student Unrest, Box 3, LBJL.

7. "Generalizations on Student Unrest," p. 1, attached to Dean Rusk, airgram to all diplomatic posts, "Student Unrest," CA-10592, Department of State, September 3, 1968, in NSF, Intelligence File, Student Unrest, Box 3, LBJL.

8. Ibid., 2.

9. Ibid., 3, 4.

10. Ibid., 6.

11. "General Action Recommendations on Student Unrest," attached to Dean Rusk, airgram to all diplomatic posts, "Student Unrest," CA-10592, Department of State, September 3, 1968, p. 1, in NSF, Intelligence File, Student Unrest, Box 3, LBJL.

12. Ibid., 2.

13. "[I]t may be desirable in special circumstances quietly to call the potential power of student unrest to the attention of friendly governments in order to guide or spur them toward essential reform." See ibid.

14. Ibid., 5.

15. Ibid.

16. Thomas Hughes, research memo to Secretary of State, "Comments from the Field on Youth and Student Unrest," Office of Intelligence and Research, De-

partment of State (hereafter INR) INR-14, September 12, 1968, 3, in White House Confidential File (hereafter WHCF), WE/MC, WE 8 Youth Programs, Box 98, LBJL. For regional assessments see Department of State, "Student Unrest in Africa," airgram, September 3, 1968; "Student Violence and Attitudes in Latin America," INR working draft, Department of State, Director of Intelligence and Research, November 1968; both in NSF, Intelligence File, Student Unrest, Box 3, LBJL.

17. "Transfer to Deputy Undersecretary for Political Affairs for Policy Guidance on Reaching Youth and Potential Leaders," Foreign Affairs Manual Circular, p. 420, Department of State, July 20, 1966, in RG 59, IAYC Records, Youth Committee Papers, 1966, Box 1, U.S. National Archives II, College Park, Md. (hereafter NA).

18. Department of State, "Foreign Affairs Manual: Vol. 11—Political Affairs," POL-14, Department of State, October 3, 1966, 112.3, in RG 59, IAYC Records, Foreign Affairs Manual, Box 4, NA.

19. Ibid.

20. The chairmanship was occupied by Lucius Battle (1962–64), Harry McPherson (1964–65), U. Alexis Johnson (1965–66), Foy Kohler (1967), Charles Bohlen (1968), and Richard Federsen (1968–71).

21. Sargent Shriver, memo to all Peace Corps Representatives, "Peace Corps Relationship with Interagency Youth Committee," 1965 (undated), Peace Corps; Washington, D.C., , in Aides Files, Harry McPherson, Youth Committee, Box 18 (1415), LBJL. For reports on the active utilization of Peace Corps for local youth efforts and its consequences, see Sargent Shriver, letter to Adam Yarmolinsky, DOD, Peace Corps, Washington, D.C., August 4, 1965, in ibid.

22. Jack Vaughn, letter to Peace Corps Representatives, Peace Corps, Washington, D.C., August 18, 1966, in Aides Files, Harry McPherson, Youth Committee, Box 18 (1415), LBJL.

23. "Minutes of the Inter-Agency Youth Committee Meeting," Department of State, March 1, 1967, in RG 59, IAYC Records, IAYC Meeting, March 1, 1967, Box 1, NA; "Draft Minutes of the Inter-Agency Youth Committee Meeting," Department of State, June 15, 1967, in RG 59, IAYC Records, IAYC Meeting, June 15, 1967, Box 1, NA.

24. Martin McLaughlin, memo to Harry McPherson, "IAYC and the Vice President," April 26, 1965, p. 1, in Aides Files, Harry McPherson, Youth Committee, Box 18 (1415), LBJL. See also Harry McPherson, memo to Vice President, August 4, 1965, in ibid.

25. "Minutes of the Inter-Agency Youth Committee Meeting," Department of State, February 21, 1968, pp. 2, 4, in RG 59, IAYC Records, IAYC Meeting, February 21, 1968, Box 1, NA.

26. Ibid., 5.

27. Robert Barnett, letter to Robert Cross, Undersecretary of Political Affairs, Department of State (hereafter G/Y), "Emphasis on Youth," EA, June 20, 1968, p. 2, in RG 59, IAYC Records, IAYC Meeting, July 1, 1968, Box 1, NA.

28. "Meeting of the Inter-Agency Youth Committee," Minutes, Department of State, July 1, 1968, pp. 3–5, in WHCF, Confidential File, WE/MC, WE 8 Youth Programs, Box 98, LBJL.

29. Both documents are attached to Robert Cross, "Agenda for IAYC Meeting on July 1, 1968," Department of State, undated, in WHCF, WE/MC, WE 8 Youth Programs, Box 98, LBJL. For a response by CU, see Julian Nugent, memo to Allan Evans, INR, "Interagency Youth Committee: Report of the Subcommittee on Information," CU/ARA, March 19, 1968, in CU, G IV, S4, 37: Youth Office: Early History, Box 161, UASC.

30. "Meeting of the Inter-Agency Youth Committee," Minutes, Department of State, September 11, 1968, 2, in WHCF, WE/MC, WE 8 Youth Programs, Box 98, LBJL.

31. Robert Cross, memo to Charles Bohlen, "Working Agenda for IAYC Meeting September 11, 1968," Department of State, G/Y, September 1968, in RG 59, IAYC Records, IAYC Meeting, September 11, 1968, Box 1, NA.

32. Robert Cross, memo to Charles Bohlen, "Suggested Introduction for Discussion of Student Unrest - IAYC, September 11, 1968," Department of State, G/Y, September 1968, in RG 59, IAYC Records, IAYC Meeting, September 11, 1968, Box 1, NA.

33. Seymour Lipset, "The Possible Effects of Student Activism on International Relations," May 2, 1969, 9 f., in National Association of International Educators (NAFSA), MC 715, conference reports and papers, 1968–76, Box 178, UASC.

34. Ibid., 11.

35. Ibid.

36. Ibid., 15.

37. Ibid., 18 f.

38. "Restless Youth," Study, no. 0613/68, CIA, September 1968, in NSF, Files of Walt Rostow, Youth and Student Movement, CIA report, Box 13, LBJL.

39. Ibid., 3.

40. Ibid., 5–6.

41. Ibid., 6 f.

42. Ibid., 8.

43. Ibid., 9–12.

44. Ibid., 16–18.

45. Ibid., 2, 13.

46. Ibid., 37.

47. According to Tom Wells, Johnson cultivated a paranoia concerning communist direction or influence on the opposition to the war. See Tom Wells, *The War Within. America's Battle over Vietnam* (Berkeley: University of California Press, 1994), 205 ff.

48. Richard Helms, memo to President, November 15, 1967, in NSF, Intelligence File, U.S. Peace Groups—International Connections, Box 3, LBJL.

49. CIA, "International Connections of US Peace Groups," Study, November 15, 1967, 1, in NSF, Intelligence File, U.S. Peace Groups—International Connections, Box 3, LBJL.

50. Ibid., 16 ff. For the government's concern about the Russell tribunal, see Walt Rostow, letter to President Johnson, White House, April 25, 1967, in NSF, International Meetings / Travel File, Germany, Presidential Trip to Adenauer, 4/4, Box 14, NA; Katzenbach, telegram to American Embassy Stockholm, "Russell Tribunal," Secretary of State, Washington, April 26, 1967, in NSF, International

Meetings / Travel File, Germany, Presidential Trip to Adenauer, 2/4, Box 14, NA; Marshall Wright, memo to Walt Rostow, "Revival of the Russell 'War Crimes Tribunal,'" National Security Council, October 26, 1967, in NSF, Country File, Vietnam, 7A—Accusations of Pernicious Allied Intent, Box 97, NA. See also Wells, *The War Within*, 141–43; Ken Coates, Peter Limqueco, and Peter Weiss, eds., *Prevent the Crimes of Silence. Reports from the Sessions of the International War Crimes Tribunal Founded by Bertrand Russell* (London: Penguin Press, 1971).

51. "Other centers of student activity are Berlin, Stockholm, Tokyo, and Mexico City," in ibid., 11 f. The "US Campaign" is also listed as one of those bases. See Appendix B, 6.

52. Ibid., 12–15.

53. Ibid., 2.

54. Walt Rostow memo to President Johnson, The White House, November 16, 1967, in NSF, Country File, Vietnam, Acc. of Pern. Allied Intent, Public Dem. [1 of 2], Box 97, LBJL. The president's approval is noted on the document.

55. Copies of the article eventually even made it back to Walter Rostow's desk through an intermediary of Tom Lambert, the journalist at the *Los Angeles Times*' Washington bureau whom he had suggested for the purpose of fulfilling the president's objective. The copies were accompanied by this message: "attached clippings on dr. dellinger and his cohorts. [S]tory should make some readers wonder. Thanks much for your help." See Tom Lambert, message, December 5, 1967, doc. 26, in NSF, Country File, Vietnam, Acc. of Pern. Allied Intent, Public Dem. [1 of 2], Box 97, LBJL.

56. Leonard Marks, memo to Walt Rostow, White House, United States Information Agency (hereafter USIA), November 16, 1967, in NSF, Country File, Vietnam, Acc. of Pern. Allied Intent, Public Dem. [1 of 2], Box 97, LBJL.

57. MACV Intelligence to, "VC on Peace Groups," Report, December 12, 1967, in NSF, Country File, Vietnam, Acc. of Pern. Allied Intent, Public Dem. [1 of 2], Box 97, LBJL.

58. Walt Rostow, memo to President, March 3, 1968, in NSF, Intelligence File, U.S. Peace Groups - International Connections, Box 3, LBJL. See also Richard Helms, "International Connections of US Peace Groups - III," SC-07248-68, February 28, 1968, in NSF, Intelligence File, U.S. Peace Groups - International Connections, Box 3, LBJL. Regrettably, Helms's second report (SC-05701-67) from December 21, 1967, has been misplaced according to the LBJL.

59. "Restless Youth," Study, 0613/68, CIA, September 1968, p. 21.

60. Ibid., 19.

61. Ibid., 14.

62. Ibid., 14 f.

63. Ibid., 8.

64. Ibid., iii.

65. Ibid., 37.

66. Ibid., 39.

67. The White House, "Cabinet Meeting of September 18, 1968," 4 f., in Cabinet Meeting 9/18/1968 [1 of 3], Box 15, LBJL.

68. Ibid.

69. Cited in Wells, *The War Within*, 209. Wells quotes from oral interviews that he conducted with these people.

70. People discarding theories of substantial communist interference were, for example, Paul Warnke and Ramsey Clark. All citations quoted in ibid., 210 f.

71. "The Student Explosion" chart, cabinet meeting, attachment A, CIA; "Escalating Tactics and Techniques of Youthful Activists," chart, cabinet meeting, attachment A, CIA, in Cabinet Papers, Cabinet Meeting 9/18/1968 [1 of 3], 15, LBJL. The charts reproduced on pages 210 and 211 have been digitally enhanced, but the changes do not alter in any substantial way the information presented in each figure.

72. See, for example, the reports by Charles Bohlen to Vice President Humphrey and the report by Ambassador at Large George McGhee to the President: Charles Bohlen, memo to Hubert Humphrey, "The U.S. Effort: Analysis of Embassy Appraisals," Department of State, Deputy Undersecretary for Political Affairs, November 11, 1968, in RG 59, IAYC Records, Youth Committee Papers, 1968, Box 1, NA; George McGhee, report to President Johnson, "World Student Unrest," George McGhee: Writings, Vol. 2, 1960–1969, pp. 332–42, 1968, in George McGhee Papers: 2001 Accession, I, 2, 1, Georgetown University Library, Special Collections, Washington, D.C. (hereafter GUL).

73. George McGhee to Secretary of State, "Report of the Student Unrest Study Group," Information Memorandum, Department of State, Ambassador at Large, January 17, 1969, 2, in NSF, Intelligence File, Student Unrest, Box 3, LBJL.

74. Ibid., 6.

75. Ibid., 7.

76. Ibid., 13.

77. The idea of special training for DOS officers on youth movements and student protest at home and abroad in week-long seminars had already been voiced in October 1968. See Leonard Sandman, memo to Labor and Social Affairs Adviser, NEA, "Proposal to Establish Training Program on Youth," October 24, 1968, in RG 59, IAYC Records, Youth Committee Papers, 1968, Box 1, NA.

78. George McGhee to Secretary of State, "Report of the Student Unrest Study Group," January 17, 1969, p. 20.

79. For an organizational history of USIS in West Germany, see Klöckner, *Public Diplomacy*, passim; Ohmstedt, *Von der Propaganda zur Public Diplomacy*, passim. See also chapter 5.

80. Hillenbrand, airgram to Department of State, "Annual Youth Activities Report," A-73, American Embassy Bonn, July 19, 1967, p. 11, in RG 59, Central Foreign Policy Files, 1967–69, EDX, GER W, 1/1/67, Box 363, NA.

81. Fritz Stern, "German Young Elites," Report for the Conference on European Youth and Young Leaders, Airlie House, May 14–15, 1967, January 9, 1967, p. 42, in Aides Files, Harry McPherson, European Youth and Young Leaders, Box 23 (1518), LBJL.

82. Morris, airgram to Department of State, "Morale in West Berlin—Psychological and Cultural Factors," A-252, U.S. Mission Berlin, November 17, 1967, p. 4, in RG 59, Central Foreign Policy Files, 1967-69, EDU GER B, 1/1/67, Box 344, NA.

83. Bruce Lancaster, airgram to Department of State, "Germany's Icono-clasts—And Some of Our Own," A-85, American Consulate Stuttgart, February 7, 1968, 1f., in RG 59, Central Foreign Policy Files, 1967–69, POL 13-2, GER W, 1/1/68, Box 2125, NA.

84. Ibid., 2.

85. Bruce Lancaster, airgram to Department of State, "Stuttgart's Revamped Youth Program," A-89, American Consulate Stuttgart, February 12, 1968, in RG 59, Central Foreign Policy Files, 1967–69, EDX, GER W, 1/1/67, Box 363, NA.

86. "Interestingly enough," according to the report, "in this case its is the youth who are less unfavorable to the U.S. with 48 per cent in West Germany opposed to U.S. policy in Viet-Nam compared to 62 per cent among Germans over 25." See USIA, Office of Policy & Research, "Is There a Generation Gap in Western Europe?" report, April 16, 1968, p. 2, in RG 306, USIA Records, Office of Research, Special Reports, 1964–82, S-19-68, Box 4, NA.

87. Ibid., 6.

88. Ibid., 2.

89. Ibid., 3.

90. Henry Cabot Lodge, airgram to Department of State, "Youth in Country Programming," A-1394, American Embassy Bonn, May 31, 1968, p. 1, in RG 59, Central Foreign Policy Files, 1967-69, EDX, GER W, 1/1/67, Box 363, NA.

91. Ibid., 2.

92. Ibid., 3.

93. Ibid., 4.

94. Ibid., 5.

95. American Embassy Bonn, airgram to Department of State, "Student Un-rest," A-1537, July 8, 1968, p. 2, in RG 59, Central Foreign Policy Files, 1967–69, POL 13-2, GER W, 5/1/68, Box 2126, NA.

96. Henry Cabot Lodge, airgram to Department of State, Student Unrest Group, "Youth Report: German Youth Organizations," A-1697, American Em-bassy Bonn, August 19, 1968; Henry Cabot Lodge, airgram to Department of State, "Youth Report: German Student Organizations," A-1769, American Em-bassy Bonn, September 6, 1968; both in RG 59, Central Foreign Policy Files, 1967–69, POL 13-2, GER W, 5/1/68, Box 2126, NA.

97. Henry Cabot Lodge, airgram to Department of State, Student Unrest Group, "Embassy Comments and Recommendations on Refair," A-1833, Ameri-can Embassy Bonn, September 25, 1968, p. 2, in RG 59, Central Foreign Policy Files, 1967–69, POL 13-2, GER W, 5/1/68, Box 2126, NA.

98. The agenda is attached to Russell Fessenden, airgram to Department of State, "Annual Youth Report - Embassy Programs," A-1990, American Embassy Bonn, November 7, 1968, pp. 10–12, in RG 59, Central Foreign Policy Files, 1967–69, POL 13-2, GER W, 5/1/68, Box 2126, NA.

99. Ibid., 9.

100. Kenneth Rush, airgram to Department of State, "Youth Officer's Meeting in Berlin," A-1221, American Embassy Bonn, November 17, 1970, pp. 1–2, in CU, IV, 5, 10: Youth Affairs—General, 1962–1970 (1 of 2), Box 162, UASC. For the specifics of the reporting according to age breakdowns and attitudes, see the attached agenda. Ibid., 6–8.

101. Ibid., 3.

102. See, for example, Russell Fessenden, airgram, "Impact of Youth and the U.S. National Interest - Phase II," A-1355, Bonn, December 18, 1970, in RG 59, IAYC Records, CA 6008, Replies and Circular Inquiry, Dec 2, 1970, Box 2, NA.

103. Kenneth Rush, letter to Elliot Richardson, Undersecretary of State, American Embassy Bonn, December 12, 1970, p. 3, in RG 59, Records of Ambassador Kenneth Rush, 1969–74, LOT 74 D430, Chrons, Box 15, NA.

104. For overall American cultural exchange efforts, see Frank Ninkovich, *Diplomacy of Ideas: U S. Foreign Policy and Cultural Relations, 1938–1950* Chicago: Imprint Publications, 2001); Volker Berghahn, *America and the Intellectual Cold Wars in Europe: Shepard Stone between Philanthropy, Academy, and Diplomacy* (Princeton: Princeton University Press, 2001); Liping Bu, *Making the World Like Us: Education, Cultural Expansion, and the American Century* (Westport, Conn.: Praeger, 2003).

105. Oliver Schmidt, "A Civil Empire by Co-Optation: German-American Exchange Programs as Cultural Diplomacy, 1945–1961." Ph.D. diss., Harvard University, 2000, p. 463. For an overview and detailed report on the German-American dimension, see the following: Karl-Heinz Füssl, "Between Elitism and Educational Reform. German-American Exchange Programs, 1945–1970," in Detlef Junker et al., eds., *The United States and Germany in the Era of the Cold War. A Handbook*, 2 vols. (New York: Cambridge University Press, 2004), 1:409–16; Ulrich Littmann, *Partners, Distant and Close: Notes and Footnotes on Academic Mobility between Germany and the United States of America (1923–1993)* (Bonn: DAAD, 1997).

106. For the Fulbright program, see Walter Johnson and Francis James Colligan, *The Fulbright Program. A History* (Chicago: University of Chicago Press, 1965); Anne Rogers Devereux, George Liston Seay, and United States Information Agency, *Minds Without Borders: Educational and Cultural Exchange in the Twenty-First Century: The Fulbright Fortieth Anniversary Washington Conference Proceedings* (Washington, DC: Smithsonian Institution, 1986); Arthur Power Dudden and Russell Rowe Dynes, *The Fulbright Experience, 1946–1986: Encounters and Transformations* (New Brunswick, NJ: Transaction Books, 1987); Richard T. Arndt and David Lee Rubin, *The Fulbright Difference, 1948–1992* (New Brunswick, N.J.: Transaction Publishers, 1993).

107. For the opinion polls, see Füssl, "Between Elitism and Educational Reform," 415 f.

108. Edward Sims, telegram to Department of State, "U.S. German Exchange Programs," American Consulate Munich, June 4, 1965, 3 f., in CU, IX, 7, p. 6: CU Program in West Germany and Berlin (Briefing Papers), 1965, Box 240, UASC.

109. Others include Michael Vester and Karl-Dietrich Wolff. See chapters 1 and 4.

110. Littmann, for example, notes a diffusion of ideas from American universities to their study centers in West Germany, as from the University of Berkeley to its affiliate at the University of Göttingen. See Littmann, *Partners, Distant and Close*, 150 f.

111. "Notes on Mr. Kohler's Summary," Department of State, 1967, May, 1, in RG 59, IAYC Records, Airlie Conference on European Youth, Box 3, NA.

112. Ibid.

113. "European Youth and Young Leaders: Notes on a Conference at Airlie House, May 14–15, 1967," Department of State, July 15, 1967, p. 10.

114. "Notes on Mr. Kohler's Summary," Department of State, 1967, May, 1.

115. George McGhee, airgram to Department of State, "Educational and Cultural Exchange: Annual Report for Germany for Fiscal Year 1966—July 1965 to June 1966," A-356, American Embassy Bonn, September 19, 1966, 1, in CU, Gr. 16, 17: Germany (Fed. Rep.), 1963–1970, Box 317, UASC.

116. Ibid., 3, 32.

117. Ibid.

118. Ibid., 2, 5.

119. Karl-Heinz Füssl, "Between Elitism and Educational Reform," in Junker, *USA and Germany*, 1:415. For an insider's view on government sponsored German-American exchange programs from 1965–75, see Littmann, *Partners, Distant and Close*, 148–82.

120. Littmann, *Partners, Distant and Close*, 150.

121. [Fulbright grantees], "Letter to President Johnson," telegram, July 12, 1967, in National Security-Defense, EX ND 19 / CO 312, ND 19 / CO 312, 6/ 29/67-7/12/67, Box 227, LBJL.

122. Charles Frankel, report to Nicholas Katzenbach, Department of State, "Weekly Report of CU Activities," CU, August 25, 1967, p. 3, in CU, I, 4, 5: Weekly Report (Frankel to Katzenbach), 1966–67, Box 21, UASC; see also Littmann, *Partners, Distant and Close*, 151 f.

123. George McGhee, airgram to Department of State, "Educational and Cultural Exchange: Annual Report for Germany For Fiscal Year 1967—July 1966 to June 1967," A-352, American Embassy Bonn, September 12, 1967, p. 1, in CU, Gr. 16, 17: Germany (Fed. Rep.), 1963–1970, Box 317, UASC.

124. Ibid., 2.

125. Ibid., 34.

126. Henry Cabot Lodge, airgram to Department of State, "Educational and Cultural Exchange: Annual Report for Germany for fiscal year July 1, 1967–June 30, 1968," A-1701, American Embassy Bonn, August 20, 1968, p. 2, in CU, Gr. 16, 17: Germany (Fed. Rep.), 1963–1970, Box 317, UASC.

127. Ibid., 7.

128. Weiss, airgram to Department of State, "Educational and Cultural Exchange: Annual Report for Germany for Fiscal Year July 1, 1968–June 30, 1969," A-898, American Embassy Bonn, September 9, 1969, p. 5, in CU, Gr. 16, 17: Germany (Fed. Rep.), 1963–1970, Box 317, UASC.

129. Ibid., 6f.

130. Ibid., 7.

131. Kenneth Rush, airgram to Department of State, "Educational and Cultural Exchange: Annual Report for Germany for Fiscal Year July 1, 1969–June 30, 1970," A-1109, American Embassy Bonn, October 13, 1969, p. 2, in CU, Gr. 16, 17: Germany (Fed. Rep.), 1963–1970, Box 317, UASC.

132. Kenneth Rush, "Educational and Cultural Exchange: Annual Report for Germany for Fiscal Year July 1, 1969–June 30, 1970," p. 1.

133. Ibid., 2, 7. For publications by Erwin Scheuch critical of the student protests, see *Die Wiedertäufer der Wohlstandsgesellschaft: Eine Kritische Untersuchung der 'Neuen Linken' und ihrer Dogmen* (Cologne: Markus Verlag, 1968); idem, "Soziologische Aspekte der Unruhe unter den Studenten," *Aus Politik und Zeitgeschichte* 36 (1968): 1–26.

134. Kenneth Rush, "Educational and Cultural Exchange,:", 8.

135. Ibid., 3–4, 5, 16.

136. Ibid., 10.

137. Department of State, Policy Planning Council, "U.S.-German Relations," November 1967, p. 4, in NSF, Country File, Germany, Box 188, Folder Germany Vol. XIV, Memos, 8/67–2/68, Box 150a, LBJL.

138. Department of State Policy Planning Council, "Where Can the Germans Go?" draft, December 19, 1967, p. 3f., in NSF, Country File, Germany, Memos, vol. 14, 8/67–2/68, Box 188, LBJL.

139. Ibid., 9.

140. Ibid., 10.

141. Henry Cabot Lodge, telegram to Secretary of State, "The German 'Establishment' and its Opponents," , Bonn 12722, American Embassy Bonn, May 29, 1968, p. 1, section 2 of 2, in NSF, Files of Walt Rostow, The Likelihood of More French-style Eruptions, Box 13, LBJL.

142. Russell Fessenden, airgram to Department of State, "The German New Left—A Current Look," A-334, American Embassy Bonn, April 8, 1969, p. 3, in RG 59, Central Foreign Policy Files, 1967–69, POL 13-2, GER W, 1/1/69, Box 2126, NA.

143. Ibid., 7.

144. Ibid., 12.

145. Hans A. Tuch, interview, August 4, 1989, in Foreign Affairs Oral History Collection, GUL.

146. Henry Kissinger, "Strains on the Alliance," *Foreign Affairs* 41 (January 1963): 269. For a thorough analysis see Holger Klitzing, *The Nemesis of Stability: Henry A. Kissinger's Ambivalent Relationship with Germany* (Trier: Wissenschaftlicher Verlag Trier, 2007).

147. Henry Kissinger, *Diplomacy* (New York: Simon and Schuster, 1994), 821.

148. WDR, "Politik am Morgen," radio broadcast, May 19, 1982; "Henry Kissinger: 'Besuch Reagans notwendig,'" *Berliner Morgenpost*, May 22, 1982.

149. For the "spiritual void" and "metaphysical boredom" spurring youthful unrest, see also Henry Kissinger, "Central Issues of American Foreign Policy," in idem, *American Foreign Policy: Three Essays by Henry Kissinger* (New York: W. W. Norton, 1969), 51–97.

150. Kenneth Rush, airgram to Department of State, "Amnesty for Demonstrators?" A-1116, American Embassy Bonn, November 7, 1969, in RG 59, Central Foreign Policy Files, 1967–69, POL 13-2, GER W, 1/1/69, Box 2126, NA.

151. Leo Goodman, airgram to Department of State, "Trends Among the Youth," A-173, American Consulate Bremen, December 30, 1969, 3f., in RG 59, Central Foreign Policy Files, 1967–69, POL 13-2, GER W, 1/1/69, Box 2126, NA.

152. Sherman P. Lloyd, "American Tragedy," April 6, 1971, in *Congressional Record*, 92nd Congress, 1st sess., vol. 117, no. 8, p. 10794.

153. McKinney Russell, report to USIA Washington, "Country Plan for USIS Germany," USIS Bonn, June 20, 1973, p. 20, in CU, I,2, 25: CPP, Germany [FY 1974], Box 14, UASC.

154. As annual assessments made by USIS Bonn hinted at in April 1974, there were no signs of a diminishing interest in the United States. McKinney Russell, report to USIA Washington, "Annual Assement Report," p. 43, USIS Bonn, April 3, 1974, p. 25, in CU, I,2, 22: CPP, Germany [FY 1974], Box 14, UASC.

155. Hans A. Tuch, interview, August 4, 1989, in Foreign Affairs Oral History Collection, GUL. For further USIS attempts to deal with this West German "successor generation" see idem, *Communicating with the World: U S. Public Diplomacy Overseas* (New York: St. Martin's Press, 1990), 152–60.

156. Jeffrey Herf, *War By Other Means: Soviet Power, West German Resistance, and the Battle of the Euromissiles* (New York: Free Press, 1991). See also the research project and digital archive "The Nuclear Crisis: Transatlantic Peace Politics, Rearmament, and the Second Cold War" at http://www.nuclearcrisis.org

157. USIA, "Agency's Ninth Seminar on Communication Problems," May 16, 1968 [?], p. 3, in George McGhee Papers, 10, Student Unrest, Box 6, GUL.

158. Policy Planning Council, Department of State, "Foreign Policy and the Generation Gap or Commending US Foreign Policy to American Students," August 21, 1968, in George McGhee Papers, 10, Student Unrest, Box 6, GUL.

159. Robert Cross, memo to Ambassadors and Principal Officers, Department of State, G/Y, March 1969, in RG 59, IAYC Records, Youth Committee Papers, 1969, Box 1, NA.

160. George McGhee, memo to Secretary of State, "United States Interest in World Youth," Department of State, Ambassador at Large, January 23, 1969, in RG 59, IAYC Records, Youth Committee Papers, 1969, Box 1, NA.

161. Robert Cross, memo to all IAYC members, "New Location for Youth Advisor," Department of State, C/Y, April 10, 1969, in RG 59, IAYC Records, Youth Committee Papers, 1969, Box 1, NA; Robert Cross, memo to Richard Pedersen, "IAYC Meeting," Department of State, C/Y, November 24, 1969; Richard Pedersen, letter to Richardson, CU, Department of State, December 15, 1969; both in RG 59, IAYC Records, IAYC Meeting, December 19, 1969, Box 1, NA.

162. Jack Vaughn, letter to Charles Bohlen, Peace Corps, 1968, in RG 59, IAYC Records, Youth Committee Papers, 1968, Box 1, NA.; Robert Cross, memo to Joseph Blatchford, Peace Corps, "Inter-Agency Youth Committee Meeting," Department of State, C/Y, April 28, 1969, in RG 59, IAYC Records, IAYC Meeting, May 8, 1969, Box 1, NA.

163. Edward Doherty to Department of State, C/Y, "Inter-Agency Youth Committee," Department of States, Policy Planning Council, May 7, 1969, in RG 59, IAYC Records, IAYC Meeting, May 8, 1969, Box 1, NA.

164. Ibid., 2 f.

165. William P. Rogers, airgram to all diplomatic posts, "Impact of Youth and the U.S. National Interest," CA-332, Department of State, January 19, 1970, in RG 59, IAYC Records, Youth Memos, Box 2, NA. See also Robert Cross, memo to Richard Pedersen, "Profile of Youth Program," Department of State, C/Y,{?}

June 23, 1969, in RG 59, IAYC Records, Youth Committee Papers, 1969, Box 1, NA.

166. See memo, Department of State, December 19, 1969, in RG 59, IAYC Records, IAYC Meeting, December 19, 1969, Box 1, NA.

167. Robert Cross, memo to IAYC Members, "Summary of Replies to CA-332: Re-evaluation of Youth Effects," Department of State, C/Y, June 18, 1970, in RG 59, IAYC Records, IAYC Meeting, June 23, 1970, Box 1, NA.

168. Dean Rusk, airgram to all European diplomatic and consular posts, "Student Unrest: Roundup of EUR Posts' Reporting," CA-237, Department of State, January 14, 1969, p. 3, in NSF, Intelligence File, Student Unrest, Box 3, NA.

169. Ibid., 2.

170. "Discussion Guide: Youth and Change in Europe," Bonn, June 11–13, 1969, in RG 59, IAYC Records, Conference of Youth Coordinators, 1966, 1969, Box 4, NA.

171. "Bonn Conference of Embassy and USIS Officers on Youth and Change in Europe," Conference Report, Bonn, June 11–13, 1969, Tab A, 3 f., in RG 59, IAYC Records, Conference of Youth Coordinators, 1966, 1969, Box 4, NA.

172. Ibid., Tab A, 7.

173. Ibid., Tab A, pp. 8, 5 ff.

174. "Minutes of the Inter-Agency Youth Committee Meeting," Department of State, June 23, 1970, 3 f., in RG 59, IAYC Records, IAYC Meeting, June 23, 1970, Box 1, NA.

175. See "Discussion Guide: Second European Youth Affairs Conference," Bonn, April 26–28, 1972, in RG 59, IAYC Records, IAYC 1-2, Bonn Conference, April 16–28, 1972, Box 6, NA.

176. US Representation at UN, telegram to Secretary of State, "World Youth Assembly - Evaluation," USUN 1536, July 22, 1970, p. 2, in RG 59, IAYC Records, IAYC Meeting, November 10, 1970, Box 1, NA.

177. John Irwin, airgram to all diplomatic posts, "Impact of Youth and the U.S. National Interest—Phase II," CA-6008, Department of State, December 2, 1970, 1 f., in RG 59, IAYC Records, Youth Memos, Box 2, NA. See also "Minutes of the Inter-Agency Youth Committee Meeting," Department of State, November 10, 1970, 1 f., in RG 59, IAYC Records, IAYC Meeting, November 10, 1970, Box 1, NA.

178. "Minutes of the Inter-Agency Youth Committee Meeting," Department of State, March 30, 1971, pp. 1–3, in RG 59, IAYC Records, IAYC Meeting, March 30, 1971, Box 1, NA.

179. William P. Rogers, airgram to all diplomatic posts, "IAYC Policy Decisions on International Youth Activities," CA-2347, Department of State, May 18, 1971, p. 1, in RG 59, IAYC Records, IAYC Meeting, March 30, 1971, Box 1, NA.

180. Ibid., 2.

181. U. Alexis Johnson, airgram to all diplomatic posts, "Sample Mission Approaches to Youth," CA-4057, Department of State, August 31, 1971, in RG 59, IAYC Records, Youth Memos, Box 2, NA.

182. William P. Rogers, airgram to all diplomatic posts, "1970 White House Conference on Children and Youth," CA-2481, Department of State, May 5,

1970, in RG 59, IAYC Records, Youth Memos, Box 2, NA; "Minutes of the Inter-Agency Youth Committee Meeting," to Department of State, June 26, 1970, p. 3, in RG 59, IAYC Records, IAYC Meeting, June 23, 1970, Box 1, NA.

183. Martin McLaughlin, memo to Charles Frankel, CU, "Foreign Students and the President's Task Force on International Education," Memo, CU/IAYC, September 20, 1965, in Aides Files, Harry McPherson, Youth Committee, Box 18, LBJL; Martin McLaughlin, memo to Harry McPherson, The White House, D.C. Lavergne, AID, and Adam Yarmolinsky, DOD, "IAYC Subcommittee on Foreign Students," Department of State, October 7, 1965, in ibid.; "Report of the Subcommittee to Review CU and AID Foreign Student Programs," undated, in ibid.

184. "Meeting of the Inter-Agency Youth Committee," Minutes, Department of State, September 11, 1968, p. 3, in WHCF, Confidential File, WE/MC, WE 8 Youth Programs, Box 98, LBJL.

185. Jacob Canter, memo to CU Office and Staff Directors, "Protest Activities on U.S. Campuses of Foreign Students Sponsored by CU," May 21, 1969, in CU, I, 1, p. 11: Policy Statement. Protest Activities of US Government Sponsored Foreign Students, Box 5, UASC.

186. Francis Colligan, "Interagency Policy Statement on Possible Protest Activities of U.S. Government Sponsored Foreign Students," memo, July 3, 1969, in CU, I, 1, p. 11: Policy Statement. Protest Activities of US Government Sponsored Foreign Students, Box 5, UASC.

187. Geraldine Sheehan, "The Foreign Student Presence—Implications for USG," memo, September 10, 1970, p. 1, in CU, G IV, S4, 37: Youth Office, Early History, Box 161, UASC.

188. Henry Kissinger, letter to U. Alexis Johnson, Undersecretary of State for Political Affairs, The White House, November 13, 1970, in RG 59, IAYC Records, Foreign Students in the U.S. (General), Box 4, NA; UASC; "IAYC Policy Decision on a Study of Foreign Students in the United States," Department of State, 1971, 03/30, "Proposal for Further In-Depth Study of Foreign Students in the U.S.," Department of State, C/Y, 1971, both in RG 59, IAYC Records, IAYC Meeting, March 30, 1971, Box 1, NA.

189. Jerry Inman to IAYC Members, "Revised Options Paper on Foreign Students in U.S.," Department of State, C/Y, January 4, 1972, 4 f., in RG 59, IAYC Records, IAYC Meeting, December 2, 1971, Box 1, NA.

190. Ibid., 5.

191. Ibid., 27.

192. John Irwin, memo to President Nixon, "Review on Foreign Students," Deputy Secretary of State, NSC Under Secretaries Committee, October 13, 1972; Henry Kissinger, memo to Chairman, NSC Under-Secretaries Committee, "Foreign Student Programs in the U.S.," The White House, October 31, 1972, in RG 59, IAYC Records, IAYC Meeting, December 13, 1972, Box 1, NA.

193. "Transcript of Press, Radio and Television News Briefing," Department of State, September 28, 1970, p. 3, in CU, IV, 5, 10: Youth Affairs—General, 1962–1970 (1 of 2), Box 162, UASC; "Minutes of the Inter-Agency Youth Committee Meeting," Department of State, November 10, 1970, p. 3, in RG 59, IAYC Records, IAYC Meeting, November 10, 1970, Box 1, NA.

194. For example, training took place at a Student Affairs Officers Conference held in Quito during October 8-10, 1969, which was organized by the USIA, and at an IAYC-sponsored regional conference of youth officers in Tokyo in July 1971. See Robert Amerson, letter to Donald Cook, Department of State, "Conference Report," USIA, November 25, 1969, in CU, IV, 5, 6: USIA: Youth Affairs, 1969, Box 162, UASC; Jerry Inman, memo to IAYC Members, "Summary Report of the Asian Conferences of Youth Committee Representatives held in Singapore and Tokyo," Department of State, August 5, 1971, in CU, G IV, S4, 38: Youth Exchanges, Box 161, UASC.

195. Memo, "Increasing Emphasis on Young Professionals within Agency Youth Programs," IOP, July 20, 1971, in CU, IV, 5, 5: Youth Affairs, General, Box 162, UASC.

196. Before his departure, Robert Cross had already complained about the lack of interest in the IAYC from other agencies and a serious weakening of the youth effort. See Robert Cross, memo to Richard Pedersen, "IAYC—Where It Stands," Department of State, C/Y, August 31, 1970, in RG 59, IAYC Records, IAYC Papers 1970, Box 1, NA.

197. Neil Boyer, memo to Richard Roth, CU/OPP, "Activities of the Department's Youth Office," CU/OPP, Department of State, August 30, 1973, in CU, IV, 5, 5: Youth Affairs, General, Box 162, UASC; John Richardson, memo to Acting Secretary, "Disposition of Youth Affairs Functions," 7323390, CU , Department of State, December 7, 1973, in CU, G IV, S4, 38: Youth Exchanges, Box 161, UASC; Richard Arndt, "Youth Affairs," memo, Executive Office of the President, Office of Management and Budget, April 10, 1974, in CU, IV, 5, 12: Youth Affairs, General, 1971–1973, Box 162, UASC. See also Budget Task Force Working Group on Youth Programs, memo, February 19, 1976, in CU, G IV, S4, 38: Youth Exchanges, Box 161, UASC.

198. William Macomber, "Charter of the Inter-Agency Youth Committee," Deputy Undersecretary for Management, January 11, 1973, in Thomas Bowman Papers, IAYC Charters and Annual Reports, July 1966–January 1973, p. 1, John F. Kennedy Library, Boston, Massachusetts (JFKL).

199. Chet Holifield, letter to Secretary of State, "A Bill to Create a Department of Youth Affairs," 0001512, Congress of the United States, House of Representatives, January 13, 1973, in RG 59, IAYC Records, CY 5, Youth Programs & Projects, Box 6, NA.

200. "Minutes of the Inter-Agency Youth Committee Meeting," Department of State, December 13, 1972, 3f., in RG 59, IAYC Records, IAYC Meeting, December 13, 1972, Box 1, NA.

201. "Guidelines for the Policy Analysis and Resource Allocation Study on Youth," draft outline, Department of State, December 12, 1972, p. 10, in RG 59, IAYC Records, IAYC Meeting, December 13, 1972, Box 1, NA.

202. Ibid., 6.

203. Ibid., 8. From the beginning of its existence, the IAYC had also entertained a steady relationship with the Department of State's Special Group (Counter-Insurgency, CI). See Martin McLaughlin, memo to Harry McPherson, "Counter-Insurgency," April 12, 1965, in Aides Files, Harry McPherson, Youth Committee, Box 18 (1415), LBJL.

204. "Kohl: Gerhard Schröder ist ein Anti-Amerikaner," interview with Helmut Kohl, *Die Welt*, April 3, 2003.

205. "Ein unheimliches Gefühl—Spiegel Gespräch mit Joschka Fischer," *Der Spiegel*, 21/2002, May 18, 2002, p. 32 [my translation].

206. For the concept of "soft power" see Joseph Nye, *Bound to Lead: The Changing Nature of American Power* (New York: Basic Books, 1990); idem, *Soft Power: The Means to Success in World Politics* (New York: Public Affairs, 2004).

Conclusion

1. Robert Cross, "World-Wide Student Unrest," speech, Department of State, C/Y, 1968, in RG 59, Records of ths Inter-Agency Youth Committee (hereafter IAYC Records), speeches (material), Box 5, U.S. National Archives II, College Park, Maryland (hereafter NA).

2. Akira Iriye, *Global Community: The Role of International Organizations in the Making of the Contemporary World* (Berkeley: University of California Press, 2002), 113 ff.

3. Ibid., 65, 115 ff. See also Akira Iriye, *Cultural Internationalism and World Order* (Baltimore: Johns Hopkins University Press, 1997), 156 ff.

4. Margaret E. Keck and Kathryn Sikkink, *Activists Beyond Borders: Advocacy Networks in International Politics* (Ithaca, N.Y.: Cornell University Press, 1998), 14f. See also Donatella Della Porta, Hanspeter Kriesi, and Dieter Rucht, eds., *Social Movements in a Globalizing World* (New York: St. Martin's Press, 1999); Ann Florini et al., eds., *The Third Force: The Rise of Transnational Civil Society* (Washington, D.C.: Brookings Institution Press, 2000); Jackie Smith and Hank Johnston, eds., *Globalization and Resistance: Transnational Dimensions of Social Movements* (Lanham, Md.: Rowman and Littlefield, 2002); Joe Bandy and Jackie Smith, *Coalitions Across Borders: Transnational Protest and the Neoliberal Order.* (Lanham, Md.: Rowman and Littlefield, 2005).

5. "Youth and Revolt—Depth and Diversity," INR paper, Department of State, November 17, 1967, 5 f., in RG 59, IAYC Records, IAYC Meeting, November 8, 1967, Box 1, NA.

6. The fact that worldwide student unrest was debated among the highly influential members of the Bilderberg group can be seen as ample evidence of its recognition as a major problem facing international relations and politics. See, for example, James Perkins, "Remarks at the Bilderberg Conference," April 27, 1968, in George McGhee Papers, 10, Student Unrest, Box 6, Georgetown University Library, Special Collections, Washington, D.C. (hereafter GUL); Graham Allison, "Young Americans' Attitudes Towards Foreign Policy for the 1970's," Bilderberg Meeting, April 17–19, 1970, in RG 59, IAYC Records, IAYC Meeting, June 23, 1970, Box 1, NA.

7. Albert Hemsing, Public Affairs Officer, Bonn (1964–67), oral history interview, 1989, Foreign Affairs Oral History Collection, GUL.

8. Umberto Eco, "The American Myth in Three Anti-American Generations," in his *On Literature* (Orlando, Fla.: Harcourt, 2004), 255–71, here 269f.

9. For a detailed analysis of the transnational image of the United States, see Martin Klimke, "America," in Akira Iriye and Pierre Saunier, eds., *The Palgrave Dictionary of Transnational History* (London: Palgrave Macmillan, 2009), 33–36.

10. "France's '68ers Earn a Right Bashing," *The Australian*, May 1, 2007. For an introduction into the extensive literature on the events of the French May of 1968, see Ingrid Gilcher-Holtey, "France," in Martin Klimke and Joachim Scharloth, eds., *1968 in Europe: A History of Protest and Activism, 1956–1977* (New York: Palgrave Macmillan, 2008), 111–24.

11. "Poland Restores Nationality to 'Forgotten' Jews," *European Jewish Press*, March 9, 2008. For an introduction into the Polish case, see Stefan Garsztecki, "Poland," in Klimke and Scharloth, *1968 in Europe*, 179–87.

12. Quoted in Tom Brokaw, *Boom! Voices of the Sixties: Personal Reflections on the '60s and Today* (New York: Random House, 2007), 346. See also the special issue "The Sixties and the 2008 Presidential Election," *The Sixties: A Journal of Politics, History and Culture*, Vol. 2, No. 1, June 2009, 49–78; Tom Hayden, *The Long Sixties: From 1960 to Barack Obama* (Boulder, CO: Paradigm Publishers, 2009).

13. For the notions of communicative and cultural memory, see Jan Assmann, *Das kulturelle Gedächtnis. Schrift, Erinnerung und politische Identität in frühen Hochkulturen* (Munich: Beck, 1992), 50–56. See also Aleida Assmann, "Memory, Individual and Collective," in Robert E. Goodin and Charles Tilly, eds., *The Oxford Handbook of Contextual Political Analysis* (Oxford: Oxford University Press, 2006), 210–24.

14. Gerard J. De Groot, *The Sixties Unplugged: A Kaleidoscopic History of a Disorderly Decade.* (Cambridge: Harvard University Press, 2008), 449.

15. Kristin Ross, *May '68 and Its Afterlives* (Chicago: University of Chicago Press, 2002), 1.

16. Elizabeth Peifer, "1968 in German Political Culture, 1967–1993: From Experience to Myth," Ph.D. diss., University of North Carolina, Chapel Hill, 1997, p. 17.

17. In order to fully understand the global dimension of the sixties, it is essential to take into account the complex relationship between such concepts as the cold war, modernization theory, and how "the Third World operated simultaneously as a political category of radical promise and of Euro-American discipline in the 1960s," as Tina Mai Chen has asserted in "Epilogue: Third World Possibilities and Problematics: Historical Connections and Critical Frameworks," in Karen Dubinsky, et al., ed., *New World Coming: The Sixties and the Shaping of Global Consciousness* (Toronto: Between the Lines, 2009), 425. Promising beginnings are Van Gosse, *Where the Boys Are: Cuba, Cold War America and the Making of a New Left,* (New York: Verso, 1993); Jennifer B. Smith, *An International History of the Black Panther Party* (New York: Garland Publishing 1999); Cynthia Young, *Soul Power. Culture, Radicalism and the Making of a U.S. Third World Left* (Durham, N.C.: Duke University Press, 2006); Quinn Slobodian, "Radical Empathy: The Third World and the New Left in 1960s West Germany," Ph.D. diss., New York University, 2008; Samantha M. R. Christiansen and Za-

chary A. Scarlett, eds., *1968 and the Global South* (New York: Berghahn Books, forthcoming).

18. See, for example, Rebecca Klatch, *A Generation Divided: The New Left, the New Right, and the 1960s* (Berkeley: University of California Press, 1999); Lisa McGirr, *Suburban Warriors: The Origins of the New American Right.* (Princeton: Princeton University Press, 2001); Stuart Hilwig, *Italy and 1968: Youthful Unrest and Democratic Culture* (London: Palgrave Macmillan, 2009).

SOURCES

Archival Collections

Germany

Archive "APO und soziale Bewegungen," Free University of Berlin

- Papers of the German SDS

Institute for Social Research, Hamburg

- Papers of the Red Army Faction (1st Generation)
- Papers of Rudi Dutschke

Press Archive, Otto-Suhr Institute, Free University Berlin

- Various press collections

Archive and Special Collections, University of Heidelberg, Heidelberg

United States

University of Arkansas Libraries, Special Collections, Fayetteville, Arkansas

- Bureau of Educational and Cultural Affairs Historical Collection (MC 468)
- NAFSA: Association of International Educators Records (MC 715)
- Council for International Exchange of Scholars (MC 703)

Lyndon B. Johnson Library, Austin, Texas

- Cabinet Papers
- NSF Files, Country File Germany
- NSF Files, Country File Vietnam
- NSF Files, Intelligence
- NSF Files, International Meetings & Travel
- NSF Files, Files of Walt Rostow
- NSF Files, Subject File
- NSF Files, National Intelligence Estimates
- NSF Files, Memos to the President (Rostow)
- Oral History Collection
- White House Central Files, CO 81, France
- White House Central Files, Confidential Files
- White House Central Files, Correspondence Germany
- White House Central Files, Judicial & Legal
- White House Central Files, NSF, Defense
- White House Central Files, USIA

- White House Central Files, Youth Programs
- White House General Files
- White House Name File

U S. National Archives, College Park, Maryland

- Record Group 59, State Department Papers
- CREST (Database of Declassified CIA documents)

Oral History Research Office, Columbia University, New York, New York

- Gregory N. Calvert (07/01-03/1987)

University of California, San Diego, Archives

- Office of the Chancellor, Marcuse (RSS1)
- Papers of Robert Elliot
- Collection of Periodicals

Wisconsin State Historical Society, Madison

- Papers of Paul Booth
- Papers of Robb Burlage
- Papers of Todd Gitlin and Nancy Hollander
- Papers of Allen Young
- Students for a Democratic Society Records (MS 177)

Oral History Interviews

- Bathrick, David, Bremen, Germany, May 21, 2004
- Birnbaum, Norman, Washington, DC, November 2, 2003
- Blagdon, Douglas, Los Angeles, CA, August 22, 2003
- Dohrn, Bernardine, Chicago, IL, July 17, 2003
- Dutschke, Gretchen, Newton, MA, November 13, 1999
- Flacks, Richard, Santa Barbara, CA, August 21, 2003
- Flores, Juan, New York, NY, October 16, 2003
- Gitlin, Todd, New York, NY, May 18, 2000
- Hayden, Tom, Boston, MA, October 15, 2003
- Klonsky, Susan, Chicago, IL, April 15, 2000
- Oglesby, Carl, Cambridge, MA, December 17, 1999, July 30, 2000
- Rassbach, Elsa, Berlin, Germany, January 28, 2002
- Reiche, Reimut, Frankfurt, Germany, January 17, 2005
- Ross, Robert, Worcester, MA, March 21, 2000
- Vester, Michael, Hannover, Germany, June 8, 2001, September 12, 2005
- Williamson, James, Cambridge, MA, June 12, 2003
- Wolff, Karl-Dietrich, Frankfurt, Germany, April 10, 2001
- Young, Allen, Orange, MA, April 26, 2000

NEWSPAPERS AND PERIODICALS

USA

New York Times
San Diego Union
San Francisco Examiner
Washington Post

Germany

Christ und Welt
Frankfurter Rundschau
Heidelberger Tageblatt
Rheinischer Merkur
Rhein-Neckar-Zeitung
Stern
Süddeutsche Zeitung

Abendroth, Wolfgang, 13, 137

Abrasimov, Pyotr, 171

Academic Senate, 71

activism: America Houses and, 187–93; antiwar movement and, 4–10, 34, 41–54, 62 (*see also* antiwar movement); apathy and, 4, 13–14, 17, 21, 23, 38, 53, 80, 132, 137; arrests and, 49, 79, 123, 133, 135, 155, 203, 283n52; Berlin problem and, 161–82; Black Power and, 108–42 (*see also* Black Power); blind, 58; bombs and, 31, 49, 57, 132, 137, 156, 165, 181–82; cross-group inspiration and, 4; cultural exchange programs and, 219–24; desertion campaigns and, 127–28, 182–87; direct action and, 8, 37, 53–60, 67–69, 73–74, 113, 115, 170, 263n66; disillusionment with government and, 6–7; fraternization and, 5–6; French Resistance and, 76; GI-organizing and, 84–86, 93, 96, 113–14, 132, 139, 182–87; global interconnectedness and, 236–37; influence on German politics, 224–28; isolationism and, 75–81; Kennedy administration and, 145; liberal arts and, 204; "Make Love Not War" slogan and, 88; militancy and, 4, 8, 25, 41, 79, 93, 101, 107, 109, 114, 125–29, 136, 141–42, 156–61, 168, 176–77, 189, 193, 195, 205, 238–39; Nazism and, 19, 33, 78, 85, 93, 129–32, 156, 172, 223; nuclear disarmament and, 4, 13, 17, 23, 28, 31–32, 44, 46, 224, 227, 236; Port Huron Statement and, 4, 8, 17–20, 24–28, 35, 48, 54, 237, 252n24; revolutionary consciousness and, 76–77; sit-ins and, 1, 8, 15, 49, 53–60, 70–72, 104, 188–90, 203; strategy conflicts and, 54–60; teach-ins and, 4, 8, 42, 50, 53–60, 70–71, 103, 120, 189, 191, 289n138; transnationalism of, 5–6; University of California at Berkeley and, 22, 32, 41, 44, 52, 61, 70–71, 73, 85, 88–89, 97, 110, 143, 151, 162, 239–43; voter registration drives and, 110. *See also* specific groups

Adams, Rebecca, 19

Adenauer, Konrad, 10

Adorno, Theodor W., 13, 22, 89, 134

African Americans: Dutschke and, 69–70; King and, 4, 109, 112, 116–17, 225, 227; Malcolm X and, 7, 69, 110–12, 119, 227; Parks and, 4. *See also* Black Power

African Student Union, 57

Agency for International Development (AID), 147

Agit 883, 125, 127–28

Alexander, Kenneth, 14

Algeria, 20, 29, 129–30

Ali, Tariq, 2, 5

Allied Psychological Warfare Division, 188

Amendt, Günter, 52, 110, 112, 119

America Houses: attacks on, 49, 144, 177, 223, 239; cultural diplomacy and, 187–93; cultural exchange programs and, 223; Dutschke and, 189, 191; establishment of, 188; Fulbright Commission and, 221; reshaping of U.S. embassy youth program and, 213; protests and, 49, 62, 66, 168, 173, 177, 187–93; sit-ins in 49

American National Mobilization Committee to End the War in Vietnam, 187

Amnesty International, 236

Angela Davis Solidarity Committee, 134–42

Anschlag Gruppe, 57

anti-authoritarianism: internationalism and, 60–67; Subversive Aktion and, 49, 54–59, 56, 62–64, 68, 73–74, 89. *See also* revolt

Anti-imperialist Week, 120

anti-Semitism, 22

antiwar movement, 5, 10, 40, 163; academics and, 88–90, 97; America Houses and, 49, 62, 66, 168, 173, 177, 187–93; American protest models and, 68–74; anti-authoritarianism and, 60–67; Berlin problem and, 161–82; corporations and, 96; cultural exchange programs and,

antiwar movement (*cont'd*)
219–24; Davis and, 134–42; democracy and, 42, 45, 52, 54, 61, 68, 85, 104; desertion campaigns and, 127–28, 182–87; direct action and, 53–60, 67–69, 73–74, 170; disharmony in, 5; draft resisters and, 76, 101; Dutschke and, 73–86, 89–99; Easter marches and, 32, 85, 102, 119, 159, 161, 177–80, 185; German opposition to Vietnam War and, 49–54; GI-organizing and, 84–86, 93, 96, 113–14, 132, 139, 182–87; growth of, 4; illegality of desertion solicitation and, 86; imperialism and, 4, 48, 63, 66–70, 79–80, 84, 87, 90–93, 97, 99, 103; International Days of Protest and, 44; International Intelligence Network and, 48; internationalism and, 41–50, 64–65, 86–100; isolationism and, 75–81; Krippendorff case and, 61–62; liberation movements and, 49, 63–64, 76–78, 83, 87, 92, 96–97, 99, 105, 107; McGhee and, 70, 143–47, 160–61, 170, 175–76, 183, 191, 196, 201, 210, 212, 220, 228, 240; "Make Love Not War" slogan and, 88; march on Washington and, 44–45; Marcuse and, 6–9, 41, 56, 64–65, 89–90, 97, 108, 129, 134, 137, 139, 141; nations series and, 48; nuclear disarmament and, 4, 13, 17, 23, 28, 31–32, 44, 46, 224, 227, 236; Oglesby and, 43–47, 78; Port Huron Statement and, 48, 54; Radical Education Project and, 48; Savio and, 41, 70; sit-ins and, 49, 53–60, 70–72; strategy conflicts and, 54–60; teach-ins and, 4, 53–60, 70–71; Third World and, 64; Tocsin and, 31–32; Washington Monument and, 42; Wolff and, 103–7. *See also* specific groups
apartheid, 4
apathy: Port Huron Statement and, 20–22; social issues and, 4, 13–14, 20–23, 38, 53, 80, 132, 137
Aptheker, Bettina, 88
Argument Club, 49, 68
Arnold, Thurman, 10
arrests, 11–12, 49, 79, 123, 133, 135, 155, 203, 283n52
arson, 177–78
Association of Socialist Student Groups, 12

Attica, 132–33
Auschwitz, Hamburg und Dresden (RAF), 132

Baader, Andreas, 127, 137
baby boomers, 3, 242
Baez, Joan, 6–7, 241
Bardot, Brigitte, 63–64
Barnes, Larry, 123–24
Barthes, Roland, 76
Bator, Francis, 171–72
Battle, Lucius, 148
"Battle at Tegeler Weg," 180–81
BBC, 5
beards, 5, 299n126
Beatles, The, 6
Beat movement, 3
Belgium, 5, 30
Bell, David, 150
Bell, Tom, 79
Berlin: "Day of International Protest against the War in Vietnam" and, 168; Easter riots and, 177–80; International Congress for Cultural Freedom and, 161; New Left and, 161–82; official receptions and, 170–71; "Peace and Freedom" rally and, 175–76; symbolism of, 161–62; U.S. Mission in, 214; *Weltanschauung* attitude and, 162–63
"Berlin: Why Not Recognize the Status Quo?" (Vester), 20
Bettelheim, Bruno, 89
Bewegung 2, 127
Bild Zeitung, 157, 177
Birnbaum, Norman, 32
Black Action Group, 122
Black Defense Group, 122
Black Liberation Army, 115, 118, 128
Black Panther: Black Community News Service, 118–19
Black Panthers, 8–9; Davis and, 134–42; Fanon and, 129–31; founding of German solidarity committees and, 116–22; Kennedy petition and, 110; Ramstein 2 and, 122–26; Red Army Faction (RAF) and, 107, 115, 127–34; Soledad Brothers and, 132–33; Solidarity Committees and, 116–26, 134–42
Black Power, 8–9, 41, 204; Anti-imperialist Week and, 120; Call for Justice Day and, 122–23; capitalism and, 69–70; Carmi-

and, 4; materialism and, 4; militancy and, 4, 8, 25, 41, 79, 93, 101, 107, 109, 114, 125–29, 136, 141–42, 156–61, 168, 176–77, 189, 193, 195, 204, 238–39; Mills and, 35–37; National Liberation Front (NLF) and, 77–78; Old Left and, 16–18, 48; Port Huron Statement and, 4; transnational origins of, 4; United States Information Agency (USIA) and, 153–54; university reform and, 163–64; U.S. discovery of German, 153–58; Vester and, 10; *Weltanschauung* attitude and, 162–63; Wolff and, 103–7
New Left Notes bulletin, 40, 75–76, 78, 80, 84, 104
New Left Review journal, 35
New Republic journal, 78
New Right, 244
New York Times, 78, 97, 156
New York University, 78
Nguyen Thi Binh, 77
Niemoeller, Martin, 11
Nitsch, Wolfgang, 52, 96–97
Nixon, Richard M., 181, 194, 241, 244; CIA and, 233; impeachment issues and, 242; Inter-Agency Youth Committee (IAYC) and, 228–34; revolutionary sabbatical and, 228–34; White House Conference on Youth and, 232
North Atlantic Treaty Organization (NATO), 25, 80, 93–96, 186, 202, 204, 213, 216, 223, 225, 227
Northern Atlantic Alliance, 187
nuclear disarmament, 4, 17, 23, 28, 224, 236; Campaign for Nuclear Disarmament (CND) and, 13–14, 32, 46; National Committee for a Sane Nuclear Policy (SANE) and, 31, 44–46, 75, 272n66; Pershing-II missiles in Germany and, 227; White House demonstration and, 31–32; Young Peoples Socialist League (YPSL) and, 32

Obama, Barack, 242
Ochs, Richard, 42
Offe, Claus, 73
Office of Intelligence and Research (INR), 152
Oglesby, Carl, 43–47, 78
Ohnesorg, Benno, 108, 129, 166, 170–72
Old Left, 16–18, 48

Ollenhauer, Erich, 12
One-Dimensional Man (Marcuse), 65, 89
On the Road (Kerouac), 16
Opposition und Ziel journal, 32
Otto-Suhr-Institute for Political Science, 61
Out of Apathy (Thompson), 14
Oxford Labour Club (OLC), 30
Oxford University, 32

pacifists, 4, 10. *See also* antiwar movement
Paris American Committee to Stop War, 205
Parks, Rosa, 4
Parmalee, Patty Lee, 85, 113–14
"Path to Vietnam, The" (Bundy), 188
"Peace and Freedom" rally, 175–76
Peace Corps, 145, 147, 197, 199, 201, 217, 228
peace movement, 18, 262n50; cold war rhetoric and, 28; Gitlin and, 31–32; International Intelligence Network and, 48; internationalism and, 46–49; North Vietnamese government and, 206; White House study of, 205–6. *See also* antiwar movement
Pedersen, Richard, 228
Peifer, Elizabeth, 243
Peirce, Robert, 93
Pells, Richard, 7
Pershing II missiles, 227
Phúc, Kim, 6
Pimental, Edward, 134
Poland, 242
police brutality, 166–67, 170
Policy Analysis and Resource Allocation Study on Youth (PARAS), 234
Politeia, 30
politics: activists' influence upon German, 224–28; America Houses and, 49, 62, 66, 144, 168, 173, 177, 188–93, 213, 221, 223, 239; apartheid and, 4; Berlin problem and, 161–82; censorship and, 60–61, 161; cold war and, 2–6, 9, 11, 17–18, 25–26 (*see also* cold war); communists and, 2, 4–5, 11, 13 (*see also* communism; corporate liberalism and, 45; cultural diplomacy and, 6, 9, 145, 187–94, 194, 200, 214, 227, 240; democracy and, 145, 214, 219 (*see also* democracy); direct action and, 8, 37, 53–60, 67–69, 73–74, 113, 115, 170,

CPSIA information can be obtained
at www.ICGtesting.com
Printed in the USA
LVHW111818100119
603456LV00008B/986/P